W9-CTY-576

DATE DUE

			PRINTED IN U.S.A.

SOMETHING ABOUT THE AUTHOR®

Something about
the Author *was named
an "**Outstanding
Reference Source**"
the highest honor given
by the American
Library Association
Reference and Adult
Services Division.*

ISSN 0276-816X

SOMETHING ABOUT THE AUTHOR®

Facts and Pictures about Authors
and Illustrators of Books for Young People

EDITED BY
DIANE TELGEN

VOLUME 75

 Gale Research Inc. • DETROIT • WASHINGTON, D.C. • LONDON

STAFF

Editor: Diane Telgen

Associate Editor: Marie Ellavich

Senior Editor: James G. Lesniak

Sketchwriters: Shelly Andrews, Joanna Brod, Bruce Ching, Pamela S. Dear,
Elizabeth A. Des Chenes, Kathleen J. Edgar, David M. Galens, Kevin S. Hile, Jeff Hill,
Anne Janette Johnson, Denise E. Kasinec, Thomas F. McMahon, Michelle M. Motowski,
Michael E. Mueller, Cornelia A. Pernik, Nancy Rampson, Susan M. Reicha, Terrie M. Rooney,
Kenneth R. Shepherd, Roger M. Valade III, Polly Vedder, and Elizabeth Wenning

Research Manager: Victoria B. Cariappa
Research Supervisor: Mary Rose Bonk
Editorial Associates: Reginald A. Carlton, Clare Collins, Andrew Guy Malonis, and Norma Sawaya
Editorial Assistants: Patricia Bowen, Rachel A. Dixon, Eva Marie Felts, Shirley Gates, Sharon McGilvray,
and Devra M. Sladics

Picture Permissions Supervisor: Margaret A. Chamberlain
Permissions Associates: Pamela A. Hayes and Keith Reed
Permissions Assistants: Susan Brohman, Arlene Johnson, and Barbara Wallace

Production Director: Mary Beth Trimper
External Production Assistant: Mary Kelley
Art Director: Cynthia Baldwin
Desktop Publisher/Typesetter: Sherrell Hobbs
Camera Operator: Willie Mathis

 This book is printed on acid-free paper that meets the minimum requirements of American National Standard for Information Sciences—Permanence Paper for Printed Library Materials, ANSI Z39.48-1984.

Library of Congress Catalog Card Number 72-27107

ISBN 0-8103-2285-4 ISSN 0276-816X

Printed in the United States of America

Published simultaneously in the United Kingdom by Gale Research International Limited
(An affiliated company of Gale Research Inc.)

I(T)P™

The trademark ITP is used under license.

10 9 8 7 6 5 4 3 2 1

Contents

Authors in Forthcoming Volumes

Below are some of the authors and illustrators that will be featured in upcoming volumes of *SATA*. These include new entries on the swiftly-rising stars of the field, as well as completely revised and updated entries (indicated with *) on some of the most notable and best-loved creators of books for children.

*Emily Arnold: Author-illustrator of various works under the name Emily Arnold McCully, including *Mirette on the High Wire,* winner of the 1993 Caldecott Medal.

Jimmy Buffett: The noted singer-songwriter who hit bestseller charts with *Tales from Margaritaville* has also written two books for children, *The Jolly Mon* and *Trouble Dolls.*

Alan and Lea Daniel: The Canadian husband-and-wife illustrating team responsible for pictures for works ranging from *The Story of Canada* to James Howe's "Bunnicula" series; entry includes exclusive interview.

Joseph F. Girzone: A former Catholic priest whose first novel was the allegory for young adults, *Kara, the Lonely Falcon,* Girzone is best known for his popular tales of Joshua, a modern-day Christ figure.

James Gurney: Creator of *Dinotopia,* a world where dinosaurs and humans interact in an intricate society, brought to life by Gurney's beautiful illustrations.

Deborah Hopkinson: Hopkinson's tale of the Underground Railroad became the children's best-seller *Sweet Clara and the Freedom Quilt.*

Holly Keller: Author-illustrator of appealing picture books such as *Horace* and *Island Baby;* entry includes exclusive interview.

*Ted Lewin: This noted illustrator later began writing his own books, including the recent autobiography *I Was a Teenage Professional Wrestler.*

Colleen O'Shaughnessy McKenna: Author of the popular middle-grade "Murphy" series about a loving if boisterous family.

*Daniel Manus Pinkwater: A favorite with kids for his wildly absurd books, including *The Snarkout Boys and the Avocado of Death* and *The Moosepire.*

*Cynthia Rylant: This prolific and talented author was the recipient of the 1993 Newbery Medal for her story of death and acceptance, *Missing May.*

Lane Smith: Smith's unique illustrations for *The Stinky Cheese Man* garnered him a 1993 Caldecott Honor citation; partnered with Jon Scieszka and on his own, Smith is responsible for many wacky, hysterically funny books, including *The Big Pets.*

*R. L. Stine: This bestselling author of the "Fear Street" and "Goosebumps" series began his career writing joke books for kids; entry includes exclusive interview.

*Elizabeth Winthrop: Author of diverse works from picture books about families to fantasy for middle readers to young adult novels; entry includes exclusive interview.

Introduction

Something about the Author (*SATA*) is an ongoing reference series that deals with the lives and works of authors and illustrators of children's books. *SATA* includes not only well-known authors and illustrators whose books are widely read, but also those less prominent people whose works are just coming to be recognized. This series is often the only readily available information source on emerging writers or artists. You'll find *SATA* informative and entertaining whether you are a student, a librarian, an English teacher, a parent, or simply an adult who enjoys children's literature for its own sake.

What's Inside SATA

SATA provides detailed information about authors and illustrators who span the full time range of children's literature, from early figures like John Newbery and L. Frank Baum to contemporary figures like Judy Blume and Richard Peck. Authors in the series represent primarily English-speaking countries, particularly the United States, Canada, and the United Kingdom. Also included, however, are authors from around the world whose works are available in English translation. The writings represented in *SATA* include those created intentionally for children and young adults as well as those written for a general audience and known to interest younger readers. These writings cover the entire spectrum of children's literature, including picture books, humor, folk and fairy tales, animal stories, mystery and adventure, science fiction and fantasy, historical fiction, poetry and nonsense verse, drama, biography, and nonfiction.

Obituaries are also included in *SATA* and are intended not only as death notices but as concise views of people's lives and work. Additionally, each edition features newly revised and updated entries for a selection of *SATA* listees who remain of interest to today's readers and who have been active enough to require extensive revision of their earlier biographies.

Two Convenient Indexes

In response to suggestions from librarians, *SATA* indexes no longer appear in each volume, but are included in alternate (odd-numbered) volumes of the series, beginning with Volume 57.

SATA continues to include two indexes that cumulate with each alternate volume: the Illustrations Index, arranged by the name of the illustrator, gives the number of the volume and page where the illustrator's work appears in the current volume as well as all preceding volumes in the series; the Author Index gives the number of the volume in which a person's Biographical Sketch or Obituary appears in the current volume as well as all preceding volumes in the series.

These indexes also include references to authors and illustrators who appear in Gale's *Yesterday's Authors of Books for Children, Children's Literature Review,* and the *Something about the Author Autobiography Series.*

Easy-to-Use Entry Format

Whether you're already familiar with the *SATA* series or just getting acquainted, you will want to be aware of the kind of information that an entry provides. In every *SATA* entry the editors attempt to give as complete a picture of the person's life and work as possible. A typical entry in *SATA* includes the following clearly labeled information sections:

- *PERSONAL:* date and place of birth and death, parents' names and occupations, name of spouse, date of marriage, and names of children, educational institutions attended, degrees received, religious and political affiliations, hobbies and other interests.

- *ADDRESSES:* complete home, office, and agent's address.

- *CAREER:* name of employer, position, and dates for each career post; military service.

- *MEMBER:* memberships and offices held in professional and civic organizations.

- *AWARDS, HONORS:* literary and professional awards received.

- *WRITINGS:* title-by-title chronological bibliography of books written and/or illustrated, listed by genre when known; lists of other notable publications, such as plays, screenplays, and periodical contributions.

- *ADAPTATIONS:* a list of films, television programs, plays, and other media which have been adapted from the author's work.

- *WORK IN PROGRESS:* description of projects in progress.

- *SIDELIGHTS:* a biographical portrait of the author's development, either directly from the person—and often written specifically for the *SATA* entry—or gathered from diaries, letters, interviews, or other published sources.

- *FOR MORE INFORMATION SEE:* references for further reading.

- *EXTENSIVE ILLUSTRATIONS:* photographs, movie stills, manuscript samples, book covers, and other interesting visual materials supplement the text.

How a SATA Entry Is Compiled

A *SATA* entry progresses through a series of steps. If the biographee is living, the *SATA* editors try to secure information directly from him or her through a questionnaire. From the information that the biographee supplies, the editors prepare an entry, filling in any essential missing details with research and/or telephone interviews. When necessary, the author or illustrator is sent a copy of the entry to check for accuracy and completeness.

If the biographee is deceased or cannot be reached by questionnaire, the *SATA* editors examine a wide variety of published sources to gather information for an entry. Biographical and bibliographic sources are consulted, as are book reviews, feature articles, published interviews, and material sometimes obtained from the biographee's family, publishers, agent, or other associates. Entries compiled entirely from secondary sources are marked with an asterisk (*).

We Welcome Your Suggestions

We invite you to examine the entire *SATA* series, starting with this volume. Please write and tell us if we can make *SATA* even more helpful to you. Send comments and suggestions to: The Editor, *Something about the Author,* Gale Research Inc., 835 Penobscot Bldg., Detroit, Michigan 48226.

Acknowledgments

Grateful acknowledgment is made to the following publishers, authors, and artists whose works appear in this volume.

MABEL ESTHER ALLAN. Jacket of *The View beyond My Father,* by Mabel Esther Allan. Copyright © 1977 by Mabel Esther Allan. Jacket painting by Bertram M. Tormey. Reprinted by permission of Dodd, Mead & Company./ Jacket of *A Dream of Hunger Moss,* by Mabel Esther Allan. Copyright © 1983 by Mabel Esther Allan. Jacket painting by Bertram M. Tormey./ Cover of *Drina Dances Again,* by Jean Estoril. Copyright © 1960 by Jean Estoril. Reprinted by permission of Scholastic Inc./ Photograph courtesy of Mabel Esther Allan.

GILLIAN AVERY. Jacket of *The Italian Spring,* by Gillian Avery. Copyright © 1964 by Gillian Avery. Illustrations by John Verney./ Photograph courtesy of Gillian Avery.

ANGELA BARRETT. Illustration by Angela Barrett from *Proud Knight, Fair Lady,* translated by Naomi Lewis. Translation copyright © 1989 by Naomi Lewis. Illustrations copyright © 1989 by Angela Barrett. Reprinted in the U.S. by permission of Penguin Books USA Inc. Reprinted in Canada and the British Commonwealth by permission of Random Century Group Ltd.

JILL BARTON. Photograph courtesy of Jill Barton.

JUDITH BERCK. Photograph Cynthia Kirk/Syntax.

RICHARD BOUGHTON. Photograph courtesy of Richard Boughton.

ALIKI BRANDENBERG. Illustration by Aliki Brandenberg from her *Digging up Dinosaurs.* Copyright © 1981, 1988 by Aliki Brandenberg. Reprinted by permission of HarperCollins Publishers./ Illustration by Aliki Brandenberg from her *Communication.* Copyright © 1993 by Aliki Brandenberg. Reprinted by permission of Greenwillow Books, a division of William Morrow and Company, Inc./ Photograph by Ian Bradshaw, courtesy of Aliki Brandenberg.

FRANZ BRANDENBERG. Jacket of *A Fun Weekend,* by Franz Brandenberg. Text copyright © 1991 by Franz Brandenberg. Illustrations copyright © 1991 by Alexa Demetria Brandenberg. Reprinted by permission of Greenwillow Books, a division of William Morrow and Company, Inc./ Photograph courtesy of Franz Brandenberg.

ROBERT CASILLA. Photograph courtesy of Robert Casilla.

JUDITH CLARKE. Jacket of *Al Capsella and the Watchdogs,* by J. Clarke. Jacket design and illustration copyright © 1991 by Michael Chesworth. Reprinted by permission of Michael Chesworth./ Photograph courtesy of Judith Clarke.

LAWRENCE CLAYTON. Cover of *Coping with a Drug-Abusing Parent,* by Lawrence Clayton, Ph.D. The Rosen Publishing Group, Inc., 1991. Copyright © 1991 by Lawrence Clayton, Ph.D. Reprinted by permission of The Rosen Publishing Group, Inc./ Photograph courtesy of Lawrence Clayton.

NORA COHEN. Photograph by Andra Munger, courtesy of Nora Cohen.

PATRICIA COMPTON. Photograph courtesy of Patricia Compton.

GARY CREW. Jacket of *Strange Objects,* by Gary Crew. Copyright © 1990 by Gary Crew. Jacket illustration copyright © 1993 by Kam Mak. Reprinted by permission of the publisher, Simon & Schuster Books for Young Readers, New York./ Photograph courtesy of Gary Crew.

VERDA CROSS. Photograph courtesy of Verda Cross.

JANE CUTLER. Photograph by Judith Holland-Steinhart.

JAMES M. DEEM. Photograph by Victoria Piloseno, courtesy of James Deem.

ALICE DELACROIX. Photograph courtesy of Alice DeLaCroix.

ANNE DE LA ROCHE SAINT ANDRE. Illustration by Sara from her *The Rabbit, the Fox, and the Wolf.* Copyright © 1990 by Sara. Reprinted by permission of Orchard Books, New York.

DAYLE ANN DODDS. Jacket of *On Our Way to Market,* by Dayle Ann Dodds. Text copyright © 1991 by Dayle Ann Dodds. Illustrations copyright © 1991 by John Gurney. Used by permission of the publisher, Simon & Schuster Books for Young Readers, New York./ Photograph courtesy of Dayle Ann Dodds.

J. ELLEN DOLCE. Illustration by J. Ellen Dolce from *My Very First Golden Bible,* as told by the Reverend Dana Forrest Kennedy. Copyright © 1991 Joshua Morris Publishing, Inc., 221 Danbury Road, Wilton, CT 06897. Used by permission of Western Publishing Company, Inc./ Photograph courtesy of J. Ellen Dolce.

MICHAEL DORRIS. Jacket of *Morning Girl,* by Michael Dorris. Text copyright © 1992 by Michael Dorris. Jacket illustration copyright © 1992 by Kam Mak. Reprinted by permission of Hyperion Books for Children./ Photograph by Louise Erdrich.

CRESCENT DRAGONWAGON. Jacket of *To Take a Dare,* by Crescent Dragonwagon and Paul Zindel. Copyright © 1982 by Zindel Productions, Inc., and Crescent Dragonwagon. Jacket photograph by Aimee Garn and Ron Boszko. Reprinted by permission of HarperCollins Publishers./ Cover of *Alligator Arrived with Apples: A Potluck Alphabet Feast,* by Crescent Dragonwagon. Illustrations copyright © 1987 by Jose Aruego and Ariane Dewey. Reprinted with the permission of Macmillan Publishing Company./ Cover of *Half a Moon and One Whole Star,* by Crescent Dragonwagon. Illustrations copyright © 1986 by Jerry Pinkney. Reprinted with permission of Macmillan Publishing Company, a division of Macmillan, Inc./ Jacket of *The Year It Rained,* by Crescent Dragonwagon. Copyright © 1985 by Crescent Dragonwagon. Copyright © 1985 by Macmillan Publishing Company, a division of Macmillan, Inc. Reprinted with permission of Macmillan Publishing Company, a division of Macmillan, Inc./ Photograph by Andrew Kilgore, courtesy of Crescent Dragonwagon.

LOIS DUNCAN. Cover of *Don't Look behind You,* by Lois Duncan. Copyright © 1989 by Lois Duncan. Reprinted by permission of Dell Books, a division of Bantam Doubleday Dell Publishing Group, Inc./ Cover of *Ransom,* by Lois Duncan. Copyright © 1966 by Lois Duncan Cardozo. Reprinted by permission of Dell Books, a division of Bantam Doubleday Dell Publishing Group, Inc./ Cover of *Summer of Fear,* by Lois Duncan. Copyright © 1976 by Lois Duncan. Reprinted by permission of Dell Books, a division of Bantam Doubleday Dell Publishing Group, Inc./ Cover of *Killing Mr. Griffin,* by Lois Duncan. Copyright © 1978 by Lois Duncan. Reprinted by permission of Dell Books, a division of Bantam Doubleday Dell Publishing Group, Inc./ Photograph courtesy of Lois Duncan.

ODETTE ELLIOTT. Photograph by Nick Hayes, courtesy of Odette Elliott.

NORMA FARBER. Cover of *I Found Them in the Yellow Pages,* by Norma Farber. Text copyright © 1973 by Norma Farber. Illustrations copyright © 1973 by Marc Brown. Reprinted by permission of Little, Brown and Company./ Cover of *As I Was Crossing Boston Common,* by Norma Farber. Text copyright © 1973 by Norma Farber. Illustrations copyright © 1975 by Arnold Lobel. Reprinted by permission of Arnold Lobel./ Photograph by Babette S. Whipple, courtesy of Norma Farber.

JAMES FARLOW. Photograph courtesy of James Farlow.

FIONA FRENCH. Illustration by Fiona French from her *Maid of the Wood.* Copyright © 1985 Fiona French. Reprinted by permission of Oxford University Press.

ANN GABHART. Cover of *Discovery at Coyote Point,* by Ann Gabhart. Copyright © 1989 by Ann Gabhart. Reprinted by permission of Avon Books, New York./ Cover of *Two of a Kind,* by Ann Gabhart. Copyright © 1992 by Ann Gabhart. Reprinted by permission of Avon Books, New York./ Photograph courtesy of Ann Gabhart.

THEODOR SEUSS GEISEL. Illustration by Theodor Seuss Geisel from his *Horton Hears A Who!* Copyright © 1954 by Dr. Seuss. Copyright © 1982 by Dr. Seuss. Reprinted in the United States and Canada by permission of Random House, Inc. Reprinted in the British Commonwealth by permission by permission of Elaine Greene Ltd./ Illustration by Theodor Seuss Geisel from his *The Cat in the Hat.* Copyright © 1957 by Dr. Seuss. Copyright © renewed 1985 by Theodor S. Geisel and Audrey S. Geisel. Reprinted in the United States and Canada by permission of Random House, Inc. Reprinted in the British Commonwealth by permission of Elaine Greene Ltd./ Illustration by Theodor Seuss Geisel from his *Green Eggs and Ham.* Copyright © 1960 by Dr. Seuss. Reprinted in the United States and Canada by permission of Random House, Inc. Reprinted in the British Commonwealth by permission of Elaine Greene Ltd./ Illustration by Theodor Seuss Geisel from his *Oh, the Places You'll Go!* Copyright © 1990 by Theodor S. Geisel and Audrey S. Geisel. Reprinted in the United States and Canada by permission of Random House, Inc. Reprinted in the British Commonwealth by permission of Elaine Greene Ltd./ Illustration by Theodor Seuss Geisel from his *How the Grinch Stole Christmas.* Copyright © 1957 by Theodor S. Geisel and Audrey S. Geisel. Copyright © renewed 1985 by Theodor S. Geisel. Reprinted in the United States and Canada by permission of Random House, Inc. Reprinted in the British Commonwealth by permission of Elaine Greene Ltd./ Photograph by Antony Di Gesu.

JAMES CROSS GIBLIN. Cover of *Chimney Sweeps: Yesterday and Today,* by James Cross Giblin. Text copyright © 1982 by James Cross Giblin. Cover art copyright © 1982 by Margot Tomes. Reprinted by permission of HarperCollins Publishers./ Cover of *The Riddle of the Rosetta Stone: Key to Ancient Egypt,* by James Cross Giblin. Copyright © 1990 by James Cross Giblin. Cover copyright © 1993 by HarperCollins Publishers. Cover background photograph reproduced courtesy of the Trustees of the British Museum. Reprinted by permission of HarperCollins Publishers./ Jacket of *The Truth about Santa Claus,* by James Cross Giblin. Copyright © 1985 by James Cross Giblin. Jacket art copyright © 1985 by Margot Tomes. Jacket copyright © 1985 by Harper & Row Publishers Inc. Reprinted by permission of HarperCollins Publishers./ Photograph © Nancy Crampton.

JUDITH GOROG. Jacket of *A Taste for Quiet and Other Stories,* by Judith Gorog. Text copyright © 1982 by Judith Gorog. Illustrations copyright © 1982 by Jeanne Titherington. Reprinted by permission of Philomel Books./ Cover of *Three Dreams and a Nightmare,* by Judith Gorog. Copyright © 1988 by Judith Gorog. Cover illustration copyright © 1988 by Richard Egielski. Reprinted by permission of The Putnam Publishing Group./ Jacket of *Winning Scheherazade,* by Judith Gorog. Atheneum, 1991. Copyright © 1991 by Judith Gorog. Jacket illustration copyright © 1991 by James E. Ransome. Reprinted by permission of James E. Ransome./ Photograph by Alison H. Speckman, courtesy of Judith Gorog.

JOHN STEVEN GURNEY. Photograph courtesy of John Steven Gurney.

CAROLYN HAYWOOD. Cover of *Eddie and His Big Deals,* by Carolyn Haywood. Copyright © 1955 by Carolyn Haywood. Cover illustration copyright © 1990 by Deborah Chabrian. Reprinted by permission of Beech Tree Books, an imprint of William Morrow and Company, Inc./ Jacket of *"B" Is for Betsy,* by Carolyn Haywood. Copyright © 1939 by Harcourt Brace Jovanovich, Inc. Copyright renewed © 1967 by Carolyn Haywood. Jacket illustration by Joe Yakovitic. Reprinted by permission of Joe Yakovetic./ Photograph courtesy of Carolyn Haywood.

MAEVE HENRY. Photograph courtesy of Maeve Henry.

ELIZABETH HILLMAN. Photograph courtesy of Elizabeth Hillman.

MARGARET HODGES. Jacket of *Persephone and the Springtime,* as retold by Margaret Hodges. Text copyright © 1973 by Margaret Hodges. Illustrations by Arvis Stewart. Reprinted by permission of Arvis L. Stewart./ Cover of *Saint George and the Dragon,* as retold by Margaret Hodges. Text copyright © 1984 by Margaret Hodges. Illustrations copyright © 1984 by Trina Schart Hyman. Reprinted by permission of Little, Brown and Company./ Cover of *Making a Difference: The Story of an American Family,* by Margaret Hodges. Copyright © 1989 by Margaret Hodges. Cover illustration copyright © 1989 by Viqui Maggio. Reprinted by permission of Viqui Maggio./ Photograph courtesy of Margaret Hodges.

ANGELA ELWELL HUNT. Cover of *Cassie Perkins #8: The Chance of a Lifetime,* by Angela Elwell Hunt. Copyright © 1992 by Angela Elwell Hunt. Front cover illustration copyright © by Ron Mazellan. Reprinted by permission of Tyndale House Publishers, Inc./ Cover of *The Case of the Terrified Track Star,* by Angela Elwell Hunt. Copyright © 1992 by Angela Elwell Hunt. Cover illustration and interior artwork by Doron Ben-Ami. Reprinted by permission of Thomas Nelson Publishers./ Cover of *Cassie Perkins #1: No More Broken Promises,* by Angela Elwell Hunt. Copyright © 1991 by Angela Elwell Hunt. Front cover illustration copyright © 1991 by Ron Mazellan. Reprinted by permission of Tyndale House Publishers, Inc./ Photograph courtesy of Angela Elwell Hunt.

ELLEN JACKSON. Photograph courtesy of Ellen Jackson.

VICTOR KELLEHER. Jacket of *Baily's Bones,* by Victor Kelleher. Jacket painting copyright © 1989 by Linda Benson. Reprinted by Dial Books for Young Readers, a division of Penguin Books USA Inc./ Jacket of *Del-Del,* by Victor Kelleher. Copyright © 1992 by Victor Kelleher. Jacket illustration by Peter Clarke.

GENE KEMP. Jacket of *The Room with No Windows,* by Gene Kemp. Copyright © 1989 by Gene Kemp. Cover illustration by Derek Brazell. Reprinted by permission of Faber & Faber Ltd.

MONA KERBY. Photograph courtesy of Mona Kerby.

MARY GRACE KETNER. Photograph © 1991 David Sixt Photography, courtesy of Mary Grace Ketner.

PAMELA LASKIN. Photograph courtesy of Pamela Laskin.

PATRICIA LAUBER. Jacket of *Journey to the Planets,* by Patricia Lauber. Copyright © 1987, 1982, by Patricia G. Lauber. Cover photographs courtesy NASA. Jacket design by Kathleen Westray. Reprinted by permission of Crown Publishers, Inc./ Jacket of *Volcano: The Eruption and Healing of Mount St. Helens,* by Patricia Lauber. Copyright © 1986 by Patricia Lauber. Jacket photograph by Lyn Topinka. Jacket design by Lyn Topinka. Reprinted by permission of Lyn Topinka./ Jacket of *Seeing Earth from Space,* by Patricia Lauber. Text copyright © 1990 by Patricia Lauber. Jacket photograph courtesy of and copyright by European Space Agency. Reprinted by permission of Orchard Books, New York./ Jacket of *Summer of Fire: Yellowstone 1988,* by Patricia Lauber. Text copyright © 1991 by Patricia Lauber. Jacket photograph copyright © Erwin and Peggy Bauer. Reprinted by permission of Orchard Books, New York./ Photograph courtesy of Patricia Lauber.

MADELEINE L'ENGLE. Cover of *A Wrinkle in Time,* by Madeleine L'Engle. Copyright © 1962 by Madeleine L'Engle Franklin. Reprinted by permission of Dell Books, a division of Bantam Doubleday Dell Publishing Group, Inc./ Cover of *A Ring of Endless Light,* by Madeleine L'Engle. Copyright © 1980 by Crosswicks, Ltd. Reprinted by permission of Dell Publishing, a division of Bantam Doubleday Dell Publishing Group, Inc./ Cover of *An Acceptable Time,* by Madeleine L'Engle. Copyright © 1989 by Crosswicks Ltd. Reprinted by permission of Dell Books, a division of Bantam Doubleday Dell Publishing Group, Inc./ Cover of *The Moon by Night,* by Madeleine L'Engle. Copyright © 1963 by Madeleine L'Engle. Reprinted by permission of Dell Books, a division of Bantam Doubleday Dell Publishing Group, Inc./ Photograph © Jerry Bauer.

AMANDA LOVERSEED. Photograph courtesy of Amanda Loverseed.

JILL MACKENZIE. Cover of *The Golden Fairy,* by Jill MacKenzie. Winston-Derek Publishers, Inc., 1991. Copyright © 1991 by Winston-Derek Publishers, Inc. Illustrations by Patricia Taber. Reprinted by permission of the publisher./ Photograph courtesy of Jill MacKenzie.

JAMES MARSHALL. Illustration by James Marshall from *The Stupids Take Off,* by James Marshall and Harry Allard. Houghton Mifflin Company, 1989. Text copyright © 1989 by Harry Allard and James Marshall. Illustrations copyright © 1989 by James Marshall. Reprinted by permission of Houghton Mifflin Company./ Illustration by James Marshall from *Miss Nelson Is Back,* by James Marshall and Harry Allard. Copyright © 1982 by Harry Allard. Copyright © 1982 by James Marshall. Reprinted by permission of Houghton Mifflin Company./ Illustration from *Fox and His Friends,* by Edward Marshall. Text copyright © 1982 by Edward Marshall. Illustration copyright © 1982 by James Marshall. All Rights Reserved. Reprinted in the United States by permission of Penguin USA. Reprinted in the British Commonwealth and the United Kingdom by permission of the Estate of James Marshall./ Illustration by James Marshall from his *George and Martha, One Fine Day.* Copyright © 1978 by James Marshall. Reprinted by permission of Houghton Mifflin Company./ Photograph used by permission of Dial Books for Young Readers, a division of Penguin Books USA Inc.

HELEN MCCANN. Photograph courtesy of Helen McCann.

TOM MCCAUGHREN. Cover of *Run with the Wind,* by Tom McCaughren. Copyright © 1983 by Tom McCaughren. Cover illustration by Debbie Rawlinson. Reprinted by permission of Wolfhound Press./ Photograph courtesy of Tom McCaughren.

LARRY MCKAUGHAN. Photograph courtesy of Larry McKaughan.

STEPHEN MOOSER. Cover of *It's A Weird, Weird School,* by Stephen Mooser. Copyright © 1989 by Stephen Mooser. Cover illustration by Carl Cassler. Reprinted by permission of Dell Books, a division of Bantam Doubleday Dell Publishing Group, Inc./ Cover of *Secrets of Scary Fun,* by Stephen Mooser. Text copyright © 1990 by Stephen Mooser. Illustrations copyright © 1990 by George Ulrich. Reprinted by permission of Dell Books, a division of Bantam Doubleday Dell Publishing Group, Inc./ Cover of *The Headless Snowman,* by Stephen Mooser. Text copyright © 1992 by Stephen Mooser. Illustration copyright © 1992 by George Ulrich. Reprinted by permission of Dell Books, a division of Bantam Doubleday Dell Publishing Group, Inc./ Cover of *The Hitchhiking Vampire,* by Stephen Mooser. Copyright © 1989 by Stephen Mooser. Cover illustration by Carl Cassler. Reprinted by permission of Dell Books, a division of Bantam Doubleday Dell Publishing Group, Inc./ Photograph courtesy of Stephen Mooser.

EVELYN CLARKE MOTT. Jacket of *Steam Train Ride,* by Evelyn Clarke Mott. Copyright © 1991 by Evelyn Clarke Mott. Cover photographs arranged by Michail J. Clarke. Reprinted by permission of Walker and Company./ Photograph courtesy of Evelyn Clarke Mott.

KILMENY NILAND. Jacket by Kilmeny Niland from her *A Bellbird in a Flame Tree.* Text copyright © 1989 by Angus & Robertson Publishers. Jacket art copyright © 1989 by Kilmeny Niland. Reprinted in the United States by permission of Tambourine Books, a division of William Morrow and Company, Inc. Reprinted in the British Commonwealth by permission of Collins/Angus & Robertson Publishers./ Photograph courtesy of Kilmeny Niland.

LYGIA BOJUNGA NUNES. Photograph courtesy of Lydia Bojunga Nunes.

GENEVIEVE O'CONNOR. Photograph courtesy of Genevieve O'Connor.

MARGARET POWER. Photograph courtesy of Margaret Power.

GLORIA TELES PUSHKER. Photograph courtesy of Gloria Teles Pushker.

DIAN CURTIS REGAN. Cover of *The Curse of the Trouble Dolls,* by Dian Curtis Regan. Illustrations by Michael Chesworth. Reprinted by permission of Henry Holt and Company, Inc./ Photograph courtesy of Dian Curtis Regan.

LYNNE REID BANKS. Jacket of *The Mystery of the Cupboard,* by Lynne Reid Banks. Text copyright © 1993 by Lynne Reid Banks. Jacket illustration copyright © 1993 by Tom Newsom. Reprinted by permission of Morrow Junior Books, a division of William Morrow and Company, Inc./ Jacket of *One More River,* by Lynne Reid Banks. Text copyright © 1992 by Lynne Reid Banks. Jacket illustration copyright © 1992 by Michael Deas. Reprinted in the United States by permission of Morrow Junior Books, a division of William Morrow and Company, Inc. Reprinted in the British Commonwealth by permission of Michael Deas./ Cover of *The Indian in the Cupboard,* by Lynne Reid Banks. Copyright © 1980 by Lynne Reid Banks. Illustrations copyright © 1981 by Brock Cole. Reprinted by Avon Books, New York./ Photograph courtesy of Lynne Reid Banks.

ANGELO G. RESCINITI. Cover of *Incredible Super Bowl Action,* by Angelo Rescinite and Ann Steinberg. Copyright © 1991 by permission of Willowisp Press, Inc./ Photograph courtesy of Angelo G. Resciniti.

ROBIN RICHMOND. Photograph courtesy of Robin Richmond.

LIZ ROSENBERG. Photograph by David Bosnick, courtesy of Liz Rosenberg.

BENGT ARNE RUNNERSTROEM. Illustration by Bengt Arne Runnerstroem from his *Cubeo Amazonas.* Copyright © 1993 by Bengt Arnee Runnerstroem. Reprinted by permission of Bengt Arne Runnerstroem./ Photograph courtesy of Bengt Arne Runnerstroem.

ANNE SAIDMAN. Photograph courtesy of Anne Saidman.

RICHARD SCARRY. Illustrations by Richard Scarry from his *Richard Scarry's Best Christman Book Ever!* Copyright © 1981 by Richard Scarry. Reprinted in the United States and Canada by permission of Random House, Inc. Reprinted in the British Commonwealth by permission of Richard Scarry./ Illustration by Richard Scarry from his *Richard Scarry's Best Counting Book Ever.* Copyright © 1975 by Richard Scarry. Reprinted in the United States and Canada by permission of Random House, Inc. Reprinted in the British Commonwealth by permission of Richard Scarry./ Illustration by Richard Scarry from his *Richard Scarry's Cars and Trucks and Things That Go.* Copyright © 1974 by Western Publishing Company, Inc. Reprinted by permission of the publisher./ Photograph courtesy of Richard Scarry.

GRETCHEN SCHIELDS. Illustration by Gretchen Schields from *The Moon Lady,* by Amy Tan. Text copyright © 1992 by Amy Tan. Illustrations copyright © 1992 by Gretchen Schields. Reprinted with permission of Macmillan Publishing Company./ Photograph Robert Foothorap Company 1992, courtesy of Gretchen Schields.

SOMETHING ABOUT THE AUTHOR®

ALIKI
  See BRANDENBERG, Aliki (Liacouras)

*   *   *

ALLAN, Mabel Esther 1915-
  (Jean Estoril, Priscilla Hagon, Anne Pilgrim)

■ Personal

Born February 11, 1915, in Wallasey, Cheshire, England; daughter of James Pemberton (a merchant) and Priscilla (Hagon) Allan. *Education:* Educated at private schools in England. *Hobbies and other interests:* Book collecting.

■ Addresses

Home—Glengarth, 11, Oldfield Way, Heswall, Wirral L60 6RQ, England. *Agent*—Curtis Brown-John Farquharson Ltd., 162-168 Regent St., London W1R 5TB, England.

■ Career

Author. Served as warden of a wartime nursery for children during World War II. *Military service:* Women's Land Army, two years during World War II.

■ Awards, Honors

Runner-up for Edgar Allan Poe Award, Mystery Writers of America, 1972, for *Mystery in Wales; Horn Book* honor list for *An Island in a Green Sea;* many of Allen's books have been Junior Literary Guild selections, including *The View beyond My Father* and *A Lovely Tomorrow.*

■ Writings

FICTION

The Glen Castle Mystery, Warne, 1948.
The Adventurous Summer, Museum Press, 1948.
Wyndhams Went to Wales, Sylvan Press, 1948.
Cilia of Chiltern's Edge, Museum Press, 1949.
Mullion, Hutchinson, 1949.
Chiltern Adventure, Blackie, 1950.
Holiday at Arnriggs, Warne, 1950.
Seven in Switzerland, Blackie, 1950.
School in Danger, Blackie, 1952.
School on Cloud Ridge, Hutchinson, 1952.
School on North Barrule, Museum Press, 1952.
Lucia Comes to School, Hutchinson, 1953.
Strangers at Brongwerne, Museum Press, 1953.
New Schools for Old, Hutchinson, 1954.
Summer at Town's End, Harrap, 1954.
Judith Teachers, Bodley Head, 1955.
Swiss School, Hutchinson, 1955.
Two in the Western Isles, Hutchinson, 1956.
At School in Skye, Blackie, 1957.
House by the Marsh, Dent, 1958.
Amanda Goes to Italy, Hutchinson, 1959.
Shadow over the Alps, Hutchinson, 1960.

MABEL ESTHER ALLAN

Holiday of Endurance, Dent, 1961.
Romance in Italy, Vanguard, 1962.
The Ballet Family, Methuen, 1963, Criterion, 1966, published under pseudonym Jean Estoril, Simon & Schuster (London), 1991.
The Sign of the Unicorn, Criterion, 1963.
New York for Nicola, Vanguard, 1963.
The Ballet Family Again, Methuen, 1964, published under pseudonym Jean Estoril, Simon & Schuster (London), 1991.
Fiona on the Fourteenth Floor, Dent, 1964, published as *Mystery on the Fourteenth Floor*, Criterion, 1965.
A Summer at Sea, Dent, 1966, Vanguard, 1967.
Missing in Manhattan, Dent, 1967, Vanguard, 1968.
The Mystery Started in Madeira, Criterion, 1967.
The Wood Street Secret, Methuen, 1968, Abelard, 1970.
The Wood Street Group, Methuen, 1969.
Climbing to Danger, Heinemann, 1969, published as *Mystery in Wales*, Vanguard, 1971.
The Wood Street Rivals, Methuen, 1970.
Dangerous Inheritance, Heinemann, 1970.
An Island in a Green Sea, Atheneum, 1972.
Time to Go Back, Abelard, 1972.
A Formidable Enemy, Heinemann, 1973, Thomas Nelson, 1974.
The Wood Street Helpers, Methuen, 1973.
Ship of Danger, Criterion, 1974.
A Chill in the Lane, Thomas Nelson, 1974.
Bridge of Friendship, Dent, 1975, Dodd, 1977.
Away from Wood Street, Methuen, 1976.

My Family's Not Forever, Abelard, 1977.
The View beyond My Father, Dodd, 1978.
A Lovely Tomorrow, Abelard, 1979, Dodd, 1980.
Wood Street and Mary Ellen, Methuen, 1979.
The Mills Down Below, Abelard, 1980, Dodd, 1981.
Pine Street Goes Camping, Abelard, 1980.
Strangers in Wood Street, Methuen, 1981.
The Horns of Danger, Dodd, 1981.
The Pine Street Problem, Abelard, 1981.
A Strange Enchantment, Abelard, 1981, Dodd, 1982.
Growing Up in Wood Street, Methuen, 1982.
Goodbye to Pine Street, Abelard, 1982.
Alone at Pine Street, Abelard, 1983.
The Crumble Lane Adventure, Methuen, 1983.
A Dream of Hunger Moss, Dodd, 1983.
A Secret in Spindle Bottom, Abelard, 1984.
Friends at Pine Street, Abelard, 1984.
Trouble in Crumble Lane, Methuen, 1984.
The Flash Children in Winter, Hodder & Stoughton, 1985.
The Pride of Pine Street, Blackie, 1985.
The Crumble Lane Captives, Methuen, 1986.
A Mystery in Spindle Bottom, Blackie, 1986.
The Road to Huntingland, Severn House, 1986.
The Crumble Lane Mystery, Methuen, 1987.
Up the Victorian Staircase: A London Mystery, Severn House, 1987.
First Term at Ash Grove, Blackie, 1988.
The Mystery of Seradina, privately printed, 1990.
Chiltern School, privately printed, 1990.
Queen Rita at the High School and Other School Stories, privately printed, 1991.
The Two Head Girls and Other School Stories, privately printed, 1992.
The Way to Glen Dradan and Other Scottish, Welsh, and Irish Stories, privately printed, 1993.

Author of over fifty other juvenile books.

UNDER PSEUDONYM JEAN ESTORIL; FICTION

Ballet for Drina, Hodder & Stoughton, 1957, Scholastic, 1989.
Drina's Dancing Year, Hodder & Stoughton, 1958, Scholastic, 1989.
Drina Dances in Exile, Hodder & Stoughton, 1959, published as *Drina Dances Alone*, Scholastic, 1989.
Drina Dances in Italy, Hodder & Stoughton, 1959, published as *Drina Dances on Stage*, Scholastic, 1989.
Drina Dances Again, Hodder & Stoughton, 1960, Scholastic, 1989.
Drina Dances in New York, Hodder & Stoughton, 1961.
Drina Dances in Paris, Hodder & Stoughton, 1962.
Drina Dances in Madeira, Hodder & Stoughton, 1963.
Drina Dances in Switzerland, Hodder & Stoughton, 1964.
Drina Goes on Tour, Brockhampton, 1965.
We Danced in Bloomsbury Square, Heinemann, 1967, published as *The Ballet Twins*, Simon & Schuster (London), 1991.
Drina, Ballerina, Simon & Schuster, 1991.

UNDER PSEUDONYM PRISCILLA HAGON

Cruising to Danger, World, 1966.
Dancing to Danger, World, 1967.
Mystery at Saint-Hilaire, World, 1968.
Mystery at the Villa Bianca, World, 1969.
Mystery of the Secret Square, World, 1970.

UNDER PSEUDONYM ANNE PILGRIM

The First Time I Saw Paris, Abelard, 1961.
Clare Goes to Holland, Abelard, 1962.
A Summer in Provence, Abelard, 1963.
Strangers in New York, Abelard, 1964.
Selina's New Family, Abelard, 1967.

OTHER

Murder at the Flood (adult novel), Paul, 1958.
The Haunted Valley and Other Poems, privately printed,
    1981.
To Be an Author: A Short Autobiography, Gill, 1982.
More about Being an Author (autobiography), Gill,
    1985.
My Background Came First: My Books and Places
    (autobiography), two volumes, privately printed,
    1988.
*The Road to the Isles and Other Places: Some Journeys
    with a Rucksack,* privately printed, 1989.

Allan's books have been translated into numerous
foreign languages, including French, German, Polish,
Italian, Norwegian, Dutch, Portuguese, and Japanese.

Manuscript collection at University of Southern Mississippi; autobiographical and bibliographical material
collected in many countries, including Uzbekistan.

■ Sidelights

Since publishing her first book in 1948, British writer
Mabel Esther Allan has been the prolific author of over
170 books for children and young adults. In her long
writing career, Allan has demonstrated much diversity,
both thematically and in the audience for her books.
Early on, Allan produced numerous conventional-type
books for young children, such as adventures, mysteries,
and school stories, in addition to romances for older girl
readers. Later in her career, however, Allan's books
became more autobiographical in scope and have dealt
with realistic topics such as British life during World
War II, the Women's Suffrage Movement, and the lives
of urban working-class youths. In *Twentieth Century
Children's Writers,* Alan Edwin Day remarks that Allan's various books show her to be a writer who "defies
... classifying and labelling authors into clearly defined
categories," and one who displays "vitality, exuberance,
and versatility."

Allan was born in Wallasey, England, a town on the
Mersey River across from Liverpool. As a young girl,
she suffered from very poor eyesight, and disliked both
school and her teachers. "I went to private schools, three
of them, where I never remember a teacher seeming
aware that I simply couldn't see," she remarked in her
autobiography, *To Be an Author.* " .... They thought

me stupid, almost beyond hope. I regarded them with
scorn and some fear." Allan found, however, great
enjoyment in books, and spent much time in Wallasey's
main library. She resolved to become a writer at the age
of eight, and her father bought her a working desk and
typewriter, upon which Allan taught herself to type.
Relying on her own knowledge of children's books as a
guide, Allan composed her first book—first in longhand
and then typewritten—when she was twelve, and a
second when she was fifteen. These early efforts were "a
tremendous task for a young girl who didn't see very
well," Allan recalled in *To Be an Author.* "All those
hours shut up alone with my typewriter set a pattern for
the rest of my life."

Allan began to sell poetry and short stories from the age
of nineteen onward, yet her desire to publish a children's book would be interrupted by the Second World
War. In 1939, one of Allan's novels was accepted for
publication, yet the threat of war resulted in its being
returned. The following year, Allan was called up to
serve in the Woman's Land Army, and was sent to
Reaseheath Agricultural College among the farm country of South Cheshire. During breaks she returned to
Wallasey, which was experiencing periodic bombing by

**A Dream of
Hunger Moss**

Mabel Esther Allan

**Young Alice learns the truth about a mysterious young
man she meets in a beloved English moor in this novel
by Allan.** (Cover illustration by Bertram M. Tormey.)

the Germans. "I never dreamed then, alone and scared in the English fields, afraid that we would lose the war, that long, long years later I would be writing about much that happened," Allan commented in *To Be an Author*. ". . . . Likewise, sitting in the air raid shelter in Wallasey during heavy raids, I would have thought anyone mad if they had told me that a book about that would one day, in the far future, be read by German young people." Allan managed to write some poetry during the war, and during one of her breaks to Wallasey produced a 120,000-word novel—most of it written in an air raid shelter.

Change in Eyesight Spurs Writing Career

Later during the war, Allan was put in charge of a wartime nursery, in which she oversaw a group of forty-eight children aged two to five, and found little time for further writing. In 1944, however, shortly before the Allied invasion of France, her sight drastically improved. She described in *To Be an Author* "the wonder of seeing what seemed to me so brilliantly. Always I had seen the world through a thick yellowish blur . . . . Even as a very young child I was far more afraid of going

When her family refuses to acknowledge her physical handicap, a sight-impaired girl in Allan's *The View beyond My Father* seeks help and friendship on her own. (Cover illustration by Tormey.)

blind than of dying." As part of her therapy, Allan wasn't allowed to do any reading and, as a result, learned to compose directly onto a typewriter, instead of transcribing from her longhand manuscript. Allan began producing numerous short stories and, in 1945, had the fortune of selling her earlier unpublished novel, *The Glen Castle Mystery*. Spurred on by her success, Allan wrote a second novel the same year, *The Adventurous Summer*, which was likewise accepted for publication.

Allan's writing career was thus launched, and she began a prolific stretch from the rest of the 1940s through the 1950s and 1960s, in which she produced numerous books that sold well, especially among young children. A lover of travel, Allan often focused her books on places she had visited and wanted to capture for herself. "[The books] simply poured out of me, as I visited new countries and was frantic to paint pictures of them. For my own pleasure. It has simply been sheer luck that other people like my books," she commented in *To Be an Author*. Allan likewise once remarked on the importance of place to her early books: "For many years *places* were all important to me as an author. The background always came first. It was partly the wish to live again experiences I had enjoyed, though formed and altered to make a story. I believe that my ability to evoke places is the thing that has given the most pleasure to readers." Two of Allan's favorite places outside of Great Britain have been New York City and Paris, which have been the setting for several of her books.

Conventional in nature, Allan's early books were, as she once commented, "all very pleasant and shallow by today's standards." Allan described the limitations of writing for young people in her early career: "I began to publish books during the days when there were many taboos in books for young people. It wasn't even possible to suggest that children sometimes hated their parents or that atheism was as desirable a state as being Protestant, Catholic, or a follower of any other religion. Unconsciously maybe this influenced me." However, one area in which Allan was considered unconventional was her portrayal of schools. "My school stories were only published in Britain and they were far ahead of their time," she once commented. ". . . . I believed passionately in co-education, which was unusual in Britain then and almost unknown in boarding schools. I believed in self-discipline and not in imposed discipline, and in learning for learning's sake and not for marks in class. I thought the boys and girls should help to run their schools and be expected to be responsible and sensible human beings, even quite young children."

Between the years of 1960 and 1970, Allan was firmly established as a top-selling children's writer. She commented in *To Be an Author:* "I worked hard, my books were translated into other languages, and I had what I must call a moderate success. For that is all it was when compared with authors who make an enormous amount of money. But the name of Mabel Esther Allan was certainly spreading around a good part of the world." While Allan's early books are today most popular among book collectors, her Drina series, originally published in the 1950s and 1960s, still enjoys a popular readership. Written under the pseudonym of Jean Estoril, the Drina books focus on the experiences of a young dancer on her way to becoming an international ballet star. In 1989 and 1990, updated editions of the original books were published in both the United States and Great Britain.

Changing World Leads to Change in Themes

Around 1970, Allan's books became more autobiographical in nature. As she once commented, she discovered that she "could be much more truthful" and "could look to the past, and write about it." Allan found herself able to address topics and concerns which she hadn't been able to do previously. "I could suggest that some people had no religious beliefs and might even be better human beings because of that," she once remarked. "I could write about young people who disliked their parents. I could also mention sexual feelings." *An Island in a Green Sea* and *Time to Go Back* were the first of Allan's books to reflect this change in direction and, together with books such as *The View beyond My Father, A Lovely Tomorrow,* and *A Strange Enchantment,* "at last go deeper than any of my earlier books," Allan added. In her 1980s book, *The Mills Down Below,* Allan wrote about political subject matter as she depicted the women's suffrage movement in Great Britain in the early part of the twentieth century. The issue is one which Allan feels close to. "I wish I had written more about women's rights, and children's rights, too," she commented in *To Be an Author.* "The older I get the more strongly I feel about such things and there is still a lot that must be done. I grew up as a second class citizen just because I was a girl, and I never even questioned it for a very long time."

In 1991, Allan began retracing the steps of her early career. She remarked: "From early 1936 to 1957 I wrote and sold about 330 short stories. At first they were for very young children, then later for older girls. I kept no copies, but when the old records were found at the bottom of a chest I began to try to find published stories. They are being found not only in Britain, but in Australia and New Zealand. I am planning to bring them together in several privately printed volumes."

Allan once commented that her long and varied life as a writer has been largely a satisfying one. "I had years of struggle and disappointment and I wouldn't relive them for anything, but it was all worth it in the end. I wouldn't have chosen any other life, though the life of an author is basically a very lonely one. When aspiring authors ask me for advice, the first thing I say is: 'Don't contemplate it unless you can stand spending a large part of your life alone, shut up with a typewriter.'" Allan has repeatedly commented that she writes for herself and for what she finds appealing, yet she enjoys having a positive affect on her readers. "I am glad where I have given pleasure, or have helped," she stated in *To Be an Author.* "And particularly glad if I have sent people to places I have loved. The first fan letter I ever had said: 'Thank you for writing such a lovely book. It made me

In *Drina Dances Again,* one of Allan's many books under the Jean Estoril pseudonym, Drina considers leaving dancing for acting after unexpected success in a play.

very happy.' That made me happy, too, but it was incidental."

■ Works Cited

Allan, Mabel Esther, *To Be an Author: A Short Autobiography,* Charles Gill & Sons, 1982.

Day, Allan Edwin, "Mabel Allan," *Twentieth Century Children's Writers,* 3rd edition, St. James, 1989.

■ For More Information See

BOOKS

Something about the Author Autobiography Series, Volume 11, Gale, 1991.

PERIODICALS

Bulletin of the Center for Children's Books, September, 1977; July-August, 1980; April, 1982; November, 1982; February, 1984.

Junior Literary Guild, March, 1980.

AVERY, Gillian (Elise) 1926-

■ Personal

Born September 30, 1926, in Reigate, Surrey, England; daughter of Norman Bates (an estate agent) and Grace Elise (Dunn) Avery; married Anthony Oliver John Cockshut (a university lecturer and writer), August 25, 1952; children: Ursula Mary Elise. *Education:* Educated at Dunottar School. *Religion:* Anglican.

■ Addresses

Home—32 Charlbury Rd., Oxford OX2 6UU, England.

■ Career

Writer and editor. *Surrey Mirror*, Redhill, Surrey, England, reporter, 1944-47; *Chamber's Encyclopaedia*, London, England, secretary, 1947-50; Clarendon Press, Oxford, England, assistant to the illustrations editor, 1950-54. *Member:* Children's Books History Society, (chair, 1987-89).

■ Awards, Honors

Carnegie commendations, 1957, for *The Warden's Niece*, and 1962, for *The Greatest Gresham*; Carnegie Medal runner-up, 1971, and *Guardian* Award, 1972, both for *A Likely Lad.*

■ Writings

JUVENILE

The Warden's Niece, illustrated by Dick Hart, Collins, 1957, published in the United States as *Maria Escapes*, illustrated by Scott Snow, Simon, 1992.
Trespassers at Charlcote, illustrated by Hart, Collins, 1958.
James without Thomas, illustrated by John Verney, Collins, 1959.
The Elephant War, illustrated by Verney, Collins, 1960, Holt, 1971.
To Tame a Sister, illustrated by Verney, Collins, 1961, Van Nostrand, 1964.
The Greatest Gresham, illustrated by Verney, Collins, 1962.
The Peacock House, illustrated by Verney, Collins, 1963.
The Italian Spring, illustrated by Verney, Collins, 1964, Holt, 1972.
Call of the Valley, illustrated by Laszlo Acs, Collins, 1966, Holt, 1968.
Ellen and the Queen, illustrated by Krystyna Turska, Hamish Hamilton, 1971, Thomas Nelson, 1974.
Ellen's Birthday, illustrated by Turska, Hamish Hamilton, 1971.
A Likely Lad, illustrated by Faith Jaques, Holt, 1971.
Jemima and the Welsh Rabbit, illustrated by John Lawrence, Hamish Hamilton, 1972.
Gillian Avery's Book of the Strange and Odd (nonfiction), illustrated by Michael Jackson, Kestrel Books, 1975.

Freddie's Feet, illustrated by Turska, Hamish Hamilton, 1976.
Huck and Her Time Machine, Collins, 1977.
Mouldy's Orphan, illustrated by Jaques, Collins, 1978.
Sixpence!, illustrated by Antony Maitland, Collins, 1979.

EDITOR

Juliana Horatia Ewing, *A Flat Iron for a Farthing*, Faith Press, 1959.
Ewing, *Jan of the Windmill*, Faith Press, 1960.
The Sapphire Treasury of Stories for Boys and Girls, Gollancz, 1960.
In the Window Seat: A Selection of Victorian Stories, illustrated by Susan Einzig, Oxford University Press, 1960, Van Nostrand, 1965.
Annie Keary, *Father Phim*, Faith Press, 1962.
(And author of introduction) *Unforgettable Journeys*, illustrated by John Verney, F. Watts, 1965.
Margaret Roberts, *Banning and Blessing*, Gollancz, 1967.
Andrew Lang, *The Gold of Fairnilee and Other Stories*, Gollancz, 1967.
Ewing, *A Great Emergency, and a Very Ill-Tempered Family*, Gollancz, 1967.
School Remembered, illustrated by Verney, Gollancz, 1967, Funk, 1968.
Charlotte Yonge, *Village Children*, Gollancz, 1967.
(And author of introduction) *Gollancz Revivals* (twelve reissued volumes of 19th century children's books), Gollancz, 1967-70.
Brenda, *Froggy's Little Brother*, Gollancz, 1968.
Mary Louisa Molesworth, *My New Home*, illustrated by L. Leslie Brooke, Gollancz, 1968.
(And author of introduction) Brenda, Mrs. Gatty, and Frances Hodgson Burnett, *Victoria-Bess and Others*, Gollancz, 1968, published in the United States as *Victorian Doll Stories*, Schocken, 1969.
G. E. Farrow, *The Wallypug of Why*, illustrated by Harry Furniss, Gollancz, 1968.
(And author of introduction) *The Life and Adventures of Lady Anne*, illustrated by F. D. Bedford, Gollancz, 1969.
Margaret Roberts, *Stephanie's Children*, Gollancz, 1969.
E. V. Lucas, *Anne's Terrible Good Nature and Other Stories for Children*, Gollancz, 1970.
Keary, *The Rival Kings*, Gollancz, 1970.
Red Letter Days, illustrated by Turska, Hamish Hamilton, 1971.

FOR ADULTS

Mrs. Ewing, Bodley Head, 1961, H. Z. Walck, 1964.
(With Angela Bull) *Nineteenth Century Children: Heroes and Heroines in English Children's Stories, 1780-1900*, Hodder & Stoughton, 1965.
Victorian People: In Life and in Literature, Holt, 1970.
The Echoing Green: Memories of Regency and Victorian Youth, Viking, 1974.
Childhood's Pattern: A Study of the Heroes and Heroines of Children's Fiction, 1770-1950, Hodder & Stoughton, 1975.
The Lost Railway (fiction), Collins, 1980.

GILLIAN AVERY

Onlookers (fiction), Collins, 1983.

(Editor, with Julia Briggs) *Children and Their Books: A Celebration of the Work of Iona and Peter Opie,* Oxford University Press, 1989.

The Best Type of Girl: A History of the Girl's Independent Schools, Deutsch, 1991.

Behold the Child: A History of American Children and Their Books 1621-1922, Random House (England), 1994.

OTHER

(Editor) *The Hole in the Wall, and Other Stories,* illustrated by Doreen Roberts, Oxford University Press, 1968.

(With others) *Authors' Choice: Stories,* illustrated by Turska, Hamish Hamilton, 1970.

Also author of introductions to reissues of Victorian children's books, Faith Press. Contributor to books, including *Winter's Tales for Children No. 2,* Macmillan, 1966; *The Eleanor Farjeon Book,* Hamish Hamilton, 1966; *Allsorts 5,* Macmillan, 1972; and *Rudyard Kipling,* Weidenfeld & Nicolson, 1972. Also editor of *Emily Pepys,* a journal, Prospect Books.

■ Sidelights

British author Gillian Avery has been writing children's novels since the 1950s. Feeling an affinity with children of the Victorian Era, she sets most of her work in this period. Avery's most popular books include *The Warden's Niece, The Elephant War,* and *A Likely Lad;* the last garnered her the *Guardian* Award and was a runner-up for the prestigious Carnegie Medal. She has also edited many books for children, including editions of the works of several Victorian children's authors, and has written and edited adult works about children in the Victorian period.

Avery was born September 30, 1926, and grew up in the town of Redhill, Surrey, England. Though she had a relatively happy childhood, her parents, educators, and neighbors did not encourage her creativity. "Books in households such as ours," Avery recalls in an essay for *Something about the Author Autobiography Series* (*SAAS*), "were not regarded as essential." In particular, "fiction was regarded as a frivolity." Nevertheless, she managed to read, sometimes in secret, and she often found herself enjoying Victorian stories for children, particularly those of author Juliana Ewing. Avery was also influenced by Arthur Mee's *Children's Encyclopaedia.* She skipped the parts about geography, natural history, and astronomy in favor of the small pieces of fiction and the biographies of famous people. Avery comments in her *SAAS* essay that "Mee was a great believer in self-help and the self-made man, and though it was not he who originally said that genius was only an infinite capacity for taking pains, this was his moral theme. It fired me also to try and be a genius."

Stifling School Leads to Sympathy for Victorians

Avery had seemingly overwhelming obstacles in the way of this goal. For her education, she was sent to a small girl's school, which she recognized as inferior even at a young age. "The headmistress ... seemed to regard the school only as a livelihood," Avery explains in *SAAS.* "She had ... no particular interest in any of her pupils.... She regarded art, music, and drama as superfluous extras, and the only purpose she appeared to see in English, history, geography, and French was as exam fodder." Avery's school experiences aided in her later identification with Victorian children, she affirms in *SAAS.* "When fifteen years later I began writing children's books, it was this memory of Us and Them that I remembered, children versus authority, with an unbridgeable gulf between them. But since by the time that I wrote children no longer seemed to fear the adult world so much as we had done, and were not likely to credit that only twenty years before it had been very different, I transferred the setting to the Victorian period, since everybody seems to accept that the Victorians were strict with their young." Ironically, the government-sponsored school near Avery's home provided a better education, but because of her father's class consciousness, he did not allow her to attend. She elaborates in her *SAAS* essay: "He saw himself as an officer and a gentleman; if he had sent his children to the state schools he would have lost caste, we would have had totally different friends; we would no longer have mixed with the children of his friends. We were just as much aware of it as our parents were, and caste then seemed to be the all-important thing."

By the time she graduated from secondary school, Avery had abandoned her ambitions of genius and decided to settle for a career in journalism. In order to learn the skills she would need, such as shorthand and typing, she enrolled in a secretarial school. She did not do well there, and when the bombing of London during World War II necessitated her departure for the safer countryside, Avery left the school never to return. Her father then found her a temporary position on the *Surrey Mirror,* a newspaper edited by one of his acquaintances. Unfortunately, there was not much work for Avery to do there, and her assignments usually consisted of covering local funerals. When the war ended, however, she received the more pleasant task of covering the numerous victory celebrations. But the end of the war also brought the return of the reporter Avery had been replacing, and so her employment with the *Surrey Mirror* was finished.

Avery then found work with publishing firms, first as a secretary for the illustrations editor at the George Newnes firm, where she worked on *Chamber's Encyclopaedia;* then with Oxford University Press, where she served as the assistant to the illustrations editor. While working at Oxford, Avery was introduced to Anthony Oliver John Cockshut, the friend of one of her childhood neighbors. In 1952 she married Cockshut, who was an Oxford scholar interested in the Victorian period. Avery acknowledges in *SAAS:* "Most of what I know and certainly my taste for Victorian literature has been derived from him, and when I came to write it was he who pared and sharpened my prose, giving me a horror of unnecessary words."

Writing Career Inspired by Homesickness

Avery "came to write," as she put it, when her husband's fellowship at Oxford ended, necessitating a move to Manchester where he got a job as a schoolteacher. Avery disliked Manchester's urban dreariness, and she was extremely nostalgic for the pleasant walks of Oxford. "Homesick for the paradise we had left," she explains in her *SAAS* essay, "I settled down one February day in 1955 to write about Oxford . . . . And I wrote about Maria, aged eleven, who in 1875 runs away from her dreadful school to Oxford, and tells her great uncle, the warden of Canterbury College, that her ambition is to be the first woman professor of Greek." This became *The Warden's Niece,* which, after a few rejections and some rewriting, was published in 1957 and remains one of her most popular books. Avery points out in *SAAS* that "it was not difficult to write about Victorian children; I had read more Victorian than contemporary fiction, and was steeped in biographies and memoirs of the period . . . . It was all written with great feeling; I drew on my longing for a proper

In this novel Avery explores the charms of nineteenth-century Italy through the eyes of an orphan taken to live with a little-known relative. (Cover illustration by John Verney.)

education and for Oxford." To her credit, more than thirty years after its initial publication, *The Warden's Niece* has been reissued in the United States as *Maria Escapes,* and "still seems fresh and appealing," according to a *Horn Book* contributor.

In the story, once Maria settles in with her uncle, she is determined to demonstrate her seriousness towards her scholastic ambition and goal to become a professor. Her uncle supports her goal and schedules her tutoring sessions. As Maria's drive for learning increases and her timidness decreases, she decides to write an article that will meet her uncle's scholarly standards and begins to zealously research a mystery concerning a seventeenth century boy. Her conviction to complete her work leads her to daringly skip her tutor's lessons and boldly invade the exclusively-for-males Bodleian Library for research. Avery's detailed knowledge of social history and setting are admired by the critics. "Avery . . . capture[s] the period and the setting," asserts Amy Kellman in the *School Library Journal.* Similarly, the *Horn Book* contributor concludes that Avery "set[s] the novel in a firm base of reality; her skill as a narrator brings it to life."

Avery continued to write children's novels, most set in the Victorian Era, throughout the 1960s and 1970s. *The Elephant War* features some of the characters from *The Warden's Niece* and concerns a protest over selling a London Zoo elephant to P. T. Barnum's circus. *A Likely Lad* is based on some of the childhood experiences of Avery's father-in-law, and *Mouldy's Orphan* explores what happens when a young girl brings a street child home to live with her family. An interesting exception to Avery's rule of Victorian settings is 1977's *Huck and Her Time Machine,* which involves a modern-day family who are able to become their Victorian-Era ancestors through the use of a time machine.

While Avery was writing and editing children's fiction, however, she also began writing some works for adults. She authored a volume about her favorite author from her childhood, *Mrs. Ewing,* in 1961, and has done several studies of Victorian children's literature in addition to the fiction works *The Lost Railway* and *Onlookers.* Since the 1980s Avery has concentrated on writing for adults. In her 1991 book, *The Best Type of Girl: A History of Girls' Independent Schools,* "Avery draws on a wide range of literature and some school archives to provide a skilfully assembled and absorbing mosaic of what school life was like," states Paul Smith in a review for the *Times Literary Supplement.* Avery describes the difficulty of establishing and maintaining appropriate schooling for young girls in England, the women who were pioneers in educational progress for girls, and the changes over time in social and cultural feelings towards girl's education. Avery experienced many of the difficulties in achieving the adequate education she elaborates on in *The Best Type of Girl,* but considers herself fortunate for not suffering from the disadvantages of lacking a good education. She concludes in *SAAS:* "My life has always apparently been shaped by a series of lucky accidents rather than by any conscious purpose on my part . . . . The lucky accidents are linked, and start with the fact that I had no education. It was the longing for one that made me write in the first place."

■ Works Cited

Avery, Gillian, essay in *Something about the Author Autobiography Series,* Volume 6, Gale, 1988, pp. 1-16.

Kellman, Amy, review of *Maria Escapes, School Library Journal,* June, 1992, p. 112.

Review of *Maria Escapes, Horn Book,* May/June, 1992, p. 339.

Smith, Paul, review of *The Best Type of Girl: A History of Girls' Independent Schools, Times Literary Supplement,* April 22, 1991, p. 3.

■ For More Information See

BOOKS

Doyle, Brian, *The Who's Who of Children's Literature,* Schocken, 1968.

PERIODICALS

Bulletin of the Center for Children's Books, September, 1975.

Growing Point, May, 1985.

Guardian, March 23, 1972.

Horn Book, August, 1968; April, 1975.

Junior Bookshelf, October, 1977.

New Statesman, November 3, 1967.

New Yorker, December 14, 1968.

Observer (London), January 27, 1991, p. 59.

Times Literary Supplement, March 25, 1977; July 7, 1978.*

B

BARRETT, Angela (Jane) 1955-

■ Personal

Born August 23, 1955, in Essex, England; daughter of Donald (an insurance broker) and Dinah Patricia (a secretary and homemaker; maiden name, Eatwell) Barrett; companion of Mike Owen (a photographer), beginning 1977. *Education:* Attended Maidstone College of Art, 1974-77, and Royal College of Art, 1977-80. *Politics:* Liberal. *Religion:* Church of England.

■ Addresses

Home—London, England. *Agent*—Caradoc King, A. P. Watt Ltd., 20 John St., London WC1, England.

■ Career

Illustrator. *Exhibitions:* Works exhibited at AOI, 1976, 1977, 1978, National Theatre, 1977, Barbican, 1983, BIB Bratislava, 1983, Michael Parkin Fine Art, 1984, Clarendon Gallery, 1985, Minneapolis, 1985, On the Wall Gallery, 1985, Folio Society, 1986, Markswood Gallery, 1988, Royal College of Art, 1989, Commonwealth Institute, 1989, Chris Beetles, 1990, and Newport Museum and Art Gallery, 1991-92.

■ Awards, Honors

W. H. Smith Illustration Award, Book Trust, 1991, for *The Hidden House.*

■ Illustrator

Frances Hodgson Burnett, *The Secret Garden,* Octopus Books, 1983.
Yehudi Menuhin and Christopher Hope, *The King, the Cat and the Fiddle,* A. & C. Black, 1983.
Hans Christian Andersen, *The Wild Swans,* translation by Naomi Lewis, A. & C. Black, 1984.
Susan Hill, *Through the Kitchen Window,* Hamish Hamilton, 1984.

James Riordan, *The Woman in the Moon,* Hutchinson, 1984, Dial Books for Young Readers, 1985.
Hope, *The Dragon Wore Pink,* A. & C. Black, 1985.
Lis Marks, *Ghostly Towers,* Octopus Books, 1985, Dial Books for Young Readers, 1986.
Hill, *Through the Garden Gate,* Hamish Hamilton, 1986.

A sense of romance and adventure fills Angela Barrett's illustrations of the medieval tales retold in Naomi Lewis's *Proud Knight, Fair Lady.*

Graham Rose, *The Sunday Times Gardeners' Almanac,* Roger Houghton, 1986.

Hill, *Can It Be True?,* Viking Kestrel, 1988.

Andersen, *The Snow Queen,* translation and introduction by Lewis, Henry Holt, 1988.

Proud Knight, Fair Lady: The Twelve Lais of Marie de France, translation by Lewis, Viking Kestrel, 1989.

Martin Waddell, *The Hidden House,* Philomel, 1990.

Hill, editor, *Walker Book of Ghost Stories,* Walker Books, 1990.

Hill, editor, *The Random House Book of Ghost Stories,* Random House, 1991.

Josephine Poole, reteller, *Snow White,* Hutchinson, 1991.

Jenny Nimm, *The Witches and the Singing Mice,* Collins, 1993.

Also book cover illustrator for novels by A. S. Byatt and Nancy Mitford published by Viking Penguin, and for books published by Gollancz, Faber & Faber, Arrow, and Macmillan. Contributor of illustrations to books and periodicals.

■ For More Information See

PERIODICALS

New York Times Book Review, July 9, 1989.

*   *   *

BARTON, Jill(ian) 1940-

■ Personal

Born March 15, 1940, in Manchester, England; daughter of James Bonet Hulme (a drafter) and Winifred Verdun (a homemaker; maiden name, Albone) Walker; married Michael Joseph Barton (in sales), April 4, 1962 (separated); children: Paul James, Nicholas John, Emma Jane. *Education:* Received degree from Manchester Polytechnic, 1988. *Politics:* "Varied." *Religion:* Church of England. *Hobbies and other interests:* Theatre, children, walking, cycling, classical music, collecting children's books, "lazing about."

■ Addresses

Home and office—15 Sidmouth Ave., Flixton, Manchester M31 2ST, England.

■ Career

Illustrator. Part-time university lecturer. Has worked variously as a laboratory assistant, secretary, and interviewer.

■ Illustrator

Iver Cutler, *Grape Zoo,* Walker Books, 1991.

Martin Waddell, *The Happy Hedgehog Band,* Walker Books, 1991.

Waddell, *The Pig in the Pond,* Walker Books, 1992.

Waddell, *Little Mo,* Walker Books, 1993.

JILL BARTON

Kathy Henderson, *The Baby Dances,* Walker Books, in press.

■ Sidelights

Jill Barton told *SATA:* "I was a late starter. I was forty-four when I decided to go to college and get a degree. I have always loved drawing (for pleasure) and I wanted to focus on illustrating good books for children. There is nothing quite like the thrill and challenge of tackling an imaginative script and I've been lucky enough to work with some fantastic authors. I don't write myself as yet, but I may one day. It's never too late."

*   *   *

BERCK, Judith 1960-

■ Personal

Born October 7, 1960, in New York, NY; daughter of Martin and Lenore (Fierstein) Berck. *Education:* Attended Harvard University.

■ Addresses

Home—604 Ramapo Rd., Teaneck, NJ 07666.

■ Career

Free-lance writer. Member, Coalition for the Homeless, 1986; member, Citizen's Committee for Children of New York City, 1987-90; consultant, New York Civil Liberties Union, fall, 1991. Advocate for homeless families.

■ Writings

No Place to Be: Voices of Homeless Children, Houghton, 1992.

■ Sidelights

Judith Berck's *No Place to Be: Voices of Homeless Children* "may be one of the saddest children's books published this year," writes Ellen Fader in *Horn Book.* Berck uses comments from more than thirty homeless children, ages nine to eighteen, to illustrate how society has failed to provide them with places to call home. Rosie Peasley suggests in *School Library Journal* that children reading the book will be profoundly affected "as they consider the degradation, discomfort, shame, and danger that is part of these young Americans' lives." A reviewer for *Voice of Youth Advocates* points out that the book provides a valuable service by making young readers aware "that there is a large population of people like themselves, who need a chance to take their place in the world."

JUDITH BERCK

■ Works Cited

Fader, Ellen, review of *No Place to Be, Horn Book,* March/April, 1992, p. 216.
Review of *No Place to Be, Voice of Youth Advocates,* April, 1992, p. 51.
Peasley, Rosie, review of *No Place to Be, School Library Journal,* June, 1992, p. 128.

■ For More Information See

PERIODICALS

Booklist, April 1, 1992, p. 1448.
Book Report, September, 1992, p.70.
Bulletin of the Center for Children's Books, June, 1992, p. 255.

*   *   *

BOUGHTON, Richard 1954-

■ Personal

Born January 23, 1954, in Portland, OR; son of Eugene (a schoolteacher) and Verne (a homemaker; maiden name, Black) Boughton; married Georgia Lucas, August 10, 1981; children: Holden, Ja'nat, Jamila, Preston. *Education:* Portland State University, B.A., 1976. *Politics:* Liberal. *Religion:* Christian.

■ Addresses

Home—359 Southeast Gilham, Portland, OR 97215.

■ Career

St. Vincent Hospital, Portland, OR, medical transcriptionist, 1992—. *Member:* Society of Children's Book Writers and Illustrators.

■ Awards, Honors

First prize, *Northwest* magazine fiction contest, 1990.

■ Writings

Rent-A-Puppy, Inc., Atheneum, 1992.

Also contributor of short stories to magazines, including "Days of Black Heat," *Writers Forum,* 1987, and *Northwest,* 1990; "Ceremonial Dress," *Northwest,* 1987; "Seals," *Stories,* 1989; and "Siyotanka Music," *Northwest,* 1990.

■ Work in Progress

Along Came Coyote, a novel; a contemporary young adult novel; researching Paul Bunyan and American Indian mythology.

RICHARD BOUGHTON

■ Sidelights

Richard Boughton told *SATA:* "I began writing straight out of college, in 1976. That was a long time ago, and it took me a long time to learn what writing was really about, the serious work that was required, and the necessity of finding one's own niche. Like many who begin to write, I had in mind writing the Great American Novel, and so soon began to fill my four drawer file cabinet, top to bottom, with poorly conceived, poorly executed, consistently unfinished novels and stories and plays and poems. I remember loving every word on every page in every doomed manuscript. And in hindsight, I think there was nothing wrong with this. For it is the proper beginning. It is the expression of the desire and the will and the commitment in hard copy. It is the learning process.

"In 1983 I became the single parent of my son. I put my whole heart and soul into this pursuit and responsibility, just as it had been put into my writing. Through him, because of him, I was influenced and inspired to return to the wonder and innocence and openness of childhood—to reenter a world of endless possibilities, extravagant schemes, spontaneous love. As a result, I wrote one or two poorly executed, unfinished children's novels. Yet, I had tied into something—something true inside myself—words that resonated, stories that led adult readers to remember and young readers to identify. In short, I began to receive crumbs of enthusiasm and support from agents and editors. And so truly, for the first time, I began to learn how to construct a novel; how to make a story, a mere manuscript, into a real-live book. I learned not only the value of, but the absolute

necessity of revision, revision, revision. The will to work until you get it right.

"Possessing this—the desire to perfect, the ability for merciless self critique, the will to completely shape and fulfill—became the key. The knob would turn, the door would open for the key that would fit—that which had been carved to fit the proper lock.

"*Rent-A-Puppy, Inc.* had its inception during a conversation with my son. When I was younger, my beagle, Felicia, had birthed six puppies. I witnessed the birth, and took care of the puppies (to whatever extent Felicia would allow), and when it came time for the puppies to go to new homes, my heart ached and I wished I could keep every one. I was telling my son about this. What if I had kept them, I wondered? How could that have been managed? Well, I could have rented them out.... Thus and therefore, *Rent-A-Puppy, Inc.* The heart speaks to the mind, the mind elucidates the heart.

"And then I had another idea. I had been reading through American Indian mythology, and had happened, in particular, upon the character of Coyote—a trickster, a hero, a vagabond, a creator. Wonderful, wonderful stories. I wanted them to continue, I wanted to express them through myself.

"Well, what if....

"And so it began again. And so it goes forever...."

*   *   *

BRANDENBERG, Aliki (Liacouras) 1929-
(Aliki)

■ Personal

Born September 3, 1929, in Wildwood Crest, NJ; daughter of James Peter and Stella (Lagakos) Liacouras; married Franz Brandenberg (an author), March 15, 1957; children: Jason, Alexa Demetria. *Education:* Graduated from Philadelphia Museum School of Art (now Philadelphia College of Art), 1951. *Hobbies and other interests:* Macrame, weaving, music, baking, traveling, reading, gardening, theater, films, museums.

■ Addresses

Home—17 Regent's Park Terrace, London NW1 7ED, England.

■ Career

Muralist and commercial artist in Philadelphia, PA, and New York City, 1951-56, and in Zurich, Switzerland, 1957-60; commercial artist, writer, and illustrator of children's books in New York City, 1960-77, and London, England, 1977—. Has also taught art and ceramics.

■ Awards, Honors

The Story of Johnny Appleseed, 1963, and *The Story of William Penn,* 1964, were named Junior Literary Guild selections; Boys' Clubs of America Junior Book Award, 1968, for *Three Gold Pieces: A Greek Folk Tale; At Mary Bloom's* was chosen by the American Institute of Graphic Arts for the Children's Book Show and as a Junior Literary Guild selection, 1976, and by the Children's Book Council for the Children's Book Showcase, 1977; New York Academy of Sciences Children's Science Book Award, 1977, for *Corn Is Maize: The Gift of the Indians;* Dutch Children's Book Council Silver Slate Pencil Award, and Garden State (NJ) Children's Book Award, both 1981, for *Mummies Made in Egypt;* Omar's Book Award (Evansville-Vandeburgh), 1986, for *Keep Your Mouth Closed, Dear;* Prix du Livre pour Enfants (Geneva), 1987, for *Feelings;* World of Reading Readers' Choice Award (Silver Burdett & Ginn), 1989, for *The Story of Johnny Appleseed;* Drexel University/Free Library of Philadelphia citation, 1991; Pennsylvania School Librarians Association Award, 1991, in recognition of outstanding contributions in the field of literature.

ALIKI

■ Writings

SELF-ILLUSTRATED; UNDER NAME ALIKI

The Story of William Tell, Faber & Faber, 1960, A. S. Barnes, 1961.
My Five Senses, Crowell, 1962.
My Hands, Crowell, 1962.
The Wish Workers, Dial, 1962.
The Story of Johnny Appleseed, Prentice-Hall, 1963.
George and the Cherry Tree, Dial, 1964.
The Story of William Penn, Prentice-Hall, 1964.
A Weed Is a Flower: The Life of George Washington Carver, Prentice-Hall, 1965.
Keep Your Mouth Closed, Dear, Dial, 1966.
Three Gold Pieces: A Greek Folk Tale, Pantheon, 1967.
New Year's Day, Crowell, 1967.
(Editor) *Hush Little Baby: A Folk Lullaby,* Prentice-Hall, 1968.
My Visit to the Dinosaurs, Crowell, 1969.
The Eggs: A Greek Folk Tale, Pantheon, 1969.
Diogenes: The Story of the Greek Philosopher, Prentice-Hall, 1969.
Fossils Tell of Long Ago, Crowell, 1972.
June 7!, Macmillan, 1972.
The Long Lost Coelacanth and Other Living Fossils, Crowell, 1973.
Green Grass and White Milk, Crowell, 1974.
Go Tell Aunt Rhody, Macmillan, 1974.
At Mary Bloom's, Greenwillow, 1976.
Corn Is Maize: The Gift of the Indians, Crowell, 1976.
The Many Lives of Benjamin Franklin, Prentice-Hall, 1977.
Wild and Woolly Mammoths, Crowell, 1977.
The Twelve Months, Greenwillow, 1978.
Mummies Made in Egypt, Crowell, 1979.
The Two of Them, Greenwillow, 1979.
Digging up Dinosaurs, Crowell, 1981, released as a book and audiocassette, HarperAudio, 1991.

We Are Best Friends, Greenwillow, 1982.
Use Your Head, Dear, Greenwillow, 1983.
A Medieval Feast, Harper, 1983.
Feelings, Greenwillow, 1984.
Dinosaurs Are Different, Crowell, 1985.
How a Book Is Made, Crowell, 1986.
Jack and Jake, Greenwillow, 1986.
Overnight at Mary Bloom's, Greenwillow, 1987.
Welcome, Little Baby, Greenwillow, 1987.
Dinosaur Bones, Crowell, 1988.
King's Day: Louis XIV of France, Crowell, 1989.
My Feet, Crowell, 1990.
Manners, Greenwillow, 1990.
Christmas Tree Memories, HarperCollins, 1991.
I'm Growing!, HarperCollins, 1992.
Milk: From Cow to Carton, HarperCollins, 1992.
Aliki's Dinosaur Dig: A Book and Card Game, HarperCollins, 1992.
My Visit to the Aquarium, HarperCollins, 1993.
Communication, Greenwillow, 1993.
Gods and Goddesses of Olympus, HarperCollins, 1994.

Aliki's books have been translated into Catalan, Danish, Dutch, Finnish, French, German, Hebrew, Japanese, Norwegian, Swedish, and Braille.

ILLUSTRATOR; UNDER NAME ALIKI

Pat Witte and Eve Witte, *Who Lives Here?,* Golden Press, 1961.
Joan M. Lexau, *Cathy Is Company,* Dial, 1961.
Paul Showers, *Listening Walk,* Crowell, 1961.
Margaret Hodges, *What's for Lunch, Charley?,* Dial, 1961.
Mickey Marks, *What Can I Buy?,* Dial, 1962.
Dorothy Les Tina, *A Book to Begin On: Alaska,* Holt, 1962.
James Holding, *The Lazy Little Zulu,* Morrow, 1962.

Aliki humorously illustrates various means of conveying information in her nonfiction work *Communication*.

Joan M. Heilbronner, *This Is the House Where Jack Lives*, Harper, 1962.

Vivian L. Thompson, *The Horse That Liked Sandwiches*, Putnam, 1962.

Arthur Jonas, *Archimedes and His Wonderful Discoveries*, Prentice-Hall, 1962.

Bernice Kohn, *Computers at Your Service*, Prentice-Hall, 1962.

Jonas, *New Ways in Math*, Prentice-Hall, 1962.

Eugene David, *Television and How It Works*, Prentice-Hall, 1962.

David, *Electricity in Your Life*, Prentice-Hall, 1963.

Holding, *Mister Moonlight and Omar*, Morrow, 1963.

Lexau, *That's Good, That's Bad*, Dial, 1963.

Judy Hawes, *Bees and Beelines*, Crowell, 1964.

Jonas, *More New Ways in Math*, Prentice-Hall, 1964.

Holding, *Sherlock on the Trail*, Morrow, 1964.

Kohn, *Everything Has a Size*, Prentice-Hall, 1964.

Kohn, *Everything Has a Shape*, Prentice-Hall, 1964.

Kohn, *One Day It Rained Cats and Dogs*, Coward, 1965.

Helen Clare, *Five Dolls in a House*, Prentice-Hall, 1965.

Rebecca Kalusky, *Is It Blue As a Butterfly?*, Prentice-Hall, 1965.

Mary K. Phelan, *Mother's Day*, Crowell, 1965.

Betty Ren Wright, *I Want to Read!*, A. Whitman, 1965.

Sean Morrison, *Is That a Happy Hippopotamus?*, Crowell, 1966.

Kohn, *Everything Has a Shape and Everything Has a Size*, Prentice-Hall, 1966.

Clare, *Five Dolls in the Snow*, Prentice-Hall, 1967.

Clare, *Five Dolls and the Monkey*, Prentice-Hall, 1967.

Clare, *Five Dolls and Their Friends*, Prentice-Hall, 1968.

Clare, *Five Dolls and the Duke*, Prentice-Hall, 1968.

Wilma Yeo, *Mrs. Neverbody's Recipes*, Lippincott, 1968.

Esther R. Hautzig, *At Home: A Visit in Four Languages*, Macmillan, 1968.

Polly Greenberg, *Oh Lord, I Wish I Was a Buzzard*, Macmillan, 1968.

Roma Gans, *Birds at Night*, Crowell, 1968.

Jane Jonas Srivastava, *Weighing and Balancing*, Crowell, 1970.

Joanne Oppenheim, *On the Other Side of the River*, Watts, 1972.

Philip M. Sherlock and Hilary Sherlock, *Ears and Tails and Common Sense: More Stories from the Caribbean*, Crowell, 1974.

Srivastava, *Averages*, Crowell, 1975.

Joanna Cole, *Evolution*, Crowell, 1987.

ILLUSTRATOR OF BOOKS BY HUSBAND, FRANZ BRANDENBERG; UNDER NAME ALIKI

I Once Knew a Man, Macmillan, 1970.

Fresh Cider and Pie, Macmillan, 1973.

No School Today!, Macmillan, 1975.

A Secret for Grandmother's Birthday, Greenwillow, 1975.

A Robber! A Robber!, Greenwillow, 1976.

I Wish I Was Sick, Too!, Greenwillow, 1976, published in England as *I Don't Feel Well*, Hamish Hamilton, 1977.

What Can You Make of It?, Greenwillow, 1977.

Nice New Neighbors, Greenwillow, 1977.

A Picnic, Hurrah!, Greenwillow, 1978.

Six New Students, Greenwillow, 1978.

Everyone Ready?, Greenwillow, 1979.

It's Not My Fault!, Greenwillow, 1980.

Leo and Emily, Greenwillow, 1981.

Leo and Emily's Big Idea, Greenwillow, 1982.

Aunt Nina and Her Nephews and Nieces, Greenwillow, 1983.

Aunt Nina's Visit, Greenwillow, 1984.

Leo and Emily and the Dragon, Greenwillow, 1984.

The Hit of the Party, Greenwillow, 1985.

Cock-a-Doodle-Doo, Greenwillow, 1986.

What's Wrong with a Van?, Greenwillow, 1987.

Aunt Nina, Good Night!, Greenwillow, 1989.

■ Sidelights

Aliki Brandenberg, who publishes under her first name only, writes children's books because she loves writing and drawing. In addition to the many stories she has written herself, Aliki has illustrated books written by others, including her husband, Franz Brandenberg. Several of her works, including the award-winning folktale *Three Gold Pieces*, reflect her Greek heritage, but Aliki has written about a variety of subjects that interest her. In all of her books, which range from fiction to history and from biography to science, Aliki's illustrations are as necessary to her stories as her words. She once said that illustrating her work "takes a long time. I have to find the right way to express the words in pictures. The words and the pictures should blend so that the pictures add to the words and make them more important."

Aliki was born in Wildwood Crest, New Jersey, where her parents, who lived in Philadelphia, were vacationing at the time. She attended school in Philadelphia and Yeadon, Pennsylvania, starting to draw during her preschool years. While in kindergarten she exhibited her first two portraits—one of her family and another of Peter Rabbit's family. "Such a fuss was made over them," she remembered in the *Third Book of Junior Authors*, "that the course of my life was decided that day." Aliki continued to draw and attend art classes on Saturdays and also took piano lessons. After she graduated from high school, she enrolled in the Philadelphia Museum School of Art.

When Aliki graduated from college in 1951 she took a job working in the display department of the J. C. Penney Company in New York City. After a year she moved back to Philadelphia and worked as a free-lance advertising and display artist. She also painted murals, started her own greeting card company, and taught classes in art and ceramics.

New Home in Europe Inspires First Book

Aliki, whose parents were natives of Greece and had taught her to speak Greek before she learned to speak English, decided in 1956 to visit that country and other places in Europe—especially Italy—traveling, painting, sketching, and learning about her heritage. While on her tour she met Franz Brandenberg, and in 1957 the two

The work involved in the discovery of dinosaurs is explained in Aliki's *Digging up Dinosaurs*. (Illustration by the author.)

married, settling in his native Switzerland. Aliki continued her free-lance art career there. While in Switzerland she learned that William Tell was Swiss, and she and Franz visited the territory where he lived. That experience inspired her to write and illustrate her first book, *The Story of William Tell,* which was published in 1960.

Later that year Aliki and her husband moved to New York City, where she was asked to illustrate several books written by other authors. That gave her the idea to write a second book of her own, *My Five Senses.* Since then, she has published more than forty of her own works. Aliki's nonfiction books start with a fascination for a certain subject, which she researches over an extended period of time. "The pleasure of these [nonfiction] books," she once wrote, "is writing complicated facts as clearly and simply as possible, so readers (and I) who know nothing about a subject learn a great deal by the time we are finished." Her fiction is written from "a lifetime of experiences"—sometimes her own and sometimes the experiences of her two children. "A word can trigger a story that has been somewhere in my mind for years," she continued. As an illustrator, Aliki tries to bring as much variety as she can to her work. "I simply could not illustrate a medieval feast the way I would a story about field mice."

Critics have praised both Aliki's illustrations and her writings, noting that her work is frequently attractive, informative, and entertaining. She is known for creating simple and accurate biographies and science books and for her warm, humorous fiction. Commenting on *Mum-*

mies Made in Egypt, Digging up Dinosaurs, Corn Is Maize, and *A Medieval Feast, Publishers Weekly* reviewer Dulcy Brainard observed that "these science primers inform, entertain and delight in a way that is particularly Aliki's, using script and different typefaces, with frieze frames and borders. One doesn't have to be a kid to devour each page, intent on not missing a single bit of information it contains." Aliki spoke about her science books with Margaret Carter in *Books for Your Children,* remarking that "It's best for me to know nothing about a subject when I begin ... that way I have to get it right. Because I am not a scientist I can perhaps approach the subject with fresh eyes."

Aliki and her family moved to England in 1977, where she and Franz have since continued their careers as children's book writers. "I'm one of those lucky people who love what they do," Aliki commented. "I also love my garden, music, theater, museums, and traveling. But I'm happiest when I'm in my studio on the top floor of our tall house in London, alone with the book I'm working on, and Mozart."

■ **Works Cited**

Aliki (publicity sheet), Greenwillow Books, 1986.

Brainard, Dulcy, interview with Aliki Brandenberg, *Publishers Weekly,* July 22, 1983, pp. 134-35.

Carter, Margaret, "Cover Artist—Aliki," *Books for Your Children,* spring, 1984, p. 9.

Third Book of Junior Authors, H. W. Wilson, 1972, pp. 8-9.

For More Information See

BOOKS

Children's Literature Review, Volume 9, Gale, 1985, pp. 15-32.

PERIODICALS

New York Times Book Review, November 18, 1979; March 8, 1981; October 16, 1983.
School Library Journal, April, 1993, p. 104.
Times Literary Supplement, March 28, 1980.
Washington Post Book World, May 9, 1982.

*   *   *

BRANDENBERG, Franz 1932-

Personal

Born February 10, 1932, in Zug, Switzerland; son of Franz and Marie (Sigrist) Brandenberg; married Aliki Liacouras (an author and illustrator), March 15, 1957; children: Jason, Alexa Demetria. *Education:* Attended boarding school in Einsiedeln, Switzerland.

Addresses

Home—17 Regent's Park Terrace, London NW1 7ED, England.

Career

Writer of children's books. Apprenticed with publisher and bookseller in Lucerne, Switzerland, 1949; worked in bookshops and publishing houses in London, Paris, and Florence, 1952-60; literary agent, New York City, 1960-72.

FRANZ BRANDENBERG

Awards, Honors

Junior Literary Guild selection, 1977, for *Nice New Neighbors,* 1979, for *Everyone Ready?,* and 1980, for *It's Not My Fault.*

Writings

ILLUSTRATED BY WIFE, ALIKI

I Once Knew a Man, Macmillan, 1970.
Fresh Cider and Pie, Macmillan, 1973.
No School Today!, Macmillan, 1975.
A Secret for Grandmother's Birthday, Greenwillow, 1975.
A Robber! A Robber!, Greenwillow, 1976.
I Wish I Was Sick, Too!, Greenwillow, 1976, published in England as *I Don't Feel Well,* Hamish Hamilton, 1977.
What Can You Make of It?, Greenwillow, 1977.
Nice New Neighbors, Greenwillow, 1977.
A Picnic, Hurrah!, Greenwillow, 1978.
Six New Students, Greenwillow, 1978.
Everyone Ready?, Greenwillow, 1979.
It's Not My Fault!, Greenwillow, 1980.
Leo and Emily, Greenwillow, 1981.
Leo and Emily's Big Idea, Greenwillow, 1982.
Aunt Nina and Her Nephews and Nieces, Greenwillow, 1983.
Aunt Nina's Visit, Greenwillow, 1984.
Leo and Emily and the Dragon, Greenwillow, 1984.
The Hit of the Party, Greenwillow, 1985.
Cock-a-Doodle-Doo, Greenwillow, 1986.
What's Wrong with a Van?, Greenwillow, 1987.
Aunt Nina, Good Night!, Greenwillow, 1989.

OTHER

Otto Is Different, illustrated by James Stevenson, Greenwillow, 1985.
Leo and Emily's Zoo, illustrated by Yossi Abolafia, Greenwillow, 1988.
A Fun Weekend, illustrated by daughter, Alexa Brandenberg, Mulberry, 1991.

Brandenberg's works have been translated into Japanese, Hebrew, French, German, Danish, and Swedish.

Sidelights

Many of the characters and situations in Franz Brandenberg's children's books are based either on his own life or on the lives of his children, Jason and Alexa. Brandenberg began his literary career by working in bookselling and publishing; a meeting with a children's book editor led to his writing career. "Writing for children is my way of perpetuating my own childhood, which was very happy," he once commented. "I enjoy sharing my experiences with children, and I hope children enjoy reading about them."

Franz Brandenberg

A FUN WEEKEND

pictures by
Alexa Brandenberg

In *A Fun Weekend* by Brandenberg, a family's countryside vacation is filled with unexpected pleasures. (Cover illustration by Alexa Brandenburg.)

Franz Brandenberg was born in Zug, Switzerland. By the time he was seven years old, his family had moved to a small village. Brandenberg had a difficult time winning acceptance because he spoke with an accent and was a much better student than the other children. To break the ice he turned into an "activities director," organizing shooting and wrestling matches, putting on magic shows and circuses, and staging plays (usually his own adaptations of fairy tales and historical events).

At the age of seventeen, Brandenberg entered a three-year apprenticeship with a publisher and bookseller in Lucerne, Switzerland. After the apprenticeship was over, he worked at other publishing houses in England, France, and Italy. While working in Florence, Italy, Brandenberg met his future wife, Aliki. He recalled their meeting in an essay for the *Fifth Book of Junior Authors:* "One Saturday morning, an American girl came into the shop and asked for a guide to Florence. I offered to guide her through the city myself.... We were married in 1957, in Berne, Switzerland."

In 1960, the couple moved to New York City, where Brandenberg began working as a literary agent representing European authors and Aliki started illustrating children's books. Brandenberg began writing his own children's books in 1969. Many of his books are based directly on the childhood experiences of family and friends. For example, Brandenberg once noted that *Everyone Ready?* "came about because I like to write about situations a small child can identify with. In our

family there is always hysteria before we go on a trip. And it was the same when I was a child. On the day my parents were to take me to boarding school, the train left as soon as I was aboard, with my parents running behind it." *It's Not My Fault!* is also based mostly on the author's childhood experiences. Because Brandenberg was the oldest of his parents' five sons, he usually won fights between the brothers for possession of important toys. "But as soon as I had the toys to myself," he remembered, "I didn't want them anymore." The last chapter in the book was inspired by one of his wife's nephews, who got into trouble at school after poking a friend who first had poked him. "The nephew got punished, but the boy who started it all got away free."

Author's Family Provides Ideas

Many of Brandenberg's other picture books also touch on family themes, including *What's Wrong with a Van?*, *Aunt Nina, Good Night!*, and *A Fun Weekend*. In *What's Wrong with a Van?* kittens Edward and Elizabeth envy their neighbors's shiny new car, comparing it to their family's run-down van. The kittens have fond memories of the van, however, and are glad when the vehicle is overhauled instead of replaced. A *Booklist* reviewer commented on the story's "intuitive understanding of a child's penchant for clinging to familiar possessions," and in *Publishers Weekly*, a reviewer praised the "charming and appealing kitten heros" of Brandenberg's "warm family story."

In *Aunt Nina, Good Night!*, which was illustrated by Aliki, Aunt Nina invites her nieces and nephews to spend the night at her house. Of course, the children have so much fun that they try to postpone going to sleep for as long as they can. "The message is simple and familiar to viewers of American children's television: love is ... horsing around with your large extended family," wrote Liz Brooks in the *Times Literary Supplement*. Denise Anton Wright, assessing *Aunt Nina, Good Night!* in *School Library Journal*, deemed it a "reassuring picture book [that] is ideal for sharing aloud with younger children."

Brandenberg is also the author of *A Fun Weekend*, which was illustrated by his daughter, Alexa. In the book Adrian and Paula's bear family take a weekend trip to the country. They make a number of stops on the way, however, and by the time they arrive the inn is full. The family must sleep in their car for the night, but they nevertheless retain their good cheer. Ann Stell praised *A Fun Weekend* in *School Library Journal*, commenting on both the lighthearted story and appealing illustrations: "The effect of story and pictures together is thoroughly disarming."

Ultimately, Brandenberg is glad that his work is such a "family affair"; he is especially happy to be working with his wife. He remarked: "I am very lucky to have my wife illustrate my books, as she, naturally, understands me better than anyone else."

■ Works Cited

Brandenberg, Franz, essay in *Fifth Book of Junior Authors and Illustrators,* edited by Sally Holmes Holtze, Wilson, 1983, pp. 45-46.

Brooks, Liz, "Animals and Others," *Times Literary Supplement,* November 24, 1989, p. 1310.

Stell, Ann, review of *A Fun Weekend, School Library Journal,* June, 1991, p. 72.

Review of *What's Wrong with a Van?, Booklist,* September 15, 1987, p. 145.

Review of *What's Wrong with a Van?, Publishers Weekly,* July 10, 1987, p. 67.

Wright, Denise Anton, review of *Aunt Nina, Good Night!, School Library Journal,* September, 1989, p. 222.

■ For More Information See

PERIODICALS

Bulletin of the Center for Children's Books, October, 1985, p. 23; October, 1988, p. 28.

Horn Book, October, 1973; May/June, 1985, p. 298; March/April, 1987, p. 198.

New York, December 17, 1973.

Publishers Weekly, October, 31, 1986, p. 62.

School Library Journal, April, 1985, p. 74; December, 1988, p. 83.*

* * *

BURCH, Joann J(ohansen)

■ Personal

Born in Denver, CO; daughter of Anker Kay Johansen and Ella Olsen Hansen Simpson; married Robert D. Burch (a lawyer); children: Berkeley, Robert, Barry. *Education:* Texas Christian University, B.A., University of Southern California, M.L.A. *Hobbies and other interests:* Travel, photography, miniatures, tennis.

■ Addresses

Home and office—1301 Delresto Drive, Beverly Hills, CA 90210.

■ Career

American Airlines, Dallas, TX, flight attendant; teacher of social studies, English, and Spanish in California and Germany; teacher of English as a second language in Los Angeles, CA. Editor of newsletters for various organizations; "professional volunteer" for various charity groups and civic organizations; Brownie and Girl Scout leader; Junior Great Books leader; president of Junior Tennis League of Southern California. *Member:* National Wildlife Federation, National Trust for Historic Preservation, National Association of Miniature Enthusiasts, Smithsonian Institute (associate), "Friends of English" at the University of California—Los Angeles, and several writing organizations.

■ Writings

Fine Print: A Story of Johann Gutenberg, Carolrhoda, 1991.

Isabella of Castile: Queen on Horseback, Franklin Watts, 1991.

Kenya, Dillon, 1992.

Also contributor of articles and photographs to periodicals.

■ Work in Progress

Chico Mendes: Defender of the Forest, Hans Christian Andersen, a work on environmental geography, and a work on the California Missions and Chumash Indians.

■ Sidelights

Joann J. Burch told *SATA:* "I was born in Denver, Colorado, the oldest of four sisters and twenty-two cousins. I grew up entertaining my younger relatives with stories that I either read to them or made up. I also wrote and directed numerous backyard dramas. When I grew up I became a teacher and a Brownie leader and continued to write skits and plays for young people to perform.

"I worked as a flight attendant and developed an ongoing passion for travel. This passion has led to numerous adventures throughout the world, including a job teaching English in Germany, an archaeological exploration of parts of South America, an African safari, and a stay in the Amazon jungle. I've sold numerous travel articles and a few photographs. These travels have inspired several of my books: a biography of [movable type inventor] Johann Gutenberg (I lived for a year not far from Mainz, Germany, his birthplace); a book on Kenya; a biography of Chico Mendes (who lost his life defending the Amazon rainforest). I am now writing a biography of Hans Christian Andersen who was born in Odense, Denmark. My grandmother was also born in Odense and my cousins still live there. I shall visit Odense soon in order to give an authentic flavor to my book as well as 'to get back to my roots.'

"Although I no longer teach, I still enjoy visiting schools and libraries to talk with young people about writing. I also love books and have found inspiration for my writing from good writers I've read. It is such a thrill to see books I have written in the hands of young readers."

C

CARKEET, David 1946-

■ Personal

Born November 15, 1946, in Sonora, CA; son of Ross (a judge) and Mary (a homemaker; maiden name, Hill) Carkeet; married Barbara Lubin (a social worker), August 16, 1975; children: Anne, Laurie, Molly. *Education:* University of California, Davis, B.A., 1968; University of Wisconsin, M.A., 1970; Indiana University, Ph.D., 1973.

■ Addresses

Home—23 Ridgemoor Dr., St. Louis, MO 63105. *Agent*—Barney Karpfinger, The Karpfinger Agency, 500 Fifth Ave., New York, NY 10110.

■ Career

University of Missouri—St. Louis, professor of English, 1973—.

■ Awards, Honors

O. Henry Award for *The Greatest Slump of All Time.*

■ Writings

NOVELS FOR YOUNG ADULTS

The Silent Treatment, HarperCollins, 1988.
Quiver River, HarperCollins, 1991.

NOVELS FOR ADULTS

Double Negative, Dial, 1980.
The Greatest Slump of All Time, HarperCollins, 1984.
I Been There Before, HarperCollins, 1985.
The Full Catastrophe, Simon & Schuster, 1990.

■ Work in Progress

A picture book, titled *Molly's Walk,* and an adult novel.

■ Sidelights

David Carkeet told *SATA:* "My two novels for young adults are about the friendship between two teenagers, Ricky and Nate, and the problems they face together. The first book, *The Silent Treatment,* is about establishing the friendship, which was initially difficult because the two boys are so different. Ricky is a 'good boy' in the standard sense. Nate is a loudmouth and a rule-breaker. But at a deeper level they are similar: Ricky is funny in his private mental life, and Nate is actually sweet and considerate of others. So the book is about the two of them, Ricky especially, working to overcome the difference that separates them and learning to focus on the fact that they really like spending time together.

"The sequel to *The Silent Treatment, Quiver River,* is about rites of passage into manhood. What does it mean in American culture to become a man? Does it mean having sex? (Nate thinks yes; Ricky thinks no, although he is not opposed to the idea.) Does it mean living away from home? Does it mean having a responsible, caring attitude toward others? Ricky and Nate are working at a summer resort in the California mountains, and as they pursue girls they also pursue a strange mystery in the area. There are signs that a young Miwok Indian, unaffected by civilization, might be living in the wild surrounding the lake.

"*Quiver River* is typical of the kind of story I like to write. I like stories with lots of things going on. I like stories with dual plots that come together in the end. In this case, the two plots are Ricky and Nate's quest for manhood and this young Miwok's attempt to undergo an ancient initiation rite. The Miwok wants the same thing as Ricky and Nate. As I wrote this novel, it was also important to me to deal with the issue of sex—to have people talk about it, be confused by it, and be driven by it in a realistic way.

"My young adult novels are heavily autobiographical. *The Silent Treatment* is set in the small California gold rush town were I was born and where I lived until I went to college. Like Ricky, I am the son of a lawyer, and I gained much of my ability and interest in writing from my father. I worked in campground maintenance at a summer resort in the Sierras and pursued girls—like Ricky—with a ridiculous lack of success.

"In general, I write the kind of young adult novels I would have loved to read when I was in high school. I think other young adult authors do the same, and, like me, they are probably frustrated by the fact that the audience for such books is large in possibility but small in practice. Most kids who were active readers when they were in elementary school either read much less when they hit junior high (they go to the mall, they play sports nonstop), or they jump beyond young adult books and go right to Stephen King. A large body of good literature is sadly under-read."

* * *

CASILLA, Robert 1959-

■ Personal

Born April 16, 1959, in Jersey City, NJ; son of Miriam (Castro) Casilla; married Carmen Torres (a real estate adjuster), May 1, 1982; children: Robert, Jr. *Education:* School of Visual Arts, B.F.A., 1982.

■ Addresses

Home and office—356 Walnut St., Yonkers, NY 10701.

■ Career

Free-lance illustrator, 1983—. *Member:* Society of Illustrators.

■ Awards, Honors

Washington Irving Children's Book Choice Award nominations, 1990 and 1992.

■ Illustrator

BIOGRAPHICAL PICTURE BOOKS; WRITTEN BY DAVID A. ADLER

Martin Luther King, Jr.: Free at Last, Holiday House, 1986.
Jackie Robinson: He Was the First, Holiday House, 1989.
A Picture Book of Martin Luther King, Jr., Holiday House, 1989.
A Picture Book of Eleanor Roosevelt, Holiday House, 1991.
A Picture Book of John F. Kennedy, Holiday House, 1991.
A Picture Book of Simon Bolivar, Holiday House, 1992.
A Picture Book of Jesse Owens, Holiday House, 1992.

OTHER

Elizabeth Howard, *The Train to Lulu's,* Bradbury Press, 1988.

ROBERT CASILLA

Myra Cohn Livingston, *Poems for Fathers,* Holiday House, 1989.
Eileen Roe, *Con mi hermano/With My Brother,* Bradbury Press, 1991.
Patricia Murkin, *The Little Painter of Sabana Grande,* Bradbury Press, 1993.
Jonelle Toriseva, *Rodeo Day,* Bradbury Press, in press.

Contributor of illustrations to the *New York Times, Daily News,* and *Black Enterprise* magazine.

■ Work in Progress

Illustrating *A Picture Book of Rosa Parks,* for Holiday House; writing and illustrating *Going to a New School.*

■ Sidelights

Robert Casilla commented: "When I illustrate biographies I try to learn as much as possible about the person I am illustrating so when I am working on the art I feel I know the person intimately. I find great rewards and satisfaction in illustrating for children. I hope to be able to help kids learn and grow and enjoy reading."

■ Works Cited

"Robert Casilla" (publicity pamphlet), Holiday House, c. 1992.

* * *

CLARKE, J.
See CLARKE, Judith

CLARKE, Judith 1943-
(J. Clarke)

■ Personal

Born August 24, 1943, in Sydney, Australia; daughter of Kenneth Edward (a production supervisor) and Sheila Iris (Grey) Clarke; married Rashmi Desai (an anthropologist), December 27, 1968; children: Yask. *Education:* University of N.S.W., B.A. (with honors), 1964; Australian National University, M.A. (with honors), 1966.

■ Addresses

Home—31 Alice St., Mt. Waverley, Melbourne, Australia, 3149.

■ Career

Full-time writer.

■ Awards, Honors

The Heroic Life of Al Capsella was shortlisted for the N.S.W. Premiers Award, 1989, and was named an editors' choice by *Booklist,* 1990, and a best book for young adults by the American Library Association, 1992; *Al Capsella and the Watchdogs* was shortlisted for the N.S.W. Premiers Award, 1990, and was\ named talking book of the year by Variety Club, 1991, and a best book for young adults by the New York Public Library, 1992.

■ Writings

The Heroic Life of Al Capsella (first book in the "Capsella" series), University of Queensland Press (Australia), 1988, Henry Holt, 1990.
The Boy on the Lake (stories), University of Queensland Press, 1989, revised edition published as *The Torment of Mr. Gully: Stories of the Supernatural,* Henry Holt, 1990.
Teddy B. Zoot, illustrated by Margaret Hewitt, Henry Holt, 1990.
Al Capsella and the Watchdogs (second book in the "Capsella" series), University of Queensland Press, 1990, revised edition published by Henry Holt, 1991.
Luna Park at Night, Pascoe Publishing (Australia), 1991.
Al Capsella on Holidays (third book in the "Capsella" series), University of Queensland Press, 1992, published as *Al Capsella Takes a Vacation,* Henry Holt, 1993.
Riff Raff, Henry Holt, 1992.

Clarke's works are sometimes published under the name J. Clarke.

■ Work in Progress

Writing a set of short stories about teenagers in tragicomical family situations; a novel.

■ Sidelights

Australian children's writer Judith Clarke explores in her works a variety of themes ranging from anxiety, to parent-child relationships, to the supernatural. In *The Torment of Mr. Gully: Stories of the Supernatural* the author relates eleven tales that depict characters who endure nightmarish confrontations with the supernatural. No individual escapes unharmed in the stories, and many even succumb to death or to strange disappearances—like the young character who vanishes into a painting. *School Library Journal* reviewer Holly Sanhuber called the narratives "disquieting" but contended that "hypnotic storytelling ... compels readers to turn the pages."

Clarke ventures into parent-child relationships in *Al Capsella and the Watchdogs,* the second work in her "Capsella" series. The story turns on the title character, an Australian teenager whose parents are, in his opinion, overprotective and too involved in his social life. One night, for instance, his mother tracks him and his friends to a party and uses a dog she has "borrowed" as an excuse to be walking the streets. The situation turns around, however, when Al's grandparents come to stay with the family, and Al's mother becomes the child whose parents constantly watch her.

In Clarke's 1990 work *Teddy B. Zoot,* the author shifts to the theme of anxiety, revolving her story around

JUDITH CLARKE

Sarah, a young student whose distress over her math abilities causes her to leave an important homework assignment at school. She gets assistance from her trusted teddy bear friend, who risks a nighttime journey in the pouring rain to retrieve the worksheet from the school. "The brave and faithful Teddy will appeal to stuffed-animal fans," declared *Booklist* contributor Kay Weisman, who added that *Teddy B. Zoot* is "an engaging first chapter book."

Clarke told *SATA:* "Although I didn't write much during the period when my own family was young—probably because I was consumed with just the kind of parental anxieties which dog the parents in the 'Capsella' novels—I can remember very clearly my first attempt at writing. I was very young, probably about four, had not gone to school yet, and had no idea of how to 'write' in the sense of forming actual letters. My mother had given me an empty notebook to draw in, and I used it to write a 'book' (it even had chapters) about a doll who'd fallen from her pram and had a series of horrendous adventures. The actual 'writing' was a kind of scribble—long wavy lines—but the story itself was a heartrending tale, and when I finished it, I gave it to my uncle to read. I watched him closely, expecting him to dissolve into sympathetic tears, but to my amazement and fury he burst out laughing. Perhaps this unsettling experience is what turned me toward comedy so many years after.

Works Focus on Parent-Child Relationships

"In my novels I'm especially concerned with the relationships between children and adults, with the conflicts of interests, misunderstandings, and the pressures they place on one another. These pressures, from the adult side, often emerge from anxiety; the parents fear what will become of their children in a difficult and dangerous world, while the children simply perceive these apprehensions as demands and restrictions. A fourteen-year-old boy once told me, 'My parents don't love me, they don't even *care,* they only worry about me.'

"I feel this kind of anxiety, which, sadly enough, often springs from love, can be dangerous because it conveys a lack of trust in the child, in his judgements, and in his nature and strength—it's as if the adult *expects* the child to come to grief because he isn't capable, and this undermines the young person's belief in himself and in his ability to act in the world outside.

"In the 'Capsella' books, which are comedies, the teenagers have relatively minor problems, but even these stem from parent-child misunderstandings. Al, in *The Heroic Life of Al Capsella,* considers his parents eccentric, unconventional, and a heavy social liability, yet when he visits his orderly grandparents he sees that conventionality, or 'being normal,' can be far more weird than eccentricity. In *Al Capsella and the Watchdogs,* Al and his friends regard their parents' anxieties about schoolwork, parties, and late-night wanderings as ridiculously unreasonable, a form of parental insanity. In *Al Capsella on Holidays,* the boys escape from parental anxieties and the dreaded prospect of dull

Al Capsella has difficulty escaping his mother's watchful eye in Clarke's humorous look at teenage life. (Cover illustration by Michael Chesworth.)

family holidays to the alluring excitements of a holiday on their own. They find themselves, however, more bored than they would have been at home.

"In *The Boy on the Lake* (or *The Torment of Mr. Gully: Stories of the Supernatural*), I've used the supernatural as an image of the fears and uncerainties which can haunt young people, especially imaginative or lonely ones. The ghosts they see may be only in their minds—the projection of their fears and bewilderment about themselves and the world outside, fears they aren't able to share with anyone for fear of being misunderstood, laughed at, or condemned as strange. They feel isolated in a world in which anything might happen, unlike the children in the comedies, who are practical, resourceful individuals who don't easily give into doubts and anxieties. And if they do, like Louis Pine in *Al Capsella on Holidays,* they're helped out by their friends.

"I do see children, in some ways, as being wiser than their elders, more courageous, less disaffected and scared by life. I feel they have enormous potential and capacity, and the disturbing idea is that this potential can be marred and even destroyed by the misunderstandings between parents and their children.

"I've put aside the fourth Al Capsella book for a time so I can work on my major project—a novel about a teenage girl, her mother, and grandmother, at a time when the grandmother, who lives in a nursing home, has lost her sense of the present and lives largely in the time of her girlhood. Her memories and the problems of her aging bring about a fuller understanding between both the mother and the grandmother, and between the mother and her teenage daughter."

■ Works Cited

Sanhuber, Holly, review of *The Torment of Mr. Gully: Stories of the Supernatural, School Library Journal,* November, 1990, p. 134.

Weisman, Kay, review of *Teddy B. Zoot, Booklist,* February 1, 1991, p. 1130.

■ For More Information See

PERIODICALS

Booklist, January 15, 1991, p. 1052; March 15, 1991, p. 1476; August, 1991, p. 2140.

School Library Journal, January, 1991, p. 70; August, 1991, p. 195.

* * *

CLAYTON, Lawrence (Otto, Jr.) 1945-

■ Personal

Born March 24, 1945, in Fallon, NV; son of Lawrence (in farm equipment sales) and Nathalie (a homemaker; maiden name, Gow) Clayton; married Janice Diane Hodge, November 25, 1977 (divorced, 1988); married Cathy Ann Renison (an artist), March 24, 1991; children: Rebecca, Larry, Amy. *Education:* Texas Wesleyan College, B.S. (summa cum laude), 1976; Texas Christian University, M.Div., 1978; Texas Woman's University, Ph.D., 1983. *Politics:* Independent. *Religion:* Methodist. *Hobbies and other interests:* Snorkling, scuba diving, collecting native American art, growing cacti, rock collecting.

■ Addresses

Office—Oklahoma Family Institute, 3900 Northwest 39th St., Oklahoma City, OK 73112.

■ Career

Diversa Inc., Newport, AR, mobile home sales representative, 1969-72; United Methodist Church, Central Texas Conference, Fort Worth, TX, pastor, 1973-81; Johnson County Mental Health Clinic, Cleburne, TX, director, 1981-83; United Methodist Counseling Services, Oklahoma City, OK, administrator, 1983-88; Clayton Clinic, Oklahoma City, owner and president, 1988-90; Oklahoma Family Institute, Oklahoma City, executive director, 1990—. Central Oklahoma Medical Group, mental health consultant, 1987-88; Fountainview, clinical director, 1990; International Certification

Reciprocity Consortium, member, 1990—, chairman of written test committee, 1991—; member of National Academy of Certified Clinical Mental Health Counselors and National Board of Certified Counselors; presenter of numerous professional workshops. *Military service:* U.S. Army, 1962-68, served in Germany and Vietnam; became staff sergeant. *Member:* American Association for Marriage and Family Therapy, American Group Psychotherapy Association, Oklahoma Drug and Alcohol Professional Counselor's Association (vice-president of certification board, 1989-91; president of certification board, 1991—), Kiwanis.

■ Awards, Honors

Careers in Psychology was named one of the best books for the teen-age, New York Public Library, 1993.

■ Writings

Assessment and Management of the Suicidal Adolescent, Essential Medical Information Systems, 1989.

(With Sharon Carter) *Coping with Depression,* Rosen Publishing, 1990, revised edition, 1992.

Coping with a Drug Abusing Parent, Rosen Publishing, 1991.

(With Carter) *Coping with Being Gifted,* Rosen Publishing, 1991.

(With J. Morrison) *Coping with a Learning Disability,* Rosen Publishing, 1992.

Careers in Psychology, Rosen Publishing, 1992.

(With B. Smith) *Coping with Sports Injuries,* Rosen Publishing, 1992.

LAWRENCE CLAYTON

Designer Drugs, Rosen Publishing, 1993.

(With R. Van Norstrand) *The Professional Drug and Alcohol Counselor Supervisor's Handbook,* Learning Publications, 1993.

Barbiturates and Other Depressants, Rosen Publishing, 1993.

Amphetamines and Other Stimulants, Rosen Publishing, 1993.

Coping with Phobias, Rosen Publishing, in press.

Coping with Being a Latchkey Kid, Rosen Publishing, in press.

Contributor to books, including *The Religion and Family Connection: Social Science Perspectives,* edited by Darwin Thomas, Brigham Young University, 1988. Contributor to periodicals, including *Growthline, Journal of Psychology and Christianity, Oklahoma Contact, Texas Methodist, Woman's Weekly,* and *Your Health.* Associate editor, *Family Perspective,* 1985—.

■ **Work in Progress**

Dysfunctional Family Roles, for Learning Publications; *Healthy Family Dynamics,* for Learning Publications; *Macrowave Perspectives in a Microwave World,* for Learning Publications; *A Field Rich and Bountiful: Careers in the Ministry;* research on suicidal family systems.

■ **Sidelights**

Lawrence Clayton told *SATA:* "I have been lucky. My life has been filled with life-changing people. The truly remarkable thing about that is that my life had a miserable beginning. We were artificially poor. My father was obsessed with money, I suppose because he was a child of the depression. My father was gone for extended periods—'selling farm implements,' he said. My brother, mother, and I tried to cling to life as best we could. We were so often hungry that we considered it a normal state of affairs. I never understood exactly how Mother found out, but one day she announced, 'Your father has another woman,' and said we were moving. Into this life walked the man destined to become my stepfather. He was both the biggest man I'd ever seen and the most generous, and he was also an alcoholic who became violently abusive. I've never been sure which form of hell was the most painful—being hungry or being afraid.

"Later I discovered that my father's previous long absences from home were largely spent in the company of his mistress in a town not too distant from the one in which I had lived. They had a huge house, several businesses, and numerous rent houses. Yet so obsessed with money was he that he played the part of a pauper, never spending as much as a dime 'foolishly' and hoarding all manner of things, even cardboard boxes.

"I consider myself lucky because throughout my life I have encountered certain individuals who pushed my life in slightly different directions until my entire course was changed. My mother maintained her dignity and

Clayton combines professional knowledge and personal experience in his book of advice for children of drug-users.

taught me to have a winning attitude. I can remember her reading *The Little Engine That Could* to me over and over. I so identified with that little engine that my life has in many ways become a parallel of its story. No hill has been too high for me to climb; no load has been too big for me to bear.

"An Episcopal lay worker was another influence. Her first task was to somehow get the old church in our town into condition to hold a service—it had been closed for many years. I was more than willing to help, but when she asked me to be the first lay reader I said I was no good at that kind of thing. She looked me right in the eye and said disdainfully, 'The problem is that you are lazy ... mentally lazy.' Never willing to admit that she was right, I set out to prove her wrong. I became their lay reader and in the process learned how to use my brain, a skill which has served me well.

Coach Fostered Positive Self-Image

"My basketball coach, Rodney Smith, became my life-changing person in my sixteenth year. Being an abused kid, I was afraid of everything. Everyone beat me up. Coach Smith changed all that. He made me see that I could compete, and he wouldn't settle for less. He demanded a more aggressive game from me. My basketball scores went from a low of two points to a high of twenty-one, even outscoring Stanley, one of my persecutors. I was elected captain of the team. Of course, this didn't put an end to Stanley's abuse. After an incident in the locker room he got the shock of his young life. I don't really know how many times I hit him; all I know is that he never managed to lay a hand on me, and when it was over he was sitting in the large chrome trash can. I knew Coach Smith would have been secretly proud. I was never again a victim of abuse.

"From my first sergeant while I was stationed at Fort Hood, Texas, I learned to become a just and caring human being. His extreme strictness was mediated by his sense of fairness and his love for his men. He didn't have a truly mean bone in his body, although he worked hard not to let the men know it.

"Dr. Alice Wonders, a sixty-four-year-old, five-foot-two-inch dynamo, radically changed my life. She got me registered in college without a high-school diploma on two conditions: that I would get a general equivalency diploma and pass the first semester. How could I let her down? I worked so hard I made the Dean's List that semester and every semester after that.

"Lydia Norie has a lot in common with Dr. Wonders—both small, caring champions of justice, possessors of great energy, and absolutely dedicated to a cause greater than themselves. To know one such person is a blessing. To know two such persons is to be enriched. To have been mentored by two such persons is to be exceedingly wealthy. Lydia was the executive of both the Oklahoma Drug and Alcohol Professional Counselor's Association and the Oklahoma Drug and Alcohol Professional Counselor's Certification Board; she held these positions for twelve years and refused to draw a salary for them. It was Lydia who persuaded me to write my first book."

*   *   *

COHEN, Nora
(Nora Tarlow)

■ Personal

Born in New Jersey; daughter of Stanley (a stockbroker and financial planner) and Iris (an infant-development researcher; maiden name Rittenberg) Willey. *Education:* Clark University, B.A.

■ Addresses

Home—Temecula, CA.

Nora Cohen and friend.

■ Career

Putnam & Grosset Group, New York City, senior editor, 1990; Harcourt, Brace, Jovanovich, San Diego, CA, free-lance editor, 1991; free-lance children's book editor and author.

■ Writings

(Under name Nora Tarlow) *An Easter Alphabet,* Putnam, 1991.
From Apple to Zipper, Aladdin Macmillan, 1993.
A Halloween Alphabet, Putnam, in press.

■ Work in Progress

Several picture books in collaboration with several illustrators.

*   *   *

COMPTON, Patricia A. 1936-

■ Personal

Born October 20, 1936, in Oakland, CA; married James R. Compton (a developer), September 11, 1982; children: Scott, Christian, Matthew. *Education:* San Francisco State University, B.A. (cum laude), 1969, M.A., 1971; post-graduate study at University of California, Berkeley, and University of California, Santa Cruz, 1972—.

■ Addresses

Home—15040 Oriole Rd., Saratoga, CA 95070.

PATRICIA A. COMPTON

■ Career

Laguna Salada School District, Pacifica, CA, art teacher, 1969-75; Pyramid Alternatives, Pacifica, art therapist, 1974-76; Laguna Salada Union School District, director and teacher at the Alternative School, 1975-76; Golden Gate University, San Francisco, CA, lecturer, 1976; J.F. Kennedy University, Orinda, CA, lecturer, 1977-78; City of Walnut Creek Civic Arts, supervisor of arts education, 1977-79; Montalvo Center for the Arts, Saratoga, CA, executive director, 1979-82; free-lance illustrator, textile designer, and writer, 1989—. Member of the San Mateo County Schools Art Committee, 1970-74; district representative, California Framework for the Arts, 1972-74. San Francisco State University and University of San Francisco, master teacher for student art teachers, 1974-76. Member of the board of directors of the Santa Clara County Arts Council, 1983-87, and the Montalvo Center for the Arts, 1985—. Member of the board of directors, Peninsula Open Space Trust, 1982—, Planned Parenthood of Santa Clara County, 1983-91, and Greenbelt Alliance, 1986-91.

■ Writings

The Terrible Eek, Simon & Schuster, 1991.

■ For More Information See

PERIODICALS

Bulletin of the Center for Children's Books, January, 1992, p. 7.
Horn Book, spring, 1992, p. 89.

Tribune Books (Chicago), October 13, 1991, p. 6.

*   *   *

CREW, Gary 1947-

■ Personal

Born September 23, 1947, in Brisbane, Australia; son of Eric (a steam engine driver) and Phyllis (a milliner; maiden name, Winch) Crew; married Christine Joy Willis (a teacher), April 4, 1970; children: Rachel, Sarah, Joel. *Education:* Attended Queensland Institute of Technology; University of Queensland, Diploma of Civil Engineering Drafting, 1970, B.A., 1979, M.A, 1984.

■ Addresses

Home—Green Mansions, 66 Picnic St., Enoggera, Queensland 4051, Australia. *Agent*—c/o Reed Australia, P.O. Box 460, Port Melbourne, Victoria 3027, Australia.

■ Career

McDonald, Wapner, and Priddle, Brisbane, Queensland, Australia, senior draftsman and drafting consultant, 1962-72; Everton Park State High School, Brisbane, English teacher, 1974-78; Mitchelton State High School, Brisbane, English teacher, 1978-81; Aspley High School, Brisbane, subject master in English, 1982; Albany Creek High School, Brisbane, subject master in English and head of English Department, 1983-88; Queensland University of Technology, creative writing lecturer, 1989—; Heinemann Octopus, series editor, 1990—. *Member:* Australian Society of Authors.

■ Awards, Honors

Book of the Year Award, Children's Book Council of Australia, and Alan Marshall Prize for Children's Literature, both 1991, both for *Strange Objects; Lucy's Bay* was short listed for the Children's Book Council of Australia's picture book of the year, 1993.

■ Writings

NOVELS

The Inner Circle, Heinemann Octopus, 1985.
The House of Tomorrow, Heinemann Octopus, 1988.
Strange Objects, Heinemann Octopus, 1990, Simon & Schuster, 1993.
No Such Country, Heinemann Octopus, 1991, Simon & Schuster, 1994.
Among Others, Heinemann Octopus, 1993.

CHILDREN'S STORY BOOKS

Tracks, illustrated by Gregory Rogers, Lothian, 1992.
Lucy's Bay, illustrated by Rogers, Jam Roll Press, 1992.
The Figures of Julian Ashcroft, illustrated by Hans DeHaas, Jam Roll Press, 1993.

First Light, illustrated by Peter Gouldthorpe, Lothian, 1993.
Gulliver in the South Seas, illustrated by John Burge, Lothian, in press.

OTHER

Contributor of short stories to anthologies, including *Hair Raising,* edited by Penny Matthews, Omnibus, 1992, and *The Blue Dress,* edited by Libby Hathorn, Heinemann, 1992. Contributor to books, including *At Least They're Reading! Proceedings of the First National Conference of the Children's Book Council of Australia,* Thorpe, 1992, and *The Second Authors & Illustrators Scrapbook,* Omnibus Books, 1992. Contributor to periodicals, including *Australian Author, Magpies,* and *Reading Time.*

■ **Adaptations**

The story "Sleeping over at Lola's" was adapted as a radio play by the Australian Broadcasting Commission; a film adaptation of *Strange Objects* is being produced by Zoic Films of Australia.

■ **Sidelights**

The novels of Australian writer Gary Crew have received critical acclaim for achieving two qualities that are difficult to combine; they have been declared intricate and enriching examples of literary writing, and they are also accessible to young readers. "His novels epitomize young adult literature in Australia to date," wrote Maurice Saxby in *The Proof of the Pudding.* "They successfully combine popular appeal with intellectual, emotional, psychological and spiritual substance." Crew's books often explore the history of Australia, but he finds that it is his own personal history that often drives his fiction. "Perhaps more than other mortals, it

GARY CREW

is the writer of children's fiction who suffers most from the desire to return to the past," he wrote in an essay in *Magpies.* "I know I cannot entirely abandon my own past. Once I would have longed to; I would have given anything to at least redress, at best forget, the forces that shaped me—but, as I grow older, and more confident in my art, I am not so certain.... A writer who cannot remember must produce lean fare. And surely, a children's writer who cannot remember is no writer at all."

Crew's past begins in Brisbane, Australia, where he was born in 1947. In his *Magpies* essay, Crew recalls that he "spent most of my childhood with the local kids racing around the neighbourhood," but there was also a sadder aspect to the author's early years. Crew began to suffer from poor health as a youngster, describing himself in a speech published in *Australian Author* as "a sickly, puny child." As a result, his rambunctious adventures soon gave way to calmer pursuits. "My mother says that I was a very quiet child, and my earliest memories suggest that she is right," Crew told *SATA.* "I was always happiest by myself, reading, drawing, or making models. I never did like crowds or noise." Crew's illness also forced him to spend a lot of time in hospitals or confined to the house, but this experience later benefited his writing in at least two ways. It first allowed him much time to read. In *Magpies,* Crew recalled that he and his sister read "anything," and this interest in books continued into adulthood, providing him with a solid literary background.

Stay at Grandmother's Provided Inspiring Setting

A second benefit of Crew's illness was that it brought him in closer contact with an influential setting that would later be featured in one of his books. "A significant period of my childhood had been spent at my great-grandmother's house in Ipswich, to the west of Brisbane," Crew related in *Australian Author.* "My great-grandmother was bedridden in this house; my widowed grandmother cared for her. Because I was always sick, there seemed to be some logic in packing me off to join them." Recalling the location in *The Second Authors & Illustrators Scrapbook,* Crew wrote that "this house was wonderful, with verandas all around, and a great big mango tree growing right up against it. We could climb over the rail and drop onto the branches of the mango. This house gave me the main idea for my second novel, *The House of Tomorrow.*" In that novel Crew writes of a teenage boy, Danny, who has difficulty coping with the increased pressures in his life. Searching for a means to order and understand the world around him, Danny finds solace in the house that is modeled on the home in Ipswich. As the author explained it in *Australian Author,* "In *The House of Tomorrow* my great-grandmother's house re-established a sense of place and belonging in a young boy's life."

Crew's stays in Ipswich had other benefits, as well. "My first public attempts at writing were letters sent from my great-grandmother's house to my parents," he wrote in *The Second Authors & Illustrators Scrapbook,* and writing and drawing later became important elements in his life. "Until I went to high school, I never seemed to be especially good at anything," Crew told *SATA*, "but at fifteen years old, I realized that I could write and draw—but that was about all I could do well!"

Despite his desire to continue his studies, Crew's drawing abilities and his family's economic status soon led him in another direction. "My parents had very little money," he told *SATA*, "so I left school at sixteen to become a cadet draftsman, working for a firm of engineers. I hated this, and at twenty-one I returned to college to matriculate by studying at night; then I went to university. All this time I was earning a living as a draftsman, but had decided to be a teacher of English because I loved books so much." Crew soon proved his abilities as a student, and he valued the opportunity to continue his delayed education. "I don't think anyone was ever more comfortable at uni[versity] than I was," he told *Scan* interviewer Niki Kallenberger, "—it was most wonderful! I would have done all the assignments on the sheets! It was a feeling of being totally at home and I was a changed person."

Chance Contest Entry Led to Career as Novelist

It was not until after he became a high school English teacher that Crew began writing fiction, and then only at the urging of his wife. "Christine cut out a piece from the paper advertising a short story contest which I entered virtually as a joke," he told Kallenberger. The story placed in the contest and later won a best short story of the year contest. Crew then turned to novels for young adults and drew inspiration from the students in his English classes. "I guess my first novels came out of my experience as a high school teacher," he told *SATA*. "I saw so many teenagers who were confused and unhappy—about themselves and the world around them." His first book, *The Inner Circle*, turned on the relationship between a black teenager, Joe, and a white one, Tony, who form a bond despite their racial differences. Saxby, analyzing the novel in *The Proof of the Pudding*, found that *The Inner Circle* is "above all, a well-told story incorporating many of the concerns of today's teenagers. The theme of personal and racial reintegration and harmony is inherent in the plot and reinforced through symbolism." The book has enjoyed great popularity in Australia, and English and Canadian editions have also been published. Crew has been pleased by its success but believes there are several flaws in the novel. "I'm not a fool in regard to approaching the book critically myself and I know the book's got phenomenal weaknesses," he told Kallenberger. "But I also see it as being a remarkable publishing oddity because it's so accessible to kids and its use in the classroom continues to astound me."

Crew's enjoyment of academic study—and research in particular—has influenced his fiction writing process. He is not an author who sits at a desk and waits for inspiration to visit him; instead, Crew actively seeks out information about a subject and collects the materials in a journal. As he told Kallenberger, a typical journal contains "clippings, drawings, scrappy notes I write to myself. I just keep it all in a carton and throw in anything, even books, that's broadly relevant.... It all goes in there and if it's a rainy day I'll look at it." Crew has also conducted computer searches to gain information on subjects, and he often employs his artistic skills in preparation for writing a book. "I think that drawing people and places before I write about them prevents me from having writer's block, and allows me to write smoothly without interruptions," he related in *The Second Authors and Illustrators Scrapbook*. "These jottings are quick and rough but they mean a great deal to me when I come to write the episode they represent; they serve as mental reminders."

Crew's explorations of Australian history began with his third novel, *Strange Objects*. The novel's hero, Stephen Messenger, is a sixteen-year-old boy who discovers a leather-bound journal and other mysterious objects in a cave. The relics are believed to have belonged to two survivors from the *Batavia*, a ship that wrecked off the coast of Australia in 1629. These relics provide Messenger with a direct link to his country's earliest European inhabitants, and they provide Crew with a means of

The discovery of a castaway's diary and a severed human hand draws a student into a seventeenth-century mystery in Crew's *Strange Objects*.

addressing the relationship between the Europeans and the aboriginal peoples who were the original inhabitants of the Australian continent. As is the case in several of Crew's books, *Strange Objects* forces the reader to consider some unpleasant aspects of the European conquest of the island and is often critical of the colonists who settled in Australia. Commenting on *Strange Objects* in *Reading Time,* Crew wrote that the book is "intended to challenge the reader to examine what has happened in our past, to re-assess what forces shaped this nation—and the effect the white invasion has had on the original inhabitants of this country."

Crew finds that, like many other things, his interest in the past stems from his childhood. When he received the Book of the Year Award from the Children's Book Council of Australia for *Strange Objects,* Crew explained the influence of his early years. "The origins of *Strange Objects* are founded deep in my memory," he stated in his acceptance speech, later published in *Reading Time.* "During the never ending sunshine of my childhood in the 50's, my parents would regularly take me and my sister Annita to the Queensland Museum.... Here we were able to stare goggle-eyed and open-mouthed at mummies stolen-away from the Torres Strait Islands, bamboo headhunters' knives complete with notches from every head taken and other so-called 'cannibal' artifacts.... When I had been made wiser by my studies, I began to understand the colonist's fear of the Indigene [or aborigines] as The Other, and to appreciate fully the fantastical and ever-changing phenomenon we call 'history'."

Australia's History Supplies Theme for Works

Crew has further explored the legacy of Australia's past in his novel *No Such Country,* which takes place in the fictional setting of New Canaan and concerns the fate of the White Father, a priest who enjoys great power in the village. Joan Zahnleiter, writing about the book in *Magpies,* noted that "the Father uses his knowledge of a particularly evil event in the past of New Canaan to blackmail superstitious fisherfolk into accepting him as the Messiah who controls their lives with his great book." Zahnleiter also found that "the book has deeply religious concepts embedded in it so that a working knowledge of the Bible enriches the reading of it. However it is a story which works well for the reader without that knowledge."

In addition to his novels, Crew has published story books for young children such as *Tracks* and *Lucy's Bay,* both including illustrations by Gregory Rogers. In *Tracks,* a young boy ventures into the strange, nighttime world of the jungle, making many unusual and beautiful discoveries. *Lucy's Bay* concerns a boy, Sam, whose sister drowns while he is taking care of her. Several years later, Sam returns to the scene of the tragedy in an attempt to come to terms with his feelings. A *Reading Time* review found *Lucy's Bay* to be "a beautiful piece of descriptive writing which places in perspective Sam's grief for his sister against the ceaseless rhythm of nature."

Looking ahead to future projects, Crew believes that his personal experiences will continue to play a large role in his books. "As a writer, I am not done with looking inward," he explained in *Australian Author.* "There is much for me still to find in my house of fiction; in those fantastical inner rooms of childhood from which, I imagine, some choose never to emerge." And in each book he writes, Crew has definite aims regarding his young audience. "My main objective in writing is to open the minds of my readers," he told *SATA,* "to say 'the world can be a wonderful place—its possibilities are open to you and your imagination.'"

■ Works Cited

Crew, Gary, essay on *Strange Objects* in *Reading Time,* Volume 35, Number 3, 1991, pp. 11-12.

Crew, Gary, "Awards: The Children's Book Council of Australia Awards, 1991 Acceptance Speeches," *Reading Time,* Volume 35, Number 4, 1991, pp. 4-5.

Crew, Gary, autobiographical essay in *The Second Authors & Illustrators Scrapbook,* Omnibus Books, 1992, pp. 32-35.

Crew, Gary, "New Directions in Fiction," *Magpies,* July, 1992, pp. 5-8.

Crew, Gary, "The Architecture of Memory," *Australian Author,* autumn, 1992, pp. 24-27.

Kallenberger, Niki, "An Interview with Gary Crew," *Scan,* November, 1990, pp. 9-11.

Review of *Lucy's Bay, Reading Time,* Volume 37, Number 2, May, 1992, p. 20.

Saxby, Maurice, *The Proof of the Pudding,* Ashton, 1993, pp. 455, 699-700.

Zahnleiter, Joan, "Know the Author: Gary Crew," *Magpies,* September, 1991, pp. 17-19.

■ For More Information See

BOOKS

Crew, Gary, "What's Next," in *At Least They're Reading! Proceedings of the First National Conference of The Children's Book Council of Australia, 1992,* Thorpe, 1992.

PERIODICALS

Magpies, May, 1991, p. 22; July, 1991, p. 37; March, 1992, p. 34.

Papers: Explorations in Children's Literature, August, 1990, pp. 51-58; April, 1992, pp. 18-26.

—Sketch by Jeff Hill

*   *   *

CROSS, Verda 1914-

■ Personal

Born September 8, 1914, in Dexter, MO; daughter of Grover Cleveland (a farmer) and Ethelinda Martha Jane (a homemaker; maiden name, Green)-Bagby; married Wentford Leeroy Cross (a farmer, chrome plater, apartment owner, and mobile home park owner); children: Delmar Lee, Billy Gene, Donald Leon. *Education:* Vocational School of Practical Nursing (Poplar Bluff, MO), L.P.N., 1969. *Politics:* "I support individuals, not their political parties." *Religion:* The Church of Jesus Christ of Latter-Day Saints.

■ **Addresses**

Home and office—270 Dawson St., Layton, UT 84041.

■ **Career**

Apartment house co-owner in Elgin, IL, 1949-57, and Poplar Bluff, MO, 1972-76; Lucy Lee Hospital, Poplar Bluff, licensed practical nurse, 1969-70; Doctors Hospital, Poplar Bluff, newborn care nurse, 1970-75; mobile home park co-owner, Poplar Bluff, 1974-86. *Member:* Relief Society (has served as president and secretary).

■ **Writings**

Great Grandma Tells of Threshing Day, illustrated by Gail Owens, Albert Whitman, 1992.

■ **Work in Progress**

Patti Finds a Gorilla Tree; Great Grandma Learns about Money; a series of eight books entitled *Swamp Angels.*

■ **Sidelights**

Verda Cross told *SATA:* "A writer should not try to write about something with which he or she is not familiar. While in school, writing assignments brought poor grades because I didn't dare write about things I had experienced. Some of my sisters felt being poor farm folk was a disgrace, and that was the only life I

VERDA CROSS

knew. They can look on it more objectively now that their circumstances have changed.

"My own children and grandchildren were different. They loved farm life and they enjoyed my stories and poems. I wrote some of them down. Years later my sister, Bernice Rabe, encouraged me to try to sell them. Due to an illness, I could not type and I couldn't afford to hire it done, so I put them away and waited. Occasionally, I would reread one and try to improve it." Cross's persistence paid off; the stories were eventually published as *Great Grandma Tells of Threshing Day.* "My books are 'cuddle' books," Cross added, "designed to be read by parents or grandparents to smaller children in hopes that the children will ask questions and learn more about their own heritage."

Cross also stated: "I believe children should be taught to work as soon as they show an interest in working. If your children want to wash dishes, let them watch you while you explain what you do and why you do it and tell them that at the next meal they can do the silverware. Or when dusting, let them dust the table legs or lower shelves and always be lavish with your praise and point out their accomplishments to others. They should not be forced to work. Instead, they should be taught that their help is appreciated.

"I believe children should be paid for some jobs to earn money for their wants and needs, but some jobs should be their own contribution to the comfort and welfare of the family and they should be highly praised for that. In this manner, children will grow up with a love of work and will understand the value of money and where it comes from. They will also learn how to spend it wisely. I try to show all this in my stories."

*   *   *

CUTLER, Jane 1936-

■ **Personal**

Born September 24, 1936, in Bronx, NY; daughter of Emanuel (a manufacturer) and Beatrice (a housewife; maiden name, Drooks) Cutler; children: Franny Nudelman, David Nudelman, Aaron Nudelman. *Education:* Northwestern University, B.A., 1958; San Francisco State University, M.A., 1982. *Hobbies and other interests:* Reading, swimming, tennis, hiking, movies, theatre.

■ **Addresses**

Agent—Linda Allen, 1949 Green St., Number 5, San Francisco, CA 94123.

■ **Career**

Writer and editor. Teaches writing at University of California, San Francisco. Has also taught writing at San Francisco State University, San Francisco. *Member:*

JANE CUTLER

Authors Guild, National Organization for Women, National Abortion Rights Action League.

■ Awards, Honors

Herbert Wilner Award for short fiction, 1982; PEN prize for short fiction, 1987.

■ Writings

Family Dinner (novel), Farrar, Straus, 1991.
No Dogs Allowed (short stories), Farrar, Straus, 1992.
Darcy and Gran Don't Like Babies (picture book), Scholastic Inc., 1993.
The War Years (novel), Farrar, Straus, 1994.
Mr. Carey's Garden (picture book) Ticknor and Fields, 1994.

Contributor of adult short stories to periodicals, including *American Girl, Redbook, North American Review,* and the *Chicago Tribune.* Also edited and wrote for text books and encyclopedias; developed reading material for children.

■ Work in Progress

A juvenile novel, *Puzzle People,* featuring a learning-disabled protagonist; a picture book about a kid and his cape; a book about a dinosaur.

■ Sidelights

Jane Cutler told *SATA:* "My own books are built around my characters: thoughtful characters, idiosyncratic characters, humorous characters. It is people who interest me most, and the books reflect this. But, like every writer, I need also to concern myself with plot—there has to be a story, after all! Fortunately, my characters have busy, active lives, which are, like most lives, full of stories."

D

DAVIS, Julia 1900-1993
(F. Draco)

OBITUARY NOTICE—See index for *SATA* sketch: Full name Julia Davis Adams, born July 23, 1900 (one source says 1904), in Clarkesburg, WV; died January 30, 1993, in Ranson, WV. Social worker, journalist, and author. Davis composed works that often focused on the history of West Virginia and her family's role in that history. In 1925, she began her career as a reporter for the Associated Press in New York City and later worked as an agent for New York's State Charities Aid Association. Davis also served as head of the adoption service of the Children's Aid Society from 1962 to 1965. Davis wrote *The Devil's Church* and *Cruise with Death* under the pseudonym F. Draco. Among her other young adult books are *Sword of the Vikings, The Shenandoah,* and *A Valley and a Song.* Davis also wrote *The Anvil,* a play.

OBITUARIES AND OTHER SOURCES:

BOOKS

International Authors and Writers Who's Who, 12th edition, International Biographical Centre, 1991.

PERIODICALS

New York Times, February 2, 1993, p. A17.

* * *

DEAN, Elinor
See McCANN, Helen

* * *

DEEM, James M(organ) 1950-

■ Personal

Born January 27, 1950, in Wheeling, WV; son of James M. and Mary Virginia (Traugh) Deem; married Susan Brontman (an elementary school librarian), May 27, 1978; children: Anna, Rachel, David, Chloe. *Education:* University of Kansas, B.S., 1971; University of Michigan, A.M., 1975, Ph.D., 1981. *Hobbies and other interests:* Travel, collecting antique pottery.

■ Addresses

Home—New Rochelle, NY. *Office*—c/o Houghton Mifflin Co., 222 Berkeley St., Boston, MA 02116.

JAMES M. DEEM

■ **Career**

Detroit Institute of Technology, Detroit, MI, director of Learning Center, 1976-78; Mohawk Valley Community College, Utica, NY, assistant professor and department chair of developmental studies, 1979-84; John Jay College of Criminal Justice, New York City, associate professor of communication skills, 1984—. *Member:* International Reading Association, American Society for Psychical Research.

■ **Awards, Honors**

Jule and Avery Hopwood Award for writing, University of Michigan, 1975.

■ **Writings**

YOUNG ADULT NOVELS

Frog Eyes Loves Pig, Crosswinds, 1988.
Frogburger at Large, Cora [Hamburg, Germany], 1990.

MIDDLE-GRADE NONFICTION

How to Find a Ghost, illustrated by True Kelley, Houghton Mifflin, 1988.
How to Catch a Flying Saucer, illustrated by Kelley, Houghton Mifflin, 1991.
How to Hunt Buried Treasure, illustrated by Kelley, Houghton Mifflin, 1992.
Ghost Hunters, illustrated by Michael David Biegel, Avon, 1992.
How to Travel through Time, Avon, 1993.
How to Read Your Mother's Mind, illustrated by Kelley, Houghton Mifflin, 1994.

OTHER

Study Skills in Practice (college textbook), Houghton Mifflin, 1993.

Contributor to books, including *Classroom Practices in Teaching English, 1980-81: Dealing with Differences,* 1980. Contributor to periodicals, including *Reading Instruction Journal, Journal of Basic Writing,* and *College Composition and Communication.*

■ **Work in Progress**

Another nonfiction book for middle readers and a young-adult novel.

■ **Sidelights**

James M. Deem told *SATA:* "I became a writer in the fifth grade. Sometime during the winter of that year, I was playing with a group of my friends in the woods behind our houses when we came across some strange tracks in the snow. They didn't look like they had been made by any familiar animals (they were *big* tracks) but they didn't exactly look human. They looked like some kind of monster tracks, and they scared us so much that we never followed them.

Searching for buried treasure can lead to an appreciation of history, as Deem explains in *How to Hunt Buried Treasure.* (Cover illustration by True Kelley.)

"That night when I went home I took out a notebook and began to write a novel. After all, I had read almost every Hardy Boys' book, and I knew that those tracks would make a great book. I wrote a title at the top of the page ('The Strange Tracks Mystery'), and then I wrote one page and stopped. I had the idea but not the ability to follow through at that point. But that's how I began my life as a writer.

"A year later I tried again, this time with a short story. I loved science fiction movies, and so I created a story called 'The Invasion of the Green-Eyed Monsters.' This time I finished it. I went on to write for the school newspaper and yearbook. By the time I got to college, I decided to become a teacher to pay the bills. At first, I taught high-school English, but after I received my master's degree I switched to teaching college students. I teach them how to develop their reading, vocabulary, and study skills, and I can think of no more rewarding work except, perhaps, writing for children.

"I have written about subjects that interested me as a child (and still interest me as an adult): ghosts, UFOs, treasure, time travel, extrasensory perception (ESP), and mummies.

"I chose to write about ghosts first, I think, because I was petrified of them when I was little. Before I was born, my grandfather had died of a heart attack while sitting on my grandmother's green damask sofa with the caned back. I remember the first time I heard this fact: I was seated on that very sofa, when my grandmother mentioned that I was sitting in the exact spot where my grandfather died. That experience—along with my already vivid imagination—convinced me to make a nightly ghost check: under the bed, in the closet, behind the door. I had to shut the closet door tight and make sure that no clothes were hanging over my desk chair (they might turn into ghosts during the night). I didn't know then that ghosts aren't the scary beings I thought they were. It was only when I grew up and began reading about experiences people claimed to have with real ghosts that I realized I had been mistaken.

"I was also interested in flying saucers when I was little. Again, the thought of them scared me, but I couldn't pass up any science-fiction movie with them in it. One night I was sure that space aliens had even invaded my bedroom. I was in bed, trying to sleep, when I heard voices whispering near me. I screamed for my parents. We looked everywhere but we couldn't find the source of the whispering. I tried to go back to sleep, but the whispering began again. I don't know how many times my parents made the trip into my bedroom that night, but we finally discovered that a broken, old radio in my room had suddenly begun to work. The whispering voices had come not from space aliens but from a radio announcer and singers.

"Recently I was working on a book on the subject of time travel. I have always wanted to know what it would be like to travel to other places and other times. In doing some historical research for this book, which was eventually published as *How To Travel through Time,* I became amazed that few people (especially children) wrote down their observations about daily life. One of the historical events I read about was the opening of the longest suspension bridge in the world (at that time) around 1850 in Wheeling, West Virginia. It took years to build. For the opening ceremony, the bridge was specially lit by 1,000 oil lights; it was lined with horse-drawn carriages carrying thousands of people. Famous politicians came to talk to the people gathered there, and a fancy banquet was held. And it appears that not one person wrote about this experience, except the reporter for the local newspaper.

"I think it's important to decide, as I did, that you are going to be a writer. Don't worry about whether you will get published or not, just start writing. Keep a daily record of writing. Don't write down what you do, write down what you think, what you feel, what you see, what you experience. Don't ask your parents for the latest game or video, ask them for a blank book with pages meant to be filled with your writing. If one child who was at the opening of that suspension bridge had written what he or she had seen, it might have helped people have a better sense of history."

DeLaCROIX, Alice 1940-

■ Personal

Born November 29, 1940, in Elwood, IN; daughter of Ermal (a farmer) and Ruby (a teacher; maiden name, Hartley) Antrim; married Robert DeLaCroix (an engineer), June 11, 1961; children: Martha, Wyatt. *Education:* Purdue University, B.S., 1962, M.S., 1963. *Hobbies and other interests:* Gardening (flowers and food), animals, reading, amateur acting, church choir, and listening to opera.

■ Addresses

Home—Penfield, NY.

■ Career

Purdue University, West Lafayette, IN, instructor in clothing and textiles, 1962-65; Harris Garden Stores, Penfield, NY, clerk, 1980-83; worked as a commercial model and voice talent in Rochester, NY, 1987-89; Fairport Schools, Fairport, NY, substitute junior high teacher, 1988-92; writer. *Member:* Society of Children's Book Writers and Illustrators.

ALICE DeLaCROIX

■ Writings

Mattie's Whisper (novel), Boyds Mills Press, 1992.

Contributor to periodicals, including *Highlights for Children.*

■ Work in Progress

Two novels for middle-grade readers, one about growing up on a farm in 1950, the second about a lonely boy who finds a friend in a lost dog.

■ Sidelights

Alice DeLaCroix told *SATA:* "While in the midst of an absolutely ordinary life, I have always been involved in things artistic, whether singing, acting, designing clothes, or writing. As a child I read a lot and liked writing. But it wasn't until I had gone through years of wonderful children's books with my own two children that I knew I wanted to be that kind of writer.

"I grew up on a farm and still love nature and animals. My first novel is about a girl who loves horses, and the novel I am working on now takes place in a small Indiana farming community. The first writing I remember doing was a short play in third grade, and, I believe, I wrote at least one play through sixth grade. It is likely I was more of a performer than a writer at that time, but the writing itch has always been with me.

"In fifth and sixth grades I read every dog story available and many biographies, the latter probably because that's what was provided in our classroom library; we had no grade school library, but each class had a few of its own books. My mother was a teacher who always inspired me to learn new things, with books being the greatest source of my discoveries. And I still picture my father with a novel in his hands, resting from the labor of farming.

"I've always enjoyed solitude and reflection—from childhood days of long walks through my daddy's fields, singing to the sky or dreaming grand dreams, to the present. Long hours alone at the computer, creating a world on paper, leave me content rather than lonely."

*   *   *

De La ROCHE SAINT ANDRE, Anne 1950- (Sara)

■ Personal

Born March 17, 1950, in Nantes, France; daughter of Jacques and Chantal (De Laubier) De La Roche Saint Andre; children: Edith, Agnes, Samuel.

■ Addresses

Home—13 Boulevard Montparnasse, Paris, France 75006.

■ Career

Illustrator and author.

■ Writings

IN ENGLISH TRANSLATION; UNDER NAME SARA; SELF-ILLUSTRATED

The Rabbit, the Fox, and the Wolf, Orchard, 1990 (published in French as *Dans la Gueule du Loup,* Epigones, 1990).
Across Town, Orchard, 1991 (published in French as *A Travers la Ville,* Epigones, 1990).

UNTRANSLATED WORKS; UNDER NAME SARA; SELF-ILLUSTRATED

La Longue Marche de Vagabonde, Epigones, 1991.
Bateau sur l'eau, Epigones, 1991.

■ Sidelights

Anne De La Roche Saint Andre has written a number of colorful books that enjoy broad audience appeal. Many of her stories—all written under the anagram-derived name "Sara"—feature animals interacting with humans in touching and humorous ways. Bringing an impres-

Sara's paper collage illustrations give an eerie tone to her picture book *The Rabbit, the Fox, and the Wolf.*

sionistic rather than realistic approach to her illustrations, De La Roche Saint Andre excels at creating striking images that linger in readers' minds. In an interview for *La Revue des Livres pour Enfants,* she commented: "Imagination is always necessary for pictures."

■ **Works Cited**

De La Roche Saint Andre, Anne, interview in *La Revue des Livres pour Enfants,* April, 1991.

*   *   *

DODDS, Dayle Ann 1952-

■ **Personal**

Born June 14, 1952, in Ridgewood, NJ; daughter of Theodore (a lawyer) and Edith (a homemaker; maiden name, Moog) Bruinsma; married Glen Dodds (an architect), December 6, 1976; children: Jaime, Greg. *Education:* California State Polytechnic University, San Luis Obispo, B.S. in Childhood Development.

■ **Addresses**

Home—4155 Willmar Dr., Palo Alto, CA 94306. *Agent*—Ginger Knowlton, Curtis Brown, Ltd., Ten Astor Pl., New York, NY 10003.

DAYLE ANN DODDS

■ **Career**

Writer, 1989—. Teacher and teacher's aide for kindergarten, first through third grades, and art classes in Palo Alto, CA, 1975-78; administrative assistant for a publishing company in Palo Alto, 1978-80; free-lance proofreader, 1980-82. *Member:* Society of Children's Book Writers and Illustrators.

■ **Awards, Honors**

Bay Area Book Reviewers Association nomination for *Wheel Away!*

■ **Writings**

Wheel Away!, illustrated by Thatcher Hurd, Harper, 1989.
On Our Way to Market, illustrated by John Gurney, Simon & Schuster, 1991.
Do Bunnies Talk?, illustrated by Arlene Dubanevich, HarperCollins, 1992.
The Color Box, illustrated by Giles Laroche, Little, Brown, 1992.
Sardines, illustrated by Jerry Smath, Simon & Schuster, 1993.
The Shape of Things, Candlewick Press, 1994.
Sing, Sophie!, Candlewick Press, 1994.

■ **Work in Progress**

More Are Mice, a picturebook, and *The Phantom Family of Lawrence O'Toole,* a middle grade novel.

■ **Sidelights**

"As a child," Dayle Ann Dodds told *SATA,* "I enjoyed reading stories of fantasy most of all. *Grimm's Fairy Tales* were probably my favorite, especially 'The Twelve Dancing Princesses,' who sneaked off into the night without being caught and danced their shoes to pieces. I was the youngest child in my family, and in many of Grimm's tales, the youngest child grew to become the smartest after all the others failed. I also loved the story of the table cloth that became filled with luscious food when the boy commanded 'Spread yourself.' What a wonderful treasure that would be to own! I read *The Wizard of Oz* over and over and the tales of Hans Christian Andersen, then my tastes took a turn to the whimsical and humorous. I loved Homer Price's misadventures, especially the donut-making machine that went out of control, and the ball of string that grew bigger and bigger. I carried this love for cumulative, building and 'out-of-control' happenings into my own stories later on.

"Drawing and riding horses were my favorite pastimes as a child. I was lucky to have my own horse, and most days after school were filled with galloping escapes through the canyons of our Southern California community, still largely rural at that time. I also loved 'putting things together.' Magazine scraps and glue became illustrated books. Light bulbs taped to soda pop bottles were transformed into brightly painted papier-mache animals. Bits of leather were cut and woven into saddles and bridles for my stable of toy horses. My favorite spot in the house was the junk drawer in the kitchen, where my mother stashed everything from magnets to glitter to broken watches. These were the jewels my treasures were made of.

"It wasn't until college that the thought of writing books for children came to me. A class on children's literature sparked a longing to relive the excitement of the stories of my youth. I found myself reading children's books once again. After all, my chosen career was teaching young children, wasn't it? I had every right to chose Robert McCloskey or Theodor Geisel as my weekend reading. I had a lovely excuse for returning to the world of children's books.

Daughter's Birth Inspired Writing Career

"The arrival of my first child, daughter Jaime, gave me the green light to begin writing my own children's books. I had taken a leave from teaching to work for an educational publishing company, where I gained some valuable experience about the putting together of illustrated books. Now I had someone to write for—my own child. I found myself getting up at 5 AM to have time to work before the baby woke up. I wrote every chance I got (which isn't much with a new baby), and I found great pleasure in knowing I had my own creative secret: I was writing children's books and no one else knew. For the first year, I literally worked in my upstairs closet, my special space where my thoughts and ideas were my own.

"My first published story, 'The Carrot Corporation,' concerned two boys who started a carrot cake business in their mother's kitchen. I got so excited that I could write something that could be published, that I began thinking along the lines of a book. For three years, I worked on story after story, making all the mistakes beginners do. My first stories were too long, too complicated, not easily illustrated as picture books.

"Next, my son Greg was born. Although a busy mother, I refused to give up on my dream to write books for children. As the children grew, my world centered around strollers, wagons, roller skates, bicycles—wheels. *Wheel Away!* was one of those ideas that comes out of nowhere and everywhere at the same time. As I stood in the shower (I did most of my creative thinking in the shower in those days), I could see the cover of the book in front of me. What resulted was a simple, cumulative tale of a wheel that gets loose from a boy's bicycle and makes a funny, noisy journey through the town. I submitted the story to Harper & Row, and to my delight, they bought it. My wishes had been answered, my dreams had come true. I was a children's book author.

"Following the success of *Wheel Away!* I began taking my writing very seriously, too seriously in fact. My ideas seamed forced and contrived. What had brought me

A simple trip to the market is nearly thwarted by a number of mishaps in this tale by Dodds. (Cover illustration by John Gurney.)

pleasure now caused frustration. On day my husband saw me struggling to pull an idea out of a now-empty magical hat (or at least it seemed that way.) He said to me, 'Dayle, if it isn't fun anymore, you shouldn't be doing it. You began writing because it brought you pleasure.' Nothing could have helped me more. That summer I wrote a fun little story about a boy taking a basket of eggs and a hen to market. I let myself off the hook. I found the words, the joy all came back.

"*Do Bunnies Talk?* One of my writing friends calls me the 'noisiest writer I know.' I love words, I love sounds, I love how words sound, alone and together. I wanted to write a book that had more than a few sounds we hear. I wanted to write an explosion of sounds. And I did.

"I am now working on a middle grade novel, which I hope to complete sometime soon. But I haven't given up on picture books. I have a few ideas up my sleeve, and as long as children keep enjoying my books, I will keep writing them!"

*   *   *

DOLCE, J. Ellen 1948-

■ Personal

Surname is pronounced "dole-chay"; born March 3, 1948, in Greenport, NY; daughter of J. Donald (a draftsperson and technician) and Janet E. (a homemaker and craftsperson; maiden name, Tuthill) Doughty; married Bill Dolce (a commercial photographer; died, 1987); married Michael S. Korsower (a teacher), June 29, 1991; children: (first marriage) Zoe Noelle. *Education:* State University of New York at New Paltz, B.S., 1970, graduate study, 1970-71. *Politics:* "Moderate Democrat." *Religion:* Protestant. *Hobbies and other interests:* Collecting antique children's books, gardening, playing the piano, reading, sculpting.

■ Addresses

Home and office—Monroe, NY.

■ Career

Free-lance illustrator, 1984—. Poppycock Players, puppeteer and puppet maker, 1972-77; taught art at a Montessori school, 1979-82.

■ Writings

"THE DAYDREAMERS" SERIES; SELF-ILLUSTRATED

If I Had a Hippo, Modern Publishing, 1988.
If I Knew How to Fly a Rocket, Modern Publishing, 1988.
If I Could Be a Circus Clown, Modern Publishing, 1988.
If I Went Sailing out to Sea, Modern Publishing, 1988.

"BABY DOLL" BOARD BOOKS; ILLUSTRATOR

Smiling Sandy, Modern Publishing, 1989.
Cuddly Casey, Modern Publishing, 1989.
Toddling Terry, Modern Publishing, 1989.
Patty Cake, Modern Publishing, 1989.

ILLUSTRATOR; PUBLISHED BY WESTERN PUBLISHING, EXCEPT AS INDICATED

Barbara Seuling, *What Kind of Family Is This,* 1985.
Bruce Isen, *Busy Saturday Word Book,* 1985.
Carol North, *The House Book,* 1985.
Jules Older, *Don't Panic,* 1986.
Leone C. Anderson, *How Come You're So Shy,* 1987.
Baby's Mother Goose, 1988.
Bill Gutman, editor, *Favorite Counting Rhymes,* Modern Publishing, 1988.

J. ELLEN DOLCE

Gutman, editor, *Favorite Lullabies,* Modern Publishing, 1988.
Joy N. Hulme, *A Stable in Bethlehem,* 1989.
Thea Feldman, adapter, *Little Red Riding Hood,* 1989.
James C. Shooter, *Baby Animals on the Farm,* 1990.
Karl Schulte, editor, *Christmas Carols,* 1990.
Dana F. Kennedy, *My Very First Golden Bible,* 1991.
Sally Bell, adapter, *The Three Little Pigs,* 1991.

■ Work in Progress

"Developing illustrations for an elf story found in an antique children's book with the notion of making them into a book."

■ Sidelights

J. Ellen Dolce told *SATA:* "My career as a children's book illustrator had its roots in my constant childhood pastime of drawing. I grew up in very rural eastern Long Island (all potato fields and truck farms) so if I wasn't at the beach or playing in the yard I was entertaining myself by making up stories and then drawing what I saw in my mind's eye. The fun part was imagining myself there in the scene I was drawing on paper; it was like being an actor in a slowly evolving graphite movie. Needless to say, this ability to amuse myself for hours by drawing made me an easy child to raise.

"Now that I'm grown up, I've had the good fortune to be able to turn my childhood passion into a career (and I think doing professionally what you always loved as a child is the best kind of job). I find I still get very wrapped up in the situations I'm depicting and project myself mentally into the scene. It's very helpful in getting the facial expressions and poses right and, by vicariously living the action on the paper, the isolation of working alone in a studio for hours is somewhat relieved.

"My latest project has been doing all the illustrations for *My Very First Golden Bible.* The idea of doing the Bible was a bit daunting at first since, with 155 illustrations, it was at least five times bigger than any book I had previously illustrated. It required doing a lot of research because, although the book is intended for very young children, I still wanted it to be as accurate as possible regarding costumes, buildings and artifacts. There's also the matter of the 2000 year time span from Abraham to Jesus, as well as locales ranging from ancient Babylon and Egypt to Palestine and the Garden of Eden. Luckily, there's plenty of material out there pertaining to biblical times, and I enjoy history and historical research. Having fifteen years of Sunday school behind me didn't hurt, either.

"I had assumed that I'd be starting with Genesis and working sequentially through to Revelations, but for some mysterious reason this wasn't the case. Ever mindful of the deadline date, I had to begin sketching as soon as I received a batch of stories, which were in no particular order. This meant I was constantly jumping back and forth between the New Testament and the Old.

The story of Moses is one of the many biblical narratives brought to life for young readers by Dolce's illustrations in *My Very First Golden Bible*.

It was all quite a challenge, especially since my specialty has always been drawing children and women, and most of the characters in the well-known Bible stories are men. To compensate, I tried to keep the action as lively as possible and the old patriarchs as friendly and approachable looking as I could make them. Many of the illustrations I had seen for other children's Bibles had seemed too somber and dark, and I wanted to avoid that but still maintain a certain dignity. In most cases I think I succeeded.

"The book took me nine months to illustrate (including pencil sketches) and it was only by following a very exacting timetable and exercising self-discipline that I was able to meet the deadline. That is always the dilemma we illustrators face: finding a way to do the best possible illustrations we can but keeping in mind how much time we have (and how much money we are being paid). I'd love to make each illustration a perfectly painted little masterpiece, but realistically that isn't possible with mass-market books. What I try to do is illustrate in a way that will appeal to children without being condescending, will satisfy my artistic criteria, and will be appropriate for the monetary and time constraints.

"I am turning more towards sculpture these days. Making three dimensional figures has always been a love of mine."

*   *   *

DORRIS, Michael A.
See DORRIS, Michael (Anthony)

DORRIS, Michael (Anthony) 1945-
(Michael A. Dorris)

■ **Personal**

Born January 30, 1945, in Louisville, KY; son of Jim and Mary Besy (Burkhardt) Dorris; married Louise Erdrich (a writer), in 1981; children: Reynold Abel (died in 1991), Jeffrey Sava, Madeline Hannah, Persia Andromeda, Pallas Antigone, Aza Marion. *Education:* Georgetown University, B.A. (cum laude), 1967; Yale University, M.Phil., 1970.

■ **Addresses**

Home—Box 358, Cornish Flat, NH 03746. *Agent*—Charles Rembar, Rembar and Curtis, 19 West Forty-fourth St., New York, NY 10036.

■ **Career**

University of Redlands, Johnston College, Redlands, CA, assistant professor, 1970; Franconia College, Franconia, NH, assistant professor, 1971-72; Dartmouth College, Hanover, NH, instructor, 1972-76, assistant professor, 1976-79, associate professor, 1979, professor of anthropology, 1979-88, adjunct professor, 1989—, chair of Native American studies department, 1979—, chair of Master of Arts in Liberal Studies program, 1982-85. University of New Hampshire, visiting assistant professor, 1973-74; University of Auckland, New Zealand, visiting senior lecturer, 1980. Director of urban bus program, summers, 1967, 1968, and 1969. Society for Applied Anthropology, fellow, 1977—; Save the Children Foundation, board member, 1991-92, advisory board member, 1992—; U.S. Advisory Committee on Infant Mortality, member, 1992—. Consultant to National Endowment for the Humanities, 1976—, and to television stations, including Los Angeles Educational Television, 1976, and Toledo Public Broadcast Center, 1978. Has appeared on numerous radio and television programs. *Member:* PEN, Authors Guild, Writers Guild, Modern Language Association of America (delegate assembly and member of minority commission, 1974-77), American Anthropological Association, American Association for the Advancement of Science (opportunities in science commission, 1974-77), National Indian Education Association, National Congress of American Indians, National Support Committee (Native American Rights Fund), Research Society on Alcoholism, National Organization for Fetal Alcohol Syndrome, Phi Beta Kappa, Alpha Sigma Nu.

■ **Awards, Honors**

Woodrow Wilson fellow, 1967 and 1980; fellowships from National Institute of Mental Health, 1970 and 1971, John Simon Guggenheim Memorial Foundation, 1978, Rockefeller Foundation, 1985, National Endowment for the Arts, 1989, and Dartmouth College, 1992; Outstanding Academic Book of 1984-85 citation, *Choice,* for *A Guide to Research on North American Indians;* Indian Achievement Award, 1985; best book

MICHAEL DORRIS

citation, American Library Association (ALA), 1988, for *A Yellow Raft in Blue Water;* PEN Syndicated Fiction Award, 1988, for "Name Games"; honorary degree, Georgetown University, 1989; National Book Critics Circle Award for general nonfiction and Governor's Writing Award, State of Washington, both 1989, and Christopher Award, Heartland Prize, and Outstanding Academic Book, *Choice,* all 1990, all for *The Broken Cord: A Family's Ongoing Struggle with Fetal Alcohol Syndrome;* Best Audio of 1990 of Author Reading His or Her Own Work citation, *Audio World,* for the audiocassette version of *The Broken Cord: A Family's Ongoing Struggle with Fetal Alcohol Syndrome;* Medal of Outstanding Leadership and Achievement, Dartmouth College, 1991; Sarah Josepha Hale Literary Award, 1991; Scott Newman Award, 1992, and Gabriel Award for National Entertainment Program, ARC Media Award, Christopher Award, Writers Guild of America award, and Media Award, American Psychology Association, all for the television film of *The Broken Cord: A Family's Ongoing Struggle with Fetal Alcohol Syndrome;* Montgomery Fellow, Dartmouth College, 1992; International Pathfinder Award, World Conference on the Family, 1992; Award for Excellence, Center for Anthropology and Journalism, 1992, for essays on Zimbabwe; Scott O'Dell Award for Historical Fiction, American Library Association, 1992, for *Morning Girl;* Citation for Excellence, Overseas Press Club, for "House of Stone"; *Morning Girl* was named to best or notable book lists by *Publishers Weekly, Horn Book Booklinks, School Library Journal, Booklist,* and *New York Times Book Review.*

■ Writings

FOR YOUNG ADULTS

Morning Girl (novel), Hyperion, 1992.
Guests, Hyperion, in press.

OTHER

Native Americans: Five Hundred Years After, with photographs by Joseph C. Farber, Crowell, 1977.
(As Michael A. Dorris; with Arlene B. Hirschfelder and Mary Lou Byler) *A Guide to Research on North American Indians,* American Library Association, 1983.
A Yellow Raft in Blue Water (novel), Holt, 1987.
The Broken Cord: A Family's Ongoing Struggle with Fetal Alcohol Syndrome (nonfiction), foreword by Louise Erdrich, Harper, 1989, published as *The Broken Cord: A Father's Story,* Collins, 1990.
(With Erdrich) *Route Two and Back,* Lord John, 1991.
(With Erdrich) *The Crown of Columbus* (novel), Harper-Collins, 1991.
Rooms in the House of Stone (nonfiction), Milkweed Editions, 1993.
Working Men (stories), Holt, 1993.
Paper Trail: Collected Essays, 1967-1992, HarperCollins, in press.

Also author of "House of Stone" and the short story "Name Games." Contributor to books, including *Racism in the Textbook,* 1976; *Separatist Movements,* 1979; and *Heaven is under Our Feet,* 1991. Contributor of articles, poems, short stories, and reviews to periodicals, including *Chicago Tribune, Life, Los Angeles Times, Mother Jones, New York Times Book Review, Parents Magazine,* and *Vogue. Viewpoint* (one source says *Viewspoint*), editor, 1967; *American Indian Culture and Research Journal,* member of editorial board, 1974—; *MELUS: The Journal of the Society for the Study of the Multi-Ethnic Literature of the United States,* member of editorial advisory board, 1977-79. Author of the screen treatment *Sleeping Lady,* Mirage Films/Sydney Pollack, 1991; author of songs with Judy Rodman, Warner-Chappell Music, 1993.

■ Adaptations

The Broken Cord: A Family's Ongoing Struggle with Fetal Alcohol Syndrome was produced for television by Universal Television and ABC-TV, 1992. *A Yellow Raft in Blue Water* and *The Broken Cord: A Family's Ongoing Struggle with Fetal Alcohol Syndrome* were released on audiocassette by HarperAudio in 1990; *The Crown of Columbus* was released on audiocassette by HarperAudio in 1991.

■ Work in Progress

Amory Goes Wild, a book for young adults, for Hyperion, 1995.

■ Sidelights

Michael Dorris is the author of a number of respected titles for adults, including the novel *A Yellow Raft in Blue Water* and the autobiographical book *The Broken Cord: A Family's Ongoing Struggle with Fetal Alcohol Syndrome.* In 1992, the five-hundredth anniversary of Christopher Columbus's discovery of the Americas, he published his first book for children, *Morning Girl,* which tells the stories of two young Bahamians living in 1492. As Morning Girl (who loves the day) and Star Boy (who prefers night) search for their own identities, Dorris evokes the natural world and its relation to the children's Native American culture. The daily adventures of the young narrators are the focus of the novel, which ends as Christopher Columbus's crew from the *Nina* lands on the island. "This sad, lovely and timely tale gives us an alternative view of America's 'discovery,'" wrote Suzanne Curley in the *Los Angeles Times Book Review.* A *Publishers Weekly* contributor called *Morning Girl* "soulful [and] affecting," and concluded: "With its spare, compelling prose, Dorris's singularly involving work should be read by both children and adults for many generations to come." And *New York Times Book Review* contributor Alice McDermott found *Morning Girl* "a warm story full of real characters and situations, told in marvelous language that makes it a pleasure to read out loud."

The idyllic lives of a young girl and her brother are changed when foreigners land on their Bahamian island in 1492. (Cover illustration by Kam Mak.)

■ Works Cited

Curley, Suzanne, review of *Morning Girl, Los Angeles Times Book Review,* September 27, 1992, p. 12.

McDermott, Alice, review of *Morning Girl, New York Times Book Review,* November 8, 1992, p. 33.

Review of *Morning Girl, Publishers Weekly,* August 10, 1992, p. 71.

■ For More Information See

BOOKS

Bestsellers 90, Issue 1, Gale, 1990.

Twentieth-Century Western Writers, St. James Press, 1991, pp. 190-191.

PERIODICALS

Commonweal, December 7, 1990, p. 728.

Los Angeles Times Book Review, June 21, 1987, p. 2; July 30, 1989, p. 1; May 12, 1991, p. 3.

Nation, October 21, 1991, p. 488.

New Republic, January 6, 1992, p. 30.

New Statesman and Society, September 7, 1990, p. 44; July 26, 1991, p. 35.

New York Times, May 9, 1987, p. 13.

New York Times Book Review, June 7, 1987, p. 7; July 30, 1989, p. 1; April 28, 1991, p. 10.

New York Times Magazine, April 21, 1991, p. 34.

Publishers Weekly, August 4, 1989, p. 73.

School Library Journal, October, 1992, p. 116.

Time, April 29, 1991, p. 76.

Times Literary Supplement, March 11, 1988, p. 276; August 24, 1990, p. 893; July 19, 1991, p. 21.

Tribune Books (Chicago), May 10, 1987, p. 6; July 23, 1989, p. 1; April 28, 1991, p. 5.

* * *

DR. SEUSS
See GEISEL, Theodor Seuss

* * *

DRACO, F.
See DAVIS, Julia

* * *

DRAGONWAGON, Crescent 1952-
(Ellen Parsons)

■ Personal

Original name, Ellen Zolotow; name legally changed; born November 25, 1952, in New York, NY; daughter of Maurice (a biographer) and Charlotte (a children's book writer; maiden name, Shapiro) Zolotow; married Crispin Dragonwagon (an archaeologist), March 20, 1970 (divorced August 10, 1975); married Ned Shank (an architectural marketing consultant and innkeeper), October 20, 1978. *Education:* Educated in Hastings-on-Hudson, NY, and Stockbridge, MA. *Hobbies and other*

CRESCENT DRAGONWAGON

interests: Gardening, reading, cooking, movies of the 1920s, '30s, and '40s, antiques, historic preservation, white water canoeing, environmentalism, theater.

■ Addresses

Home—Route 4, Box 1, Eureka Springs, AR 72632.

■ Career

Writer, inkeeper, lecturer. Co-owner (with husband), Dairy Hollow House (a country inn and restaurant), Eureka Springs. Former participant in artist in the schools programs in Arkansas and Georgia; lecturer at numerous national conferences, including National Council of Teachers of English Conference, 1980, American Association of School Librarians Conference, 1982, and Professional Association of Innkeepers International Conference, 1992. Member of board, Walton Arts Center, Fayetteville, AR. *Member:* Professional Association of Innkeepers International, Society of Children's Book Writers and Illustrators, American Society of Journalists and Authors, Poets & Writers, Independent Innkeepers Association, Historic Preservation Alliance of Arkansas, WORDS: Arkansas Literary Society.

■ Awards, Honors

Outstanding Science Trade Book for Children, National Science Teachers Association/Children's Book Council, 1976, for *Wind Rose;* American Library Association Notable Book citation, 1982, for *To Take a Dare;* Georgia and Colorado Children's Choice award nominations, 1983, for *I Hate My Brother Harry;* National Council Teachers of English Choice Book, 1984, for *Jemima Remembers;* Parents' Choice Award, and Social Sciences Book of the Year, both 1984, both for *Always, Always;* *New York Times* Notable Book citation, 1985, for *The Year It Rained;* Notable Children's Book in Social Studies, and Wisconsin Children's Center Best Books citation, both 1987, both for *Diana, Maybe;* "Reading Rainbow Book," 1989, for *Half a Moon and One Whole Star;* Golden Kite Award, Society of Children's Book Writers, 1990, and National Conference of Christians and Jews Recommended Reading List for Children and Young Adults citation, 1990-91, all for *Home Place;* Notable Children's Trade Book in social studies, National Council for the Social Studies/Children's Book Council, 1990, for *Home Place* and *Winter Holding Spring;* Porter Fund Award for Literary Excellence, 1991, for body of work; James Beard Award, and Julia Child/IACP Cookbooks award nomination, both 1992-93, both for *Dairy Hollow House Soup & Bread.*

■ Writings

CHILDREN'S BOOKS

(Under pseudonym Ellen Parsons) *Rainy Day Together,* Harper, 1970.

Strawberry Dress Escape, illustrated by Lillian Hoban, Scribner, 1975.

When Light Turns into Night, illustrated by Robert A. Parker, Harper, 1975.

Wind Rose, illustrated by Ronald Himler, Harper, 1976.

Will It Be Okay?, illustrated by Ben Shecter, Harper, 1977.

Your Owl Friend, illustrated by Ruth Bornstein, Harper, 1977.

If You Call My Name, illustrated by David Palladini, Harper, 1981.

I Hate My Brother Harry, illustrated by Dick Gackenbach, Harper, 1983.

Katie in the Morning, illustrated by Betsy Day, Harper, 1983.

Coconut, illustrated by Nancy Tafuri, Harper, 1984.

Jemima Remembers, illustrated by Troy Howell, Macmillan, 1984.

Always, Always, illustrated by Arieh Zeldich, Macmillan, 1984.

Alligator Arrived with Apples: A Potluck Alphabet, illustrated by Jose Aruego and Ariane Dewey, Macmillan, 1985.

Half a Moon and One Whole Star, illustrated by Jerry Pinkney, Macmillan, 1986.

Diana, Maybe, illustrated by Deborah Kogan Ray, Macmillan, 1987.

Dear Miss Moshki, illustrated by Diane Palmisciano, Macmillan, 1988.

Margaret Ziegler Is Horse-Crazy, illustrated by Peter Elwell, Macmillan, 1988.

I Hate My Sister Maggie, illustrated by Leslie Morrill, Macmillan, 1989.

This Is the Bread I Baked for Ned, illustrated by Isadore Seltzer, Macmillan, 1989.

The Itch Book, illustrated by Joseph Mahler, Macmillan, 1990.

Winter Holding Spring, illustrated by Himler, Macmillan, 1990.

Home Place, illustrated by Pinkney, Macmillan, 1990.

Alligators and Others, All Year Long, illustrated by Aruego, Macmillan, 1992.

Annie Flies the Birthday Bike, Macmillan, 1992.

Brass Button, Macmillan, 1993.

OTHER

The Commune Cookbook, Simon & Schuster, 1971.

The Bean Book (cookbook), Workman, 1973.

Putting up Stuff for the Cold Time (cookbook), Workman, 1973.

Stevie Wonder (biography), Flash Books, 1976.

Message from the Avocadoes (poetry), August House, 1981.

(With Paul Zindel) *To Take a Dare* (young adult novel), Harper, 1982.

The Year It Rained (novel), Macmillan, 1985.

(With Jan Brown) *The Dairy Hollow House Cookbook,* illustrated by Jacquie Froelich, Macmillan, 1986.

Dairy Hollow House Soup & Bread: A Country Inn Cookbook, Workman, 1992.

Contributor to popular magazines, including *Cosmopolitan, Ladies' Home Journal, McCall's, New Age, New York Times, New York Times Book Review, Organic Gardening,* and *Seventeen.*

■ Adaptations

Wind Rose was made into a motion picture by Phoenix Films in 1983.

■ Work in Progress

An adult novel, *Common Knowledge;* a book of adult poetry, *Death Is Not Like Going to Mexico.*

■ Sidelights

The daughter of two noted authors, Crescent Dragonwagon has made writing a way of life since she was very young. "From the time I learned the alphabet I wrote stories, beginning with drawing accompanied by a few words," the author commented. She explained: "Because my parents are writers, it seemed evident to me that when things happen to you in life, you write about them, and eventually they become books. Writing seemed natural, not esoteric or difficult." Her parents also gave her insight into the publishing process; unafraid of potential rejection, Dragonwagon published her first book before she was twenty. "Most of life since has been focused in my writing: strong feelings and experiences, interesting people, overheard bits of conversa-

tion, almost everything that strikes me has a way of turning up in my work, sometimes surprising me greatly."

An early book for children, "*Wind Rose* is typical of my writing process, beginning with an incident which sparked the idea," the author continued. "Never having had a child myself, I took my own feelings about being in love and attached them to the actual conception and birth of this child (the daughter of a friend) and wrote the book." The result is "a rather special children's book about conception and birth," as Linda Wolfe describes it in the *New York Times Book Review,* consisting of a poem in which a mother explains to her child how and why she was conceived. "Certainly one of the most attractive and beautiful introductions to the subject of birth," a *Publishers Weekly* reviewer comments, "Ms. Dragonwagon's text is honest and intensely personal." *Wind Rose* stands out from other books explaining where babies come from by aiming "to show the feeling side—*why* people have babies (under ideal circumstances) as opposed to simply *how*," Melinda Schroeder notes in *School Library Journal.* "Gentle and joyous," the critic continues, "this celebrates the wonder of creation on a level young children will appreciate and find reassuring."

Nighttime quietly fills the world of a young girl in this poem written by Dragonwagon and illustrated by Jerry Pinkney.

Aladdin Books

Alligator Arrived with Apples
A Potluck Alphabet Feast

by Crescent Dragonwagon   *pictures by* Jose Aruego & Ariane Dewey

Food and fun are celebrated in *Alligator Arrived with Apples,* **one of Dragonwagon's books for younger children.** (Cover illustration by Jose Aruego and Ariane Dewey.)

Dragonwagon's later children's books have also earned praise for their personal, delicate approach. *Diana, Maybe,* in which a little girl dreams of meeting her half-sister, has a "sensitive quality" that shows the child's feelings "in a natural way," Lorraine Douglas comments in *School Library Journal.* Jane Saliers similarly observes that "children will recognize their own collisions between dream and reality" in *Margaret Ziegler Is Horse-Crazy.* Telling of a little girl's depression when she discovers that horseback riding is not all that she had imagined, the book is "a skillfully-conveyed story of dreams, disappointment, and recovered pride," the critic writes in *School Library Journal.*

Sense of Place Distinguishes Work

Other books by Dragonwagon are tender portraits of distinctive places. *The Itch Book,* for instance, details a day in Arkansas so hot that even the animals itch. "Composed in poetic prose replete with descriptive phrasing, this glimpse into an Ozark day is modern American folklore at its best," Cathy Woodward comments in *School Library Journal.* Dragonwagon's sketch of local life is "a great book to share with children," the critic adds. *Home Place* similarly conjures up a special area; while hiking in the country, a family comes upon the remnants of a house and wonders about the people who once lived there. With its imagined scenes of a loving family, "this mood piece captures that quiet, reflective feeling a country hike can prompt," Denise Wilms writes in *Booklist. Home Place* earned Dragonwagon the Golden Kite Award from the Society of Children's Book Writers and Illustrators.

Dragonwagon's first novel, *To Take a Dare,* was written with the aid and encouragement of Paul Zindel, himself famous for such young adult books as *The Pigman.* "I had started a number of novels but never finished them," the author once related. "I knew that Paul worked with other writers. One day, I bit the bullet and wrote him a letter asking if he would work with me. He agreed. I wanted his assurance to finish my novel if I reached the point that I couldn't, and he gave it to me. As it turned out ninety-eight percent of *To Take a Dare* is my writing, but I feel I couldn't have written it without his encouragement."

To Take a Dare "stakes a claim to be this season's most talked about 'Young Adult' novel—sure to scandalize many parents at the same time that it hooks a large audience of worldly wise teens," Joyce Milton suggests in the *New York Times Book Review*. Narrated by Chrysta, a sixteen-year-old runaway, *To Take a Dare* offers a frank look at adolescent drinking, drug abuse, and sex. "It's almost a certainty that [the book] will be a target of censors because of the uncompromising, flat-out raw language the narrator and others use and because of Chrissie's experiences," a *Publishers Weekly* critic remarks.

The book opens with this declaration by Chrysta: "On my thirteenth birthday my father called me a slut once too often, my dog was hit by a car, and I lost my virginity—what was left of it." After running away from home Chrysta develops a painful venereal disease that leaves her permanently sterile; she is also threatened with rape by her boss and with death by a twelve-year-old runaway she has befriended. But after living on the

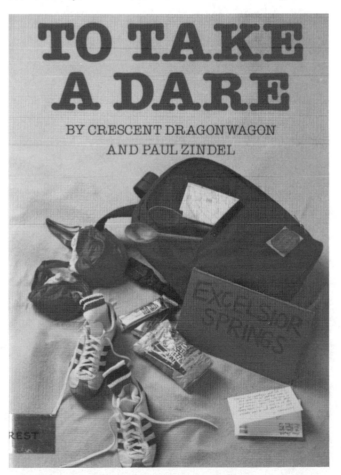

In this 1982 work, Dragonwagon portrays the struggle of a runaway to make a new home for herself and her friends. (Cover illustration by Aimee Garn and Ron Boszko.)

road for three years, Chrysta arrives in a small resort town and finds a job as a cook. She begins to make friends who stay with her through hard times, and begins a caring relationship with a young man. Her experiences, both good and bad, "somehow teach her she has a lot of strength, love and other good qualities in spite of her unhappy childhood," Karen Ritter summarizes in *School Library Journal*. As the *Publishers Weekly* critic concludes: "The novel is strong stuff but it is a voice that should be heard."

Portrait of Mental Illness Highlights Novel

Dragonwagon's second novel, *The Year It Rained,* provides similarly intense material in its account of a young woman struggling with mental illness, among other problems. In a narrative that ranges through past and present, seventeen-year-old Elizabeth Stein tells of her parents' bitter divorce, her father's alcoholism, her strained relationship with her mother, her hollow relationships with boyfriends, her conflicts at school, and her own suicide attempts. "Elizabeth takes the reader through, among and around these situations, looking hard at every person and every detail from a bittersweet present perspective of comparative calm—calm brought about by successful treatment with vitamins of what has finally been diagnosed as biochemically based schizophrenia," Natalie Babbitt observes in the *New York Times Book Review.*

Elizabeth's monologue "lends a decided cathartic impact" to this "affecting, introspective novel," a *Booklist* reviewer similarly comments. But Roger Sutton finds Elizabeth's character "insufferable." He writes in *School Library Journal* that she never matures, and at the end of the novel she remains "as self-centered and self-important as [she was] to begin with." *New Statesman and Society* writer Nicci Gerrard, however, believes that an "often narcissistic self-questioning" is common to young adult novels of this type, while Tim Wynne-Jones of the Toronto *Globe and Mail* remarks that Elizabeth's character "is better than most; she shows some compassion for those around her, and that in itself rescues The Year It Rained from formula." Gerrard likewise finds a "striking" aspect of the novel in "how well-written, discomforting and entirely unpatronising" it is. While the book is marketed as "young adult," Gerrard adds, "any adult might enjoy [it]."

Babbitt concurs with this assessment; the book "would be ideal to read at age 17," she asserts, "but also at 30, and again at 45 when one's own children are circling 17—it faces so unflinchingly the anguished and so often unsuccessful attempts to get past all the precious but heavy baggage of love between mother and child and on into some kind of mutual understanding that can set both free." Although the author herself considers *The Year It Rained* more of an adult novel, "for the sensitive teenager, it's going to be a really good book," she told Bo Emerson of the *Atlanta Journal-Constitution*. "The truth is," she added, "I think all of the categories are stupid."

Along these lines, Dragonwagon once commented: "I have always seen myself as a writer first. Not a children's book writer as such, or a novelist, or a poet, or a magazine writer, or a cookbook author—though I have done each of these types of writing. Writing is the lens through which I focus on the world and the things in it which trouble me, or interest me, or give me pleasure. The particular subject or feeling I am looking at through the lens determines what form the finished piece of writing will take. The exception to this rule is when I'm working on a novel, however; for there the characters soon take over and do it *their* way, from *their* perspective—which may be very different from mine.

"I feel lucky to have a profession which allows me to explore so many interests, while allowing me to stay true to the main and abiding interest in my life: writing. I have always known that this is what I wanted to do—and that, too, is lucky. It makes possible the persistent striving which underlies craft, talent, experience, gift and good fortune.

"I also feel writing is a highly utilitarian profession. To quote from a poem of mine called 'Looking for Bones in

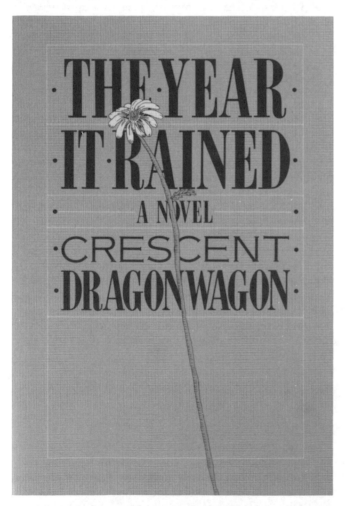

A girl suffering from mental illness searches for health and independence in Dragonwagon's novel *The Year It Rained.*

Her House,' 'She can write about anything that happens to her!'"

■ Works Cited

Babbitt, Natalie, "Love, and Learn to Bear It," *New York Times Book Review,* November 10, 1985, p. 35.

Douglas, Lorraine, review of *Diana, Maybe, School Library Journal,* January, 1988, p. 64.

Emerson, Bo, "'Year It Rained' Exposes Story of a Teen's Life," *Atlanta Journal-Constitution,* March 23, 1986.

Gerrard, Nicci, "Rites of Passage," *New Statesman and Society,* July 7, 1989, pp. 38-40.

Milton, Joyce, "Three for the Road," *New York Times Book Review,* April 25, 1982, p. 49.

Ritter, Karen, review of *To Take a Dare, School Library Journal,* May, 1982, p. 68.

Saliers, Jane, review of *Margaret Ziegler Is Horse-Crazy, School Library Journal,* June-July, 1988, p. 90.

Schroeder, Melinda, review of *Wind Rose, School Library Journal,* April, 1976, p. 60.

Sutton, Roger, "High School Confidential," *School Library Journal,* December, 1985, p. 43.

Review of *To Take a Dare, Publishers Weekly,* March 19, 1982, p. 71.

Wilms, Denise, review of *Home Place, Booklist,* August, 1990, p. 2171.

Review of *Wind Rose, Publishers Weekly,* January 19, 1976, p. 102.

Wolfe, Linda, review of *Wind Rose, New York Times Book Review,* May 23, 1976, p. 16.

Woodward, Cathy, review of *The Itch Book, School Library Journal,* June, 1990, p. 99.

Wynne-Jones, Tim, review of *The Year It Rained, Globe and Mail* (Toronto), June 28, 1986.

Review of *The Year It Rained, Booklist,* November 15, 1985.

■ For More Information See

BOOKS

Something about the Author Autobiography Series, Volume 14, Gale, 1992.

PERIODICALS

Bulletin of the Center for Children's Books, May, 1984; September, 1984; March, 1985; March, 1986; May, 1986.

Los Angeles Times, December 21, 1986.

New York Times Book Review, October 26, 1986.

School Library Journal, March, 1990.

Wilson Library Bulletin, February, 1986.

DUNCAN, Lois 1934-
   (Lois Kerry)

■ Personal

Original name, Lois Duncan Steinmetz; born April 28, 1934, in Philadelphia, PA; daughter of Joseph Janney (a magazine photographer) and Lois (a magazine photographer; maiden name, Foley) Steinmetz; married second husband, Donald Wayne Arquette (an electrical engineer), July 15, 1965; children: (first marriage) Robin, Kerry, Brett; (second marriage) Donald Jr., Kaitlyn (deceased). *Education:* Attended Duke University, 1952-53; University of New Mexico, B.A. (cum laude), 1977.

■ Addresses

Agent—Claire Smith, Harold Ober Associates, 425 Madison Ave., New York, NY 10017.

■ Career

Writer; magazine photographer; instructor in department of journalism, University of New Mexico, 1971-82. Lecturer at writers' conferences. *Member:* National League of American Pen Women, Society of Children's Book Writers and Illustrators, Phi Beta Kappa.

■ Awards, Honors

Three-time winner during high school years of *Seventeen* magazine's annual short story contest; Seventeenth Summer Literary Award, Dodd, Mead & Co., 1957, for *Debutante Hill;* Best Novel Award, National Press Women, 1966, for *Point of Violence;* Edgar Allan Poe Award nominations, Mystery Writers of America, 1967, for *Ransom,* 1969, for *They Never Came Home,* 1985, for *The Third Eye,* 1986, for *Locked in Time,* and 1989, for *The Twisted Window;* Zia Award, New Mexico Press Women, 1969, for *Major Andre: Brave Enemy;* grand prize winner, Writer's Digest Creative Writing Contest, 1970, for short story; Theta Sigma Phi Headliner Award, 1971; Ethical Culture School Book Award, Library of Congress' Best Books citation, and *English Teacher's Journal* and University of Iowa's Best Books of the Year for Young Adults citation, all 1981, and Best Novel Award, National League of American Pen Women, 1982, all for *Stranger with My Face;* Notable Children's Trade Book in the Field of Social Studies, National Council for Social Studies and the Children's Book Council, 1982, for *Chapters: My Growth as a Writer;* Child Study Association of America's Children's Books of the Year citation, 1986, for *Locked in Time* and *The Third Eye;* Children's Book Award, National League of American Pen Women, 1987, for *Horses of Dreamland;* Margaret A. Edwards Award, 1991, *School Library Journal*/Young Adult Library Services Association, for body of work.

Duncan has also received several American Library Association Best Books for Young Adults citations and *New York Times* Best Books for Children citations, as

LOIS DUNCAN

well as numerous librarians', parents' and children's choice awards from organizations in the states of Alabama, Arizona, California, Colorado, Florida, Indiana, Iowa, Massachussetts, Nevada, New Mexico, Oklahoma, Tennessee, Texas, South Carolina, and Vermont, in addition to groups in England.

■ Writings

YOUNG ADULT NOVELS

Debutante Hill, Dodd, 1958.
(Under pseudonym Lois Kerry) *Love Song for Joyce,* Funk, 1958.
(Under pseudonym Lois Kerry) *A Promise for Joyce,* Funk, 1959.
The Middle Sister, Dodd, 1961.
Game of Danger, Dodd, 1962.
Season of the Two-Heart, Dodd, 1964.
Ransom, Doubleday, 1966, published as *Five Were Missing,* New American Library, 1972.
They Never Came Home, Doubleday, 1969.
I Know What You Did Last Summer, Little, Brown, 1973.
Down a Dark Hall, Little, Brown, 1974.
Summer of Fear, Little, Brown, 1976.
Killing Mr. Griffin, Little, Brown, 1978.
Daughters of Eve, Little, Brown, 1979.

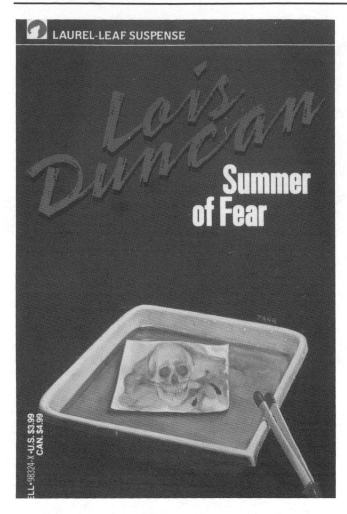

LAUREL-LEAF SUSPENSE

Lois Duncan

Summer of Fear

ELL•98324-X•U.S. $3.99 CAN. $4.99

Rachel cannot ignore her unsettling suspicions about her visiting cousin Julia in this mystery novel by Duncan.

Stranger with My Face, Little, Brown, 1981.
The Third Eye, Little, Brown, 1984 (published in England as *The Eyes of Karen Connors,* Hamish Hamilton, 1985).
Locked in Time, Little, Brown, 1985.
The Twisted Window, Delacorte, 1987.
Don't Look Behind You, Delacorte, 1989.

JUVENILE

The Littlest One in the Family, illustrated by Suzanne K. Larsen, Dodd, 1960.
Silly Mother, illustrated by Larsen, Dial, 1962.
Giving Away Suzanne, illustrated by Leonard Weisgard, Dodd, 1963.
Hotel for Dogs, illustrated by Leonard Shortall, Houghton, 1971.
A Gift of Magic, illustrated by Arvis Stewart, Little, Brown, 1971.
From Spring to Spring: Poems and Photographs, photographs by the author, Westminster, 1982.
The Terrible Tales of Happy Days School (poetry), illustrated by Friso Henstra, Little, Brown, 1983.
Horses of Dreamland, illustrated by Donna Diamond, Little, Brown, 1985.

Wonder Kid Meets the Evil Lunch Snatcher, illustrated by Margaret Sanfilippo, Little, Brown, 1988.
The Birthday Moon (poetry), illustrated by Susan Davis, Viking, 1989.
Songs from Dreamland (poetry), illustrated by Kay Chorao, Knopf, 1989.
The Circus Comes Home, photographs by father, Joseph Janney Steinmetz, Delacorte, 1992.

OTHER

Point of Violence (adult), Doubleday, 1966.
Major Andre: Brave Enemy (young adult nonfiction), illustrated by Tran Mawicke, Putnam, 1969.
Peggy (young adult nonfiction), Little, Brown, 1970.
When the Bough Breaks (adult), Doubleday, 1974.
How to Write and Sell Your Personal Experiences (nonfiction), Writers Digest, 1979.
Chapters: My Growth as a Writer (autobiography), Little, Brown, 1982.
A Visit with Lois Duncan (videotape), RDA Enterprises, 1985.
Dream Songs from Yesterday (audio cassette), Silver Moon Productions, 1987.
Songs from Dreamland (audio cassette), Silver Moon Productions, 1987.
Our Beautiful Day (audio cassette), Silver Moon Productions, 1988.
The Story of Christmas (audio cassette), Silver Moon Productions, 1989.
Who Killed My Daughter?: The True Story of a Mother's Search for Her Daughter's Murderer, Delacorte, 1992.
Psychics in Action (audio cassette series), Silver Moon Productions, 1993.

Contributor of over five hundred articles and stories to periodicals, including *Good Housekeeping, Redbook, McCall's, Woman's Day, The Writer, Reader's Digest, Ladies' Home Journal, Saturday Evening Post,* and *Writer's Digest.* Contributing editor, *Woman's Day.*

■ **Adaptations**

Summer of Fear was made into the television movie *Strangers in Our House* by NBC-TV, 1978; Listening Library made cassettes of *Down a Dark Hall,* 1985, *Killing Mr. Griffin,* 1986, *Summer of Fear,* 1986, and *Stranger with My Face,* 1986; RDA Enterprises made cassettes of *Selling Personal Experiences to Magazines,* 1987, and *Songs from Dreamland,* 1987.

■ **Work in Progress**

The Magic of Spider Woman, juvenile fiction for Scholastic, 1995; *The Psychic Connection,* with William G. Roll, young adult nonfiction, for Delacorte, 1995.

■ **Sidelights**

Lois Duncan's young adult novels of suspense and the supernatural have made her a favorite of adult critics and young readers alike. According to *Times Literary Supplement* reviewer Jennifer Moody, Duncan is "popular ... not only with the soft underbelly of the literary world, the children's book reviewers, but with its most hardened carapace, the teenage library book borrower." "Duncan understands the teenage world and its passionate concerns with matters as diverse as dress, death, romance, school, self-image, sex and problem parents," *Times Literary Supplement* contributor Sarah Hayes notes. But while other writers for young adults show life in a humorous, optimistic light, the critic explains, "Duncan suggests that life is neither as prosaic nor as straightforward as it seems at first." As a result, Leigh Dean comments in the *Children's Book Review Service,* Duncan's readers look for "unconventional characters, and situations steeped in danger, magic, and intrigue."

Duncan started writing stories for magazines as a teenager and progressed to book-length manuscripts as she matured. One of her first efforts was a love story for teens, *Debutante Hill,* that the young housewife wrote to pass the lonely hours while her first husband was attending law school. She entered the book in Dodd, Mead and Company's "Seventeenth Summer Literary Contest." "It was returned for revisions because in it a

An ordinary school bus ride becomes a terrifying ordeal for five students in Duncan's *Ransom.*

young man of twenty drank a beer," Duncan related in her *Something about the Author Autobiography Series* (*SAAS*) entry. "I changed the beer to a Coke and resubmitted the manuscript. It won the contest, and the book was published." Duncan thinks the story "sweet and sticky and pap," but a reviewer for the *Christian Science Monitor* states in a 1959 review that Duncan "writes exceptionally well, and has the happy ability to make a reader care what happens to her characters."

When her first marriage ended in divorce, Duncan returned to magazine writing to support her family. In 1965, she married engineer Don Arquette, and since "the financial pressure was off, I also felt free to turn back to my non-lucrative, but immeasurably enjoyable, hobby of writing teenage novels," she recalled in *SAAS.* Over the years young adult novels had changed, however, and Duncan found she was no longer constricted by many of the taboos of the fifties. The result of this newfound freedom was 1968's *Ransom,* an adventure story of five teenagers kidnapped by a schoolbus driver. Duncan's publisher refused to handle the book, since it deviated from her former style. Doubleday took it on instead, and *Ransom* became a runner-up for the prestigious Edgar Allan Poe Award. Reviewers also praised the book; Dorothy M. Broderick says in the *New York Times Book Review* that the character of Glenn Kirtland, whose consistently selfish behavior endangers the whole group, "sets the book apart and makes it something more than another good mystery."

Supernatural Events Befall Everyday Characters

Duncan's style "is a simple one," Audrey Eaglen comments in *Twentieth-Century Children's Writers.* "She places an individual or a group of normal, believable young people in what appears to be a prosaic setting such as a suburban neighborhood or an American high school; on the surface everything is as it should be, until Duncan introduces an element of surprise that gives the story an entirely new twist." These elements are often supernatural; *Summer of Fear* features a young witch who charms herself into an unsuspecting family, while *Down a Dark Hall* involves a girls' boarding school whose students are endangered by the malevolent ghosts of dead artists and writers.

In a similar fashion, *Stranger with My Face* details a young girl's struggle to avoid being possessed by her twin sister, who uses astral projection to take over others' bodies. While the novel's premise might be difficult to accept, "Duncan makes it possible and palatable by a deft twining of fantasy and reality, by giving depth to characters and relationships, and by writing with perception and vitality," states Zena Sutherland of the *Bulletin of the Center for Children's Books.* This depth is typical of all of Duncan's mystic novels; as Eaglen comments, "an element of the occult is an integral part of [Duncan's] fast-moving plot, but it is always believable because Duncan never carries her depiction of the supernatural into the sometimes goofy realms that a writer such as Stephen King does. Character and plot are always predominant; the books are first and foremost good mysteries made even more interesting for young readers by some aspect of the unusual."

Duncan doesn't rely solely on supernatural events to provide suspense, however. In *Killing Mr. Griffin,* a teenage boy guides a group of friends into kidnapping their strict high school teacher and intimidating him into giving less homework. The teacher dies when he misses his heart medication, and the students try to cover up their involvement. "Lois Duncan breaks some new ground in a novel without sex, drugs or black leather jackets," comments Richard Peck in the *New York Times Book Review.* "But the taboo she tampers with is far more potent and pervasive: the unleashed fury of the permissively reared against any assault on their egos and authority.... The value of the book lies in the twisted logic of the teenagers and how easily they can justify anything."

While Peck likes the beginning of *Killing Mr. Griffin,* he criticizes the ending for descending "into unadulterated melodrama.... The book becomes an 'easy read' when

LAUREL-LEAF SUSPENSE

DELL-94515-1·U.S. $3.99
CAN. $4.99

A group of teenage boys try to hide their involvement in the accidental death of their teacher in *Killing Mr. Griffin.*

it shouldn't." But Duncan points to her readers to explain the style of her writing, for she has had to learn to tailor her work to a generation of teens more familiar with television than books. "Television has had an enormous effect upon youth books," she writes in her *SAAS* entry. "Few of today's readers are patient enough to wade through slow paced, introductory chapters as I did at their ages to see if a book is eventually going to get interesting." Television "has conditioned its viewers to expect instant entertainment," the author continued, and because of this, "writers have been forced into utilizing all sorts of TV techniques to hold their readers' attention."

Daughters of Eve also features a dangerous leader—a faculty adviser who leads a high school girls' club into increasingly more violent acts in the name of feminism. The book's portrayal of a negative feminist element has drawn some strong remarks from critics. "It has an embittered tone of hatred that colors the characterization," suggests Sutherland in her *Bulletin of the Center for Children's Books* review. Jan M. Goodman presents a similar assessment in *Interracial Books for Children Bulletin:* Duncan "clearly places a harsh value judgment on violent solutions, and ... she leaves the impression that fighting for women's rights leads to uncontrollable anger and senseless destruction.... The book's deceptive interpretation of feminism plus its dangerous stereotypes make it a harmful distortion of reality." But Natalie Babbitt finds the work "refreshing" and likes the fact that "there are no lessons." In the *New York Times Book Review,* she compares the book to William Golding's classic *Lord of the Flies* and concludes that *Daughters of Eve* "is strongly evenhanded, for it lets us see that women can be as bloodthirsty as men ever were."

Bizarre Coincidences Characterize Daughter's Death

While the extraordinary events she features in her books are fiction, "the things I have written about as fiction in suspense novels are now part of our everyday lives," Duncan commented. She often bases her characters on family and friends; for instance, "the character 'April' in *Don't Look behind You* was based upon the personality of my youngest daughter, Kait," the author revealed. This resemblance developed into a tragic coincidence in 1989, the year Duncan's story of a girl in a witness relocation program was published. "In that book, which was published in June, 1989, April was chased by a hitman in a Camaro," the author related. "One month later, in July 1989, Kait was chased down and shot to death by a hitman in a Camaro." As a result, Duncan noted, "we are currently involved in a police investigation like the one in *Killing Mr. Griffin.* We are working with a psychic like the one in *The Third Eye.*"

Duncan related the story of Kait's tragic murder and her family's subsequent attempts to solve it in *Who Killed My Daughter?: The True Story of a Mother's Search for Her Daughter's Murderer.* After the local police classified the killing as a random drive-by shooting—despite

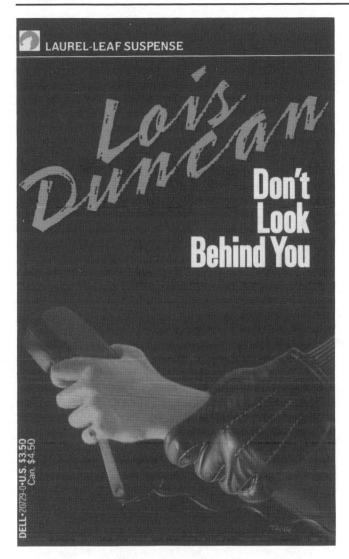

LAUREL-LEAF SUSPENSE

Lois Duncan

Don't Look Behind You

DELL-20729-0-U.S. $3.50 Can. $4.50

In Duncan's *Don't Look behind You* a girl learns to cope with a new life as her family goes into hiding as part of a witness protection program.

information that Kait's boyfriend was involved in illegal activities—the frustrated family turned to various psychics for further clues. Although several remarkable coincidences turned up during the psychic investigations, the case was still unsolved at the time Duncan's book was published. "Reading like the suspense mysteries that have made her famous, Duncan's account ... is horrifying and at the same time thought provoking," Barbara Lynn remarks in *School Library Journal*, adding that "all the elements of a suspenseful mystery are here." *Booklist* reviewer Ilene Cooper similarly finds *Who Killed My Daughter?* a "page-turner," and praises it in particular as superior to many "true-crime" books: "For one thing, Duncan's personal involvement makes the telling much more intense, the grief more cutting." The critic goes on to predict wide readership for the volume, something Duncan hopes will lead to a break in the case.

The author added: "Those who have seen the videotape *A Visit with Lois Duncan* met Kait at age twelve. She is the first person on the tape—the girl who says, 'My

favorite book is *Stranger with My Face,* where Laurie's spirit can leave her body and go anywhere it wants to!' My romantic, adventurous daughter has done just that now; it is some small comfort to know that she loved that concept."

■ Works Cited

Babbitt, Natalie, review of *Daughters of Eve, New York Times Book Review,* January 27, 1980, p. 24.

Broderick, Dorothy M., review of *Ransom, New York Times Book Review,* June 5, 1966, p. 42.

Cooper, Ilene, review of *Who Killed My Daughter?, Booklist,* April 15, 1992, p. 1482.

Dean, Leigh, review of *Chapters: My Growth As a Writer, Children's Book Review Service,* spring, 1982, p. 116.

Duncan, Lois, *Something about the Author Autobiography Series,* Volume 2, Gale, 1986.

Eaglen, Audrey, "Lois Duncan," *Twentieth-Century Children's Writers,* 3rd edition, edited by Tracy Chevalier, St. James Press, 1989, pp. 303-304.

Goodman, Jan M., review of *Daughters of Eve, Interracial Books for Children Bulletin,* Volume 11, number 6, 1980, pp. 17-18.

Hayes, Sarah, "Fatal Flaws," *Times Literary Supplement,* January 29-February 4, 1988, p. 119.

Lynn, Barbara, review of *Who Killed My Daughter?, School Library Journal,* August, 1992, p. 190.

Moody, Jennifer, "The Onset of Maturity," *Times Literary Supplement,* March 26, 1982, p. 343.

Peck, Richard, "Teaching Teacher a Lesson," *New York Times Book Review,* April 30, 1978, p. 54.

Sutherland, Zena, review of *Daughters of Eve, Bulletin of the Center for Children's Books,* January, 1980, pp. 92-93.

Sutherland, Zena, review of *Stranger with My Face, Bulletin of the Center for Children's Books,* April, 1982, p. 146.

"Widening Horizons: Debutante Hill," *Christian Science Monitor,* February 5, 1959.

■ For More Information See

BOOKS

Children's Literature Review, Volume 29, Gale, 1993.
Contemporary Literary Criticism, Volume 26, Gale, 1983.

PERIODICALS

Bulletin for the Center of Children's Books, February, 1974; July-August, 1987.

Horn Book, April, 1977; February, 1982.

New York Times Book Review, June 8, 1969; November 10, 1974; March 6, 1977.

School Library Journal, November, 1981; July, 1989.

DYCK, Peter J. 1914-

■ Personal

Born December 4, 1914, in Lysanderhoh, Russia; son of John J. and Renate (Mathies) Dyck; married Elfrieda Klassen (a nurse), October 14, 1944; children: Ruth Scott, Rebecca. *Education:* Attended University of Saskatchewan, 1939-40, and Bethel College, 1951-52; Bethany Theological Seminary, M.Div., 1958; Goshen College, B.A., 1959. *Hobbies and other interests:* Photography.

■ Addresses

Home—23 Main St., Akron, PA 17501.

■ Career

Writer. Lecturer at schools, churches, and retreats.

■ Awards, Honors

Knighted by Queen Juliana of the Netherlands, 1950; honorary doctorate of divinity, University of Waterloo (Kitchener, Ontario, Canada), 1974.

■ Writings

A Leap of Faith, Herald Press, 1990.
The Great Shalom, Herald Press, 1990.
(With wife, Elfrieda Dyck) *Up from the Rubble,* Herald Press, 1991.
Shalom at Last, Herald Press, 1992.

Also author of *Story Time Jamboree,* 1993.

E–F

ELLIOTT, Odette 1939-

■ Personal

Born November 17, 1939, in Tunbridge Wells, England; daughter of Donald and Claudine (Gibbs) Durrant; married Donald Elliott (a minister), July 14, 1962; children: Rachel, Josephine, Roger, Ben. *Education:* Newcastle University, B.Ed. (with honors). *Religion:* Protestant. *Hobbies and other interests:* Camping and traveling in France, gardening, walking, music, enjoying London parks.

■ Addresses

Home—35 Meyrick Rd., Willesden, London NW10 2EL, England. *Office*—c/o Andre Deutsch, Scholastic Children's Books, 719 Pratt St., London NW1 0AE, England.

■ Career

International Voluntary Service, Leicester, England, secretary and assistant administrator of overseas work camp exchange scheme, 1980-83; University College London, London, England, secretary and administrator, 1984-87; Centre for Policy on Ageing, London, secretary and administrator, 1988-92; Horizon House Publications, London, secretary, 1993—; writer. School governor. Founder of a Save the Children fund group in Gateshead, England. *Member:* Writers Guild.

■ Writings

ILLUSTRATED BY AMANDA WELCH

Under Sammy's Bed, Andre Deutsch, 1989, Penguin, 1991.
Sammy Goes Flying, Andre Deutsch, 1990, Penguin, 1992.
Sammy and the Telly, Andre Deutsch, 1991.
Sammy's Christmas Workshop, Andre Deutsch/Scholastic, 1992.

ODETTE ELLIOTT

■ Work in Progress

Holly and the Sea Dancers, a fantasy story; *Class I and Mrs. Joy* (tentative title), a collection of stories.

■ Sidelights

Odette Elliott told *SATA:* "I have wanted to write children's books ever since I was very young. I have a copy of something I wrote in a school exercise book when I was nine. It says: 'When I am grown up I want to be an author and write some poems. My reason is because I love writing and it makes me happy to do it.' I have scribbled in notebooks ever since the age of twelve.

When I was a young teenager I spent many hours sitting in my bedroom, writing my current 'book.' You may ask why it was so many years before I had a book published. It is a good question!

"I was married when I was twenty-two. My husband was a minister of a local church. In those days it was rare for a minister's wife to continue a formal job, so I became involved in the life of the church. I visited young and old and joined in all the church activities, including playgroups at the church. We soon had two daughters and then moved to Malaysia for a period of three years.

"While in Malaysia, I ran a playgroup four days a week and met many young characters. Again you could ask why I did not write stories at this stage of my life. Perhaps it was because the climate was so humid and tiring.

"On our return to England we adopted Roger. He was a nine-week-old baby. He was born in London and was of Afro-Caribbean origin. The big sisters Rachel and Jo enjoyed their little brother. Later we adopted another son, a little brother for Roger and the whole family. He is also of Afro-Caribbean origin. His name is Ben and the 'Sammy' stories are based on him, as he is quite a character! It was Ben who invented an imaginary world under his bed. He always tried to keep up with his older sisters and brother. He is pleased that 'Sammy' is based on him!

"I was pleased for many reasons to have my first 'Sammy' book published. When Roger was small, we always tried to find books depicting black children who looked like him. This was not easy at that time. He particularly loved *Pete's New Chair* and other stories by Ezra Jack Keats because he could identify with the characters. Now at last I had written a book, and Sammy looks just like Roger and Ben did. Fortunately today there are many more books representing children of mixed race and minority groups.

"I have written four 'Sammy' stories and at present I am working on a short story which is a fantasy. It will be called *Holly and the Sea Dancers.* I have also been asked to write some short stories about five- and six-year-old children for a collection. It might be called *Class I and Mrs. Joy.*"

* * *

ESTORIL, Jean
See ALLAN, Mabel Esther

* * *

FARBER, Norma 1909-1984

■ Personal

Born August 6, 1909, in Boston, MA; died of a vascular disease, March 21, 1984, in Cambridge, MA; daughter of G. Augustus and Augusta (Schon) Holzman; married Sidney Farber (a doctor; deceased), July 3, 1928; children: Ellen, Stephen, Thomas, Miriam. *Education:* Wellesley College, A.B., 1931; Radcliffe College, M.A., 1932.

■ Career

Musician, poet, and author of picture books for children. Appeared as a soprano singer in solo recitals and with small ensemble groups and orchestras. *Member:* Phi Beta Kappa.

■ Awards, Honors

Premier Prix in singing, Jury Central des Etudes Musicales (Belgium), 1936; Children's Book Showcase Award, Children's Book Council, and National Book Award, American Academy and Institute of Arts and Letters, both 1976, both for *As I Was Crossing the Boston Common; New York Times* Best Illustrated Children's Book of the Year, 1978, for *There Once Was a Woman Who Married a Man;* Golden Rose Award, New England Poetry Club; prizes for poetry from Poetry Society of America; *This Is the Ambulance Leaving the Zoo* was a Junior Literary Guild selection.

■ Writings

FOR CHILDREN

Did You Know It Was the Narwhale?, Atheneum, 1967.

NORMA FARBER

I Found Them in the Yellow Pages, illustrated by Marc Brown, Little, Brown, 1973.

Where's Gomer?, illustrated by William Pene du Bois, Dutton, 1974.

As I Was Crossing the Boston Common, illustrated by Arnold Lobel, Dutton, 1975.

This Is the Ambulance Leaving the Zoo illustrated by Tomie de Paola, Dutton 1975.

A Ship in a Storm on the Way to Tarshish, illustrated by Victoria Chess, Greenwillow Books, 1977.

Six Impossible Things Before Breakfast: Stories and Poems, illustrated by de Paola, Addison-Wesley, 1977.

How the Left-Behind Beasts Built Ararat, illustrated by Antonio Frasconi, Walker, 1978.

There Once Was a Woman Who Married a Man, illustrated by Lydai Dabcovich, Addison-Wesley, 1978.

The Wanderers from Wapping, illustrated by Charles Mikolaycak, Addison-Wesley, 1978.

How Does It Feel to Be Old?, illustrated by Trina S. Hyman, Dutton, 1979.

Never Say Ugh! to a Bug, illustrated by Jose Aruego, Greenwillow Books, 1979.

There Goes Feathertop!, illustrated by Brown, Dutton, 1979.

Small Wonders, illustrated by Kazue Mizumura, Coward, 1979.

Up the Down Elevator, Addison-Wesley, 1979.

How the Hibernators Came to Bethlehem, illustrated by Barbara Cooney, Walker, 1980.

Mercy Short: A Winter Journal, North Boston, 1692-93, Dutton, 1982.

How to Ride a Tiger, illustrated by Claire Schumacher, Houghton Mifflin, 1983.

All Those Mothers at the Manger, illustrated by Megan Lloyd, Harper & Row, 1985.

(And selecter with Myra Cohn Livingston) *These Small Stones: Poems,* Harper & Row, 1987.

FOR ADULTS; POETRY COLLECTIONS

The Hatch, Scribner, 1955.

Look to the Rose, privately printed, 1958.

A Desperate Thing: Marriage Is a Desperate Thing, Plowshare Press, 1973, also published as *A Desperate Thing: Marriage Poems,* Plowshare Press, 1973.

(Translator with Edith Helman) Pedro Salinas, *To Live in Pronouns: Selected Love Poems,* Norton, 1974.

Household Poems, Hellric Publications, 1975.

Something Further: Poems, Kylix Press, 1979.

Shekhina: Forty Poems, Capstone Editions, 1984.

OTHER

Also author of a play, *Mary Chesnut's Diary,* produced in Cambridge, Massachusetts, 1961. Contributor of poetry to periodicals, including *America, Christian Century, Horn Book, Nation, New Catholic World, New Republic, New Yorker, Poetry,* and *Saturday Review.*

■ **Sidelights**

"It was the wonders and miracles of life that captured Norma Farber's imagination in her work for young

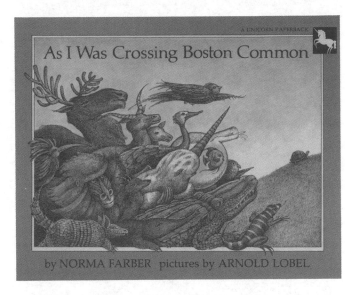

A parade of unusual animals fill this rhyming alphabet book by Farber. (Cover illustration by Arnold Lobel.)

people, a devotion to the seemingly obscure to which she held a glittering magnifying glass," wrote Myra Cohn Livingston in *Twentieth-Century Children's Writers.* Farber is remembered for the variety of her books for children, which include nonsense verse, instructional stories, and retellings of biblical tales. According to Livingston, Farber brought to her work, all of which was composed in rhyme, "a gift of music and of observation, expanding horizons of reality and of fantasy."

Born, raised, and educated in Boston, Massachusetts, Farber was an outstanding scholar and a member of Phi Beta Kappa national honor society, receiving her A.B. from Wellesley College in 1931 and her M.A. from Radcliffe College in 1932. In 1928, at the age of eighteen, she married Sidney Farber, then a recent Harvard Medical School graduate. Early in their marriage, the Farbers lived in Europe, where Dr. Farber was continuing his studies. They had four children: Ellen, Stephen, Thomas, and Miriam.

Throughout her life, Farber wrote poems for her contemporaries. During her youth when she graduated from Girls' Latin School, she wrote and read what she described in an autobiographical sketch for the *Fifth Book of Junior Authors and Illustrators* as "a solemn, grandiloquent piece in Spenserian stanzas." Farber began publishing her poetry in periodicals in the early 1950s and received encouragement from John Holmes and John Hall Wheelock, noted poets of the day. In addition to her writing, Farber was also an accomplished singer, performing as a soprano in the United States and abroad. In 1936 she received the Premier Prix for her performance in the Jury Central des Etudes Musicales in Belgium.

After years of writing poetry for adults, Farber began penning stories and poetry for children in the 1960s. As Farber noted in her autobiographical sketch, "For the

I FOUND THEM IN THE YELLOW PAGES

BY NORMA FARBER

ILLUSTRATED BY MARC BROWN

Farber used an ordinary phone book to find examples of the many careers young readers could have as grown-ups. (Cover illustration by Marc Brown.)

last twenty years I've been quite as eager to 'reach' youngsters as to communicate with my own aging peers. For I've discovered that certain stories I'd like to tell, certain moods I want to share, certain problems I need to explore, require the fresh ear and attention of a child encouraging me."

Love of Language Inspired Work for Children

"It dawned on me a while ago that I have two obsessions [in my children's books]: the alphabet, and Noah's Flood," Farber once told *SATA*. "My picture books *Did You Know It Was the Narwhale?* and *Where's Gomer?* testify to the second preoccupation. Alphabet poems and stories enchant me because these twenty-six letters are the warp and woof, the living texture of our spoken and written communication. I just can't celebrate the English language loudly enough."

Did You Know It Was the Narwhale?, Farber's first published children's book, appeared in 1967. Next came *I Found Them in the Yellow Pages*, an alphabet book written in verse, followed by another story about Noah and the Great Flood, *Where's Gomer?* Farber's highly praised *As I Was Crossing the Boston Common* earned the Children's Book Showcase Award in 1976 and was also nominated for the National Book Award. Narrated

by a turtle, the story describes the variety of rare animals he encounters as he crosses the Boston Common one day. The turtle journeys through the alphabet of unusual creatures, from the angwantibo to the zibet.

How Does It Feel to Be Old?, written in verse and published in 1979, was Farber's more serious response to her granddaughter's questions about aging. Norma Bagnall, writing in *Dictionary of Literary Biography*, described this work as "at once lighthearted, warm, and serious. Its fresh perspective is welcome and different ... in that it is told from the point of view of the grandmother—a grandmother who is vibrant and appreciative of all life's experiences, one who can respond with humor, empathy, and love without ever regressing to the trite and sentimental."

Farber wrote in her autobiographical sketch, "I should admit that I can be tempted, even in my seventies, to undertake new and difficult assignments. I welcome a challenge, a *dare!* Love to try something I've never tried before, especially if it seems to be way beyond me." Living out this attitude, Farber tried her hand at writing a novel in 1982. Entitled *Mercy Short: A Winter Journal, North Boston, 1692-93*, the work appeals to both young adult and older audiences. The story, written in diary form, is set in Boston during the Salem witch trials and is based on actual people and accounts. The book's main focus is Mercy Short, a seventeen-year-old indentured servant who is suspected of witchcraft and counseled by minister Cotton Mather. Caught up in the hysteria surrounding the witch hunts, Short believes her fits of delirium are the work of demons and attempts to describe such occurrences in her diary, written in seventeenth-century dialect.

In *Mercy Short*, Farber uses the title character's accounts to delineate Mather's attempts to exorcise the girl of these spirits. But the cleric's puritanical efforts only serve to increase the painful memories Short associates with her earlier life—she survived the murder of her parents and her subsequent kidnapping by Indians; she endured the death of the son she bore to an Indian lover; and she persevered a forced march to Quebec before her ransoming to Mather's church. The story concludes on a positive note as Short writes that she is being courted. However, a postscript written by Mather states that the troubled young woman was later excommunicated from the church for adultery. Farber planned a sequel to her novel as she had become so involved with the characters. She died in 1984 before the work could be completed.

■ Works Cited

Bagnall, Norma, *Dictionary of Literary Biography*, Volume 61: *American Writers for Children since 1960: Poets, Illustrators, and Nonfiction Authors*, Gale, 1987, pp. 50-56.

Farber, Norma, entry in *Fifth Book of Junior Authors and Illustrators*, H. W. Wilson, 1983, pp. 111-12.

Livingston, Myra Cohn, entry on Farber, *Twentieth-Century Children's Writers,* 3rd edition, St. James Press, 1989.

■ For More Information See

PERIODICALS

Bulletin of the Center for Children's Books, January, 1983, pp. 87-88.
Horn Book, December 1974; February 1976; June 1977; February 1978; August 1979; February 1980; December 1982, pp. 655-656.
Kirkus Reviews, November 1, 1982, p. 1195.
Publishers Weekly, April 30, 1973.
School Library Journal, October, 1982, p. 160.
Wilson Library Bulletin, November 1987.*

*   *   *

FARLOW, James O(rville, Jr.) 1951-

■ Personal

Born February 7, 1951, in Greensburg, IN; son of James O., Sr. (an electrical engineer) and Arlene M. (a homemaker; maiden name, Tomany) Farlow; married Karen A. Beckerman (a homemaker), 1978; children: Jill C., Erin M. *Education:* Indiana University, B.A. (with honors), 1972; Yale University, M.Phil., 1974, Ph.D., 1980. *Politics:* "On occasion, with great discretion." *Religion:* Christian. *Hobbies and other interests:* Reading, birding, model railroading.

■ Addresses

Home—207 West 13th St., Auburn, IN 46706. *Office*—Department of Geosciences, Indiana University-Purdue University at Fort Wayne, 2101 Coliseum Blvd. E., Fort Wayne, IN 46805.

■ Career

Indiana University-Purdue University at Fort Wayne, lecturer in geology, 1978-79; Hope College, Holland, MI, assistant professor of geology, 1979-81; Indiana University-Purdue University at Fort Wayne, assistant professor, 1982-87, associate professor, 1987-90, professor of geology, 1990—. Consultant to Texas Department of Parks and Wildlife, 1985—. *Member:* Society of Vertebrate Paleontology, Paleontological Society, Indiana Academy of Sciences, Society of Sigma Xi, Phi Beta Kappa.

■ Awards, Honors

Scientific researcher of the year, Fort Wayne Sigma Xi Club, 1986; honorary Master of Science degree, Wagner Free Institute of Science, 1990; college science teacher of the year, Fort Wayne Sigma Xi Club, 1992.

JAMES O. FARLOW

■ Writings

A Guide to Lower Cretaceous Dinosaur Footprints and Tracksites of the Paluxy River Valley, Somervell County, Texas (guidebook), Geological Society of America, Baylor University, 1987.
On the Tracks of Dinosaurs: A Study of Dinosaur Footprints (children's book), F. Watts, 1991.
(With R. E. Molnar) *Meat-Eating Dinosaurs* (children's book), F. Watts, in press.
The Dinosaurs of Dinosaur Valley State Park, Texas Department of Parks and Wildlife, in press.

Author of introduction and annotations for *Bones for Barnum: Adventures of a Dinosaur Hunter,* by R. T. Bird, Texas Christian University Press, 1985. Contributor to books, including *Behold the Mighty Dinosaur!,* 1981; (with others) *The Origins of Angiosperms and Their Biological Consequences,* 1987; *Dinosaur Tracks and Traces,* 1989; *The Dinosauria,* 1990; *Mysteries of Life and the Universe: New Essays from America's Finest Writers on Science,* 1992; and (with M. F. Schult) *Trace Fossils,* 1992. Contributor of science fiction short stories to *Analog Science Fiction/Science Fact,* and scientific articles to journals and magazines, including *Evolution, Science, Nature, Paleobiology, American Midland Naturalist, Modern Geology, Ecology, American Journal of Science, Journal of Paleontology,* and *Geology.*

■ Work in Progress

Another children's book and articles for professional journals.

■ Sidelights

James O. Farlow told *SATA:* "Because I am a professional paleontologist, most of my writing consists of technical articles about dinosaurs and other extinct animals written for other paleontologists. Some of my papers describe newly discovered fossils, and others offer speculative interpretations about the ecology and behavior of prehistoric beasts. Among the topics I have researched are the horns and frills of ceratopsian dinosaurs like *Triceratops,* the plates of *Stegosaurus,* the teeth of meat-eating dinosaurs, and dinosaur footprints, the subject of my first children's book.

"The idea for a children's book about dinosaur tracks came to me while I was doing field work on these fossils in Texas. One evening I happened to be in a bookstore in Austin. Because I frequently give presentations about dinosaurs to school groups, I like to keep informed about what the juvenile literature on the topic is like, and so I browsed through the dinosaur books in the children's section of the Austin bookshop. What impressed me was how similar most of the dinosaur books seemed to be, and I wondered if it was possible to write a children's dinosaur book that took a truly different slant on the subject. It then hit me that I'd never seen a children's book devoted to what I was myself studying: what can be learned about dinosaurs from research on their fossilized footprints.

"I have found writing for children to be much harder than writing for my professional colleagues. There are many technical terms which nicely encapsulate a concept, and for which there are no equivalents in everyday usage, particularly among words familiar to juvenile audiences. I nonetheless find writing for children to be very rewarding, and I now consider this an important part of my work as a science educator. Children have an intense curiosity about the world around them, and dinosaurs provide a splendid vehicle for further stimulating that interest. The number of scientific topics that can be introduced to children in the context of dinosaur studies is almost unlimited, and includes such seemingly disparate matters as mathematics, geology, anatomy, ecology, and evolution.

"The critical thing is to provide children with dinosaur literature that is scientifically accurate and up to date, illustrated by pictures that are themselves defensible as scientific hypotheses about the life appearance of dinosaurs. There are far too many slap-dash dinosaur books on the juvenile market—quickie tomes thrown together to make a buck, their texts the distillates of years of outdated information, and their illustrations copied from previously published artwork that was itself swiped from originals of dubious quality. We can do much better than that, a challenge I put before myself,

and before anyone else who wants to write about dinosaurs for children."

*   *   *

FRENCH, Fiona 1944-

■ Personal

Born June 27, 1944, in Bath, Somerset, England; daughter of Robert Douglas (an engineer) and Mary G. (Black) French. *Education:* Croydon College of Art, Surrey, N.D.D., 1966. *Hobbies and other interests:* Collecting "blue and white" china and old editions of children's books.

■ Addresses

Home—50, The Street, Sustead, Norfolk NR11 8RX, England. *Agent*—Pat White, Rogers Coleridge and White, 20 Powis Mews, London W11 1JN, England.

■ Career

Long Grove Psychiatric Hospital, Epsom, Surrey, children's art therapy teacher, 1967-69; assistant to the painter Bridget Riley, 1967-72; Wimbledon School of Art, design teacher, 1970-71; Leicester and Brighton polytechnics, design teacher, 1973-74; free-lance illustrator, 1974—.

■ Awards, Honors

Children's Book Showcase award, 1973, for *The Blue Bird;* Kate Greenaway commended book, Library Association, 1973, for *King Tree;* Kate Greenaway Medal, 1987, for *Snow White in New York.*

■ Writings

SELF-ILLUSTRATED CHILDREN'S BOOKS

Jack of Hearts, Harcourt, 1970.
Huni, Oxford University Press, 1971.
The Blue Bird, Walck, 1972.
King Tree, Walck, 1973.
City of Gold, Walck, 1974.
Aio the Rainmaker, Oxford University Press (London), 1975, (New York), 1978.
Matteo, Oxford University Press (London), 1976, (New York), 1978.
Hunt the Thimble, Oxford University Press, 1978.
The Princess and the Musician, Evans, 1981.
(Reteller) *John Barleycorn,* Abelard-Schuman, 1982.
Future Story, Oxford University Press, 1983, Peter Bedrick, 1984.
Maid of the Wood, Oxford University Press, 1985.
Snow White in New York, Oxford University Press (Oxford), 1986, (New York), 1987.
The Song of the Nightingale, Blackie, 1987.
(Reteller) *Cinderella,* Oxford University Press (Oxford), 1987, (New York), 1988.
Rise & Shine, Little, Brown, 1989, published in England as *Rise, Shine!,* Methuen, 1989.

The Magic Vase, Oxford University Press, 1991.
Anancy and Mr. Dry-Bone, Little, Brown, 1991.
King of Another Country, Oxford University Press, 1992.

ILLUSTRATOR

Margaret Mayo, *The Book of Magical Birds,* Kaye & Ward, 1977.
(With Joanna Troughton) Richard Blythe, *Fabulous Beasts,* Macdonald Educational, 1977.
(With Kim Blundell and George Thompson) Carol Crowther, *Clowns and Clowning,* Macdonald Educational, 1978.
Oscar Wilde, *The Star Child,* abridged by Jennifer Westwood, Evans Brothers, 1979.
Josephine Karavasil, *Hidden Animals: Investigator's Notebook,* Dinosaur, 1982.
Jennifer Westwood, *Fat Cat,* Abelard-Schuman, 1984.
Westwood, *Going to Squintum's: A Foxy Folktale,* Blackie, 1985.

OTHER

Un-Fairy Tales (adult fiction), privately printed, 1966.

■ Sidelights

Fiona French's work has been praised for both its strong attention to detail and deep sense of atmosphere. Many

Many of Fiona French's storybooks are based on myths and folk tales, as in her self-illustrated *Maid of the Wood.*

of her books feature mythical themes and characters found in folktales and mythology from around the world. This diverse cultural presentation allows French's readers to experience a broad base of artistic and storytelling styles. "I treat each book as a new venture, during which I discover information I never knew before," the author once commented, adding that she intends her books "for younger children, and put details in the pictures which might hold their attention even if they cannot read and are 'being read to.'"

French spent much of her childhood in Devon and Surrey. She was raised in an English convent school while other members of her family lived in the Middle East. As a child, French's interests included art, history, geography, and literature. The author was eventually able to put these interests to use when she attended art school, taught at several art colleges and technical schools, and acted as assistant to painter Bridget Riley.

French started writing and illustrating her own books in 1970. Her themes—ranging from greed and envy to African tribal legend—are brought to life through a variety of imaginative settings and characters. French's first book, *Jack of Hearts,* is based on playing cards, as the "four Kings"—hearts, diamonds, clubs, and spades—celebrate the birthday of the Jack of Hearts. *King Tree* takes place in a French garden much like the one at Versailles, where courtiers dressed as trees act out the nomination process for "King of the Trees." In another vein, *City of Gold* tells of a fight between good and evil as two brothers engage in a dramatic struggle with the Devil. *Snow White in New York*—one of the author's most popular works—retells the familiar story in a 1920s jazz setting, while *King of Another Country* offers an African moral fable.

In a review of *King Tree* for *Library Journal,* Margaret Maxwell calls French's illustrations "skillfully done." "A sumptuous picture book," agrees a reviewer for the *Times Literary Supplement,* who adds that the text yields "nice ironic touches as well as great visual pleasure." Genivieve Stuttaford, writing in *Publishers Weekly,* terms *Snow White in New York* to be full of "astonishing pictures" in a "suave and witty" setting. And Marilyn Iarusso, in a review of *King of Another Country* for *School Library Journal,* praised the author's "brilliantly colored and patterned double-page illustrations."

When not working on new material of her own, French has illustrated works for other many other authors. These illustrations, echoing those found in the author's original tales, all feature French's trademark mix of whimsy, color, and style. Margaret R. Marshall concludes in *Twentieth Century Children's Writers* that French "produces not only authentic detail but an almost tangible atmosphere, a feat perceivable in her gloriously rich illustrative style and in the entirely suitable economy and relevance of the texts."

■ Works Cited

Iarusso, Marilyn, review of *King of Another Country, School Library Journal,* April, 1993.

Review of *King Tree, Times Literary Supplement,* June 15, 1973, p. 686.

Marshall, Margaret R., essay in *Twentieth Century Children's Writers,* 3rd edition, St. James Press, 1989.

Maxwell, Margaret, review of *King Tree, Library Journal,* September 15, 1973, p. 2639.

Stuttaford, Genivieve, review of *Snow White in New York, Publishers Weekly,* February 13, 1987, p. 93.

■ For More Information See

PERIODICALS

Junior Bookshelf, February, 1993, p. 12.

Library Journal, June 15, 1972, p. 3796.

New York Times Book Review, October 22, 1989, p. 55.

Publishers Weekly, March 24, 1989, p. 67; November 30, 1990, p. 71.

School Library Journal, July, 1989, p. 64; March, 1990, p. 153.

Times Educational Supplement, June 9, 1989, p. B10; November 7, 1990, p. R4.

G

GABHART, Ann 1947-

■ Personal

Born September 15, 1947, in Anderson County, KY; daughter of Johnson Hanks (a farmer) and Olga Elizabeth (a clerk and homemaker; maiden name, Hawkins) Houchin; married Darrell Wayne Gabhart (a records analyst), November 19, 1964; children: Johnson Wayne, Tarasa Ann, Daniel Christopher. *Religion:* Baptist. *Hobbies and other interests:* Reading, walking, children, dogs.

■ Addresses

Home and office—1307 Harry Wise Rd., Lawrenceburg, KY 40342. *Agent*—Ann Elmo Agency, 60 East 42nd St., New York, NY 10165.

■ Career

Writer, 1975—. Vice-president, Academic Booster Club, 1989 and 1990; volunteer worker for Academic Booster Club and Library of the Blind and Physically Handicapped; teacher for Community Education.

■ Writings

FOR YOUNG ADULTS

A Chance Hero, Silhouette, 1985.
The Look of Eagles, Silhouette, 1986.
The Gifting, Crosswinds, 1987.
A Kindred Spirit, Crosswinds, 1987.
Only in Sunshine, Avon, 1988.
Wish Come True, Avon, 1988.
For Sheila, Avon, 1991.
Bridge to Courage, Avon, 1993.

FOR CHILDREN

Discovery at Coyote Point, Avon, 1989.
Two of a Kind, Avon, 1992.

HISTORICAL ROMANCE NOVELS

A Forbidden Yearning, Warner Books, 1978.

A Heart Divided, Warner Books, 1980.

■ Work in Progress

A young adult book for Avon; a sequel to *Two of a Kind;* researching steamships during the 1850s and Cherokees in Tennessee.

ANN GABHART

■ Sidelights

Ann Gabhart told *SATA:* "When I was ten years old, I was an avid Hardy Boys mystery book fan and I thought it would be the most wonderful thing to be able to solve a mystery the way they did. Fortunately for me, there weren't any jewel thieves or kidnappers for me to try to nab around my quiet rural area, so I had to write my own mystery. Thus I was launched on a two-fold adventure. The first was the adventure of the mystery I had so much fun writing and starring in as a kid, and the second was the beginning of the much greater adventure of being a writer.

"When I was ten, it seemed natural to decide to write a book, and since that time, I've not had to think about it at all. I write. Although no one in my family had ever attempted to write fiction, my grandmother once dreamed of writing and my grandfather was a book lover and collector. An aunt introduced me to my first typewriter—an old Underwood number five—and I felt the magic in the keys even before I could make words.

"The first novels I published were historical romances for adults. I had not really thought about writing for young adults until I'd been working professionally for a number of years. Then I spotted an announcement regarding a contest for a first juvenile fiction novel, and I decided to give it a try since I was having difficulty selling my current work. The historical romance field was changing, and I was not changing fast enough with it. So I tried to come up with an idea that combined the normal problems of a fifteen-year-old boy coming to terms with the person he is with something a bit strange—a deep woods that people often get lost in—and a secret regarding the death of the hero's mother. The novel, *A Chance Hero,* was not finished in time for the contest, but it was accepted for publication by Silhouette First Love, a young adult line that has since stopped publishing for young readers.

"I enjoy writing for young people because they are so open and ready to be entertained by a good story. They enjoy being surprised by something different even while they're searching for something familiar to embrace in the stories they read. Even when the problems my characters have are serious ones, I try to make all my stories upbeat. It's my hope and intention that reading about my characters will make my readers feel better about themselves and how they fit into the world around them. More than anything, that is the focus of my work—that everyone is different, but that our differences are what make each of us special and unique and lovable. My goal is to have my readers close the book wishing the story could continue, while knowing the ending was right and being confident that the characters in my story are ready to face whatever challenges the future might hold for them.

Mystery Provides Focus for Children's Books

"Central to most of my plots is some bit of mystery. In *A Chance Hero,* it is Big Foot. In my newest book, *Bridge to Courage,* it is the hero's fear of heights and the reason behind that phobia. In between I wrote *The Gifting,* which is about an old woman recluse who has healing powers, some of which she can pass on. *A Kindred Spirit* involves Erin's imaginary childhood playmate, who suddenly begins haunting her again. In *Wish Come True,* Alyssa believes a mirror is making her wishes come true, and in *For Sheila,* Sydney is helped through her grief for her sister by a mysterious little white dog that just may be a ghost. *Discovery at Coyote Point* centers on the mystery of the disappearance of Ance's father.

"Most of my books are set in rural areas or small towns because I grew up and still live in the country, and it is what I know. In *Discovery at Coyote Point,* I take that one step further and use a unique place on my mother's farm as a setting for my story. The desire to use this setting was the beginning of the idea for the story. The area, a wild place with cliffs and caves and trees that have been allowed to grow undisturbed for years, made a perfect setting for the story of a young boy who has a special feeling for animals. In the story he befriends a coyote, or perhaps the coyote befriends him.

"I like animals, especially dogs, and so I'm always glad when I can have an animal character to help the hero. In

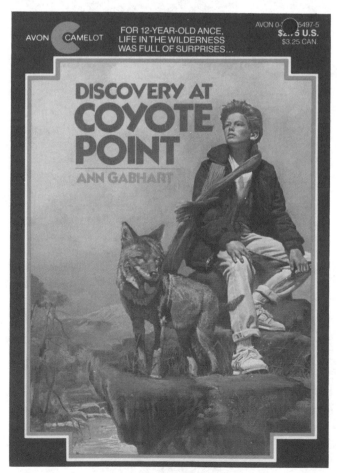

FOR 12-YEAR-OLD ANCE, LIFE IN THE WILDERNESS WAS FULL OF SURPRISES...

AVON CAMELOT

AVON 0-   6497-5
$2. 5 U.S.
$3.25 CAN.

DISCOVERY AT COYOTE POINT

ANN GABHART

Living in the remote wilderness of Coyote Point teaches a city boy important lessons about himself and his family in this novel by Gabhart.

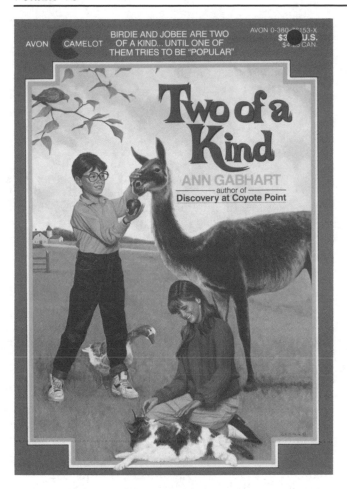

In Gabhart's *Two of a Kind,* a new student has an opportunity to join the popular crowd at school—if she participates in their disruptive classroom pranks.

Two of a Kind, I use a menagerie of animals that are a bit odd to help the young heroine discover that being a bit different from the average kid, if there is such a thing as an average kid, doesn't mean nobody will like her.

"I like to work even when the words come hard to the page. I usually work every weekday between six and eight hours unless I'm doing temporary secretarial work to stretch my family's income. After years of having a desk in my kitchen, I now have my own office with two large windows so that I can watch the birds at my bird feeder, see the squirrels running through the trees along the fence row, and spot the occasional deer or coyote passing through our field below the house. I suppose that makes it easy to see why I like getting my characters out in the woods. It's something I like to do myself, and often while I'm walking in the woods with my dogs, I work out kinks in my story line or let my characters talk to me so I'll understand them better.

Reading Widely Inspires Writing Talent

"I always tell young people who express an interest in writing that one of the best things they can do is read. I try to encourage them to expand their reading interests to include different types of books with all kinds of subjects. Next I tell them that writing is the same as

anything else a person might want to do. Even if you have talent, you still need to practice to develop that talent. So I tell them to practice regularly the way an athlete practices until they feel the same ease in putting words together that a professional basketball player feels dribbling down the court. Last but not least, I tell them that persistence is perhaps the best friend of any aspiring writer. Persistence is what keeps a writer going when the ideas stop flowing or when the rejections come, as they do for most writers at times.

"I am currently at work on another middle reader story with the same characters that are in *Two of a Kind.* Honaker and Riggs are a special team that I hope to keep together for a while. I am also researching an idea for an adult novel, but it is still in the planning stages. I have never been able to discuss my work in progress, perhaps because I need to keep the freshness of the idea inside me instead of letting it all spill out in spoken words. When the characters start talking to each other in my head, I know it's time to begin writing my story.

"Writing a book is a long process from the initial idea to the finished product ready for a bookstore shelf. Each new book brings its own thrill. I've had eleven books published. Several of these have been reprinted in various forms in foreign countries. My main wish as a writer of books for young people is to be able to make young people fall in love with reading the way I did long ago when I made my first trip to the library and checked out a book called *Black Penny.* Since then it's been one adventure after another waiting for me inside the covers of a book. I'm happy to have been able to put some of those adventures inside the covers for other people who love to read."

*   *   *

GEISEL, Theodor Seuss 1904-1991 (Theo. LeSieg, Dr. Seuss; Rosetta Stone, a joint pseudonym)

■ Personal

Surname is pronounced *Guy*-zel; born March 2, 1904, in Springfield, MA; died September 24, 1991; son of Theodor Robert (superintendent of Springfield, MA, public park system) and Henrietta (Seuss) Geisel; married Helen Palmer (an author and vice-president of Beginner Books), November 29, 1927 (died, October 23, 1967); married Audrey Stone Diamond, August 6, 1968. *Education:* Dartmouth College, A.B., 1925; graduate study at Lincoln College, Oxford, 1925-26, and Sorbonne, University of Paris.

■ Addresses

Home—La Jolla, CA 92037. *Office*—Random House, Inc., 201 East 50th St., New York, NY 10022. *Agent*—International Creative Management, 40 West 57th St., New York, NY 10019.

THEODOR SEUSS GEISEL

■ Career

Author and illustrator. Free-lance cartoonist, beginning 1927; advertising artist, Standard Oil Company of New Jersey, 1928-41; editorial cartoonist, *PM* (magazine), New York City, 1940-42; publicist, War Production Board of U.S. Treasury Department, 1940-42; founder and president, Beginner Books, Random House, Inc., New York City, 1957-91. Correspondent in Japan, *Life* (magazine), 1954. Trustee, La Jolla (CA) Town Council, beginning 1956. *Military service:* U.S. Army, Signal Corps, Information and Education Division, 1943-46; became lieutenant colonel; received Legion of Merit. *Exhibitions:* One-man art exhibitions at San Diego Arts Museum, 1950, Dartmouth College, 1975, Toledo Museum of Art, 1975, La Jolla Museum of Contemporary Art, 1976, and Baltimore Museum of Art, 1987. *Member:* Authors League of America, American Society of Composers, Authors and Publishers (ASCAP), Sigma Phi Epsilon.

■ Awards, Honors

Academy Awards, 1946, for *Hitler Lives,* 1947, for *Design for Death,* and 1951, for *Gerald McBoing-Boing;* Randolph Caldecott Honor Awards, Association for Library Services for Children, American Library Association, 1948, for *McElligot's Pool,* 1950, for *Bartholomew and the Oobleck,* and 1951, for *If I Ran the Zoo;*

Young Reader's Choice Award, Pacific Northwest Library Association, 1950, for *McElligot's Pool;* L.H.D., Dartmouth College, 1956, American International College, 1968, and Lake Forest College, 1977; Lewis Carroll Shelf Award, 1958, for *Horton Hatches the Egg,* and 1961, for *And To Think That I Saw It on Mulberry Street;* Boys' Club Junior Book Award, Boys' Club of America, 1966, for *I Had Trouble in Getting to Solla Sollew.*

Peabody Award, 1971, for animated cartoons *How the Grinch Stole Christmas* and *Horton Hears a Who;* Critics' Award, International Animated Cartoon Festival, and Silver Medal, International Film and Television Festival of New York, both 1972, both for *The Lorax;* Los Angeles County Library Association Award, 1974; Southern California Council on Literature for Children and Young People Award, 1974, for special contribution to children's literature; named "Outstanding California Author," California Association of Teachers of English, 1976; Emmy Award, 1977, for *Halloween Is Grinch Night;* Roger Revelle Award, University of California, San Diego, 1978; winner of Children's Choice Election, 1978; grand marshal of Detroit's Thanksgiving Day Parade, 1979; D. Litt., Whittier College, 1980; Laura Ingalls Wilder Award, Association for Library Services for Children, American Library Association, 1980.

"Dr. Seuss Week" proclaimed by State Governors, March 2-7, 1981; Regina Medal, Catholic Library Association, 1982; National Association of Elementary School Principals special award, 1982, for distinguished service to children; Pulitzer Prize, 1984, for his "special contribution over nearly half a century to the education and enjoyment of America's children and their parents"; PEN Los Angeles Center Award for children's literature, 1985, for *The Butter Battle Book;* D.H.L., University of Hartford, 1986; honored with special program by Academy of Motion Picture Arts and Sciences, 1989; in 1993 Random House established the Dr. Seuss Picture Book Award, a biannual award given in Geisel's honor to a children's book author/illustrator.

■ Writings

UNDER PSEUDONYM DR. SEUSS; SELF-ILLUSTRATED

And To Think That I Saw It on Mulberry Street, Vanguard, 1937.
The 500 Hats of Bartholomew Cubbins, Vanguard, 1938.
The Seven Lady Godivas (adult humor), Random House, 1939.
The King's Stilts, Random House, 1939.
Horton Hatches the Egg, Random House, 1940.
McElligot's Pool, Random House, 1947.
Thidwick, the Big-Hearted Moose, Random House, 1949.
Bartholomew and the Oobleck, Random House, 1949.
If I Ran the Zoo, Random House, 1950.
Scrambled Eggs Super!, Random House, 1953.
Horton Hears a Who!, Random House, 1954.
On Beyond Zebra, Random House, 1955.

Signs of Civilization! (booklet), La Jolla Town Council, 1956.

If I Ran the Circus, Random House, 1956.

The Cat in the Hat, Random House, 1957, French/English edition published as *Le Chat au Chapeau*, Random House, 1967, Spanish/English edition published as *El Gato Ensombrerado*, Random House, 1967.

How the Grinch Stole Christmas, Random House, 1957.

The Cat in the Hat Comes Back!, Beginner Books, 1958.

Yertle the Turtle and Other Stories, Random House, 1958.

Happy Birthday to You!, Random House, 1959.

One Fish, Two Fish, Red Fish, Blue Fish, Random House, 1960.

Green Eggs and Ham, Beginner Books, 1960.

The Sneetches and Other Stories, Random House, 1961.

Dr. Seuss' Sleep Book, Random House, 1962.

Hop on Pop, Beginner Books, 1963.

Dr. Seuss' ABC, Beginner Books, 1963.

(With Philip D. Eastman) *The Cat in the Hat Dictionary, by the Cat Himself*, Beginner Books, 1964.

Fox in Socks, Beginner Books, 1965.

I Had Trouble in Getting to Solla Sollew, Random House, 1965.

The Cat in the Hat Songbook, Random House, 1967.

Dr. Seuss' Lost World Revisited: A Forward-Looking Backward Glance (adult nonfiction), Award Books, 1967.

The Foot Book, Random House, 1968.

I Can Lick 30 Tigers Today and Other Stories, Random House, 1969.

I Can Draw It Myself, Random House, 1970.

Mr. Brown Can Moo! Can You?, Random House, 1970.

The Lorax, Random House, 1971.

Marvin K. Mooney, Will You Please Go Now?, Random House, 1972.

Did I Ever Tell You How Lucky You Are?, Random House, 1973.

The Shape of Me and Other Stuff, Random House, 1973.

There's a Wocket in My Pocket!, Random House, 1974.

Oh, the Thinks You Can Think!, Random House, 1975.

The Cat's Quizzer, Random House, 1976.

I Can Read with My Eyes Shut!, Random House, 1978.

Oh, Say Can You Say?, Beginner Books, 1979.

The Dr. Seuss Storybook (includes *Scrambled Eggs Super!*), Collins, 1979.

Hunches in Bunches, Random House, 1982.

The Butter Battle Book, Random House, 1984.

You're Only Old Once, Random House, 1986.

The Tough Coughs as He Ploughs the Dough: Early Writings and Cartoons by Dr. Seuss, edited by Richard Marschall, Morrow, 1986.

Oh, the Places You'll Go!, Random House, 1990.

Six by Seuss: A Treasury of Dr. Seuss Classics (includes *And To Think That I Saw It on Mulberry Street, The 500 Hats of Bartholomew Cubbins, Horton Hatches the Egg, How the Grinch Stole Christmas, The Lorax,* and *Yertle the Turtle*), Random House, 1991.

UNDER PSEUDONYM THEO. LeSIEG

Ten Apples Up on Top!, illustrations by Roy McKie, Beginner Books, 1961.

I Wish That I Had Duck Feet, illustrations by B. Tobey, Beginner Books, 1965.

Come Over to My House, illustrations by Richard Erdoes, Beginner Books, 1966.

The Eye Book, illustrations by McKie, Random House, 1968.

(Self-illustrated) *I Can Write-By Me, Myself*, Random House, 1971.

In a People House, illustrations by McKie, Random House, 1972.

The Many Mice of Mr. Brice, illustrations by McKie, Random House, 1973.

Wacky Wednesday, illustrations by George Booth, Beginner Books, 1974.

Would You Rather Be a Bullfrog?, illustrations by McKie, Random House, 1975.

Hooper Humperdinck...? Not Him!, Random House, 1976.

Please Try to Remember the First of Octember!, illustrations by Arthur Cummings, Beginner Books, 1977.

Maybe You Should Fly a Jet! Maybe You Should Be a Vet, illustrations by Michael J. Smulin, Beginner Books, 1980.

The Tooth Book, Random House, 1981.

Sam-I-Am's persistence convinces a friend to try an unusual—but tasty—dish in the popular Dr. Seuss book *Green Eggs and Ham*.

1990's *Oh, the Places You'll Go!* was the last book written and illustrated under Geisel's famous pseudonym, Dr. Seuss.

OTHER BOOKS

(Illustrator) *Boners*, Viking, 1931.

(Illustrator) *More Boners*, Viking, 1931.

(Under pseudonym Dr. Seuss) *My Book about Me, by Me, Myself: I Wrote It! I Drew It!*, illustrations by McKie, Beginner Books, 1969.

(Under pseudonym Dr. Seuss) *Great Day for Up!*, illustrations by Quentin Blake, Random House, 1974.

(With Michael Frith, under joint pseudonym Rosetta Stone) *Because a Little Bug Went Ka-Choo!*, illustrated by Frith, Beginner Books, 1975.

Dr. Seuss from Then to Now (museum catalog), Random House, 1987.

(Under pseudonym Dr. Seuss) *I Am Not Going To Get Up Today!*, illustrations by James Stevenson, Random House, 1987.

SCREENPLAYS

Your Job in Germany (documentary short subject), U.S. Army, 1946, released under the title *Hitler Lives*, Warner Brothers.

(With wife, Helen Palmer Geisel) *Design for Death* (documentary feature), RKO Pictures, 1947.

Gerald McBoing-Boing (animated cartoon), Columbia, 1951.

(With Allen Scott) *The 5,000 Fingers of Dr. T* (musical), Columbia, 1953.

TELEVISION SCRIPTS

How the Grinch Stole Christmas, Columbia Broadcasting System, Inc. (CBS-TV), 1966 (also available on videotape from Metro-Goldwyn-Mayer-United Artists [MGM-UA]).

Horton Hears a Who, CBS-TV, 1970 (also available on videotape from MGM-UA).

The Cat in the Hat, CBS-TV, 1971.

Dr. Seuss on the Loose, CBS-TV, 1973.

Hoober-Bloob Highway, CBS-TV, 1975.

Halloween Is Grinch Night, American Broadcasting Companies, Inc. (ABC-TV), 1977.

Pontoffel Pock, Where Are You?, ABC-TV, 1980.

The Grinch Grinches the Cat in the Hat, ABC-TV, 1982.

The Butter Battle Book, Turner Network Television (TNT-TV), 1989.

Also author of *The Lorax*.

OTHER

Dr. Seuss Presents Favorite Children's Stories (recording), Camden, 1972.

Contributor of cartoons and prose to magazines, including *Judge, College Humor, Liberty, Vanity Fair,* and *Life*.

A collection of Geisel's manuscripts, drawings, and other memorabilia is held by the University of California, San Diego.

■ **Adaptations**

Dr. Seuss' animated cartoon character Gerald McBoing-Boing appeared in several other UPA pictures, including *Gerald McBoing-Boing's Symphony*, 1953, *How Now McBoing-Boing*, 1954, and *Gerald McBoing-Boing on the Planet Moo*, 1956. In December of 1956, Gerald McBoing-Boing appeared in his own animated variety show, *The Gerald McBoing-Boing Show*, which aired on CBS-TV on Sunday evenings and ran through October of 1958. Several Dr. Seuss books are available on cassette, including *Yertle the Turtle and Other Stories*, from Random House.

■ **Sidelights**

They have become part of our imaginations' landscape: the crusty Grinch who stole Christmas, gentle Horton the elephant, the Cat in the Hat, and the persistent Sam-I-Am with his green eggs and ham. All these and many more are the creations of Theodor Seuss Geisel, better known to generations of readers as Dr. Seuss. Since publishing his first children's book over fifty years ago, Geisel became perhaps the most successful writer in the whole field of children's literature. His books for young readers have sold more than one hundred million copies and have been translated into almost every language on the globe. Animated television specials based on his stories have won Emmy and Peabody awards, and he was the recipient of a special Pulitzer Prize in recognition of his achievements. As Ralph Novak put it in

People magazine, "Certainly no author has shown a greater understanding or love of children."

Geisel brought significant changes to the world of children's book publishing in late 1957 when he released *The Cat in the Hat.* With one slim volume, Dr. Seuss challenged the idea that primers for young readers were limited to dull stories by the restricted vocabulary. The adventuresome Cat in the Hat runs amok while Mother is away, leaving a horrible mess for the two astonished children who are so well-behaved. The remarkable qualities of the story are its rhyme—done with only 223 words—and its quirky illustrations that are as silly as the tale itself.

By the time *The Cat in the Hat* appeared, however, Dr. Seuss had already built a reputation around those effortless rhymes and silly drawings. *New York Times Book Review* correspondent Ellen Lewis Buell noted of the author's works: "This deft combination of easy words, swift rhymes and batty nonsense convinced thousands of hitherto skeptical children that reading could be fun—just as the grown-ups said."

Born on March 2, 1904, Theodor Seuss Geisel grew up in Springfield, Massachusetts. He was an avid reader and loved to draw, but he did not spend his childhood planning to become a children's author. In fact, he remembered in *Reader's Digest* that his first foray into art class was anything but successful. His high school teacher told him, "You will never learn to draw, Theodor. Why don't you just skip this class for the rest of the term." In a *Parade* magazine feature, Geisel claimed that the lack of formal art lessons actually assured that he would develop a distinctive style of his own. "I've capitalized on my mistakes," he said. "Since I can't draw, I've taken the awkwardness and peculiarities of my natural style and developed them. That's why my characters look that way."

College Years Start of Cartooning Career

From high school Geisel moved to Dartmouth College, where he became editor of the college humor magazine, *Jack-o-Lantern.* In the pages of that periodical first appeared the bizarre cartoon animals that would eventually become the backbone of his book illustrations. Even so, the work with *Jack-o-Lantern* was a sideline. Geisel graduated from Dartmouth and entered Oxford University, intending to pursue a doctorate in English literature. Within a year he had changed his mind about academia—a fellow student, Helen Palmer, encouraged him to pursue cartooning. He took her advice, and married her as well. They returned to the United States, and soon Geisel was selling drawings and prose pieces to magazines such as *College Humor, Vanity Fair, Liberty,* and *Life.*

One of his cartoons caught the attention of the Standard Oil Company. He was signed to a contract to create grotesque, enormous insects to illustrate the famous slogan "Quick, Henry! The Flit!" Those characters and others created for Standard Oil appeared on billboards nationwide and made a name for Geisel as an illustrator. He still had other lofty ambitions, however. He wanted to write serious fiction and humor for adults.

Geisel's first children's book came about quite by accident. He was crossing the Atlantic on a cruise ship when he became caught up in the monotonous rhythm of the ship's engine. He began to put words to the rhythm, and the result was *And To Think That I Saw It on Mulberry Street.* Set in his hometown of Springfield, Geisel's work tells the story of a boy whose imagination transforms a simple horse-drawn wagon into a fabulous parade of exotic beasts and vehicles. The author drew the illustrations himself, finished the work in 1937, and set about trying to find a publisher for it.

He met with more than twenty-five rejections before a fellow Dartmouth alumnus—encountered quite by chance—accepted the work for Vanguard Press. As Myra Kibler recounted in the *Dictionary of Literary Biography,* "Such a fortunate meeting is the stuff of fantasy, an appropriate beginning for the career of Dr. Seuss. Geisel used his middle name, his mother's maiden name, for his children's books, saving his last name for greater, more serious writing. To that he added the Dr. in a flippant gesture to the doctorate he never

The antics of Geisel's troublesome feline in *The Cat in Hat* make this book fun for beginning readers.

finished." Thus, in 1937, the career of Dr. Seuss was launched.

Early Work Traditional Yet Distinctive

Any lofty ambitions Theodor Geisel may have retained were soon shelved in the face of his pseudonym's fantastic success. He was not long a "Dr." by default, however—his alma mater Dartmouth was one of several universities which conferred honorary doctorates on him over the years. By the time the Second World War interrupted his work, Geisel had published several well-received children's books, including *The 500 Hats of Bartholomew Cubbins, The King's Stilts,* and the ever-popular *Horton Hatches the Egg.* The latter book introduces Horton the elephant, who is tricked into sitting on a nest by a lazy bird. Kibler wrote of *Horton Hatches the Egg:* "[Geisel] is not yet inventing words—that comes later. But his work has acquired that distinctive Seuss sound. Similarly, animals in the drawings are still recognizable as lion, moose, giraffe, or hippopotamus. The elephant-bird that hatches as a result of Horton's faithful labor is the first 'brand new' creature. But just the situation of the immense elephant sitting in the tree on the small egg opens a whole new world of incongruities."

Some of Geisel's books impart a message of responsibility for others, as in *Horton Hears a Who,* in which Horton protects a tiny, but vocal, friend.

During World War II, Geisel and his wife aided the war effort by writing and producing films for the Allied cause. Two of these short subjects, *Hitler Lives* and *Design for Death,* won Academy Awards for best documentary features. After the war, Geisel settled in La Jolla, California, and returned to his work for children. In quick succession he released *McElligot's Pool, Thidwick, The Big-Hearted Moose, Bartholomew and the Oobleck, If I Ran the Zoo,* and *Horton Hears a Who!* These books added a new dimension to Dr. Seuss's earlier work: they suggest to the reader that individuals can and should be responsible for the welfare of others. This is a theme Geisel has warmed to over the years in the face of environmental deterioration and threat of nuclear attack. More recent Dr. Seuss works such as *The Lorax* and *The Butter Battle Book* take strong stands on the dangers of indifference to world affairs.

In 1957 Geisel released his first book specifically aimed at beginning readers, *The Cat in the Hat.* The author said he was motivated to write the book after reading a *Life* magazine article called "Why Johnny Can't Read." The article suggested that beginning primers were dull and that children saw reading as a job rather than a pleasure. Geisel set to work on a story that would be both easy to read *and* fun—but the task was not as simple as it seemed. In *Women's Day* he remembered his labors over *The Cat in the Hat:* "Writing children's books is hard work, a lot harder than most people realize, and that includes most writers of children's books. And it never gets any easier. I remember thinking that I might be able to dash off *The Cat in the Hat* in two or three weeks. Actually, it took over a year. You try telling a pretty complicated story using less than two hundred and fifty words! No, don't, not unless you're willing to rewrite and rewrite and rewrite."

Cat in the Hat's Success Launches Imprint

Hard work aside, *The Cat in the Hat* was a stunning success for Geisel. Buell maintained that the volume "immediately made publishing history." By 1960, Random House—Geisel's publisher for a number of years—made the author head of Beginner Books, a subsidiary company aimed specifically at the market for the youngest readers. Not only did Beginner Books first publish such Dr. Seuss classics as *Green Eggs and Ham* and *One Fish, Two Fish, Red Fish, Blue Fish,* it also helped popularize the work of writers such as P. D. Eastman and Robert Lopshire.

How the Grinch Stole Christmas was also first published in 1957. Geisel claimed this tale of the stingy, slinking Grinch remained one of his favorite works. The author told *Women's Day:* "In any story things happen and characters have motives that are good or bad. So every storyteller is a moralist whether he knows it or not. Children have a strong ethical sense anyway. They want to see virtue rewarded and arrogance or meanness punished. You don't want to hit them over the head with the moral, of course; you have to work it in sideways. But it has to be there. If the Grinch steals Christmas, . . . he has to bring it back in the end. I must say, though, when I was doing that one I was kind of rooting for the Grinch."

By his eightieth birthday in 1984, Geisel was considered the dean of humorous children's writers. Translations of his books were selling all over the world, some of his best-loved stories had been made into award-winning television shows, and almost every honor the children's publishing industry bestows had found its way onto his shelf. Humorist Bennett Cerf, Geisel's publisher at Random House, declared in the *Saturday Evening Post:* "I've published any number of great writers, from William Faulkner to John O'Hara, but there's only one genius on my authors' list. His name is Ted Geisel."

The author himself was not so eager to sing his own praises. In the same article, Geisel replied: "If I were a genius, why do I have to sweat so hard at my work? I know my stuff all looks like it was rattled off in twenty-three seconds but every word is a struggle and every sentence is like the pangs of birth."

Geisel commented further on his work in *Books Are by People:* "The most important thing about me is that I work slavishly—write, rewrite, reject and polish incessantly.... I am trying to capture an audience. Most every child learning to read has problems, and I am just saying to them that reading is fun." Geisel told *Publishers Weekly* that all of his books have to pass the strictest of tests: *he* must find that reading them is fun. "When I write a book," he said, "I have only one person in mind. I'm writing it for myself."

■ Works Cited

Buell, Ellen Lewis, review of *The Cat in the Hat Comes Back, New York Times Book Review,* October 5, 1958, p. 36.
Crichton, Jennifer, "Dr. Seuss Turns 80," *Publishers Weekly,* February 10, 1984, pp. 22-3.
Freeman, Don, "Dr. Seuss at 72—Going Like 60," *Saturday Evening Post,* March, 1977.
Gordon, Arthur, "The Wonderful Wizard of Soledad Hill," *Women's Day,* September, 1965.
Hopkins, Lee Bennett, *Books Are by People,* Citation Press, 1969.
Kibler, Myra, "Theodor Seuss Geisel," *Dictionary of Literary Biography,* Volume 61: *American Writers for Children since 1960: Poets, Illustrators, and Nonfiction Authors,* Gale, 1987.
Kupferberg, Herbert, "A Seussian Celebration," *Parade,* February 26, 1984, pp. 4-6.
Novak, Ralph, review of *You're Only Old Once!, People,* March 31, 1986.
Stewart-Gordon, James, "Dr. Seuss: Fanciful State of Childhood," *Reader's Digest,* April, 1972.

■ For More Information See

BOOKS

Children's Literature Review, Gale, Volume 1, 1976, Volume 9, 1985.

A grumpy Grinch devises a plan to cancel Christmas in a nearby town, but instead finds himself joining in the holiday spirit in *How the Grinch Stole Christmas.*

Cott, Jonathan, *Pipers at the Gates of Dawn: The Wisdom of Children's Literature,* Random House, 1983.
Lanes, Selma G., *Down the Rabbit Hole: Adventures and Misadventures in the Realm of Children's Literature,* Atheneum, 1972.

PERIODICALS

Newsweek, January 16, 1984.
New York Times, May 21, 1986.

OBITUARIES:

PERIODICALS

School Library Journal, November, 1991. pp. 12, 14.*

*   *   *

GIBLIN, James Cross 1933-

■ Personal

Surname is pronounced with a hard "g"; born July 8, 1933, in Cleveland, OH; son of Edward Kelley (a lawyer) and Anna (a teacher; maiden name, Cross) Giblin. *Education:* Attended Northwestern University, 1951; Western Reserve University (now Case Western

JAMES CROSS GIBLIN

Reserve University), B.A., 1954; Columbia University, M.F.A., 1955.

■ Addresses

Home—200 East 24th St., Apt. 1606, New York, NY 10010. *Office*—Clarion Books, 215 Park Ave. S., New York, NY 10003.

■ Career

Free-lance writer, 1955—. Worked as a temporary typist, and at the British Book Centre, 1955-59; Criterion Books, Inc., New York City, assistant editor, 1959-62; Lothrop, Lee & Shepard Co., New York City, associate editor, 1962-65, editor, 1965-67; Seabury Press, Inc., New York City, editor-in-chief of Clarion Books (for children), 1967-79, vice-president, 1975-79; Houghton Mifflin Company, New York City, editor and publisher of Clarion Books, 1979-89, contributing editor, 1989—. Adjunct professor at Graduate Center of the City University of New York, 1979-83. *Member:* Society of Children's Book Writers and Illustrators (member of board of directors), Authors Guild, Children's Book Council (president, 1976), Children's Reading Round Table of Chicago.

■ Awards, Honors

Golden Kite Award for nonfiction, Society of Children's Book Writers and Illustrators, 1982, and American Book Award for children's nonfiction, 1983, both for *Chimney Sweeps: Yesterday and Today;* Golden Kite Award for nonfiction, 1984, for *Walls: Defenses throughout History;* Boston Globe-Horn Book Award Nonfiction Honor Book, 1986, for *The Truth about Santa Claus;* Golden Kite Award for nonfiction, 1989, for *Let There Be Light: A Book about Windows.*

American Library Association notable children's book citations, 1980, for *The Scarecrow Book,* 1981, for *The Skyscraper Book,* 1982, for *Chimney Sweeps: Yesterday and Today,* 1985, for *The Truth about Santa Claus,* 1986, for *Milk: The Fight for Purity,* 1987, for *From Hand to Mouth,* 1988, for *Let There Be Light: A Book about Windows,* 1990, for *The Riddle of the Rosetta Stone: Key to Ancient Egypt,* and 1991, for *The Truth about Unicorns;* several of Giblin's books have been Junior Library Guild selections.

■ Writings

CHILDREN'S NONFICTION

(With Dale Ferguson) *The Scarecrow Book,* Crown, 1980.

The Skyscraper Book, illustrated by Anthony Kramer, photographs by David Anderson, Crowell, 1981.

Chimney Sweeps: Yesterday and Today, illustrated by Margot Tomes, Crowell, 1981.

Fireworks, Picnics, and Flags: The Story of the Fourth of July Symbols, illustrated by Ursula Arndt, Clarion Books, 1983.

Walls: Defenses throughout History, Little, Brown, 1984.

The Truth about Santa Claus, Crowell, 1985.

Milk: The Fight for Purity, Crowell, 1986.

From Hand to Mouth; or, How We Invented Knives, Forks, Spoons, and Chopsticks & the Table Manners to Go with Them, Crowell, 1987.

Let There Be Light: A Book about Windows, Crowell, 1988.

The Riddle of the Rosetta Stone: Key to Ancient Egypt, Crowell, 1990.

The Truth about Unicorns, illustrated by Michael McDermott, Harper, 1991.

Edith Wilson: The Woman Who Ran the United States, illustrated by Michele Laporte, Viking, 1992.

George Washington: A Picture Book Biography, illustrated by Michael Dooling, Scholastic, 1992.

Be Seated: A Book about Chairs, HarperCollins, 1993.

OTHER

My Bus Is Always Late (one-act play; first produced in Cleveland, OH, at Western Reserve University, 1953), Dramatic Publishing, 1954.

Writing Books for Young People (adult nonfiction), The Writer, Inc., 1990.

Also author of a play based on William Styron's novel *Lie Down in Darkness.* Contributor of articles and stories for children to *Cricket* and *Highlights for Children,* and of articles for adults to *Children's Literature in Education, Horn Book, Publishers Weekly, The Writer,* and *Writer's Digest.*

■ Sidelights

James Cross Giblin has not only been a major figure in the field of children's book publishing, editing many important authors during his years at Clarion Books, but he has also written more than a dozen books for young readers himself. He has won awards and critical acclaim for his nonfiction children's books, including

Chimney Sweeps: Yesterday and Today, The Truth about Santa Claus, and *Let There Be Light: A Book about Windows.* As Giblin once explained: "Nonfiction books for children aged eight to twelve [give] me the opportunity to pursue my research interests, meet interesting and stimulating experts in various fields, and share my enthusiasms with a young audience. I try to write books that I would have enjoyed reading when I was the age of my readers."

Giblin was born July 8, 1933, in Cleveland, Ohio. He grew up in nearby Painesville, a shy, bookish child. Early in his young life he enjoyed the comic strip "Blondie" and, with the help of his mother, began drawing his own strips. He recalled in an essay for *Something about the Author Autobiography Series (SAAS):* "I filled sketchbook after sketchbook with action-filled pictures drawn in boxes like those of the comics. Mother helped me to print the words I wanted to put in the balloons, and later I learned how to print them myself." He also enjoyed going to the movies as a youngster; he noted in *SAAS:* "My favorites weren't films made for children but spy movies set in Germany and Nazi-occupied areas such as *Casablanca.* I also liked melodramas starring emotional actresses like Bette Davis and Greer Garson, especially if they took place in exotic settings ... or had to do with World War II."

Giblin traces the history of the tradition of Santa Claus in this 1985 work. (Cover illustration by Margot Tomes.)

In junior high, Giblin worked on the school paper, which helped him overcome some of his shyness. He reminisced in his autobiographical essay in *Sixth Book of Junior Authors:* "Robert K. Payne, my ninth-grade English teacher, did more than anyone to draw me out of my isolation. Mr. Payne encouraged his classes to try new things, including a mimeographed class newspaper. And he was determined that I should not only contribute pieces to the paper but also edit it." Giblin continued: "I backed away from the responsibility at first, as I backed away from so many things then. But Mr. Payne was persistent, and at last I allowed myself to become involved. Once I did, I discovered that I loved working with my classmates on the paper and thinking up ideas for each new issue."

When Giblin got to high school, however, he discovered a new interest. He answered a notice in the local paper about auditions for a community theater production of the play *Outward Bound,* and, as he recalled in *SAAS:* "My parents drove me to the barn theatre on the outskirts of town, and I nervously entered the rustic auditorium. When I arrived home three hours later— one of the actors had given me a ride—I couldn't restrain my excitement. 'I got a part! I got a part!' I shouted as I raced through the darkened house to the back porch, where my parents were sitting. The director had cast me as the idealistic young Reverend Duke in the play, which tells the story of a group of English people traveling on an ocean liner who gradually realize that they have died and are on their way to Heaven ... or to Hell." He further recounted: "As a shy youth of sixteen I might be reluctant to reveal my feelings, but I found I had no trouble expressing them through the character of the Reverend Duke. When the play was over and I walked to the center of the stage to take my bow, the applause seemed like an endorsement not just of my acting but of me personally. I felt a surge of confidence that I had never known before.... After *Outward Bound* I was hooked on the theatre. I tried out for and got parts in all of the Le Masque Club productions ... at Harvey High School, and the following summer I was cast in the small but funny role of the Lost Private in a professional production of the comedy *At War with the Army* at Rabbit Run Theatre in nearby North Madison."

Acting Developed into Interest in Writing

Following high school graduation, Giblin went off to study drama at Northwestern University. He was not happy there, however, and after a semester transferred to Western Reserve University (now Case Western Reserve University), near his parents' home. There he did well, winning a contest to co-star in a radio drama in New York City with actress Nina Foch in addition to starring in many university stage productions. But Giblin's ambitions were gradually changing with his experience. He noted in *SAAS:* "The actor has very little control over his situation, and I now knew that I wanted control. So I turned my attention to directing and playwriting." An experience with an old woman on a bus inspired him to write his first play, *My Bus Is*

Always Late, which was produced locally and published by the Dramatic Publishing Company in 1954.

Soon after, Giblin decided to earn a M.F.A. in playwriting from Columbia University in New York. After completing his degree, he remained in New York City to write, supporting himself by working as a temporary office employee. He became involved in a project to adapt William Styron's novel *Lie Down in Darkness* into a play, but due to various complications, the project fell through. This failure deeply affected Giblin; he explained in *SAAS:* "I'd put almost a year of hard work and anticipation into *Lie Down in Darkness.* I'd drawn on my deepest feelings in order to write it, and in the process it had become my personal statement as much as Styron's. I tried to start a new play in that late spring of 1957, but I discovered, painfully, that I'd already expressed most of what I had to say in *Lie Down in Darkness.*"

After a recuperative visit to Painesville, Giblin returned to New York with the intent of finding a more dependable career. He started out as a special-order clerk at the British Book Centre, then joined the staff of Criterion Books in 1959, first as a publicity director and later as an editor. He enjoyed the work, especially when given the opportunity to edit children's books. Deciding to

In *The Riddle of the Rosetta Stone,* Giblin suspensefully relates the discovery of a stone tablet that provided the key to deciphering ancient hieroglyphs.

concentrate solely on works for children, he moved to Lothrop, Lee and Shepard in 1962.

While working at Lothrop, he started to think about writing his own books for children. Giblin recalled in *SAAS:* "In 1964, after editing J. J. McCoy's career book, *The World of the Veterinarian,* I decided to try writing a similar book about publishing and drafted an outline for it and several sample chapters." Though a publisher expressed some interest in the book, it was decided that its market would be too small. Giblin had ambivalent feelings, as he noted in his autobiographical essay in *Sixth Book of Junior Authors:* "I really wasn't sorry. While part of me wanted to resume my writing career, another part—remembering the *Lie Down in Darkness* experience—hung back from making the necessary commitment to it."

Publishing Career Leads to Own Children's Books

In the late 1960s, Giblin went to work for Seabury Press, and became instrumental in developing its children's division, Clarion Books. In the 1970s, a trip to China inspired him to try a book project of his own again— "an anthology of Chinese writings about the doings of Chinese young people in the years since the Communist Revolution of 1949," as he described it in *SAAS.* But this time the project did not go through because it was considered too political. By then, however, Giblin was writing again—contributing articles about children's books to periodicals, and lecturing at conferences of children's book writers and librarians.

In 1980, Giblin collaborated with Dale Ferguson on his first children's book, *The Scarecrow Book.* Since then, he has—on his own—penned thirteen more works of nonfiction for children, among them *The Skyscraper Book, Walls: Defenses throughout History,* and *The Truth about Unicorns.* In 1989 he decided he was having too much difficulty juggling his role as editor-in-chief of Clarion Books with his expanding career as a writer, so he retired to contributing editor status. Giblin has also written a guide for aspiring authors entitled *Writing Books for Young People.*

The author's children's books are concerned with explaining the historical developments of a variety of subjects. He has considered milk pasteurization, Fourth of July celebrations, and eating utensils among numerous other topics. Book critics have frequently praised Giblin's ability to tell a complex historical tale in simple and understandable terms. Elizabeth S. Watson, in her *Horn Book* review of *The Riddle of the Rosetta Stone: Key to Ancient Egypt,* stated that "the author has done a masterful job of distilling information, citing the highlights, and fitting it all together." *New York Times Book Review* contributor Philip M. Isaacson was likewise pleased with Giblin's work in *Let There be Light,* noting that the author "has condensed a daunting body of material to provide young readers with a great deal of information about the evolution and technology of windows."

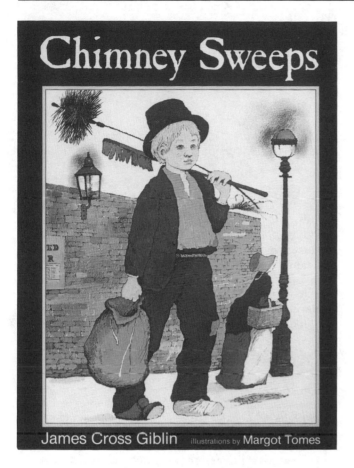

Chimney Sweeps

James Cross Giblin   illustrations by Margot Tomes

The job of the old-fashioned chimney sweep has a rich history, as Giblin describes in this book. (Cover illustration by Tomes.)

Critics have also pointed out that Giblin's accounts, while easy to understand, are loaded with valuable detail. "Giblin's relaxed, affable manner belies the amount of information he offers," wrote Amy L. Cohn in a *School Library Journal* review of *Chimney Sweeps: Yesterday and Today.* This information is derived, critics have noted, from the author's painstaking research. "Giblin has such a flair for historic detail and research that he translates hordes of tales into a singular creation of Santa Claus," proclaimed a *School Library Journal* review of *The Truth about Santa Claus.* An evaluation of the same book in *Bulletin of the Center for Children's Books* also emphasized Giblin's command of his subject, stating that the author had done "his usual good job of research and well-organized presentation."

Giblin has commented on the enjoyment he derives from investigating the factual details of his subjects and how important this task is to his work. "I love research," the author told *Publishers Weekly* interviewer Wendy Smith. "I love going down to Washington on a vacation week and using the Library of Congress. I enjoy making things clear for readers—maybe 'clear' is a unifying word in my work as an author and editor."

■ Works Cited

Cohn, Amy L., review of *Chimney Sweeps: Yesterday and Today, School Library Journal,* January, 1983, p. 75.

Giblin, James Cross, autobiographical sketch in *Sixth Book of Junior Authors,* H. W. Wilson, 1989.

Giblin, James Cross, essay in *Something about the Author Autobiography Series,* Volume 12, Gale, 1991, pp. 83-102.

Isaacson, Philip M., review of *Let There Be Light: A Book about Windows, New York Times Book Review,* March 12, 1989.

Smith, Wendy, "PW Interviews James Giblin," *Publishers Weekly,* July 26, 1985, p. 169.

Review of *The Truth about Santa Claus, Bulletin of the Center for Children's Books,* September, 1985.

Review of *The Truth about Santa Claus, School Library Journal,* October, 1985, p. 192.

Watson, Elizabeth S., review of *The Riddle of the Rosetta Stone: Key to Ancient Egypt, Horn Book,* November/December, 1990, p. 758.

■ For More Information See

BOOKS

Children's Literature Review, Volume 29, Gale, 1993.

PERIODICALS

Bulletin of the Center for Children's Books, October, 1983; February, 1985; November, 1986; December, 1987.

Chicago Tribune Book World, April 11, 1982.

Horn Book, February, 1983, pp. 62-63; January/February, 1989, pp. 33-34.

New York Times Book Review, November 21, 1982, p. 43.

Publishers Weekly, November 15, 1985, p. 56.

School Library Journal, March, 1987, pp. 113-15; October, 1988, pp. 27-31.

Washington Post Book World, November 10, 1991.

*   *   *

GIBSON, Betty 1911-

■ Personal

Born July 14, 1911, in Brandon, Manitoba, Canada; daughter of Jesse (in construction) and Margaret (a dressmaker; maiden name, Calderbank) Gibson. *Education:* University of Manitoba, bachelor of paedagogy, 1958, B.A., 1959, B.Ed., 1959; Harvard University, Ed.M., 1962. *Religion:* Christian (Anglican).

■ Addresses

Home and office—333 Fifteenth St., No. 316, Brandon, Manitoba R7A 6P4, Canada.

■ Career

Elementary school teacher, 1929-35, primary supervisor, 1945-55, and assistant superintendent for kindergarten to fourth grade, 1965-75, all in Brandon, Manitoba, Canada; Kingsmead Girls College, Johannesburg, South Africa, teacher, 1936-44; Brandon University, professor of early childhood education, 1956-65; writer.

■ Writings

A Time for Learning, a Time for Joy, Manitoba Department of Education, 1972.
The Story of Little Quack, illustrated by Kady MacDonald Denton, Kids Can Press (Toronto), 1990.

■ Sidelights

Betty Gibson told *SATA:* "I do not really consider myself an author in spite of the success of *The Story of Little Quack.* My life has centered around teaching and producing material to help teachers. I was also interested in providing stories to encourage reluctant readers.

"After retirement I volunteered at the Betty Gibson School (yes, it was named for me). Kady Denton and I worked to encourage young children to write and illustrate their own stories. Kady and the principal became interested in some of my stories, and Kady encouraged me to send materials to publishers. Kids Can Press bought *The Story of Little Quack* and Kady illustrated it. The illustrations won the Christie Award for best children's book illustration in 1990.

"The publication of the book has given me a great deal of pleasure and brought renewed acquaintance with many former students—particularly those from the education faculty at Brandon University. *A Time for Learning, a Time for Joy* was written on assignment from the Manitoba Department of Education as a sourcebook in early childhood education. It has had a wide circulation and is still in demand, but it is of course just for teachers.

"I wish I had sought publication of some of my stories while I was active in the classroom."

*   *   *

GOROG, Judith (Katharine Allen) 1938-

■ Personal

Born December 16, 1938, in Madison, WI; daughter of Henry Allen (a pilot and electrical engineer) and Harriett Donner (a secretary; maiden name, Teckemeyer) Kelley; married Istvan Gorog (a technology researcher, developer, and manufacturer), November 13, 1965; children: Antonia, Nicole, Christopher. *Education:* Attended San Jose State College (now San Jose State University), 1957-59; University of California, Berkeley, B.A., 1961; Mills College, M.A., 1963. *Politics:* Social Democrat. *Hobbies and other interests:* Cooking,

skiing, hiking, swimming, reading, storytelling, people-watching, sailing, going to open-air markets and hardware stores, theatre, opera, ballet, chamber music, traveling, friends.

■ Addresses

Home—Lancaster, PA. *Agent*—Joanna Cole Literary Agency, 404 Riverside Dr., New York, NY 10025.

■ Career

Writer and editor. Mobil Research and Development, Princeton, NJ, editor, 1965-67; RCA-Astro Electronics, Hightstown, NJ, production editor and writer, 1969-71; free-lance editor and writer, 1971-75. Has worked as a park director, a teaching assistant, and a scanner of bubble chamber film. *Member:* PEN, Authors Guild, Society of Children's Book Writers and Illustrators, Writers Who Love Libraries.

■ Writings

FOR CHILDREN

A Taste for Quiet and Other Disquieting Tales (includes "Critch," "Queen Pig," "A Story about Death," and "Those Three Wishes"), illustrated by Jeanne Titherington, Philomel Books, 1982, published as *When Flesh Begins to Creep,* Gollancz, 1986.
Caught in the Turtle (novel), illustrated by Ruth Sanderson, Philomel Books, 1983.
No Swimming in Dark Pond and Other Chilling Tales (includes "No Swimming in Dark Pond," "Tim the Alien," and "Will"), afterword by Dr. Caroline Bauer, Philomel Books, 1987.
Three Dreams and a Nightmare and Other Tales of the Dark (includes "At the Sign of a Beckoning Finger," "Mall Rat," and "Perfect Solution"), Philomel Books, 1988.
In a Messy, Messy Room and Other Strange Stories (includes "The Angel," "In a Messy, Messy Room," and "Smelly Sneakers"), illustrated by Kimberly Bulcken Root, Philomel Books, 1990.
Winning Scheherazade (novel), Atheneum, 1991.
On Meeting Witches at Wells, Philomel Books, 1991.
Please Do Not Touch, Scholastic, Inc., 1993.
The Sitter's Find, Scholastic, Inc., 1994.
Tiger Lily, illustrated by Floyd Cooper, Philomel Books, 1994.

Work represented in anthologies, including *100 Great Fantasy Short Short Stories,* edited by Isaac Asimov, Terry Carr, and Martin H. Greenberg, Doubleday, 1984; *The Ghost Treasury,* selected by Linda Sonntag, illustrated by Annabel Spenceley, Putnam, 1987; *A Treasury of Spooky Stories,* selected by Jane Olliver, illustrated by Spenceley, Kingfisher, 1992; *Read All About It!,* edited by Jim Trelease, Learning Tree, 1993; and *Don't Give Up the Ghost,* edited by David Gale, Dell, 1993.

JUDITH GOROG

A Taste for Quiet and Other Disquieting Tales has been translated into Spanish as *El gusto por la tranquilidad,* Mondadori, 1990.

■ Work in Progress

Ol' Bones and Other Grave Delights, for Scholastic, Inc., 1995; *Zilla Sasparilla and the Mud Baby,* illustrated by Amanda Harvey, for Candlewick Press, 1995; *Bed and Breakfast and* . . .

■ Sidelights

"Judith Gorog very well may be the Stephen King-type mistress of bump-in-the-night scary stories for the young," Catherine L. Kissling noted in the *Cleveland Plain Dealer.* Gorog, who identified herself as "the only short story writer I know" in an interview for *SATA,* is the author of short story collections and novels for children. Her narratives, often described as fantastical or supernatural, evoke the traditions of oral storytelling and folktales and are filled with the characteristics of often-told, haunting tales. "My point is that I am not writing to write scary stories," Gorog told Leonard S. Marcus in an interview published in *The Lion and the Unicorn: A Critical Journal of Children's Literature.* "I am more interested in the weird and the kooky and the funny and the strange and the 'what if' and the 'maybe.' I might write a story structured like a Grimm's fairytale but I don't write it to scare people. It is scary because we

do fear losing someone we love. We have other equally strong fears that a story can tap."

Gorog told *SATA* that she "was only in Madison, Wisconsin, long enough to be born." Her parents soon moved to Yardley, Pennsylvania, where her father pursued his love of airplanes by attending a pilot training school. When she was four years old, Gorog, her mother, and her two-year-old brother moved to Texas, where they stayed with relatives who owned a hotel. "My mother was ill, and I was pesky, so the family took me across the river to a school run by nuns. Because I could read, they told the nuns I was six, and I began school. I loved the notebook they gave me, with a picture in color on the cover of Roy Rogers, Dale Evans, and their horses. That was the first evidence of a lifelong passion for notebooks and for stationary stores and their contents."

Childhood Reading Stimulates Imagination

Later, when Gorog's mother remarried, the family moved to California. By then, Gorog was a "voracious" reader who "took out the maximum seven books allowed downstairs in the children's room of the San Leandro Public Library, then went upstairs to check out six more from the adult section." She had a club with another girl and told *SATA* that, together, they "did plays and made-up things." In her grammar school, it was a privilege for a sixth-grader to be asked to baby-sit for the younger classes; when Gorog was asked, she would "tell the kindergartners the Greek myths," placing herself "in all the important roles." Aside from reading and storytelling, radio was another of Gorog's addictions. After bedtime, she would stop reading under the covers with a flashlight to listen, in the dark, to the plays her parents heard on the radio in the living room. "Radio is wonderful because your imagination is so much more vivid than even the best television," she remarked.

Gorog's interests in writing and reading were not always encouraged. "In those days, what your parents said was, 'Get your nose out of that book and go outside!' They also said, 'Get your nose out of that book and cut the grass, or weed the garden!' My mother would never permit comic books in the house. I went to read them in the laundry room of my friend's house, where the newspapers were kept before they were given to the paper drive. My friend got mad at me more than once, saying I was no fun because I only came to read her comics." But, Gorog told *SATA,* there were often library books in the house. "My mother read historical novels, and my stepfather once gave me a surprise I have never forgotten. On the coffee table I saw a copy of American playwright Arthur Miller's *Death of a Salesman.* I was struck by the title, but never dared to touch the book. Because my stepfather was a salesman for the yellow pages of the telephone book, I thought that the play had something to do with his work. Knowing that he read that play, which must have been new at the time, gives me a glimpse into him, but [provides] more questions than answers. I am blown away by that."

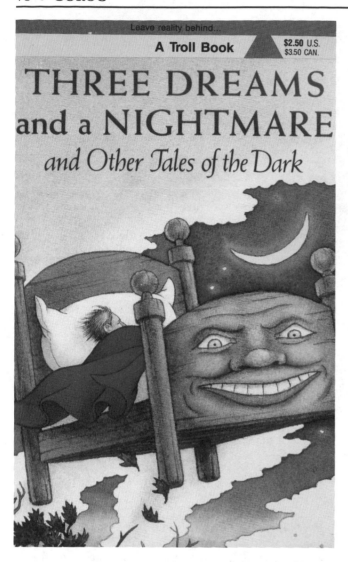

Gorog's stories in this collection combine everyday elements with fantasy to create a world of mystery and suspense.

Gorog also spent some years growing up in Wiesbaden, Germany, after her mother divorced and then married again. Because she moved so often, Gorog was frequently the tall, skinny, new girl in school, an experience she described as "painful." But the new school and life in Wiesbaden were different. "It was an Air Force high school, with mostly military kids who had moved more times than I had, and some civilian kids who had never moved before in their lives. It gave me a certain perspective, and friends. I loved living in Europe. For me, moving there from the suburbs was like dying and going to heaven. I could walk everywhere, along beautiful streets, with gardens, fountains, benches, statues. There were coffee houses, a stable where I took horseback riding lessons. There were theaters, an opera house, a special library for Americans with thousands of books in English. You could walk and look in shop windows. There were cheap bus tours to Paris, Basel, anywhere. I only took a few because I was saving for college, and I was so sure I would be back soon. But it was ten years before I got back to Europe, more than thirty before I got back to Paris. So much for 'soon.'"

Gorog returned to California to attend San Jose State College (now San Jose State University), where she stayed until she transferred to the University of California, Berkeley, two years later in 1959. Times were tough there, according to Gorog. Laughing, she told *SATA:* "We were repressed in those days. Even though I had transferred with an A average in all subjects, my advisor in the English department—the English department!— told me that I should not be there because I was taking the place that a man could occupy. That's my advisor." Nevertheless, Gorog admitted: "If I could choose to be anywhere for the rest of my life, I would be in Berkeley." She added: "In those days I thought academia was an ideal world, that ideas were important and that everyone was kind to one another in a search for truth and beauty." While working as a park director, a teaching assistant, and later as a scanner of bubble chamber film, Gorog continued to write. "I'd always wanted to write and I always thought that whatever other work I did to earn a living, I would write."

After graduating from Berkeley in 1961, and after some indecision about whether or not to join the Peace Corps, Gorog went Mills College, where she hoped to earn an M.A. with a collection of short stories. "That idea hit the wall when the professor who 'taught' fiction thought mine was awful. Professor Franklin Walker, who wrote about the literary history of California, very kindly asked me to be his student. I did a research project on a beautiful writer of not very good poetry and one published short story who died young. She was lovely, and her life was very sad, and I did excellent research and found, and met, a number of people who had known her, including her sister. Her poetry was published after her death, bound in silver birch. I still have the copy I found in a used bookstore."

Family Life Inspires Writing

In 1965 Gorog moved to New Jersey, where she worked as an editor and technical writer. During those years, she told *SATA,* "I was one painfully blocked writer." In 1968, Gorog and her husband moved to Frascati, Italy, where her husband had a fellowship. She kept diaries and did one free-lance editing and writing job, but wrote no fiction. Then, when her first child was born in 1971, her situation changed. "There is nothing for a blocked writer like having a baby. There is NO time to write, and so you do." In 1976, Gorog tried to get a short story, "Critch," published as a picture book. "Editor Ann Beneduce said she liked it and wanted to do it, but the market for picture books, especially by an unknown writer, was nil. She asked if I had more stories, perhaps enough to make a collection. At that, I began to write sometimes two stories a week."

Gorog's newfound productivity proved successful. Her first book of stories, *A Taste for Quiet and Other Disquieting Tales,* was published in 1982. In "Critch," Gorog tells the story of an unusual witch—she wears her shoes on the wrong feet and her clothes inside-out—who has trouble making her spells turn out right. In another tale, "A Story about Death," a mother must trick Death, whom Gorog described in her interview as "a greedy child, an absolutely insatiable and very messy child." Death walks into the kitchen one morning and demands that the mother give up one of her children. The mother outwits and diverts Death with food and clever illusions. Gorog told *SATA:* "There *are* things that come from fears. I wrote that story right after my youngest child was three months old, and ill with pneumonia." Of the resulting story, Gorog said, "When I wrote it, I was afraid I would never write anything better."

A Taste for Quiet has received attention from librarians and storytellers, helped along by word of mouth. "An interesting irony is that one of the most successful stories—the one that keeps getting reprinted and reprinted—I kind of composed that while making the beds," Gorog admitted. "That was 'Those Three Wishes.'" The story recounts the plight of a girl who receives three wishes from a snail whose life she has reluctantly spared. At the end of the brief story, she accidentally wishes for the wrong thing: that she were dead. "In book talks I tell kids that the story's a cheap shot," Gorog said. "You take an existing form, which is simple as 1-2-3. You take a character and you crank her up so that she's loathsome. The only response that an audience ever has is a startled laugh."

Critics Applaud Spooky Tales

A Taste for Quiet garnered solid reviews. *Times Literary Supplement* reviewer Gerald Mangan admired the stories' "authentic folk flavour" and the "nice symbolic weight" of "A Story about Death." In *Science Fiction and Fantasy Book Review,* Diane Parkin-Speer called the book a "fine collection" and noted: "The writing style is deceptively simple, understated with flashes of wry humor, altogether aesthetically satisfying." Kathryn Morton, writing in the *Virginian-Pilot/Ledger-Star,* declared: "What a delightful invention this writer has, what graceful energy, light-handed humor; and all the while underneath, there seem to be cellos weaving sober wisdom."

Gorog's next story collection, *No Swimming in Dark Pond and Other Chilling Tales,* contains the same sort of stories as *A Taste for Quiet.* The main character in "No Swimming in Dark Pond" is a woman whose husband has left her. She becomes independent, but possessive as well. She tries to drive everyone away from Dark Pond, where she lives, by tricking them into believing that a monster lurks in the depths of the water. In "Tim the Alien," young Tim literally turns into an extraterrestrial after eating a box of alien cookies. After his sister sells him to a zoo, Tim finds that the animals don't like living in the zoo but have nowhere else to go. Tim and the animals construct a spaceship in order to make their escape. "Gorog's demons aren't recognizable by their pitchforks and horns," Leonard Marcus explained in *Parenting Magazine.* But they are easily enough encountered, the author implies, in any neighborhood—or even in oneself. Stranger than most children's fiction, her tales cut right to the quick of a child's own reality. "For lovers of the bizarre and unusual, *No Swimming in Dark Pond* is a treasure found," wrote Julia Holmes in the *San Diego Union.* And *Los Angeles Times Book Review* contributor Joan Lowery Nixon stated, "Judith Gorog writes her imaginative, poetic tales with a simplicity that quickly moves each story directly to its startling conclusion." Nixon also noted that several of the stories in *No Swimming in Dark Pond* are "the kind of wonderfully gossipy stories that people love to repeat."

In a Messy, Messy Room and Other Strange Stories, Gorog's fourth short story collection, consists of five tales; the title narrative describes a boy who loves his messy room until night falls. In "Smelly Sneakers," the winner of the annual smelly sneakers contest arrives home to find that the intense odor of his shoes has eaten away his feet. A *Kirkus Reviews* contributor called the author a "remarkably original storyteller," and Molly Kinney, writing in the *School Library Journal,* identified *In a Messy, Messy Room* as an "absurdly wonderful collection.... Full of zany fun, weird and wacky characters and situations, this easily read collection will surely be popular."

Questions of the origin and the end of life and the human race are raised in Gorog's *A Taste for Quiet and Other Disquieting Tales.* (Cover illustration by Jeanne Titherington.)

Gorog's *Winning Scheherazade* is based on the traditional tale of a woman who saves herself from death by her incredible storytelling abilities. (Cover by James A. Ransome.)

Gorog is also the author of the novel *Caught in the Turtle* and the two books *Winning Scheherazade* and *On Meeting Witches at Wells,* both of which she described as "stories set into frames." *Caught in the Turtle* followed the publication of *A Taste for Quiet* by a year; it relates the story of Kate Balazs, who goes with her father on a business trip to California and becomes friends with Piper, who is hiding out from a man she fears. A *School Library Journal* contributor called the novel "very entertaining with extremely likable characters." In *On Meeting Witches at Wells,* graduating eighth-graders make pillows fashioned to give them stories throughout their lives. Though the pillows are made every year, this year there is a certain urgency: the students must not only make pillows for themselves but for all of the grades below them because an ancient spring under the school is taking back the land. As the students sew, apparitions from all times and places relate their stories. In the *School Library Journal,* JoAnn Rees wrote: "Readers encounter in these stories some of Gorog's best work—her buildup of the school's past and the first few tales have a lovely, otherworldly quality."

"As a child, I devoured folktales and fairytales by the yard," Gorog told *SATA.* "As an adult, I have expanded my reading into all sorts of nonfiction, biographies, histories, newspapers, and through my children, MTV, and other places. In my head, I make up worlds. I have a teller's voice, personality, and history in mind as the tale unfolds. Writings offers me a saving grace. What I read, see, hear, and taste often affect me so that I always want to wave things at my family and friends, urging them to read! see! taste! By writing stories, I can structure this input, these playful ideas, these odds and ends; and with luck the stories find readers who are amused, nudged, perhaps affected. I believe artists are the most fortunate people because we require almost nothing, but can give our characters worlds."

■ Works Cited

Review of *Caught in the Turtle, School Library Journal,* December, 1983, p. 82.

Gorog, Judith, telephone interview with Roger M. Valade III for *Something about the Author,* April 22, 1993.

Holmes, Julia, review of *No Swimming in Dark Pond and Other Chilling Tales, San Diego Union,* May 17, 1987.

Review of *In a Messy, Messy Room and Other Strange Stories, Kirkus Reviews,* May 2, 1990.

Kinney, Molly, review of *In a Messy, Messy Room and Other Strange Stories, School Library Journal,* July, 1990, p. 76.

Kissling, Catherine L., review of *In a Messy, Messy Room and Other Strange Stories, Cleveland Plain Dealer,* October 21, 1990.

Mangan, Gerald, review of *When Flesh Begins to Creep* (also known as *A Taste for Quiet and Other Disquieting Tales*), *Times Literary Supplement,* April 11, 1986, p. 390.

Marcus, Leonard, review of *No Swimming in Dark Pond and Other Chilling Tales, Parenting Magazine,* October, 1987.

Marcus, Leonard S., "Night Visions: Conversations with Alvin Schwartz and Judith Gorog," *The Lion and the Unicorn: A Critical Journal of Children's Literature,* June, 1988, pp. 44-62.

Morton, Kathryn, review of *A Taste for Quiet and Other Disquieting Tales, Virginian-Pilot/Ledger-Star,* April 27, 1983.

Nixon, Joan Lowery, review of *No Swimming in Dark Pond and Other Chilling Tales, Los Angeles Times Book Review,* September 27, 1987, p. 9.

Parkin-Speer, Diane, review of *A Taste for Quiet and Other Disquieting Tales, Science Fiction and Fantasy Book Review,* March, 1983.

Rees, JoAnn, review of *On Meeting Witches at Wells, School Library Journal,* January, 1992, p. 109.

■ For More Information See

PERIODICALS

Bulletin of the Center for Children's Books, July-August, 1987.

Kirkus Reviews, December 1, 1982, p. 1295; July 1,
    1988, p. 974; March 15, 1991, p. 392; September
    15, 1991.
School Library Journal, March, 1983, p. 192; March,
    1987, p. 158; November, 1988, p. 125; April, 1991,
    p. 118.

                      —*Sketch by Roger M. Valade III*

                      *   *   *

GURNEY, John Steven 1962-

■ Personal

Born January 11, 1962, in Lancaster, PA; son of Allan
B. (a market research consultant) and Caroline E. (a
hydrologic technician; maiden name, Whiteside) Gurney; married Kathleen Gatto (a dancer and choreogra-
pher), September 20, 1987. *Education:* Received B.F.A.
from Pratt Institute; attended New York Academy of
Fine Art and the Stevenson Academy of Traditional
Painting. *Politics:* Democrat. *Religion:* Catholic.

■ Addresses

Home and office—261 Marlborough Rd., New York,
NY 11226.

■ Career

Illustrator. *Exhibitions:* Work has been exhibited by the
Society of Illustrators, the Society of Publication De-
signers, and numerous galleries in the New York City
metropolitan area. *Member:* Children's Book Illustrators Group (officer).

■ Illustrator

William F. Buckley, Jr., *The Temptation of Wilfred
    Malachy,* Workman Publishing, 1985.
(Contributor) *The Classic Mother Goose,* Running Press,
    1987.
Dan Elish, *The Worldwide Dessert Contest,* Orchard
    Books, 1988.
(Co-illustrator) Della Rowland, *A World of Cats,* Con-
    temporary Books, 1989.
Clement Clarke Moore, *The Night before Christmas,*
    Scholastic, Inc., 1989.
Debbie Dadey and Marcia Jones, *Vampires Don't Wear
    Polka Dots,* Scholastic, Inc., 1990.
(Contributor) *The Classic Treasury of Children's Poetry,*
    Running Press, 1990.
Dayle Ann Dodds, *On Our Way to Market,* Simon &
    Schuster, 1991.
Brothers Grimm, *Hansel and Gretel,* Andrews &
    McMeel, 1991.
Dadey and Jones, *Werewolves Don't Go to Summer
    Camp,* Scholastic, Inc., 1991.
Dadey and Jones, *Santa Claus Doesn't Mop Floors,*
    Scholastic, Inc., 1991.
Lydia Maria Child, *Over the River and through the
    Woods,* Scholastic, Inc., 1992.

JOHN STEVEN GURNEY

The Jumbaroo, Wright Group, 1992.

Also illustrator of "Kermit Tales" series of story cards,
Jim Henson Productions, 1989-91; and of book covers
for Ace, Berkley, Atheneum, Pocket Books, and Orchard
Books. Illustrator for magazines, advertisements, greeting cards, and puzzles.

■ Sidelights

John Steven Gurney told *SATA:* "I grew up in Bucks
County, Pennsylvania, where my earliest artistic influences were the animated films of Walt Disney, *Mad*
magazine and, much later, N. C. Wyeth. When I was ten
years old I attended a class where the students created
illustrations while listening to selected stories read by
the teacher, artist Jean Burford. I knew then that I
wanted to be an illustrator.

"During high school I pursued interests in wrestling,
saxophone, and tennis while attending Saturday classes
at the Philadelphia College of Art. I also had the
privilege of studying with and working for the renowned
illustrator William A. Smith during this period.

"I received a partial scholarship to study illustration a
Pratt Institute, and was named Outstanding Senior
upon graduating. During the summers I helped to fund
my education by doing caricatures on the Atlantic City
boardwalk. After college I spent several months hitchhiking through Europe to experience the various cultures and artistic traditions.

Things keep going wrong on a trip to the market in the rhymed tale *On Our Way to Market*, written by Dayle Ann Dodds and illustrated by Gurney.

"While at Pratt I won a national poster contest for Molson's Golden Ale, and my illustration ran as an advertisement in *Rolling Stone* magazine. The exposure led to my first illustrated children's book, *The Temptation of Wilfred Malachy*, written by the noted columnist William F. Buckley, Jr.

"Since then I have illustrated many children's books, and for me the preparation is as important as the painting. I took photographs from precarious rooftop heights to obtain interesting 'flying reindeer' angles for *The Night before Christmas*. I revisited my rural childhood surroundings for *On Our Way to Market*. Recently, I had to track down a one-horse open sleigh to pose models for *Over the River and through the Woods*."

*   *   *

GWYNNE, Fred(erick Hubbard) 1926-1993

OBITUARY NOTICE—See index for *SATA* sketch: Born July 10, 1926, in New York, NY; died of complica-

tions of pancreatic cancer, July 2, 1993, in Taneytown, MD. Actor, author, illustrator, and copywriter. After serving with the U.S. Navy during World War II and graduating from Harvard University, Gwynne played Stinker in the 1952 Broadway production of *Mrs. McThing,* which starred noted American actress Helen Hayes. After a stint as a copywriter with the advertising firm of J. Walter Thompson, Gwynne returned to the stage, resuming a nearly forty-year career during which he showed his versatility in wide-ranging roles on stage, television, and screen. In the theatre, Gwynne earned recognition for his portrayals of such characters as Big Daddy in Tennessee Williams's *Cat on a Hot Tin Roof,* which he counted among his favorite roles, and Claudius in William Shakespeare's *Hamlet.* In 1979, he won an Obie Award for his performance in *Grand Magic.* After making his film debut in 1954 as Slim in *On the Waterfront,* Gwynne also acted in numerous motion pictures, including *The Cotton Club* and *My Cousin Vinny,* where he played a mob member and a judge respectively. He was most widely known, however, for his roles in two 1960s television series. From 1961 to 1963 he played Officer Francis Muldoon, half of a mismatched team of policemen on *Car 54, Where Are You?* He later became Herman Munster, a Frankenstein look-alike and a star of *The Munsters,* a popular situation comedy which featured a ghoulish family as they try to adapt to suburban life. After his acting career peaked, Gwynne wrote several well-received books for children, including *Ick's ABC's,* which combines lessons about the alphabet with information on environmental stewardship, *A Little Pigeon Toad* in 1988, and *Easy to See Why,* a book set for publication at the time of his death. He also illustrated both his own work and books by other authors.

OBITUARIES AND OTHER SOURCES:

BOOKS

Who's Who in America, 46th edition, Marquis, 1990.

PERIODICALS

Chicago Tribune, July 4, 1993, sec. 2, p. 7.
Los Angeles Times, July 3, 1993, p. A30.
New York Times, July 3, 1993, p. 8.
Times (London), July 5, 1993, p. 17.
Washington Post, July 3, 1993, p. B6.

H

HAGON, Priscilla
See ALLAN, Mabel Esther

* * *

HAYWOOD, Carolyn 1898-1990

■ Personal

Born January 3, 1898, in Philadelphia, PA; died of a stroke January 11, 1990, in Philadelphia, PA; daughter of Charles and Mary Emma (Cook) Haywood. *Education:* Graduated from the Philadelphia Normal School for Girls; attended Pennsylvania Academy of the Fine Arts.

■ Career

Writer, illustrator, portrait and mural painter. Teacher at Friends Central School, Philadelphia, PA; assistant in studio of Violet Oakley. *Member:* Pennsylvania Academy of the Fine Arts (fellow), Philadelphia Water Color Club.

■ Awards, Honors

Boys' Clubs of America Junior Book Award, 1956, for *Eddie and His Big Deals;* named Distinguished Daughter of Pennsylvania, by governor, 1967; Utah Children's Book Award, 1981.

■ Writings

"BETSY" SERIES; SELF-ILLUSTRATED, EXCEPT WHERE INDICATED

"B" Is for Betsy, Harcourt, 1939.
Betsy and Billy, Harcourt, 1941.
Back to School with Betsy, Harcourt, 1943.
Betsy and the Boys, Harcourt, 1945.
Betsy's Little Star, Morrow, 1950.
Betsy and the Circus, Morrow, 1954.
Betsy's Busy Summer, Morrow, 1956.
Betsy's Winterhouse, Morrow, 1958.
Snowbound with Betsy, Morrow, 1962.

CAROLYN HAYWOOD

Betsy and Mr. Kilpatrick, Morrow, 1967.
Merry Christmas from Betsy, Morrow, 1970.
Betsy's Play School, illustrated by James Griffin, Morrow, 1977.

"EDDIE" SERIES; SELF-ILLUSTRATED, EXCEPT WHERE INDICATED

Little Eddie, Morrow, 1947.
Eddie and the Fire Engine, Morrow, 1949.
Eddie and Gardenia, Morrow, 1951.
Eddie's Pay Dirt, Morrow, 1953.
Eddie and His Big Deals, Morrow, 1955.
Eddie Makes Music, Morrow, 1957.
Eddie and Louella, Morrow, 1959.
Annie Pat and Eddie, Morrow, 1960.
Eddie's Green Thumb, Morrow, 1964.
Eddie, the Dog Holder, Morrow, 1966.
Ever-Ready Eddie, Morrow, 1968.
Eddie's Happenings, Morrow, 1971.

Eddie's Valuable Property, Morrow, 1975.
Eddie's Menagerie, illustrated by Ingrid Fetz, Morrow, 1978.

JUVENILE; SELF-ILLUSTRATED

Two and Two Are Four, Harcourt, 1940.
Primrose Day, Harcourt, 1942.
Here's a Penny, Harcourt, 1944.
Penny and Peter, Harcourt, 1946.
Penny Goes to Camp, Morrow, 1948.
The Mixed-Up Twins, Morrow, 1952.
Here Comes the Bus, Morrow, 1963.
Robert Rows the River, Morrow, 1965.
Taffy and Melissa Molasses, Morrow, 1969.
Away Went the Balloons, Morrow, 1973.
"C" Is for Cupcake, Morrow, 1974.

JUVENILE

A Christmas Fantasy, illustrated by Glenys and Victor Ambrus, Morrow, 1972.
A Valentine Fantasy, illustrated by G. and V. Ambrus, Morrow, 1976.
The King's Monster, illustrated by V. Ambrus, Morrow, 1980.

Eddie competes with his new neighbor to collect the most and the best items in this humorous story by Haywood. (Cover illustration by Deborah Chabrian.)

Halloween Treats, illustrated by Victoria de Larrea, Morrow, 1981.
Santa Claus Forever, illustrated by G. and V. Ambrus, Morrow, 1982.
Make a Joyful Noise: Bible Verses for Children, illustrated by Lane Yerkes, Westminster, 1983.
Happy Birthday from Carolyn Haywood, illustrated by Wendy Watson, Morrow, 1984.
Summer Fun, illustrated by Julie Durrell, Morrow, 1986.
Hello, Star, illustrated by Durrell, Morrow, 1987.

Also illustrator and calligrapher of *Book of Honor,* a collection of the biographies of Pennsylvania women. Contributor to *Jack and Jill.*

Haywood's books have been translated into Norwegian, French, German, and Japanese. Her works are housed in the Kerlan Collection at the University of Minnesota, the de Grummond Collection at the University of Southern Mississippi, the Pennsylvania Academy of Fine Arts, and the Philadelphia Free Library.

■ **Adaptations**

Santa Claus Forever (audiocassette), Random House, 1985.

■ **Sidelights**

Carolyn Haywood wrote children's books for almost half a century, illustrating most of them herself. She is best remembered for her characters Betsy and Eddie, average children who have adventures which are not out of the reach of most of their loyal fans, who range in age from five to eleven. In addition to these famous works, Haywood created popular holiday stories including *A Valentine Fantasy, Halloween Treats,* and *Santa Claus Forever,* and published adaptations such as *Make a Joyful Noise: Bible Verses for Children.* She also contributed stories to the popular children's magazine *Jack and Jill.*

Haywood was born January 3, 1898, in Philadelphia, Pennsylvania. She liked art from an early age, and spent most of her time as a child drawing and painting, determined to become an artist when she reached adulthood. After graduating from the Philadelphia Normal School for Girls, however, she taught in a private institution—Friends Central School in Philadelphia—for a year before enrolling at the Pennsylvania Academy of the Fine Arts. Haywood studied under artists such as Elizabeth Shippen Elliott and Jessie Wilcox Smith, themselves the students of famed American illustrator Howard Pyle. Also during her years at the academy she was a studio assistant to mural artist Violet Oakley, another protege of Pyle's. In addition, Haywood was awarded the Cresson European Scholarship and thus was able to study art in Europe for a time.

Haywood's work with Oakley influenced her to paint murals as well; she did some for local Philadelphia banks and one for a public school. But she is best known

"B" IS FOR Betsy

Carolyn Haywood

In this first book in the popular "Betsy" series, Betsy finds many things to like about her first days at school—including her new friends. (Cover illustration by Joe Yakovetic.)

for her self-illustrated children's books. As Haywood recalled for Lee Bennett Hopkins in *More Books by More People:* "I came to write my first book when I showed some illustrations to Elizabeth Hamilton, who was at that time editor of children's books at Harcourt, Brace, Jovanovich. She suggested that I write a story and I wrote *'B' Is for Betsy.*" Thus one of Haywood's most popular characters made her debut when the title was published in 1939. *"B" Is for Betsy* follows the adventures of the six-year-old title character during her first year of school and describes such episodes as a visit to a farm and a trip to the circus. The Betsy books continued with titles such as *Back to School with Betsy, Betsy's Little Star,* and *Betsy's Play School.* Haywood followed Hamilton, her editor, when she moved to the Morrow publishing company from Harcourt.

Everyday Children Populate Haywood's Books

In 1947, Haywood published *Little Eddie,* the first book in her series about seven-year-old Eddie Wilson. In the work, Eddie attempts to join a baseball team, find homes for some stray cats, and get elected president of the United States, often with humorous results. Hay-

wood followed that work with efforts like *Eddie and the Fire Engine, Eddie and Louella, Eddie, the Dog Holder,* and *Eddie's Menagerie.* The success of both of Haywood's major characters has been attributed by critics to their ordinariness—they are characters that the majority of children can relate to, dealing with problems that the readers might have themselves, though the problems are complex enough to give the stories a great deal of interesting action. Anne Pellowski, writing in *Horn Book,* judged that Haywood's stories "depict the little ups and downs of everyday life with such good humor and interest that the reader is convinced there is nothing more delightful than being between six and nine and growing up."

Betsy and Eddie also show up in other Haywood books. Her 1986 book *Summer Fun* involves not only new characters but Betsy and Eddie as well, in addition to some of her other creations, including Annie Pat. But it was an Eddie book, *Eddie and His Big Deals,* which garnered Haywood one of her most prestigious prizes—the Boys' Clubs of America Junior Book Award in 1956. Haywood was also named a Distinguished Daughter of Pennsylvania by that state's governor in 1967 and won the Utah Children's Book Award in 1981, for her body of work.

During the 1970s, Haywood stopped illustrating her own books and let other artists, such as Glenys and Victor Ambrus, decorate her works. One of these works, *Santa Claus Forever,* especially met with critical acclaim. In this seasonal tale, Santa Claus becomes disenchanted with his job after a series of freak accidents—a chimney brick falls and hits him, his suit gets singed in someone's fireplace, etc. But when he sees the man who proposes to replace him and hears his dubious plans for improvement, Santa changes his mind about retiring. As a reviewer for *Bulletin of the Center for Children's Books* put it, "the humor and sentiment of pictures and story, and the happy solution to a problem should make this Christmas tale a great favorite with the read-aloud audience."

Haywood also published work for adults; notably *Book of Honor,* a collection of biographies of famous women from Pennsylvania, for which she provided illustrations and calligraphy. She died on January 11, 1990, after publishing her last children's book, *Hello, Star,* in 1987. Critics cite Haywood's talent for capturing the everyday events of childhood as the reason for her enduring popularity. In particular, Pellowski praised the author's "uncanny ability in observing children and somehow in getting their speech, their actions, and their interactions expressed in a simple, natural style."

■ Works Cited

Hopkins, Lee Bennett, *More Books by More People,* Citation, 1974.

Pellowski, Anne, "Dick and Jane Invade the Third World," *Horn Book,* April, 1973, pp. 113-118.

Review of *Santa Claus Forever, Bulletin of the Center for Children's Books,* October, 1983.

For More Information See

BOOKS

Children's Literature Review, Volume 22, 1991.

OBITUARIES:

PERIODICALS

New York Times, January 12, 1990.
Washington Post, January 15, 1990.*

*   *   *

HENRY, Maeve 1960-

Personal

Born November 16, 1960, in Dublin, Ireland; daughter of Eamonn (an economist) and Denise (a teacher; maiden name Kirk) Henry; married John Fernandes (a computer operator), June 16, 1990; children: Emily Rachel. *Education:* Oxford University, B.A., 1983. *Religion:* Russian Orthodox.

Addresses

Agent—Felicity Bryan, 2A North Parade, Oxford, OX2 6PE, England.

Career

Oxford Intensive School of English, Oxford, England, English and foreign language teacher, 1987—.

Awards, Honors

Observer/Goldenlay poetry competition prize, 1976, for "The Golden Egg."

Writings

The Witch King, Orchard Books, 1987.
A Gift for a Gift, Heinemann, 1990.
Listen to the Dark, Heinemann, 1993.

Work in Progress

Dancing with Velsford, a young adult novel, for Heinemann, to be finished in 1993.

Sidelights

Maeve Henry told *SATA:* "I have written poetry for pleasure since I was nine or ten years old and started (and abandoned!) my first novel in the long summer holidays when I was eleven. Since then I have been writing around the edges of full-time education, and chose a job that would allow me time in the winter months to write. It's a necessary obsession; Rilke said 'if you don't *have* to write—don't.'

"There are two main strands to my writing, family relationships and what may lie behind the physical

MAEVE HENRY

nature of the world. None of my writing, except a novel now in progress, has been directly autobiographical. Often a book starts with a picture in my head; I need to fill in the before and after. Once it started from a situation my sister was describing to me. I felt an extraordinary inner shift, which meant the beginning of a book. The biggest influence on my writing is probably my mother, who taught me to look at relationships with clarity as well as charity. The context of my fiction is Russian Orthodox, although so far this has never been an explicit part of any book."

■ For More Information See

PERIODICALS

Bulletin of the Center for Children's Books, June, 1988.

*   *   *

HILLMAN, Elizabeth 1942-

■ Personal

Born March 21, 1942, in Worcestershire, England; married Stuart Hillman, May 25, 1963 (divorced October, 1992). *Education:* San Diego State University, B.A. (with high honors), 1972. *Hobbies and other interests:* Reading, studying Portuguese and international folklore.

■ Addresses

Home—41 Love Lane, Oldswinford, Stourbridge, West Midlands DY8 2DH, England.

■ Career

San Diego State University Library, San Diego, CA, clerk, 1970-74; National Steel and Shipbuilding Co., CA, engineering aide, 1975-80. *Member:* Phi Kappa Phi.

■ Writings

Tudo Bem! (Haiku chapbook), Pereira Press (Brazil), 1989.
Apitos Da Brisa (Haiku chapbook), Pereira Press, 1989.
Min-Yo and the Moon Dragon, illustrated by John Wallner, Harcourt, 1992.

■ Work in Progress

Breeze Whistles, a collection of poems; *Saquarema Stories,* "strange tales of a small town in Brazil"; a new children's book, involving extensive research in South American folklore and geography.

■ Sidelights

Elizabeth Hillman told *SATA:* "I wrote my first poem at the age of six and a half, and when we began writing compositions at school a few months later, I knew that I was going to be a writer. Later, of course, I was scared that it was just wishful thinking, but fortunately, many small press editors (bless them) accepted about 300 of my poems, and quite large magazines bought articles and short stories. Harcourt Brace Jovanovich accepted *Min-Yo and the Moon Dragon,* my first children's book, and I was extremely fortunate in having John Wallner illustrate it with his wonderful rich and lively paintings.

"I've tried just about every type of writing, from limericks and rhyming children's stories to haiku and fantasy poems, from inspirational stories in women's magazines and esoteric horror tales to articles on the history of everyday items and unusual recipe ideas from overseas. In order of importance, my reasons for writing are because I enjoy being drunk with words, juggling them to make new patterns, and whenever I discover an interesting thing, I have a great wish to share with everyone else. I'm still bewitched by the alchemy of literature—that I can make cryptic little black marks on a piece of paper, and others can scan those marks and an imaginary world springs to being in their minds; it has to be a kind of magic.

"My ex-husband Stuart and I were fortunate in being able to travel a good deal; from England, we moved to Canada for a year, and because of the harsh winter, we quickly moved to southern California, where we lived for fourteen years. Stuart was then employed by the State Department, and we were posted to Panama. I had long wanted to write a novel set in Brazil, and had researched the subject for about ten years, and I had hoped that someday we would visit Brazil; as it happened, a sudden vacancy came up at the Consulate in Rio de Janeiro, and we had the great joy of living there for three years. I was able to explore the capital cities of Argentina, Paraguay, Uruguay, Chile, Bolivia, and Venezuela, as well as a good many parts of Brazil, including the obligatory Amazon excursion, which was fascinating. Seeing for myself how the ordinary people live, talking to them, and hearing their folklore first-hand has given me a lifetime of ideas to write about. I suppose that is the basis of my writing method, and what I would advise to all writers: constant observation of people, places, sensations, even the smallest details, and absorbing them into your own mind."

*   *   *

HITE, Sid 1954-

■ Personal

Born April 12, 1954, in Richmond, VA. *Education:* Attended a community college for one year.

■ Addresses

Home—Sag Harbor, NY.

■ Career

Writer; has also worked in various odd jobs.

ELIZABETH HILLMAN

■ Writings

Dither Farm, Holt, 1992.

■ Work in Progress

A novel.

■ Sidelights

"I grew up outside of the small, country town of Bowling Green, Virginia," Sid Hite told *SATA.* "A stoplight went up at the main intersection when I was sixteen. Most of my childhood was spent outdoors—either playing baseball, basketball and football, or exploring the vast stretches of woods that still exist in Caroline County.

"Instead of pursuing a formal education, I traveled extensively after leaving high school, managing to step foot in twenty countries by the time I was twenty-one. I fell in love with novels in my late teens, and decided then I wanted to write one myself."

* * *

HODGES, Margaret Moore 1911-

■ Personal

Born Sarah Margaret Moore, July 26, 1911, in Indianapolis, IN; daughter of Arthur Carlisle (in business) and Anna Marie (Mason) Moore; married Fletcher Hodges, Jr. (a museum curator), September 10, 1932; children: Fletcher, Arthur Carlisle, John Andrews. *Education:* Vassar College, A.B. (with honors), 1932; Carnegie Institute of Technology (now Carnegie-Mellon University), M.L.S., 1958. *Politics:* Republican. *Religion:* Episcopalian. *Hobbies and other interests:* Traveling, reading, folklore, and gardening.

■ Addresses

Home—5812 Kentucky Ave., Pittsburgh, PA 15232. *Office*—University of Pittsburgh, Library and Information Science Building, Bellefield Ave., Pittsburgh, PA 15260.

■ Career

Carnegie Library of Pittsburgh, Pittsburgh, PA, special assistant and children's librarian, 1953-64; Pittsburgh Public Schools, story specialist in compensatory education department, 1964-68; University of Pittsburgh, Graduate School of Library and Information Science, lecturer, 1964-68, assistant professor, 1968-72, associate professor, 1972-75, professor 1975-77, professor emeritus, 1978—. Storyteller on program "Tell Me a Story," WQED-TV, 1965-76. *Member:* American Library Association (member of Newbery-Caldecott committee, 1960), Pennsylvania Library Association, Distinguished Daughters of Pennsylvania (elected, 1970), Pittsburgh Bibliophiles, Pittsburgh Vassar Club, Zonta International.

■ Awards, Honors

Carnegie Library staff scholarship, 1956-58; American Library Association Notable Book citation, *New York Times* ten best picture books of the year award, both 1964, runner-up for Caldecott Award, and Silver Medal, Bienal (Brazil), both 1965, all for *The Wave; Lady Queen Anne: A Biography of Queen Anne of England* was selected as best book for young adults by an Indiana author, 1970; *The Making of Joshua Cobb* was selected as a *New York Times* outstanding juvenile book, 1971; American Library Association Notable Book citation, 1972, for *The Fire Bringer: A Paiute Indian Legend;* John G. Bowman Memorial grant, 1974; Distinguished Alumna, Carnegie Library School and Graduate School of Library and Information Science, 1976; Outstanding Pennsylvania Children's Author award, Pennsylvania School Librarians Association, 1977; Daughter of Mark Twain Award, 1980; *New York Times* Best Illustrated Children's Book Award, 1984, Carolyn W. Field Award for best children's book by a Pennsylvania author, *Horn Book* Honor Book Award, and Caldecott Award, all 1985, all for *Saint George and the Dragon: A Golden Legend;* "Margaret Hodges Day" citation from University of Pittsburgh School of Library and Information Science, 1985; Keystone State Reading Award, 1985; Margaret Hodges scholarship established, 1989; American Library Association Best Books for Young Adults citation, 1989, for *Making a Difference: The Story of an American Family;* Notable Children's Trade Book citation, National Council for Social Studies and Children's Book Council, 1989, for *The Arrow and the Lamp: The Story of Psyche;* Parents' Choice Honor for Story Books, and Children's Book Council award, both 1990, for *Buried Moon;* American Library Association Notable Books List, 1991, for *St. Jerome and the Lion;* Park Tudor [Tudor Hall] Distinguished Alumna Award, 1992.

■ Writings

FICTION

One Little Drum, illustrated by Paul Galdone, Follett, 1958.

What's for Lunch, Charley?, illustrated by Aliki, Dial, 1961.

A Club against Keats, illustrated by Rick Schreiter, Dial, 1962.

The Secret in the Woods, illustrated by Judith Brown, Dial, 1963.

The Hatching of Joshua Cobb, illustrated by W. T. Mars, Farrar, Straus, 1968.

Sing Out, Charley!, illustrated by Velma Ilsley, Farrar, Straus, 1968.

The Making of Joshua Cobb, illustrated by W. T. Mars, Farrar, Straus, 1971.

The Freewheeling of Joshua Cobb, illustrated by Pamela Johnson, Farrar, Straus, 1974.

The High Riders, Scribner, 1980.

The Avenger, Scribner, 1982.

MARGARET MOORE HODGES

NONFICTION

Lady Queen Anne: A Biography of Queen Anne of England (Junior Literary Guild selection), illustrated with photographs, Farrar, Straus, 1968.

Hopkins of the Mayflower: Portrait of a Dissenter, Farrar, Straus, 1972.

Knight Prisoner: The Tale of Sir Thomas Malory and His King Arthur, decorations by Don Bolognese and Elaine Raphael, Farrar, Straus, 1976.

Making a Difference: The Story of an American Family, illustrated with photographs, Scribner, 1989.

RETELLINGS

The Wave (adapted from Lafcadio Hearn's *Gleanings in Buddha Fields*), illustrated by Blair Lent, Houghton, 1964.

The Gorgon's Head: A Myth from the Isles of Greece, illustrated by Charles Mikolaycak, Little, Brown, 1972.

The Fire Bringer: A Paiute Indian Legend, illustrated by Peter Parnall, Little, Brown, 1972.

Persephone and the Springtime: A Greek Myth, illustrated by Arvis Stewart, Little, Brown, 1973.

The Other World: Myths of the Celts, illustrated by Eros Keith, Farrar, Straus, 1973.

Baldur and the Mistletoe: A Myth of the Vikings, illustrated by Gerry Hoover, Little, Brown, 1974.

The Little Humpbacked Horse: A Russian Tale (adapted from a translation by Gina Kovarsky of a poem by Peter Pavlovich Yershov), illustrated by Chris Conover, Farrar, Straus, 1980.

Saint George and the Dragon: A Golden Legend (adapted from Edmund Spenser's *Faerie Queen*), illustrated by Trina Schart Hyman, Little, Brown, 1984.

If You Had a Horse: Steeds of Myth and Legend, illustrated by D. Benjamin Van Steenburgh, Scribner, 1984.

The Voice of the Great Bell (adapted from Lafcadio Hearn's *Some Chinese Ghosts*), illustrated by Ed Young, Little, Brown, 1989.

The Arrow and the Lamp: The Story of Psyche, illustrated by Donna Diamond, Little, Brown, 1989.

Buried Moon, illustrated by Jamichael Henterly, Little, Brown, 1990.

The Kitchen Knight: A Tale of King Arthur, illustrated by Trina Schart Hyman, Holiday House, 1990.

St. Jerome and the Lion, illustrated by Barry Moser, Orchard Books, 1991.

Hauntings: Ghosts and Ghouls from around the World, illustrated by David Wenzel, Little, Brown, 1991.

Brother Francis and the Friendly Beasts, illustrated by Ted Lewin, Scribner, 1991.

The Golden Deer, illustrated by Daniel San Souci, Scribner, 1992.

Don Quixote and Sancho Panza, illustrated by Stephen Marchesi, Scribner, 1992.

Of Swords and Sorcerers, Adventures of King Arthur and His Knights, illustrated by David Frampton, Scribner, 1992.

Saint Patrick and the Peddler, illustrated by Paul Brett Johnson, Orchard, 1993.

The Hero of Bremen, illustrated by Charles Mikolaychak, Holiday House, 1993.

EDITOR

Kathleen Monypenny, *The Young Traveler in Australia,* Dutton, 1954.

H. M. Harrop, *The Young Traveler in New Zealand,* Dutton, 1954.

Lucile Iremonger, *The Young Traveler in the West Indies,* Dutton, 1955.

Geoffrey Trease, *The Young Traveler in Greece,* Dutton, 1956.

(With others) *Stories to Tell to Children,* Carnegie Library of Pittsburgh, 1960.

Tell It Again: Great Tales from around the World, illustrated by Joan Berg, Dial, 1963.

Constellation: A Shakespeare Anthology, Farrar, Straus, 1968.

(With Susan Steinfirst) Elva S. Smith, *The History of Children's Literature: A Syllabus with Selected Bibliographies,* 2nd edition, American Library Association, 1980.

OTHER

Also author of radio scripts; contributor to journals.

Collections of Hodges's works are housed in the Kerlan Collection at the University of Minnesota, in the de Grummond Collection at the University of Southern Mississippi, and in the Elizabeth Nesbitt Room at the University of Pittsburgh.

■ Sidelights

Award-winning writer, storyteller, and children's librarian Margaret Moore Hodges sees herself not as a creator "but rather as a sort of midwife, simply bringing out life that already existed in itself," she remarked in her essay in *Something about the Author Autobiography Series* (*SAAS*). She also once described her writing as falling into several types: "real life stories based on the adventures and misadventures of my three sons, the retelling of folk tales and myths in picture book format, and biography written to bring to life a few little-known or disregarded characters who contributed in an important way to history." However she might describe her work, it has earned her regional and national honors.

Stories and books were an important part of Hodges's early years. When her mother died six months after the

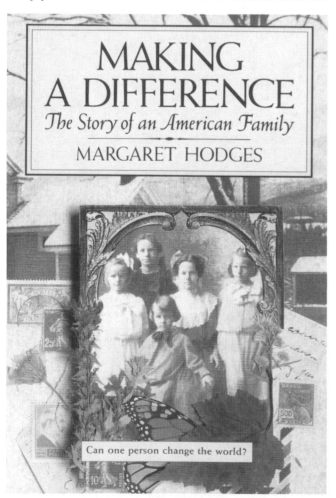

Hodges relates the way one woman overcame her poverty to raise five children who each became successful and important Americans. (Cover illustration by Viqui Maggio.)

author's birth, Hodges's father brought an older cousin, Margaret Carlisle, into the household to take care of the family, which included Hodges, her brother John, her father, and her paternal grandfather. Hodges heard "superb storytelling" at Sunday school, and both her cousin Margaret and her father gave her books and read to her. Robert Louis Stevenson's poems, Beatrix Potter's *Tale of Peter Rabbit*, and George Macdonald's *The Princess and the Goblin* and its sequel, *The Princess and Curdie*, were early loves. Lewis Carroll, Rudyard Kipling, and Charles Dickens followed. Long poems such as Kipling's "The Ballad of East and West" and Browning's "The Pied Piper of Hamelin," learned during this period, became useful for Hodges later in storytelling programs for children.

Hodges began writing at an early age, producing her first work at public school Number 60 in Indianapolis—a paragraph titled "Miss Matty's Library" that was published in the school magazine. Around the same time she sent a poem to *St. Nicholas*, a children's magazine that encouraged contributions from its readers and awarded them with silver and gold badges. Later at Vassar College, she majored in English and took an active part in theater, studying the Stanislavsky method of acting developed at the Moscow Art Theatre. This method, which relies largely on the actor's establishing empathy with the character being portrayed, was also to help her in her storytelling.

Children Provide Material for First Books

Hodges graduated from Vassar and married Fletcher Hodges, Jr., in 1932. The couple moved to Pittsburgh in 1937, where they have lived since; they have three sons. Before their children went off to school, Hodges had, as a volunteer, written scripts for a radio program called "The Children's Bookshelf." In 1953, at the request of the Carnegie Library of Pittsburgh's Boys and Girls Department, she took a paid job as radio storyteller for the library's "Let's Tell a Story," which later became WQED-TV's "Tell Me a Story." Working in the Boys and Girls Room was part of the inspiration for her first book, *One Little Drum*, which was based on the real-life adventures of her children, as were several of the books that followed.

One of Hodges's early works, *The Hatching of Joshua Cobb*, tells of the adventures of a ten year old boy at camp, away from home for the first time. Within a two week period, his fears and worries fade away as he makes friends, learns to swim, and enjoys camp life. Jean C. Thomson, writing in the *Library Journal*, notes that Hodges "handles her small charge well, good-naturedly detailing the ... metamorphosis." And a reviewer in the *Bulletin of the Center for Children's Books* calls *The Hatching of Joshua Cobb* "pleasantly low-keyed and smoothly written."

Joshua Cobb continues his adventures in *The Making of Joshua Cobb*, which follows him into the Fifth Form at boarding school. "Hatched" from his shell at camp, Josh is now trying to discover himself and voice his independence. His self-confidence gradually grows; by the end of the year, he is elected class president. "A skillful handling of a school situation," declares a reviewer in *Horn Book.* Another critic in *Publishers Weekly* praises the "believable characters" and "relaxed and natural atmosphere" in Hodges's book. *Library Journal* contributor Sandra Scheraga concludes that *The Making of Joshua Cobb* is "an enjoyable, non-offensive pleasantry."

The final book in the trilogy, *The Freewheeling of Joshua Cobb,* takes Josh on a summer vacation bike trip with his former camp counselor, Dusty, and a group of friends. The only outsider in the group is a last minute substitute, a girl named Cassandra who insists her name is "Crane" and eats health food. By the end of the trip, the group has accepted her as a friend. While *Library Journal* contributor Scheraga calls *The Freewheeling of Joshua Cobb* "a colorless paean to bicycling and hosteling," other critics were more enthusiastic. A reviewer in *Horn Book* notes the "fresh background" of the story, and praises Hodges's talent in knowingly portraying the "personality changes" of the characters. Another reviewer concludes in the *Bulletin of the Center for Children's Books:* "The writing style has vitality, the characters individuality."

Works Reflect Interest in History and Folktales

Hodges turns to the distant past for inspiration in preparing the volume *Lady Queen Anne: A Biography of Queen Anne of England.* "In spite of my long-held prejudice against history," she wrote in *SAAS,* she found the historical research "pure delight." In this factual story of Queen Anne's life, Hodges not only covers the monarch's friends, family, marriage, and children, but the time period as well, including politics, dress, literature, food, and social customs. A *Publishers Weekly* reviewer uses the terms "worthwhile" and "interesting" in describing *Lady Queen Anne.* And Nathan Berkowitz in the *Library Journal* praises Hodges's work as a "broad, thorough treatment" of the monarch's life, and a "good introduction to the lives and era of the later Stuarts."

In *Knight Prisoner: The Tale of Sir Thomas Malory and His King Arthur,* Hodges focuses on the widely known fifteenth-century English translator of Arthurian legend. While there is little information actually available about Thomas Malory, the author of *Morte d'Arthur,* Hodges "makes the most of the ascertainable facts and speculations," notes a reviewer in *Horn Book.* Told in flashbacks, the book presents Malory recalling episodes of his life and his experiences with some of the most famous people of the time, including Joan of Arc, King Henry V, and King Edward IV. While a reviewer in the *Bulletin of the Center for Children's Books* remarks that the multitude of historical and literary detail may "prove too difficult" for some readers, *Knight Prisoner* "has both biographical and historical interest." Ruth M. McConnell concludes in the *School Library Journal:* "The overall result is a most readable political and social history."

Persephone and the Springtime
A GREEK MYTH

Retold by MARGARET HODGES
Illustrated by ARVIS STEWART

This ancient Greek myth, as retold by Hodges, provides an explanation of why there are different seasons throughout the year. (Cover illustration by Arvis Stewart.)

Hodges is also a reteller of tales, as in her book *The Little Humpbacked Horse: A Russian Tale.* Based on a translation of a poem by Peter Pavlovich Yershov drawn from a Russian folktale, *The Little Humpbacked Horse* is the story of a younger son, Ivan, whose ownership of a magical, humpbacked horse changes his life. The horse not only carries Ivan on land and through the air, but also offers advice. *School Library Journal* contributor Patricia Dooley praises Chris Conover's illustrations and Russian motifs, and calls the little horse "shaggy and appealing as an equine Ugly Duckling who never gets transformed." An "admirably clear and smooth English translation," comments a *Horn Book* reviewer. And a *Publishers Weekly* critic declares *The Little Humpbacked Horse* "one of the most outstanding productions this year—handsome in all aspects."

Caldecott Award-winning *Saint George and the Dragon: A Golden Legend* is another of Hodges's retellings, based on the first book of Edmund Spenser's *Faerie Queen.* Saint George, the hero, rescues a maiden and slays a dragon to save her family, and eventually the hero and his love marry and live happily ever after. The main portion of the story, though, is George's three-day battle with the dragon. "The dragon in full action virtually bursts off the page," proclaims Rosalie Byard in the *New York Times Book Review,* praising Trina Schart Hyman's illustrations. Byard also notes that Hodges "offers a faithful translation of Spenser's detailed account" of

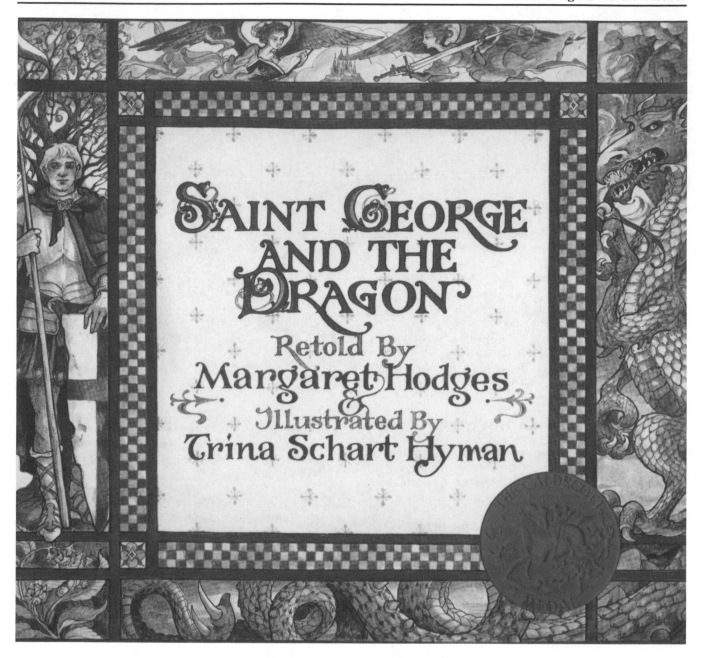

This retelling of a tale from *The Faerie Queen* by Edmund Spenser earned Hodges numerous awards. (Cover illustration by Trina Schart Hyman.)

the battle. A reviewer in the *Bulletin of the Center for Children's Books* calls Hodges's adaptation "capable," highlighting her use of Spenserian language without becoming bogged down in it. *School Library Journal* contributor Janice M. Del Negro declares the action "fast-paced and immediate," and comments that Hodges's *Saint George and the Dragon* "has made [Spenser's *Faerie Queen*] a coherent, palatable story suitable for a wide range of ages."

Hodges returns to folktales for her inspiration in producing *If You Had a Horse: Steeds of Myth and Legend.* A collection of nine tales drawn from different cultures and times, the volume features horses as the unifying theme. Celtic, Norse, Greek, and Arabian are among the folktales' cultures of origin. A reviewer in the *Bulletin of*

the *Center for Children's Books* praises Hodges's "smooth narrative style." A critic in *Publishers Weekly* judges that Hodges "intensifies the effects of the nine legends" in *If You Had a Horse* with her convincing approximation of the "speaking manners of the original storytellers." And Gayle W. Berge in the *School Library Journal* claims "all these tales have broad appeal, action and drama."

In *Making a Difference: The Story of an American Family,* Hodges creates another collection, this time a collective biography of the six members of the Sherwood family—mother and five children—during the first half of this century. The book traces the lives of these extraordinary people who faced adversity, overcame straitened circumstances, and excelled in their chosen fields. The mother, widowed shortly after her last child was born, raised her children to believe in and fight for issues larger than themselves. Her daughters, all graduates of Vassar, embraced literature, social action, preservation, and medicine, while her son, a Princeton graduate, became an international economist. A *Publishers Weekly* reviewer notes the "tremendous amount of research" necessary to create the volume, which includes letters, journal entries, and reminiscences, and remarks on "Hodges's dedication to historical fact, her eye for detail and interest in truth." A *Horn Book* contributor praises *Making a Difference* as a "carefully crafted, ... seamless" book, and comments that the transitions between life stories "serve both as introductions and as linking devices—a remarkable achievement." Jean Fritz, writing in the *New York Times Book Review,* calls *Making a Difference* "well written," and concludes: "For all those readers who have been crying for good nonfiction about memorable women, here is your book."

Stories Drawn from Many Times and Places

In *The Arrow and the Lamp: The Story of Psyche,* Hodges returns to the field of myth and legend with her retelling of the ancient Greek myth of Psyche, a mortal whose love for a god changes her existence. A beautiful woman, Psyche angers the goddess Aphrodite merely by looking so attractive that mortal men ignore the deity. Aphrodite sends her son Eros (or Cupid) to punish Psyche, but he falls in love with her instead. They marry, with the condition that Psyche can never look at her husband in the light. Curiosity overpowers her, and one night she lights a lamp in order to see Eros clearly. She loses him at that moment, earning him back only after completing a series of impossible tasks that make her one of the immortals, too. A critic in the *Bulletin of the Center for Children's Books* praises Hodges's work as "a haunting myth well adapted by an experienced storyteller." Connie C. Rockman in the *School Library Journal* judges *The Arrow and the Lamp* a "smooth, straightforward retelling."

St. Jerome and the Lion is another of Hodges's storytelling adaptations. In this volume, Hodges tells the tale of the Christian Saint Jerome pulling a thorn from a lion's paw. The grateful beast stays at Jerome's monastery, assuming the job of guarding the donkey. But one night when he falls asleep on watch, the donkey is stolen. Almost all the monks think that the lion ate the donkey, except for Jerome. Eventually the donkey is returned, and the lion is redeemed and Jerome's wisdom reconfirmed. Shirley Wilton in *School Library Journal* labels *St. Jerome and the Lion* a "moral tale" and a "gentle story." Another critic in the *Bulletin of the Center for Children's Books* remarks on the "compassion" in Hodges's "simple and dignified adaptation." And a reviewer in *Publishers Weekly* calls Hodges's book a "sensitive adaptation" with "language and rhythms sensitively attuned to contemporary readers."

In *Hauntings: Ghosts and Ghouls from around the World,* Hodges retells sixteen ghost stories drawn from cultures the world over, including Europe, the Orient, America, and India. The theme of restless spirits unites the collection, as do similarities among the tales. Several retellings describe humans bargaining with Death, as in the Japanese story "Snow," the Brothers Grimm's "Godfather Death," and the "Lord of the Dead" taken from the *Mahabarata*. The tales are "more mysterious than they are scary," judges Maeve Visser Knoth in *Horn Book,* calling *Hauntings* "one fresh, readable volume." "Hodges's polished retellings retain the flavor of the originals," declares Margaretret A. Chang in the *School Library Journal*. And Hodges's "meaty retellings" win praise from Denia Hester in *Booklist.*

Hodges returns to historical figures with her biographical retelling of the life of Saint Francis of Assisi as told in *Brother Francis and the Friendly Beasts*. A young man born into a wealthy family, Francis rejects a life of leisure to become a wandering monk, spending the rest of his days preaching and enjoying nature. *School Library Journal* contributor Eva Elisabeth Von Ancken labels *Brother Francis and the Friendly Beasts* as "superficial," claiming that Hodges's book has no depth and that no attempt has been made to understand "the man's character." Other critics were more positive, with a reviewer in the *Bulletin of the Center for Children's Books* calling Hodges's adaptation "graceful and smooth." A reviewer in *Horn Book* judges *Brother Francis and the Friendly Beasts* "a graceful production."

Hodges has spent a good portion of her life writing and telling stories for children. "The art of storytelling thrilled me because I saw it as the best way to lead children to good literature, to leap the boundaries between literacy and illiteracy, and to bring marvelous old tales to listeners of all ages," explains Hodges in her *SAAS* essay. Her stories, whether told aloud, retold from history and legend, or set down from her own experience and that of her family, serve the same purpose, bringing the joy of reading to children and encouraging them to continue learning. Hodges continues to find compelling subject matter for her books and to speak to curious young audiences about the process of researching and writing.

■ Works Cited

Review of *The Arrow and the Lamp: The Story of Psyche, Bulletin of the Center for Children's Books,* February, 1990, pp. 138-39.

Berge, Gayle W., review of *If You Had a Horse: Steeds of Myth and Legend, School Library Journal,* January, 1985, p. 76.

Berkowitz, Nathan, review of *Lady Queen Anne: A Biography of Queen Anne of England, Library Journal,* September 15, 1969, p. 3218.

Review of *Brother Francis and the Friendly Beasts, Bulletin of the Center for Children's Books,* November, 1991, p. 64.

Review of *Brother Francis and the Friendly Beasts, Horn Book,* September/October, 1991, p. 611.

Byard, Rosalie, review of *Saint George and the Dragon: A Golden Legend, New York Times Book Review,* November 4, 1984, p. 22.

Chang, Margaretret A., review of *Hauntings: Ghosts and Ghouls from around the World, School Library Journal,* November, 1991, p. 129.

Del Negro, Janice M., review of *Saint George and the Dragon: A Golden Legend, School Library Journal,* January, 1985, p. 76.

Dooley, Patricia, review of *The Little Humpbacked Horse: A Russian Tale, School Library Journal,* December, 1980, pp. 44, 53.

Review of *The Freewheeling of Joshua Cobb, Bulletin of the Center for Children's Books,* March, 1975.

Review of *The Freewheeling of Joshua Cobb, Horn Book,* October, 1974, p. 137.

Fritz, Jean, review of *Making a Difference: The Story of an American Family, New York Times Book Review,* July 23, 1989, p. 28.

Review of *The Hatching of Joshua Cobb, Bulletin of the Center for Children's Books,* November, 1967, p. 43.

Hester, Denia, review of *Hauntings: Ghosts and Ghouls from around the World, Booklist,* November 15, 1991, p. 624.

Hodges, Margaret Moore, *Something about the Author Autobiography Series,* Volume 9, Gale, 1990, pp. 183-201.

Review of *If You Had a Horse: Steeds of Myth and Legend, Bulletin of the Center for Children's Books,* January, 1985, p. 87.

Review of *If You Had a Horse: Steeds of Myth and Legend, Publishers Weekly,* November 30, 1984, p. 89.

Review of *Knight Prisoner: The Tale of Sir Thomas Malory and His King Arthur, Bulletin of the Center for Children's Books,* April, 1977, p. 126.

Review of *Knight Prisoner: The Tale of Sir Thomas Malory and His King Arthur, Horn Book,* December, 1976, pp. 632-33.

Knoth, Maeve Visser, review of *Hauntings: Ghosts and Ghouls from around the World, Horn Book,* November/December, 1991, pp. 747-48.

Review of *Lady Queen Anne: A Biography of Queen Anne of England, Publishers Weekly,* May 19, 1969, p. 71.

Review of *The Little Humpbacked Horse: A Russian Tale, Horn Book,* February, 1981, p. 61.

Review of *The Little Humpbacked Horse: A Russian Tale, Publishers Weekly,* November 14, 1980, p. 55.

Review of *Making a Difference: The Story of an American Family, Horn Book,* September, 1989, pp. 636-37.

Review of *Making a Difference: The Story of an American Family, Publishers Weekly,* April 28, 1989, p. 80.

Review of *The Making of Joshua Cobb, Horn Book,* June, 1971, p. 287.

Review of *The Making of Joshua Cobb, Publishers Weekly,* March 22, 1971, p. 53.

McConnell, Ruth M., review of *Knight Prisoner: The Tale of Sir Thomas Malory and His King Arthur, School Library Journal,* December, 1976, p. 60.

Rockman, Connie C., review of *The Arrow and the Lamp: The Story of Psyche, School Library Journal,* December, 1989, p. 108.

Review of *Saint George and the Dragon: A Golden Legend, Bulletin of the Center for Children's Books,* October, 1984, p. 27.

Review of *St. Jerome and the Lion, Bulletin of the Center for Children's Books,* September, 1991, p. 12.

Review of *St. Jerome and the Lion, Publishers Weekly,* July 5, 1991, p. 64.

Scheraga, Sandra, review of *The Freewheeling of Joshua Cobb, Library Journal,* September 15, 1974, p. 2270.

Scheraga, review of *The Making of Joshua Cobb, Library Journal,* April 15, 1971, p. 1504.

Thomson, Jean C., review of *The Hatching of Joshua Cobb, Library Journal,* September 15, 1967, p. 118.

Von Ancken, Eva Elisabeth, review of *Brother Francis and the Friendly Beasts, School Library Journal,* December, 1991, pp. 110-11.

Wilton, Shirley, review of *St. Jerome and the Lion, School Library Journal,* September, 1991, p. 246.

■ For More Information See

PERIODICALS

Publishers Weekly, November 23, 1984, p. 75.
School Library Journal, May, 1989, pp. 129-30.

—*Sketch by Terrie M. Rooney*

*　　*　　*

HOY, Nina
See ROTH, Arthur J(oseph)

*　　*　　*

HUNT, Angela Elwell 1957-

■ Personal

Born December 20, 1957, in Winter Haven, FL; daughter of James (an engineer at NASA's Kennedy Space Center) and Frankie (a retired telephone operator) Elwell; married Gary A. Hunt (a youth pastor), May, 1980; children: Taryn Li, Tyler Jordan. *Education:* Liberty University, B.S. (magna cum laude), 1980. *Politics:* Republican. *Religion:* Christian. *Hobbies and other interests:* Quilting, gardening, singing.

■ Addresses

Agent—Curtis Lundgren, Curtis Bruce Agency, P.O. Box 967, Plover, WI 54467.

■ Career

Writer, 1983—. Worked as an English teacher and held a full-time secretarial position prior to 1983. *Member:* Authors Guild, Society of Children's Book Writers and Illustrators.

■ Awards, Honors

Lorna Balian Prize, Abingdon Press, and "Children's Choice" award, 1987, for *If I Had Long, Long Hair;* Evangelical Christian Publishing Association Gold Medal nominations, 1991, for *A Gift for Grandpa,* and 1993, for *The True Princess;* Campus Life "Book of the Year" nomination, 1991, for *If God Is Real, Where on Earth Is He?;* Chicago Women in Publishing honorable mention for design, 1992, for *Calico Bear.*

■ Writings

"CASSIE PERKINS" SERIES; YOUNG ADULT NOVELS

No More Broken Promises, Tyndale House, 1991.
A Forever Friend, Tyndale House, 1991.
A Basket of Roses, Tyndale House, 1991.
A Dream to Cherish, Tyndale House, 1992.
The Much-Adored Sandy Shore, Tyndale House, 1992.
Love Burning Bright, Tyndale House, 1992.
Star Light, Star Bright, Tyndale House, 1993.
The Chance of a Lifetime, Tyndale House, 1993.
The Glory of Love, Tyndale House, 1993.

"NICKI HOLLAND" SERIES; YOUNG ADULT MYSTERIES

The Case of the Mystery Mark, Here's Life/Thomas Nelson, 1991.

ANGELA ELWELL HUNT

The Case of the Phantom Friend, Here's Life/Thomas Nelson, 1991.
The Case of the Teenage Terminator, Here's Life/Thomas Nelson, 1991.
The Case of the Terrified Track Star, Here's Life/Thomas Nelson, 1992.
The Case of the Counterfeit Cash, Here's Life/Thomas Nelson, 1992.
The Case of the Haunting of Lowell Lanes, Here's Life/Thomas Nelson, 1992.
The Case of the Birthday Bracelet, Thomas Nelson, 1993.
The Secret of Cravenhill Castle, Thomas Nelson, 1993.
The Riddle of Baby Rosalind, Thomas Nelson, 1993.

"THEYN CHRONICLES" SERIES; HISTORICAL FICTION

Afton of Margate Castle, Tyndale House, 1993.
The Troubadour's Quest, Tyndale House, 1994.
Ingram of the Irish, Tyndale House, 1995.

OTHER

(With husband, Gary Hunt) *Surviving the Teenage Years,* Here's Life, 1988, published as *Too Young to Drive, Too Old to Ride: Surviving Your Child's Middle School Years,* 1993.
If I Had Long, Long Hair, illustrated by L. Diane Johnson, Abingdon Press, 1988.
(With Gary Hunt) *Mom and Dad Don't Live Together Anymore,* Here's Life, 1989.
The Tale of Three Trees, illustrated by Tom Jonke, Lion Publishing, 1989.
The Adoption Option, Victor Books, 1989.
(With Gary Hunt) *Now That You've Asked Her Out,* Here's Life/Thomas Nelson, 1989.
(With Gary Hunt) *Now That He's Asked You Out,* Here's Life/Thomas Nelson, 1989.
Calico Bear (picture book), illustrated by Natalie Carabetta, Tyndale House, 1991.
A Gift for Grandpa, illustrated by Terry Julien, D. C. Cook, 1991.
If God Is Real, Where on Earth Is He?, Here's Life/Thomas Nelson, 1991.
(With Charles Dyer) *The Rise of Babylon: Sign of the End Times,* Tyndale House, 1991.
Loving Someone Else's Child, Tyndale House, 1992.
The Singing Shepherd, illustrated by Peter Palagonia, Lion Publishing, 1992.
The True Princess, illustrated by Diana Magnuson, D. C. Cook, 1992.
(With Laura Krauss Calenberg) *Beauty from the Inside Out: Becoming the Best You Can Be,* Thomas Nelson, 1993.
Howie Hugemouth, Standard Publishing, 1993.
Pulling Yourself Together When Your Family's Falling Apart, Tyndale House, 1994.

Contributor to *Christianity Today.*

■ Work in Progress

Another historical fiction series set in ancient Egypt.

■ **Sidelights**

Angela Elwell Hunt has become one of the major writers
of Christian fiction for teenage girls and young children.
Her "Nicki Holland" mystery stories and "Cassie Perkins" series present teenagers who (respectively) solve
mysteries and learn to live their lives in a Christian
context. Her picture book for young children, *The Tale
of Three Trees,* a retelling of an old folktale, has become
an international bestseller, which has sold more than
200,000 copies.

"My mother didn't work until after I had left home,"
Angela Hunt told an interviewer for *Something about
the Author* (*SATA*), "when she went back to being a
telephone operator, which is what she'd been before I
was born. My father worked at Cape Kennedy on the
space shuttle until recently. My father wasn't much of a
reader, but my mother was always a great reader, and
she instilled in me a love for reading. That was my
favorite thing to do—go sit in my room with a good
book (the thicker the better). My mother enjoyed ...
not romance novels, exactly, but mainstream classic
novels with romance added (which incidentally, I find
that I'm writing now for adults). That was the sort of
thing I really enjoyed, and she as well. I read *Gone with*

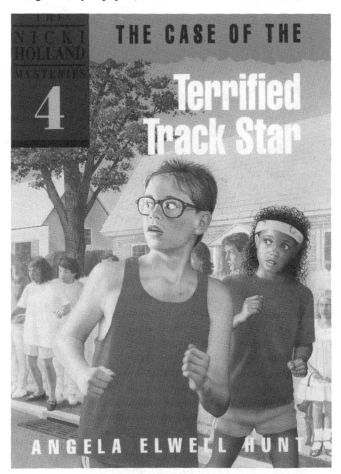

THE CASE OF THE
Terrified
Track Star

ANGELA ELWELL HUNT

**An unknown enemy tries to prevent the town track star
from running in an important race in this book in
Hunt's "Nicki Holland" series.** (Cover illustration by
Doron Ben-Ami.)

the Wind in sixth grade. My favorite volume after that
was *Jane Eyre.* I just really, really loved a good story,
particularly one, I think, with a heroine—a woman as
the central figure.

"My parents are both devout Christians. I am a Christian and have been since I was six or seven. I was very
active in church from a young age—those formative
years. It's who I am. Of course, it comes through my
writing. I don't always even intend to put it in there, but
I'm sure that it shines through. I hope so, anyway.

"In sixth grade, I had a teacher named Deanna Barcher,
who says she recognized in me the soul of a poet.
Nobody else was pointing me out as being different, or
more talented than any of my peers, but she praised me
in class and she praised the poems that I wrote. And this
praise propelled me to try to do more and to do better.
In high school I had an excellent writing teacher, Mrs.
Janet Williams. I had her for several different English
classes—including American Literature and English
Literature—as well as a creative writing class and a
career writing class and that sort of thing. She was very
good in teaching foundational skills and basic organization that a lot of teachers don't teach. She instilled in us
a love of literature. I can still see her sitting on her stool
acting out scenes from *Of Mice and Men.* She really
made it come to life for me. If I have any skill at all, it
came from her.

"I went to community college for two years right after
high school and majored in vocal performance. Then I
took a year off to travel with a singing group—a sort of
God and Country thing. We did churches and Kiwanis
Clubs and Rotary Clubs—even cut some albums. It was
a great year. The leader of that group, Derric Johnson,
was sort of a mentor to all of us. One night as we were all
driving from place to place, he said to me, 'Ang, what do
you want to do?' and I said, 'Well, I guess I'll finish
college as a music major.' And he said, 'What are you
really going to do with that degree?' He said, 'Unless you
want to go full-time on the road or teach, what do you
really want to do with it?'

Plans Writing Career

"Thinking about it, I didn't think I had the stamina to
be a professional singer, because I developed nodes on
my vocal chords after about 6 weeks on the road. My
overriding concern, however, was that I've always
wanted to be married and be a mom, and I really wanted
a career where I could place my family first. Then Pastor
Derric said to me, 'You know, you're really good with
words. Why don't you think about doing something in
an English-related field?' And so, when I went to
Liberty, I switched over to an English major. The college
was very good as far as training in literature went. But
once I decided to strike out and actually begin free-lance
work, I sort of taught myself. I got every 'how-to' book
that *Writer's Digest* has published! I started seeing what
worked and what didn't, and what got me sales and what
didn't.

"I graduated from college on a Monday and got married that Tuesday! I met Gary Hunt at college. He was older than me—I was only 21 and he was nearly 30—and he was always surrounded by kids. I know enough about kids to know that they can spot a fake a mile away. We started dating, and I found that the kids were right— he's a very genuine, wonderful guy.

"I began writing in 1983 when I quit my full-time secretarial job and decided to stay home and wait for the baby we planned to adopt. The baby came and so did the writing work, slowly, as I learned to improve my craft. I began by writing letters, brochures, radio ad copy—pretty much anything anybody would pay me to write. From there I advanced to magazine writing, and after five years, I sold my first book, *If I Had Long, Long Hair.*

"Since that beginning ten years ago, I've lost track of the number of magazine articles, and I stay busy writing an average of one book a month. Longer books of 600-plus pages take longer, of course, but I like staying busy and I've never, *ever* had a case of writer's block. There are just too many things to write about!

"I think I have a real advantage in writing for young people because my husband is a youth pastor and I spend hours with teenagers every week. I listen to them and learn what their problems are. Plus, I have a keen memory and I remember what it feels like to be scared and unsure of yourself. At the same time, I remember how much fun being a teenager can be!

"Cassie Perkins" Books Based on Experience

"Most of my characters are parts of me, but Cassie Perkins is more me than any of the others. Because those stories are written in first person, I think it's only natural that it should come through. Like Cassie, I trained as a professional soprano, and, like Cassie, my Dad worked at the space center. I was also very scientifically inclined and that part of me comes out in Cassie's brother Max—my love for research and exploration. And a lot of things that Cassie gets into were things that are taken from my experience, although I changed them subtly.

"A lot of my experiences are reflected and used in my books. That's what writers do. Our lives are really all we've got to draw from. For instance, in *The Chance of a Lifetime,* when Cassie's performing in a singing group full-time, they're caught in a flood. Well, I was in the same situation, except I was caught with my fellow singers in a blizzard. I even used my diary, the journal that I kept while we were stuck in the blizzard, to augment the book. Everywhere that Cassie and her friends sing came right out of my journals, because I wanted to make sure I had driving distances accurate. I thought, 'If we did it, I know it's possible.'

"However, Cassie's life and mine part over her problems with her home life. I've never gone through a divorce, my parents are still happily married after many, many years—nearly forty. But my husband and I work with middle-school young people day-in and day-out at church. We have a youth group of about 250 kids whom we work with every year on a first-name basis. Of that group, I would say 75% of them are from divorced homes. So Cassie's experience dealing with her step-siblings and her new dad—that comes from the experiences of the kids that I work with every day."

Hunt's "Nicki Holland" mysteries are drawn not so much from her own experiences as from those of her children. "I'm very careful not to be so specific in my books that I embarrass my children, because my daughter is a big Nicki Holland fan," she states in her *SATA* interview. "I think Cassie Perkins is a tad too sophisticated for her yet, but she and her friends love Nicki Holland. I wanted to do something that would make her feel included, but I didn't want to make them ethnically diverse just for the sake of having a token black girl, a token brain, a token red-head... The final result made for a very interesting mix because they all bring special talents and gifts that aren't related to their race. Meredith, the black girl, happens to be the brain, because I had just read an article that said that a lot of black girls are afraid of appearing too brainy because their peers accuse them of trying to be white if they try to get good grades. So, I thought, 'That's good. Let's turn

None of Cassie's successes prepare her for the break-up of her parents' marriage in this novel by Hunt. (Cover illustration by Mazellan.)

CASSIE PERKINS
The Chance
of a Lifetime

Cassie is going on a nationwide
singing tour as one of the best young singers
in the country! This will be her big chance . . .
but what will it cost her?

Angela Elwell Hunt

Cassie's chance to get her big break as a singer is
complicated by some confusing and dangerous events in
The Chance of a Lifetime. (Cover illustration by Ron
Mazellan.)

the tables here a little bit and offer some challenges
here.' The characters are all very different."

Picture Book Earns Praise from Readers

Perhaps Hunt's best-known work, however, is the picture book *The Tale of Three Trees.* "I had heard the
story many, many times about the three trees on the
mountaintop," Hunt recalls in her *SATA* interview.
"The first one wants to hold treasure, the second one
wants to be a sailing ship, and the third one just wants to
stay on the mountain and point to God. And their
dreams come true, but not at all in the way that they
expect. When I sat down to write it up, I changed it a
bit—I was not working from a printed copy, and I
wasn't sure how it went, so I just made it suit my fancy.
Later, when I found a copy of the original, I discovered
that the differences were minor—for instance, in the
original, the first tree wants to be a baby's cradle. In my
story, it ends up being the manger that held the infant
Jesus, which, of course, was the greatest treasure of the
world.

"There are little twists in it that are different, but the
story seems to have a timeless appeal. I get letters from
people who interpret the message in many different
ways. Once, I heard from a blind lady who heard the
story at a convention for people with disabilities and she
said, 'All of the sudden, I saw that my blindness was a
gift from God, that He can still use me in a special way.'
I had never, ever conceived of the story in that light. She
said that this story had just helped her to see that God
can use her, even in her blindness and with her differing
abilities. People come up at conventions all the time and
tell me how much that book means to them, and I'm just
stunned. It's really a very simple story, but a lot of
people find a lot of profound meaning in it.

"Things are so confusing now, I want to write about the
solid things we can hold on to like love, honesty,
friendship, and eternal truth. I want my readers to know
that no matter how gray things may seem, there's still
hope on the horizon.

"I guess I'm an optimist; I just know I like happy
endings. Even if things aren't *perfect* at the end of a
story, at least there's hope for the future. So whether my
book is about Cassie looking for hope, or Nicki Holland
searching for the answer to a mystery, or the little girl
wishing for long, long hair, we can all find what we're
looking for. We just have to learn to look in the right
places."

■ Works Cited

Hunt, Angela Elwell, interview for *Something about the
Author,* May 3, 1993.

J–K

JACKSON, Ellen B. 1943-

■ Personal

Born April 27, 1943, in Los Angeles, CA; daughter of Merrill O. (an accountant) and Carol (a children's librarian; maiden name, Goldstein) Jackson. *Education:* University of California, Los Angeles, B.A., 1967; California Family Study Center, M.A., 1977. *Politics:* "Liberal Democrat." *Hobbies and other interests:* Hiking, tidepooling and beachcombing after a storm, playing alto and soprano recorder, fiber arts.

■ Addresses

Home—1430 Pacific Ave., Santa Barbara, CA 93109.

■ Career

Writer. Monte Vista Street School, Los Angeles, CA, kindergarten teacher, 1969-79; Santa Barbara County Schools, Santa Barbara, CA, curriculum writer, 1984-87. *Member:* Society of Children's Book Writers and Illustrators, Amnesty International, Peace Resource Center.

■ Awards, Honors

National Writer's Club certificate, 1991.

■ Writings

PICTURE BOOKS

The Bear in the Bathtub, illustrated by Margot Apple, Addison-Wesley, 1981.
The Grumpus under the Rug, Follett, 1981.
Ants Can't Dance, illustrated by Frank Remkiewicz, Macmillan, 1990.
Boris the Boring Boar, illustrated by Normand Chartier, Macmillan, 1992.
The Tree of Life (nonfiction), Prometheus, 1993.
Yellow, Mellow, Green and Brown, Hyperion Press, 1994.
Cinder Edna, Lothrop, 1994.

ELLEN B. JACKSON

The Winter Solstice (nonfiction), Millbrook Press, 1994.

OTHER

Top of the World, Children's Story Scripts, 1991.
Quick Wits and Whiskers, Children's Story Scripts, 1991.
Families Are for Finding, Children's Story Scripts, 1991.
Earthquake Safety, Horizon, 1991.
Household Safety, Horizon, 1991.

Stranger Danger (safety advice for kids), Horizon, 1991.

Contributor of articles for adults to newspapers, including *Critical Times,* 1992; also contributor of children's stories to periodicals, including "Dragons in the Drapes," *Humpty Dumpty's,* 1990.

■ Work in Progress

Lots of Knots, Ticknor and Fields, forthcoming.

■ Sidelights

Ellen B. Jackson has written over a dozen books for children, ranging from nonfiction books with safety advice about earthquakes and strangers to fiction books with witty tales about animal and human characters. One of her early books, *The Bear in the Bathtub,* is a funny tale of a young boy, Andrew, who hates to take baths. He learns to appreciate taking a bath each night, however, when a huge bear inhabits the bathtub. Unable to bathe for days, Andrew experiences the consequences of being dirty—his friends no longer wish to be near him. Unfortunately, no one, not even his parents, the police, or the fire fighters, is able to remove the bear from the tub. Finally, Andrew comes up with an idea and solves the problem. Critics appreciate the humor Jackson imparts in her stories. "Jackson accents the mirth by relating the nonsense with a straight face," writes a contributor to *Publishers Weekly.* "This amusing, well-written story reads aloud well," asserts Pamela Warren Stebbins in a *School Library Journal* review.

Jackson, who has been a free-lance writer for over ten years, told *SATA:* "At present I live in a house one block from the beach in Santa Barbara, California, with my eccentric dog Bailey. I read in many different fields including science, sociology, fiction, eastern philosophy, and history. I do volunteer work for Amnesty International and the Peace Resource Center in Santa Barbara."

■ Works Cited

Review of *The Bear in the Bathtub, Publishers Weekly,* April 17, 1981, p. 62.
Stebbins, Pamela Warren, review of *The Bear in the Bathtub, School Library Journal,* September, 1981, p. 109.

■ For More Information See

PERIODICALS

School Library Journal, September, 1992, p. 206.

KELLEHER, Victor (Michael Kitchener) 1939-

■ Personal

Born July 19, 1939, in London, England; son of Joseph (a builder) and Matilda (a dressmaker; maiden name, Newman) Kelleher; married Alison Lyle (a potter and sculptor), January 2, 1962; children: Jason, Leila. *Education:* University of Natal, B.A., 1961; University of St. Andrews, Diploma in Education, 1963; University of the Witwatersrand, B.A. (with honors), 1969; University of South Africa, M.A., 1970, D.Litt. et Phil., 1973. *Religion:* Atheist. *Hobbies and other interests:* Films, politics, domestic architecture, travel.

■ Addresses

Home—1 Avenue Rd., Glebe, New South Wales 2037, Australia.

■ Career

University of the Witwatersrand, Johannesburg, South Africa, junior lecturer in English, 1969; University of South Africa, Pretoria, lecturer, 1970-71, senior lecturer in English, 1972-73; Massey University, Palmerston North, New Zealand, lecturer in English, 1973-76; University of New England, Armidale, Australia, lecturer, 1976-79, senior lecturer, 1980-83, associate professor of English, 1984-87; writer. *Member:* Australian Society of Authors.

■ Awards, Honors

Patricia Hackett Prize, *Westerly* magazine, 1978, for story, "The Traveller"; Literature Board of the Australia Council senior writer's fellow, 1982; West Australian Library Association, West Australian Young Readers' Book Award, 1982, for *Forbidden Paths of Thual,* and West Australian Young Readers' Special Award, 1983, for *The Hunting of Shadroth;* Australian Children's Book of the Year Award, Children's Book Council of Australia, 1983, for *Master of the Grove;* Australian Science Fiction Achievement Award, National Science Fiction Association, 1984, for *The Beast of Heaven;* Honour Award, Children's Book Council of Australia, 1987, for *Taronga;* Australian Peace Prize, 1987, for *The Makers;* Koala Award, 1991, for *The Red King;* Honour Award, Children's Book Council of Australia, and West Australian Hoffmann Award, both 1992, both for *Brother Night; Del-Del* was short-listed for the Carnegie Medal in Great Britain.

■ Writings

Voices from the River (novel), Heinemann, 1979.
Africa and After (stories), University of Queensland Press, 1983, published as *The Traveller: Stories of Two Continents,* 1987.
The Beast of Heaven (novel), University of Queensland Press, 1984.

Em's Story: A Novel, University of Queensland Press, 1988.

Wintering, University of Queensland Press, 1990.

Micky Darlin', University of Queensland Press, 1992.

FOR YOUNG ADULTS

Forbidden Paths of Thual, illustrated by Anthony Maitland, Penguin Books, 1979.

The Hunting of Shadroth, Penguin Books, 1981.

Master of the Grove, Penguin Books, 1982.

Papio: A Novel of Adventure, Penguin Books, 1984, published as *Rescue!*, Dial, 1992.

The Green Piper, Penguin Books, 1984.

Taronga, Penguin Books, 1986.

The Makers, Penguin Books, 1987.

Baily's Bones, Penguin Books, 1988.

The Red King, Penguin Books, 1989.

Brother Night, illustrated by Peter Clarke, Walker Books, 1990.

Del-Del, illustrated by Clarke, MacRae Books/Random House, 1991.

To The Dark Tower, MacRae Books/Random House, 1992.

OTHER

Work represented in anthologies, including *Introduction 6*, Faber, 1977. Contributor of articles and stories to magazines.

■ Sidelights

Award-winning author Victor Kelleher writes for both juvenile and adult audiences. His younger readers delight in the fantasy and adventure found in such novels as *The Hunting of Shadroth* and *Taronga*, while his older readers are exposed to the darker thoughts of Kelleher's futuristic fantasy as found in *The Beast of Heaven*. Kelleher once commented that he began writing in 1973, after he left Africa, as a means of therapy. Soon his writing became an end in itself, and his first novels, *Voices from the River* and *Forbidden Paths of Thual*, were published in 1979. Since then, the author has described his adult fiction as falling into "the category of contemporary realism."

Forbidden Paths of Thual is "an interesting, refreshing, worthwhile" young adult book according to Norman Culpan writing in the *School Librarian*. Quen, the protagonist, is the sole character capable, with the aid of a friendly fox, of freeing his land from the ruthless soldiers called grey Mollags. He is the only one who can overcome his own weaknesses and resist the temptations of cruelty and greed. Audrey Laski sums up Kelleher's story in the *Times Educational Supplement:* "It rests on one boy to dare everything that is necessary to defeat the conquerors."

Kelleher's next two books echo the single protagonist and animal companion of *Forbidden Paths of Thual*. *The Hunting of Shadroth* presents Tal, a boy with psychic talents who can see into the future, and his friendly cat-like aide called a Feln. Shadroth, the object of Tal's quest, is a physical beast representing the

Two siblings sense that danger lurks near their new home in an isolated part of Australia in this suspenseful mystery by Kelleher. (Cover illustration by Linda Benson.)

violent tendencies of Tal's people, a creature Tal must subdue, if not destroy. David Churchill, writing in the *School Librarian*, notes that *The Hunting of Shadroth* "is written with care and elegance." *Times Literary Supplement* contributor Edward Blishen comments in his conclusion: "The whole story is a morality, but without ever ceasing to be a story. There are satisfactory terrors . . . and the final struggle rises to one climax only to reveal another beyond it."

In *Master of the Grove*, Kelleher turns to sorcery and a war-ravaged land as backdrops for a quest by Derin, who has lost his memory, yet must complete a journey he does not understand with a witch who dislikes him. Ultimately, he must defeat an evil sorcerer who is at the root of all the strife in the land. "The story of a sorcerer's misuse of his knowledge may seem hackneyed, but it allows Kelleher to explore the theme of the responsibilities and temptations of power in a lively and well-fashioned narrative," declared Neil Philip in the *Times Educational Supplement*. Many critics offered mixed reviews, with *School Librarian* contributor Dennis Hamley calling *Master of the Grove* a "worthy, well-crafted book," but noting that "the style is ponderous."

Dominic Hibberd also praised *Master of the Grove* in the *Times Literary Supplement* as "quite a good story," though he felt it contains too much material and big ideas to flesh out in its two hundred pages—the tale "becomes too ingenious because the book is too full."

Kelleher switches from writing for younger readers to an adult audience with his novel *The Beast of Heaven,* published in 1984. Set in a world destroyed by a nuclear holocaust, the book tells the tale of a group of gentle nomads who subsist on "mustools," a mushroom and toadstool combination, and milk from the animals they call Houdin, the beasts of heaven. Their peace-filled world turns violent as the Houdin's aggressiveness increases. The land is also slowly losing its ability to support life. "*The Beast of Heaven* is an engrossing fable," judges Paulette Minare in the *Science Fiction Review. Fantasy Review* contributor Michael J. Tolley declares this book a "poignant, readable novel, not without charm." And *Analog*'s Tom Easton proclaims *The Beast of Heaven* "a fable for our times, a warning, a chastisement, well equipped with portentous symbolism."

YA Novels Filled with Supernatural Elements

Kelleher returns to children's fiction with the award-winning novel *Taronga.* Set in a post-"cataclysm" Australia, where cities are destroyed and people go hungry, *Taronga* is the story of telepathic, fourteen-year-old Ben and his experiences at the gang-controlled Taronga Park Zoo. His gift allows him to control the animals in the zoo, earning him the position, shared with an Aboriginal girl named Ellie, of keeper of the big cats. Released at night to frighten and repel the hungry, the cats must be put back into their cages each morning. Ellie and Ben decide to free all the zoo animals. "It makes a very violent story with complex strategies," remarks Dorothy Atkinson in the *School Librarian.* And Colin Greenland notes in the *Times Literary Supplement* that "once again Victor Kelleher portrays the child's world as a miserable, shadowy place occupied by corrupt and violent adults."

In *Baily's Bones,* Kelleher takes a look at the supernatural, including ghosts, ghostly possession, and mystery. He also delves into the often violent relationship between the Aborigines and the early Australian settlers. When a vengeful spirit named Baily takes control of their mentally handicapped older brother, Kenny, Alex and Dee must reconstruct the tragic events surrounding Baily's death in order to save Kenny's life and put Baily's ghost to rest. "Their efforts come to a climax in a stunning conclusion," determines a reviewer in *Horn Book.* Jeanette Larson, writing in the *School Library Journal,* declares: "This haunting tale is well told" and an "exciting story." *Voice of Youth Advocates* contributor Deborah L. Dubois has a similar viewpoint, commenting in her conclusion that "this is an exciting suspense novel ... that will appeal to most young adults."

Kelleher returns to fantasy worlds with his novel *The Red King.* The book's medieval overtones, and the battle staged between good and evil, invite comparisons with Tolkien's *The Hobbit.* The heroine, Timkin, is a skilled acrobat rescued by a self-serving magician from the punishing disease sent by the Red King that kills all her companions. The magician plans to use Timkin's talent to help him steal the Red King's gold. *School Library Journal* contributor Bruce Anne Shook mentions that "excitement and suspense are maintained throughout the story .... Fantasy lovers will find this to be an intriguing tale that provides not only high adventure but also some challenging food for thought about the nature of good and evil." Laura Moss Gottlieb in the *Voice of Youth Advocates* also notes the "thought-provoking questions" the novel raises, and judges the writing as "excellent."

"This is fantasy at its very best for young teens," declares Gladys Hardcastle in the *Voice of Youth Advocates,* describing *Brother Night.* Peter Clarke's illustrations add to the story, combining with the words "to bring a perilous quest through the shadowy realm of dark and light forces brilliantly to life," according to Hardcastle. *Brother Night* is the story of twin boys, one handsome and one grotesque, separated at birth. They

A girl struggles to free her younger brother from the possession of an evil spirit in Kelleher's *Del-Del*. (Cover illustration by Peter Clarke.)

are supposed to be the children of Jenna the Moon Witch and Solmak the Sun Lord. Undertaking a dangerous journey, one seeks vengeance and the other wants only to bury their mother. Ultimately, the boys learn more about themselves and their heritage than they ever imagined. *School Library Journal* reviewer JoAnn Rees finds *Brother Night* "competently written, but no more," claiming the characters were like "cardboard cutouts"—either good or evil with no in-between. A critic for the *Bulletin of the Center for Children's Books* concludes: "Darker-toned than much juvenile fantasy, this is an adept and satisfying blend of action and atmosphere."

Kelleher moves into a modern setting with *Del-Del,* the story of a traumatized young genius. After the death of his eldest sister, seven-year-old Sam retreats into an obnoxious, uncaring persona he calls Del-Del. For four years, the family tries everything they can think of, including exorcism, to rescue Sam. But it is his sister Beth, by risking her life, who restores Sam to himself and the family. A reviewer in *Publishers Weekly* notes that Kelleher "plots an unusual course for a sibling death theme, with confusing results" and a "pat resolution." The reader never gets "caught up in the horror, because it seems silly," claims Caroline S. McKinney in the *Voice of Youth Advocates. School Library Journal* contributor Sara Miller, however, praises *Del-Del* as a "tense, involving story," and calls it "a psychological thriller that's guaranteed to hold readers' attention."

Kelleher's fiction, especially for juveniles, generally tends to focus on the darker elements of literature and life. In his novels, many of the adult characters are forbidding or distant figures, and his young heroes and heroines are willing to risk all they have for what they believe. Futuristic, and at the same time moral in tone, Kelleher entertains while he imparts his lessons and views. Kelleher once wrote: "My children's fiction, which is aimed primarily at the young adult group of readers, ranges from realism to fantasy. Regardless of the type of novel I'm writing, I always try to create a fast pace and strong story line. Equally important to me is the idea of a serious subtext which raises issues that are, I hope, both challenging and pertinent to all my readers, irrespective of their age."

■ Works Cited

Atkinson, Dorothy, review of *Taronga, School Librarian,* May, 1988.

Review of *Baily's Bones, Horn Book,* March, 1990, p. 207.

Blishen, Edward, "Moral Beasts," *Times Literary Supplement,* March 27, 1981.

Review of *Brother Night, Bulletin of the Center for Children's Books,* June, 1991, p. 241.

Churchill, David, review of *The Hunting of Shadroth, School Librarian,* June, 1981, p. 154.

Culpan, Norman, review of *Forbidden Paths of Thual, School Librarian,* December, 1979, pp. 388, 391.

Review of *Del-Del, Publishers Weekly,* June 15, 1992.

Dubois, Deborah L., review of *Baily's Bones, Voice of Youth Advocates,* April, 1990.

Easton, Tom, review of *The Beast of Heaven, Analog,* April, 1987.

Gottlieb, Laura Moss, review of *The Red King, Voice of Youth Advocates,* June, 1990, p. 116.

Greenland, Colin, "Animal Liberation," *Times Literary Supplement,* January 1, 1988, p. 21.

Hamley, Dennis, review of *Master of the Grove, School Librarian,* June, 1982, p. 155.

Hardcastle, Gladys, review of *Brother Night, Voice of Youth Advocates,* October, 1991, p. 244.

Hibberd, Dominic, "The Elements of Fantasy," *Times Literary Supplement,* March 26, 1982.

Larson, Jeanette, review of *Baily's Bones, School Library Journal,* November, 1989, p. 111.

Laski, Audrey, review of *Forbidden Paths of Thual, Times Educational Supplement,* November 11, 1983.

McKinney, Caroline S., review of *Del-Del, Voice of Youth Advocates,* June, 1992, p. 110.

Miller, Sara, review of *Del-Del, School Library Journal,* June, 1992, p. 136.

Minare, Paulette, review of *The Beast of Heaven, Science Fiction Review,* May, 1986, p. 7.

Philip, Neil, "Action Men All," *Times Educational Supplement,* April 23, 1982.

Rees, JoAnn, review of *Brother Night, School Library Journal,* May, 1991, p. 111.

Shook, Bruce Anne, review of *The Red King, School Library Journal,* July, 1990, p. 89.

Tolley, Michael J., review of *The Beast of Heaven, Fantasy Review,* September, 1984, p. 31.

■ For More Information See

PERIODICALS

Publishers Weekly, July 5, 1985, p. 58.
School Librarian, September, 1985, pp. 256, 259.
Times Literary Supplement, April 12, 1985.

—*Sketch by Terrie M. Rooney*

*   *   *

KELLY, Fiona
See WELFORD, Sue

*   *   *

KEMP, Gene 1926-

■ Personal

Born December 27, 1926, in Wigginton, Staffordshire, England; daughter of Albert (an electrician) and Alice (Sutton) Rushton; married Norman Charles Pattison, August 20, 1949 (divorced May, 1958); married Allan William George Kemp (a National Union of Railwaymen divisional officer), August 23, 1958; children: (first marriage) Judith Eve; (second marriage) Chantal Alice, Richard William. *Education:* University of Exeter, B.A.

(with honors), 1945; M.A., 1984. *Politics:* Labour. *Religion:* Church of England. *Hobbies and other interests:* Politics, amateur archaeology, gardening, and reading folklore, myths, and adult literature.

■ Addresses

Home and office—6 West Ave., Exeter, Devon EX4 4SD, England. *Agent*—Gerald Pollinger, Lawrence Pollinger Ltd., 18 Maddox St., Mayfair, London W1R 0EU, England.

■ Career

Free-lance writer. Saint Sidwell's School, Exeter, England, teacher, 1963-77. Lecturer at Rolle College, 1974-75.

■ Awards, Honors

Carnegie Medal and Children's Rights Workshop Other Award, both 1977, both for *The Turbulent Term of Tyke Tiler;* Whitbread award runner-up, 1984, for *Charlie Lewis Plays for Time;* Smarties Award shortlist, 1986, 1990; Kurt Maschler Award shortlist, 1992, for *The Mink War.*

■ Writings

The Prime of Tamworth Pig, illustrated by Carolyn Dinan, Faber, 1972, Merrimack Book Service, 1979.

Tamworth Pig Saves the Trees, illustrated by Dinan, Faber, 1973, Merrimack Book Service, 1978.

Tamworth Pig and the Litter, illustrated by Dinan, Faber, 1975, Merrimack Book Service, 1978.

The Turbulent Term of Tyke Tiler, Faber, 1977.

Christmas with Tamworth Pig, illustrated by Dinan, Faber, 1977, Merrimack Book Service, 1979.

Gowie Corby Plays Chicken, Faber, 1979.

(Editor) *Ducks and Dragons: Poems for Children* (anthology), illustrated by Dinan, Faber, 1980.

Dog Days and Cat Naps (short stories), illustrated by Dinan, Faber, 1980.

Clock Tower Ghost, illustrated by Dinan, Faber, 1981.

No Place Like, Faber, 1983.

Charlie Lewis Plays for Time, illustrated by Vanessa Julian-Ottie, Faber, 1984.

The Well, illustrated by Chantal Fouracre, Faber, 1984.

Jason Bodger and the Priory Ghost, Faber, 1985.

Mr. Magus Is Waiting for You, illustrated by Alan Baker, Faber, 1986.

Juniper: A Mystery, illustrated by Chloe Cheese, Faber, 1986.

Tamworth Pig Stories, illustrated by Dinan, Faber, 1987.

Crocodile Dog, illustrated by Elizabeth Manson-Bahr, Heinemann, 1987.

I Can't Stand Losing, Faber, 1987.

Room with No Windows, Faber, 1989.

Just Ferret, Faber, 1990.

Matty's Midnight Monster, illustrated by Diann Timms, Faber, 1991.

The Mink War, illustrated by Andrew Davidson, Faber, 1992.

Tamworth Pig Rides Again, Faber, 1992.

Puffin Book of Ghosts and Ghouls, Puffin, 1992.

Roundabout (short stories), Faber, 1993.

The Wacky World of Wesley Baker, Viking Kestrel, in press.

Kemp's works have been translated into a dozen languages, including Japanese.

■ Adaptations

Mr. Magus Is Waiting for You was adapted for television and broadcast on HTV.

■ Sidelights

Gene Kemp spent many years as a teacher before she formed a small literary kingdom writing stories about the fictional Cricklepit School and its interesting inhabitants. Because of its sense of humor and dialogue that realistically imitates the way children speak, one of these books, *The Turbulent Term of Tyke Tiler,* became a best-seller in England and was very popular in the United States as well. Kemp has also produced a series about Tamworth Pig, a little boy's "pet" who can talk and who mounts crusades for various causes. She is best known for her ability to create realistic characters who must struggle with the problems dealt them. As a *Junior Bookshelf* reviewer summarized: "Gene Kemp has an understanding of modern children which enables her to write of them with humour and tolerance."

Kemp was born in Wigginton, Staffordshire, England. Many of her adventures at an early age are chronicled in the semi-autobiographical novel *The Well,* written in 1984. The story, about a young girl who grows up in a rural area and is harassed by her brother, was seen as heartwarming by many reviewers. Rodie Sudbery, for example, commented in *School Librarian* that "the book is very readable, and leaves one feeling that one would have liked more."

Kemp was an English student at the University of Exeter. She found, however, that her teachers did not have the same interest in learning that she had. "I was told to read so many stanzas of *The Faerie Queen,* toddled back home and was gripped, I read it all, then read it all again," she told Virginia Makins in the *Times Educational Supplement.* "When my tutor heard she said: 'Don't do that, we don't get carried away with things.' That's the attitude I've been fighting for the rest of my life." As if to counter this event, Kemp decided to become a teacher. She finally settled into Saint Sidwell's primary in Exeter, a school that was remarkably like the Cricklepit Combined School she was to write about later.

The first children's books Kemp published are about her character Tamworth Pig—a talking pig who is interested in a variety of causes, most notably conservation and promoting vegetarianism. Her books follow the adven-

ff

THE ROOM WITH NO WINDOWS
Gene Kemp

Gene Kemp has been praised for her novels portraying realistic young characters and their problems. (Cover illustration by Derek Brazell.)

tures of the crusading pig and his human friend, Thomas. Thomas has two favorite toy animals, Rabbit and Hedgecock, who are remarkably lucid and aid him in his adventures. These books are written in the spirit of A. A. Milne's *Winnie the Pooh* stories. While they were well-received by a variety of reviewers, Kemp told Makins she considered them to be only "nice little books in the conventional style." She wanted to write books that would be more provocative—and more relevant—to today's children.

Kemp had a breakthrough with her 1977 book *The Turbulent Term of Tyke Tiler*. The book follows the adventures of the disruptive but intelligent Tyke, whose best friend is a slow but charming child. Through an ingenious twist in the story Kemp reveals that eleven-year-old Tyke of Cricklepit School is actually a girl instead of a boy. The book was praised as a feminist work of art and served as a testament to the power of being female for many young readers. Mary Cadogan commented in *Twentieth-Century Children's Writers* that the book "demolishes many accepted ideas about aspirational and experiential differences between boys and girls." After this success, Kemp left teaching to write full-time. She has produced several other stories

about the Cricklepit School, including *Gowie Corby Plays Chicken, Juniper,* and *Charlie Lewis Plays for Time.* Kemp has also written supernatural stories, like *The Clock Tower Ghost* and *Jason Bodger and the Priory Ghost.*

"What then is the charm of Gene Kemp?" asked Elizabeth J. King in *School Librarian.* "Her writing often seems deceptively simple but her books usually have finely-drawn characters, lots of humour, and a narrative that keeps you guessing until the end." Furthermore, King reported that Kemp's writing style is street-savvy and relevant as well as accessible to children. King concluded, "from the very first page, she establishes direct contact between the reader and writer, and the reader is immediately hooked."

■ Works Cited

Cadogan, Mary, essay in *Twentieth-Century Children's Writers,* 3rd edition, edited by Tracy Chevalier, St. James Press, 1989, pp. 517-18.
Review of *Jason Bodger and the Priory Ghost, Junior Bookshelf,* December, 1985, p. 278.
King, Elizabeth J., "Children's Writers: 13—Gene Kemp," *School Librarian,* December, 1986, pp. 309-13.
Makins, Virginia, "Turbulent Terms," *Times Educational Supplement,* September 30, 1983, p. 41.
Sudbery, Rodie, review of *The Well, School Librarian,* June, 1985, p. 139.

■ For More Information See

BOOKS

Children's Literature Review, Volume 29, Gale, 1993.

PERIODICALS

Books for Keeps, July, 1990.
Bulletin of the Center for Children's Books, June, 1980; May, 1982; September, 1984.
Children's Literature in Education, autumn, 1979; autumn, 1984.
School Librarian, December, 1986, pp. 309-15.
School Library Journal, March, 1980, p. 133; August, 1980, p. 65; September, 1986, p. 136.
Spectator, June 2, 1990.
Times Literary Supplement, December 14, 1979, p. 124; June 29, 1984, p. 737; December 20, 1985, p. 1460; May 15, 1987, p. 529; May 11, 1990, p. 509.

*   *   *

KERBY, Mona 1951-

■ Personal

Given first name is Ramona; born February 5, 1951, in Dallas, TX; daughter of Raymond R. (a business executive) and Bette (a school principal; maiden name, Rudd) Nolen; married Steve Alan Kerby (a college teacher), November 27, 1974. *Education:* Attended Austin College, 1969-71; Texas Wesleyan University,

B.A., 1973; Texas Christian University, M.Ed., 1975; Texas Woman's University, M.L.S., 1980, Ph.D., 1984. *Hobbies and other interests:* Reading, knitting, movie-going.

■ Addresses

Home—6916 Martha Ln., Fort Worth, TX 76112. *Office*—Little Elementary School, 3721 Little Rd., Arlington, TX 76021.

■ Career

Thornton Elementary School, Arlington, TX, kindergarten teacher, 1973-77; Morton Elementary School, Arlington, kindergarten teacher, 1977-78; J. B. Little Elementary School, Arlington, librarian, 1978—; writer of children's books, 1987—. Texas Woman's University, adjunct professor in library and information science, 1989—. Texas Association of School Librarians, chair, 1989-90; Texas Library Association, scholarship and research committee member, 1991—; J. B. Little Parent Teacher Association, member of executive board. *Member:* Society of Children's Books Writers and Illustrators, Authors Guild, American Library Association, Texas Library Association, Beta Phi Mu Honor Society, Alpha Chi Honor Society.

MONA KERBY

■ Awards, Honors

Teacher of the Year Award, J. B. Little Elementary, 1982; *Asthma* and *Cockroaches* were named Outstanding Science Trade Books for Children, both 1989; Siddie Jo Johnson Award for Outstanding Library Service to Children in the State of Texas, 1990; National Endowment for the Humanities Teacher Scholar Award, 1993.

■ Writings

Investigating the Effectiveness of School Library Instruction, University Microfilms, 1984.
Friendly Bees, Ferocious Bees, illustrated by Anne Green, Watts, 1987.
38 Weeks Till Summer Vacation, illustrated by Melodye Rosales, Viking, 1989.
Asthma, Watts, 1989.
Beverly Sills: America's Own Opera Star, illustrated by Sheila Hamanaka, Viking, 1989.
Cockroaches, illustrated by Green, Watts, 1989.
Amelia Earhart: Courage in the Sky, illustrated by Eileen McKeating, Viking, 1990.
Samuel Morse, Watts, 1991.

■ Sidelights

Mona Kerby told *SATA:* "I am a library teacher, and whether or not I'm standing in front of my class or sitting at my desk hammering out words, I want my students to share my joy of books and ideas.

"So far, I've published three science books, three biographies, and one fiction book. I wrote *38 Weeks Till Summer Vacation* because I wanted my students to laugh. Some things in the book really happened—either in my childhood or at the school where I teach. Other things I just made up.

"I wasn't exactly thrilled when my editor asked me to write *Cockroaches.* But when I found Joanna Cole's book on the subject, I felt I was in good company (with Joanna, not the bugs). I read, learned, and taught cockroaches. My students enthusiastically tried every experiment. We learned, and had fun, too.

"Books, writing, and teaching—it's a good life."

■ For More Information See

PERIODICALS

Bulletin of the Center for Children's Books, April, 1987.

*   *   *

KERRY, Lois
See DUNCAN, Lois

KETNER, Mary Grace 1946-

Personal

Born July 1, 1946, in Kerrville, TX; daughter of John Henry (an auto mechanic and shop owner) and Grace Virginia (a homemaker; maiden name, Goss) Klingemann; married Jennings F. Ketner (a certified public accountant), December 19, 1970; children: John Travis, Katherine Heidel. *Education:* Texas Lutheran College, B.A., 1968; Southwest Texas State University, M.Ed., 1978. *Politics:* Democrat. *Religion:* Unitarian Universalist.

Addresses

Home—13710 Castle Grove, San Antonio, TX 78231-1910.

Career

School teacher in Hondo, TX, and San Antonio, TX, 1968-74; First Unitarian Church, San Antonio, director of religious education, 1982-88; writer. Institute of Texan Cultures, docent, 1989—; University of Texas at San Antonio Children's Chorus, public relations chair, 1989—; San Antonio Storytellers Association, cofounder and secretary, 1991—. Also works as a workshop facilitator and speaker. *Member:* Society of Children's Book Writers and Illustrators, San Antonio Writers' Guild, Texas Storytellers Association, Daughters of the Republic of Texas.

Awards, Honors

Best Children's Books of 1991 citation, Banks Street College, for *Ganzy Remembers.*

Writings

Ganzy Remembers (picture book), illustrated by Barbara Sparks, Atheneum, 1991.

Also author of "Lifetimes: The Texas Experience," a daily radio spot produced by the Institute of Texan Cultures, 1993—.

Work in Progress

Picture books and juvenile fiction.

Sidelights

Mary Grace Ketner commented: "In January of 1990, a teacher at my daughter's middle school asked if I could teach for her for six weeks in April and May while she was on maternity leave. The steady income had a strong appeal, but things seemed to be moving right along with the publication of *Ganzy Remembers,* and, of course, I didn't want to shortchange any parties or book signings that might come about when the book was released. I told the teacher I would have to think about it.

MARY GRACE KETNER

"The next day I called my editor to ask what date Atheneum anticipated for *Ganzy*'s publication. 'Go ahead and take the job,' she said. 'We have it on our calendar for 1991.'

"1991! Disappointed, I hung up the phone. My daughter was sitting at the kitchen table with me.

"'Kate,' I said, 'Do you know I'll be almost forty-five years old when my book is published?'

"'Yes, Mom,' she said sympathetically. 'But your picture will only be forty-two.'"

*   *   *

KNEBEL, Fletcher 1911-1993

OBITUARY NOTICE—See index for *SATA* sketch: Born October 1, 1911, in Dayton, OH; committed suicide February 26, 1993, in Honolulu, HI. Journalist and author. Knebel was perhaps best known for his Cold War thriller, *Seven Days in May,* written with Charles W. Bailey, and for his satiric syndicated daily column, "Potomac Fever," which he wrote for thirteen years beginning in 1951. He began his writing career as a reporter for local newspapers, including the *Coatesville Record* in Coatesville, PA. In 1936, he joined the *Cleveland Plain Dealer,* becoming the Washington correspondent a year later. Knebel's books, mostly novels geared toward adults and young adults, include *Night of Camp David,* for which he won an Ohioana Book Award in 1966, *Trespass, Dark Horse, Crossing in Berlin,* and *Dave Sulkin Cares!*

OBITUARIES AND OTHER SOURCES:

BOOKS

Contemporary Novelists, 5th edition, St. Martin's, 1991.

PERIODICALS

New York Times, February 28, 1993, p. 44.
Washington Post, February 28, 1993, p. B7.

*   *   *

KRAUSS, Ruth (Ida) 1911-1993

OBITUARY NOTICE—See index for *SATA* sketch: Born July 25, 1911, in Baltimore, MD; died July 10, 1993, in Westport, CT. Author of children's books, poetry, and plays. Widely known for her children's books, Krauss introduced the ideas of using minimal text and precise language and working in close collaboration with the illustrator. She herself had studied art at the Parsons School of Fine and Applied Art. Krauss issued her first book, *A Good Man and His Good Wife,* in the mid-1940s. Among her other works is *The Carrot Seed,* a collaborative effort with her husband, who illustrated it and many of her other books. Some of her volumes, like *A Hole Is to Dig* and *Somebody Else's Nut Tree,* were illustrated by renowned illustrator Maurice Sendak. Krauss's other books included *Love Poems for Children* and *Big and Little,* and she also wrote adult poem-plays for the theater.

OBITUARIES AND OTHER SOURCES:

BOOKS

The Writers Directory: 1992-1994, St. James Press, 1991, p. 561.

PERIODICALS

New York Times, July 15, 1993, p. D22.

L

LASKIN, Pamela L. 1954-

■ Personal

Born September 4, 1954, in Queens, NY; daughter of Carl Laskin (an engineer) and Frances Laskin Kornbluh; married Ira Reiser (a physician); children: Craig, Samantha. *Education:* Harpur College, B.A. (with honors), 1975, M.A. (with honors), 1981. *Politics:* Democrat. *Religion:* Jewish.

■ Addresses

Home—414 Fifth Street, Brooklyn, NY 11215.

■ Career

City College of the City University of New York, adjunct instructor in English, 1981—; Pratt Institute, Brooklyn, NY, adjunct instructor in creative writing and children's literature, 1989—. Tutors and performs poetry at a public school. *Member:* Children's Book Society, Poetry Society of America, Poets and Writers.

■ Awards, Honors

Received award in a Poetry Society of America contest, 1985; third prize, *Humanist* magazine's "Teaching Children How to Write" competition, 1987.

■ Writings

A Little off the Top, Marvel, 1985.
Music from the Heart, Bantam, 1989.
(With Addie Alexander Moskowitz) *Wish upon a Star: A Story for Children with a Parent Who Is Mentally Ill,* illustrated by Margo Lemieux, Magination, 1991.

Contributor of poetry and short fiction to periodicals, including *New York Quarterly, Kalliope, Central Park, Sassy,* and *Young Miss.*

PAMELA L. LASKIN

■ Work in Progress

Getting to Know You, Stepmother at My Door, and *Visitation Rites,* all young adult novels; a picture book titled *Steve's Specialness.*

■ Sidelights

Pamela L. Laskin told *SATA:* "I write because I am. This may sound a bit philosophical and perhaps a trifle dramatic, but writing is the essence of my heart, spirit, and soul. Most recently, my children have taken over this role dramatically, but I still find writing to be my great provider.

"How is writing a provider? It saturates my soul with music, dance, and passion; it fills a great loneliness. Whatever emotion I am feeling, writing helps to articulate and give credence to that feeling. I feel a multitude of emotions intensely and passionately—love, lust, joy, sorrow, rage—but writing, my provider, allows me to place these emotions within the context of a form.

"What I love the most about writing is the language. From the time I was very young, I loved words. They seemed like magic. I could draw on this magic and create any painting I desired. I started writing poetry when I was seven. I was a painter with words; I am one now.

"The gift my family has given me is the ability to view life from a child's perspective. This has enabled me to write for children. I believe children are the world's greatest poets, and poetic language lends itself well to children's fiction. I am using this language now when I write picture books about emotionally sensitive issues, such as *Steve's Specialness*, which is about a young boy and his retarded brother.

"I want to write great children's books, not simply books that are great. By this I mean that I want to write books—as I have done already—that will entertain and excite children, and also books about significant issues—provocative and timely issues—that will enable children to think as well as feel.

"*Wish upon a Star* is about a young girl and her emotionally disturbed mother. I have written other children's books about coping with schizophrenia. Currently I'm working on a young adult novel about a boy whose dad is homosexual and has acquired immunodeficiency syndrome (AIDS)."

*   *   *

LAUBER, Patricia (Grace) 1924-

■ Personal

Born February 5, 1924, in New York, NY; daughter of Hubert Crow (an engineer) and Florence (Walker) Lauber; married Russell Frost III, 1981. *Education:* Wellesley College, B.A., 1945. *Hobbies and other interests:* Theatre, music, animals, sailing, and travel.

■ Addresses

c/o Bradbury Press, 866 Third Ave., New York, NY 10022.

■ Career

Writer of children's books, 1954—. *Look,* New York City, writer, 1945-46; *Scholastic Magazines,* New York City, writer and editor, 1946-55; Street & Smith, New York City, editor in chief of *Science World,* 1956-59; Grolier, Inc., New York City, chief editor, science and mathematics, *The New Book of Knowledge,* 1961-67; consulting editor, *Scientific American Illustrated Library,* 1977-80. Consultant, National Science Resources

PATRICIA LAUBER

Center, National Academy of Sciences-Smithsonian Institution.

■ Awards, Honors

New York Times Notable Book citation, 1982, for *Journey to the Planets;* American Book Award nominations for children's nonfiction, 1982, for *Seeds: Pop, Stick, Glide,* and 1983, for *Journey to the Planets; Washington Post*/Children's Book Guild Award, 1983, for overall contribution to children's nonfiction literature; New York Academy of Sciences Honor Book citations, 1986, for *Tales Mummies Tell,* 1987, for *Volcano: The Eruption and Healing of Mount St. Helens,* 1988, for *From Flower to Flower,* and 1990, for *The News about Dinosaurs;* Newbery Honor Book, and *Horn Book* Fanfare Book, both 1987, both for *Volcano: The Eruption and Healing of Mount St. Helens;* Award for Outstanding Contribution to Children's Literature, Central Missouri State University, 1987; Eva L. Gordon Children's Science Author Award, American Nature Study Society, 1988; Orbis Pictus Honor Book citations, National Council of Teachers of English, 1989, for *The News about Dinosaurs,* and 1990, for *Seeing Earth from Space;* Lifetime Achievement Commendation, National Forum on Children's Science Books, Carnegie-Mellon University, 1992.

■ Writings

JUVENILE NONFICTION

Magic up Your Sleeve, Teen-Age Book Club, 1954.

(Editor) *Jokes and More Jokes,* Scholastic, 1955.

Battle against the Sea: How the Dutch Made Holland, Coward, 1956 (published in England as *Battle against the Sea: The Challenge of the Dutch and the Dikes,* Chatto & Windus, 1963), revised edition, 1971.

Highway to Adventure: The River Rhone of France, Coward, 1956.

Valiant Scots: People of the Highlands Today, Coward, 1957.

Penguins on Parade, illustrated by Douglas Howland, Coward, 1958.

Dust Bowl: The Story of Man on the Great Plains, Coward, 1958.

Rufus, the Red-Necked Hornbill, illustrated by Polly Cameron, Coward, 1958.

The Quest of Galileo, illustrated by Lee J. Ames, Doubleday, 1959.

Changing the Face of North America: The Challenge of the St. Lawrence Seaway, Coward, 1959, revised edition, 1968.

All about the Ice Age, Random House, 1959.

Our Friend the Forest: A Conservation Story, illustrated by Anne Marie Jauss, Doubleday, 1959.

All about the Planets, Random House, 1960.

The Quest of Louis Pasteur, illustrated by Ames, Doubleday, 1960.

Getting to Know Switzerland, illustrated by J. L. Pellicer, Coward, 1960.

The Story of Numbers, Random House, 1961.

Icebergs and Glaciers, Garrard, 1961.

The Mississippi: Giant at Work, Garrard, 1961.

Famous Mysteries of the Sea, Thomas Nelson, 1962.

All about the Planet Earth, Random House, 1962.

Your Body and How It Works, Random House, 1962.

The Friendly Dolphins, Random House, 1963, revised edition, Scholastic, 1994.

Penguins, Garrard, 1963.

The Congo: River into Central Africa, Garrard, 1964.

The Surprising Kangaroos and Other Pouched Mammals, Random House, 1965.

Big Dreams and Small Rockets: A Short History of Space Travel, Crowell, 1965.

Volcanoes, Garrard, 1965.

The Story of Dogs, Random House, 1966.

The Look-It-Up Book of Mammals, illustrated by Guy Coheleach, Random House, 1967.

The Look-It-Up Book of Stars and Planets, illustrated by John Polgreen, Random House, 1967.

The Look-It-Up Book of the Fifty States, illustrated by Herbert Borst, Random House, 1967.

Bats: Wings in the Night, Random House, 1968.

The Planets, Random House, 1969.

This Restless Earth, Random House, 1970.

Who Discovered America?: Settlers and Explorers of the New World before the Time of Columbus, Random House, 1970, new edition, HarperCollins, 1992.

Of Man and Mouse: How House Mice Became Laboratory Mice, Viking, 1971.

Satellite images of the Earth provide a wealth of information about how our world is working and changing in this book by Lauber.

Earthquakes: New Scientific Ideas about How and Why the Earth Shakes, Random House, 1972.

Everglades: A Question of Life or Death, photographs by Patricia Caulfield, Viking, 1973.

Cowboys and Cattle Ranching, Crowell, 1973.

Who Needs Alligators?, Garrard, 1974.

Life on a Giant Cactus, Garrard, 1974.

Too Much Garbage, illustrated by Vic Mays, Garrard, 1974.

Great Whales, Garrard, 1975.

Earthworms: Underground Farmers, Garrard, 1976.

Sea Otters and Seaweed, Garrard, 1976.

Mystery Monsters of Loch Ness, illustrated by Mays, Garrard, 1978.

Tapping Earth's Heat, illustrated by Edward Malsberg, Garrard, 1978.

What's Hatching out of That Egg?, Crown, 1979.

Seeds: Pop, Stick, Glide, photographs by Jerome Wexler, Crown, 1981.

Journey to the Planets, Crown, 1982, 4th revised edition, 1993.

Tales Mummies Tell, Crowell, 1985.

Volcanoes and Earthquakes, Scholastic, Inc., 1985.

What Big Teeth You Have!, illustrated by Martha Weston, Crowell, 1986.

Get Ready for Robots!, illustrated by True Kelley, Crowell, 1986.

Volcano: The Eruption and Healing of Mount St. Helens, Bradbury, 1986.

From Flower to Flower: Animals and Pollination, photographs by Wexler, Crowell, 1986.

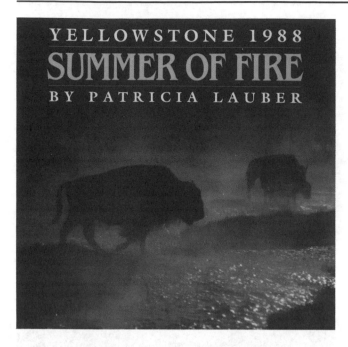

YELLOWSTONE 1988 SUMMER OF FIRE
BY PATRICIA LAUBER

Lauber's concern for the natural environment inspired her to present this look at the renewal of life after a forest fire in Yellowstone National Park.

Dinosaurs Walked Here and Other Stories Fossils Tell, Bradbury, 1987.
Snakes Are Hunters, illustrated by Holly Keller, Crowell, 1987.
Lost Star: The Story of Amelia Earhart, Scholastic, Inc., 1988.
Voyagers from Space: Meteors and Meteorites, illustrated by Mike Eagle, Crowell, 1989.
The News about Dinosaurs, illustrated by John Gurche, Douglas Henderson, and Gregory Paul, Bradbury, 1989.
Seeing Earth from Space, Orchard Books, 1990.
An Octopus Is Amazing, illustrated by Keller, Crowell, 1990.
How We Learned the Earth Is Round, illustrated by Megan Lloyd, Crowell, 1990.
Living with Dinosaurs, illustrated by Henderson, Bradbury, 1991.
Great Whales, the Gentle Giants, illustrated by Pieter Folkens, Henry Holt, 1991.
Summer of Fire: Yellowstone 1988, Orchard Books, 1991.
Be a Friend to Trees, illustrated by Keller, HarperCollins, 1994.
How Animals Live Where They Do, Scholastic, 1994.
What Do You See?, Crown, 1994.
Alligators: A Success Story, Holt, 1994.
Earthworms: Farmers of the Underground, Holt, 1994.
Who Eats What?, illustrated by Keller, HarperCollins, in press.
How Dinosaurs Came to Be, illustrated by Henderson, Bradbury, in press.

JUVENILE FICTION

Clarence, the TV Dog, Coward, 1955.

Clarence Goes to Town, Coward, 1957, Random House, 1967.
Found: One Orange-Brown Horse, Random House, 1957.
The Runaway Flea Circus, Random House, 1958.
Clarence Turns Sea Dog, Coward, 1959, Random House, 1965.
Adventure at Black Rock Cave, Random House, 1959.
Champ, Gallant Collie, Random House, 1960.
Curious Critters, Garrard, 1969.
Clarence and the Burglar, illustrated by Paul Galdone, Coward, 1973.
Clarence and the Cat, illustrated by Galdone, Coward, 1977.
Home at Last: A Young Cat's Tale, illustrated by Mary Chalmers, Coward, 1980.

OTHER

Contributor of short stories and light essays to adult magazines. Former editor, Coward-McCann's "Challenge Books" series, and Garrard's "Good Earth Books" series; free-lance editor, *Scientific American Illustrated Library.*

■ Work in Progress

A book of light fiction and three nonfiction works.

■ Sidelights

Through such award-winning books as *Volcano: The Eruption and Healing of Mount St. Helens* and *Journey to the Planets,* Patricia Lauber has made science an entertaining as well as enriching reading experience for children. "Children are born curious, wanting and needing to understand the world around them, wanting to know why, how, and what: the very questions that scientists ask," the author remarked in *The Lion and the Unicorn.* Contrary to the popular perception of science as dry and lifeless, Lauber continued, "I believe that the best science books have a story line: that one thing leads to another, that it is possible to build tension so that the reader really wants to find out what happens next." Lauber's own work, whether describing nature's marvels, animals both prehistoric and living, or technological matters, informs readers with clear explanations, up-to-date information, and illustrations carefully selected by the author for their interest and accuracy.

In *The Quest of Galileo,* for instance, "the story of the man who destroyed the Aristotelian view of the universe is told clearly and forthrightly," Isaac Asimov writes in *Horn Book,* and "extraordinarily good is the description of the experiments Galileo conducted and the conclusions he drew therefrom." Similarly, in *Tales Mummies Tell* Lauber makes science accessible to children "by illustrating how it can answer questions any normal youngster would find interesting," *Washington Post Book World* contributor Michael Guillen notes. With her uncomplicated yet interesting explanations of scientific principles, the critic adds, "Lauber makes science more attractive and not, thank goodness, merely more respectworthy."

Lauber earned her first American Book Award nomination for 1982's *Seeds: Pop, Stick, Glide,* a book Steve Matthews of *School Library Journal* calls "the Mercedes of the introductory seed books." The critic explains: "The text is vivid and assumes very little on the part of readers, except a willingness to perceive the natural world." "The text is remarkable," Marion P. Harris similarly comments in *Appraisal: Children's Science Books.* "It manages to go into sufficient depth to surprise and fascinate an adult reader, yet uses sentence structure and vocabulary that will allow comfortable reading by intermediate readers." As Matthews concludes: "*Seeds* not only informs, it fosters an appreciation of the plant world and makes wondrous what is too often seen as commonplace."

Journey to the Planets has received similar praise; a *Kirkus Reviews* writer calls it "a stimulating experience for the eyes, mind, and imagination." In her review, Margaret L. Chatham of *School Library Journal* predicts that Lauber's colorfully illustrated guide to our solar system will become popular "because Lauber has the rare ability to explain things simply without compromising scientific accuracy." The critic's forecast proved accurate, for *Journey to the Planets* has already inspired three additional updates; *Appraisal* contributor Diane F. Holzheimer notes of one that Lauber's "metaphors and concrete examples draw the reader in and make these remote and awesome places real."

In her nonfiction works for children, such as this look at the planets of our solar system, Lauber presents scientific concepts in accurate and yet entertaining detail.

Volcano Chosen for Newbery Honor

A less remote but equally awesome event was the 1980 volcanic eruption of Mount St. Helens in the state of Washington, and Lauber's *Volcano: The Eruption and Healing of Mount St. Helens* "is told in a gripping style and with extraordinary photographs," Elizabeth S. Watson describes in *Horn Book.* "Evident throughout the book are Patricia Lauber's careful scholarship and talent for distilling material to present it in an extremely smooth narrative." "Not only is the eruption carefully explained, but nature's slow rebuilding process is delineated," Frances Bradburn recounts in *Wilson Library Bulletin.* As a result, the critic continues, "children are given the privilege of experiencing a year in the life of a volcano and its surrounding areas, a year in which they witness the miraculous power of two of nature's greatest forces—an active volcano and life's resilient rebirth."

Although Lauber had kept abreast of the developments in the volcano's eruption, "I had not thought of doing a book specifically on Mount St. Helens—until I saw the photo," the author related in a Junior Literary Guild publicity article. "It was a close-up of a hardy green plant that had pushed its way up through a crack in the crust of ash and put out a pink flower. It made me think about doing a book that would explain not only why and how the volcano erupted but also how life came back to a region as barren as the moon." This portrayal of the area's renewal makes *Volcano,* "while written for children, [a book] that will appeal to the curious and full of wonder of all ages," Bradburn writes. "From Patricia Lauber's masterly book we learn that solid information can be captivating in the hands of a gifted writer," Jo Carr comments in *Horn Book.* The judges for the 1987 Newbery Awards, the critic concludes, "showed great wisdom in choosing this perfect book for a Newbery Honor Book."

Although she is best known for her award-winning nonfiction, Lauber has also written several stories for children. Her first, *Clarence the TV Dog,* came from her experiences with her own dog and proved popular enough to inspire four more "Clarence" books. A friendly dog who watches television and catches a burglar by untying his shoelaces, Clarence, as well as his family, is "believable and funny, simpler than life and twice as natural," *New York Times Book Review* writer Marjorie Fischer comments of the first book. *Clarence Goes to Town* is similarly funny, the critic adds in another review, "a fine mixture of the probable and improbable—sensible nonsense."

Speaking of her origins as an author, Lauber once commented: "'How did you become a writer?' is a question that I long found very difficult to answer. Finally, I realized what the problem was: I don't think that I 'became' a writer; I think I was born wanting to write. As a very small child, I loved stories and being read to and soon learned to read myself, because then I could have as many stories as I wanted.

Lauber relates the findings of scientists who witnessed the powerful eruption of Mount St. Helens in 1980 and the natural recovery of the surrounding landscape that followed.

"When I had learned to read, and also to print and to spell a few words, I made a wonderful discovery—I could make up stories and poems myself and put them on paper. The spelling wasn't very good, but people seemed to enjoy what I wrote anyhow. This encouraged me . . . .

"I write about anything that interests me—dogs, horses, forests, birds, mysteries, life in other countries. Some of my books are fiction, and some are nonfiction, but all are based on what I've seen around me. I like to stand and stare at things, to talk with people, and to read a lot. From this I'm always learning something I didn't know before. Some time later, when I've had a chance to think things over, I write down what I heard, saw, felt, and thought."

"And that," the author concluded, "is about as close as I can come to answering another question people often ask me. 'Where do you get your ideas?' My ideas come from everywhere—from things I read, from things people tell me about, from things I see about me, from things I experience. The important aspect is that they must interest me very much, because then I want to share them with other people."

■ Works Cited

Asimov, Isaac, review of *The Quest of Galileo, Horn Book*, October, 1959, p. 396.

Bradburn, Frances, "Middle Books," *Wilson Library Bulletin*, April, 1987, pp. 48-49.

Carr, Jo, "Filling Vases, Lighting Fires," *Horn Book*, November-December, 1987, pp. 710-713.

Chatham, Margaret L., review of *Journey to the Planets, School Library Journal*, August, 1982, p. 118.

Fischer, Marjorie, "Gifted Pooch," *New York Times Book Review*, November 13, 1955, p. 36.

Fischer, Marjorie, "A Dog Has His Day," *New York Times Book Review*, November 17, 1957, p. 38.

Guillen, Michael, review of *Tales Mummies Tell, Washington Post Book World*, May 12, 1985.

Harris, Marion P., review of *Seeds: Pop, Stick, Glide, Appraisal: Children's Science Books*, fall, 1981, pp. 24-25.

Holzheimer, Diane F., review of *Journey to the Planets, Appraisal: Children's Science Books*, winter, 1988, pp. 39-40.

Review of *Journey to the Planets, Kirkus Reviews*, May 15, 1982, pp. 606-607.

Lauber, Patricia, "What Makes an Appealing and Readable Science Book?," *The Lion and the Unicorn*, Volume 6, 1982, pp. 5-9.

Lauber, Patricia, quoted in Junior Literary Guild publicity packet, April-September, 1986, p. 33.

Matthews, Steve, review of *Seeds: Pop, Stick, Glide, School Library Journal*, April, 1981, p. 114.

Watson, Elizabeth S., review of *Volcano: The Eruption and Healing of Mount St. Helens, Horn Book*, September-October, 1986, p. 609.

■ For More Information See

BOOKS

Children's Literature Review, Volume 16, Gale, 1989.

de Montreville, Doris, and Donna Hill, editors, *Third Book of Junior Authors*, H. W. Wilson, 1972.

PERIODICALS

Bulletin of the Center for Children's Books, September, 1986.

New York Times Book Review, April 26, 1959.

*   *   *

L'ENGLE, Madeleine (Camp Franklin) 1918-

■ Personal

Surname pronounced "leng-*el*"; given name, Madeleine L'Engle Camp; born November 29, 1918, in New York, NY; daughter of Charles Wadsworth (a foreign correspondent and author) and Madeleine (a pianist; maiden name, Barnett) Camp; married Hugh Franklin (an actor), January 26, 1946 (died September, 1986); children: Josephine (Mrs. Alan W. Jones), Maria (Mrs. John Rooney), Bion. *Education:* Smith College, A.B. (with honors), 1941; attended New School for Social Research, 1941-42; Columbia University, graduate study, 1960-61. *Politics:* "New England." *Religion:* Anglican.

■ Addresses

Home—924 West End Ave., New York, NY 10025; Crosswicks, Goshen, CT 06756. *Agent*—Robert Lescher, 67 Irving Place, New York, NY 10003.

■ Career

Active career in theatre, 1941-47; teacher with Committee for Refugee Education during World War II; St. Hilda's and St. Hugh's School, Morningside Heights, NY, teacher, 1960-66; Cathedral of St. John the Divine, New York City, librarian, 1966—. University of Indiana, Bloomington, member of faculty, summers, 1965-66 and 1971; writer-in-residence, Ohio State University, Columbus, 1970, and University of Rochester, New York, 1972. Lecturer. *Member:* Authors Guild (president), Authors League of America, PEN.

■ Awards, Honors

And Both Were Young was named one of the Ten Best Books of the Year, *New York Times,* 1949; Newbery Medal from the American Library Association, 1963, Hans Christian Andersen Award runner-up, 1964, and Sequoyah Children's Book Award from the Oklahoma State Department of Education, and Lewis Carroll Shelf Award, both 1965, all for *A Wrinkle in Time; Book World's* Spring Book Festival Honor Book, and one of *School Library Journal's* Best Books of the Year, both 1968, both for *The Young Unicorns;* Austrian State Literary Prize, 1969, for *The Moon by Night;* University of Southern Mississippi Silver Medallion, 1978, for "an outstanding contribution to the field of children's literature"; American Book Award for paperback fiction, 1980, for *A Swiftly Tilting Planet;* Smith Medal, 1980; Newbery Honor Book, 1981, for *A Ring of Endless Light;* Books for the Teen Age selections, New York Public Library, 1981, for *A Ring of Endless Light,* and 1982, for *Camilla;* Sophie Award, 1984; Regina Medal, Catholic Library Association, 1984; *A House Like a Lotus* was exhibited at the Bologna International Children's Book Fair, 1985; Adolescent Literature Assembly Award for Outstanding Contribution to Adolescent Literature, National Council of Teachers of English, 1986.

■ Writings

PICTURE BOOKS

Dance in the Desert, illustrated by Symeon Shimin, Farrar, Straus, 1969.

Everyday Prayers, illustrated by Lucille Butel, Morehouse, 1974.

Prayers for Sunday, illustrated by Lizzie Napoli, Morehouse, 1974.

Ladder of Angels: Scenes from the Bible Illustrated by the Children of the World, Seabury, 1979.

The Glorious Impossible, illustrated by Giotto, Simon & Schuster, 1990.

JUVENILE FICTION

And Both Were Young, Lothrop, 1949, reprinted, Delacorte, 1983.

Camilla, Crowell, 1965, reprinted, Delacorte, 1981.

Intergalactic P.S.3, Children's Book Council, 1970.

The Sphinx at Dawn: Two Stories (illustrated by Vivian Berger), Harper, 1982.

"AUSTIN FAMILY" SERIES

Meet the Austins (ALA Notable Book), illustrated by Gillian Willett, Vanguard, 1960.

The Moon by Night, Farrar, Straus, 1963.

The Twenty-Four Days before Christmas: An Austin Family Story, illustrated by Inga, Farrar, Straus, 1964, new edition, illustrated by Joe De Velasco, Shaw, 1984.

A Ring of Endless Light (ALA Notable Book), Farrar, Straus, 1980.

The Anti-Muffins (illustrated by Gloria Ortiz), Pilgrim, 1981.

"TIME FANTASY" SERIES

A Wrinkle in Time (Junior Literary Guild selection), Farrar, Straus, 1962.

A Wind in the Door, Farrar, Straus, 1973.

A Swiftly Tilting Planet, Farrar, Straus, 1978.

A House Like a Lotus, Farrar, Straus, 1984.

Many Waters, Farrar, Straus, 1986.

Madeleine L'Engle's Time Quartet, Dell, 1987.

An Acceptable Time, Farrar, Straus, 1989.

"CANNON TALLIS MYSTERY" SERIES

The Arm of the Starfish (*Horn Book* honor list; Junior Literary Guild selection), Farrar, Straus, 1965.

The Young Unicorns, Farrar, Straus, 1968.

Dragons in the Waters, Farrar, Straus, 1976.

MADELEINE L'ENGLE

FOR ADULTS: FICTION

The Small Rain: A Novel, Vanguard, 1945, published as
    Prelude, 1968, new edition under original title,
    Farrar, Straus, 1984.
Ilsa, Vanguard, 1946.
Camilla Dickinson, Simon & Schuster, 1951, also pub-
    lished for young adults as *Camilla.*
A Winter's Love, Lippincott, 1957, reprinted, Ballan-
    tine, 1983.
The Love Letters, Farrar, Straus, 1966.
The Other Side of the Sun, Farrar, Straus, 1971.
A Severed Wasp (sequel to *The Small Rain*), Farrar,
    Straus, 1982.
Certain Women, Farrar, Straus, 1992.

NONFICTION

(Editor with William B. Green) *Spirit and Light: Essays
    in Historical Theology,* Seabury, 1976.
And It Was Good: Reflections on Beginnings, Shaw,
    1983.
Dare to Be Creative, Library of Congress, 1984.
(With Avery Brooke) *Trailing Clouds of Glory: Spiritual
    Values in Children's Books,* Westminster, 1985.
A Stone for a Pillow: Journeys with Jacob, Shaw, 1986.
Sold into Egypt: Joseph's Journey into Human Being,
    Shaw, 1989.
The Rock That Is Higher: Story as Truth, Shaw, 1993.

"CROSSWICKS JOURNALS" (AUTOBIOGRAPHY)

A Circle of Quiet, Farrar, Straus, 1972.
The Summer of the Great-Grandmother, Farrar, Straus,
    1974.
The Irrational Season, Seabury, 1977.
Two Part Invention: The Story of a Marriage, Farrar,
    Straus, 1988.

POETRY

Lines Scribbled on an Envelope and Other Poems,
    Farrar, Straus, 1969.
The Weather of the Heart, Shaw, 1978.
Walking on Water: Reflections on Faith and Art, Shaw,
    1980.
A Cry Like a Bell, Shaw, 1987.

PLAYS

18 Washington Square, South: A Comedy in One Act
    (first produced in Northampton, MA, 1940), Baker,
    1944.
(With Robert Hartung) *How Now Brown Cow,* first
    produced in New York, 1949.
The Journey with Jonah, illustrated by Leonard Everett
    Fisher (one-act; first produced in New York City,
    1970), Farrar, Straus, 1967.

OTHER

Contributor of articles, stories, and poems to periodicals, including *McCall's, Christian Century, Commonweal, Christianity Today,* and *Mademoiselle.* Collections
of L'Engle's manuscripts are housed at Wheaton College, at the Kerlan Collection of the University of
Minnesota, Minneapolis, and at the de Grummond
Collection of the University of Southern Mississippi.

■ Work in Progress

A new "Austin Family" book centering on Vicky Austin
and set in Antarctica.

■ Adaptations

Miramax is producing a film of *A Wrinkle in Time* for
release in 1994, and the book was recorded by Newbery
Award Records, 1972, and adapted as a filmstrip with
cassette by Miller-Brody, 1974; *A Wind in the Door* was
recorded and adapted as a filmstrip with cassette by
Miller-Brody; *Camilla* was recorded as a cassette by
Listening Library; *A Ring of Endless Light* was recorded
and adapted as a filmstrip with cassette by Random
House. *And Both Were Young, The Arm of the Starfish,
Meet the Austins, The Moon by Night, A Wrinkle in
Time,* and *The Young Unicorns* have been adapted into
Braille; *The Arm of the Starfish, Camilla, Dragons in the
Waters, A Wind in the Door,* and *A Wrinkle in Time*
have been adapted as talking books; *The Summer of the
Great-Grandmother* is also available on cassette.

■ Sidelights

Madeleine L'Engle is a writer who resists easy classifica-
tion. She has successfully published plays, poems,
essays, autobiographies, and novels for both children
and adults. She is probably best known for her "Time
Fantasy" series of children's books, including *A Wrinkle
in Time, A Wind in the Door,* and *A Swiftly Tilting
Planet.* These novels combine elements of science
fiction and fantasy with L'Engle's constant themes of
family love and moral responsibility.

As the daughter of a respected journalist and a gifted
pianist, L'Engle was surrounded by creative people from
birth. She wrote her first stories at the age of five. She
was an only child; in her autobiographies she writes of
how much she enjoyed her solitude and of the rich
fantasy life she created for herself.

Speaking of her childhood, L'Engle explains in *The
Summer of the Great-Grandmother:* "[My mother] was
almost forty when I was born .... Once she and Father
had had their long-awaited baby, I became a bone of
contention between them. They disagreed completely on
how I ought to be brought up. Father wanted a strict
English childhood for me, and this is more or less what I
got—nanny, governesses, supper on a tray in the nursery, dancing lessons, music lessons, skating lessons, art
lessons."

Her father's failing health sent her parents to Switzerland and young Madeleine to a series of boarding
schools, where she found herself very unpopular because
of her shy, introspective ways. "I learned," L'Engle
recounts in *The Summer of the Great-Grandmother,* "to
put on protective coloring in order to survive in an
atmosphere which was alien; and I learned to concentrate. Because I was never alone ... I learned to shut
out the sound of the school and listen to the story or
poem I was writing when I should have been doing

A Companion to *A Wrinkle in Time*

MADELEINE L'ENGLE

An Acceptable Time

A girl is transported through a time gate to a world three thousand years in the past in L'Engle's fantasy novel.

schoolwork. The result of this early lesson in concentration is that I can write anywhere."

L'Engle became involved in theatre at Smith College, acting as well as writing plays. Soon after graduation, she was made an understudy for a Broadway production. Later she was given a few small roles and the position of assistant stage manager for Anton Chekhov's *Cherry Orchard*. The play ran for two years, and one of the performers, Hugh Franklin, eventually became L'Engle's husband. Throughout her career in the theatre, the author's writing continued, and both her theatre and boarding school experiences are evident in her first published novel. *The Small Rain* features Katherine Forrester, the daughter of a concert pianist. As a young child, Katherine plays a small role in a Broadway production, and the actors, stage hands, and dressing rooms become her world. Later, as a boarding school student, she finds solace in her music and becomes increasingly dedicated to it. *The Small Rain* thus illustrates "one of L'Engle's predominant themes: that an artist must constantly discipline herself; otherwise her talent will become dissipated and she will never achieve her greatest potential," commented Marygail G. Parker in the *Dictionary of Literary Biography*.

After publishing several books in the late 1940s, L'Engle's career as a writer was postponed in favor of raising her own family. During the 1950s, she and her husband operated a general store in rural Connecticut. L'Engle still wrote stories in her spare time, but these were invariably rejected by magazines. As she recounts in *A Circle of Quiet:* "During the long drag of years before our youngest child went to school, my love for my family and my need to write were in acute conflict. The problem was really that I put two things first. My husband and children came first. So did my writing." On her fortieth birthday, in 1958, discouraged by several years of rejections, she renounced writing completely, but found that she was unable to stop. She explains, "I had to write. I had no choice in the matter. It was not up to me to say I would stop, because I could not. It didn't matter how small or inadequate [was] my talent. If I never had another book published, and it was very clear to me that this was a real possibility, I still had to go on writing." Soon thereafter, things began to change for the author, and her writing began to sell again.

Award-winning Novel Initially Rejected by Publishers

Selling *A Wrinkle in Time,* however, proved a challenge. The juvenile novel was rejected by 26 publishers in two years. Reasons given vary. The book was neither science fiction nor fantasy, impossible to pigeon hole. "Most objections," L'Engle recalled in an interview with *Children's Literature in Education,* "were that it would not be able to find an audience, that it was too difficult for children." Speaking to Michael J. Farrell in the *National Catholic Reporter,* L'Engle commented that *A Wrinkle in Time* "was written in the terms of a modern world in which children know about brainwashing and the corruption of evil. It's based on Einstein's theory of relativity and Planck's quantum theory. It's good, solid science, but also it's good, solid theology. My rebuttal to the German theologians [who] attack God with their intellect on the assumption that the finite can comprehend the infinite, and I don't think that's possible."

The book was finally accepted by an editor at Farrar, Straus. "He had read my first book, *The Small Rain,* liked it, and asked if I had any other manuscripts," L'Engle recalled for *More Books by More People.* "I gave him *Wrinkle* and told him, 'Here's a book nobody likes.' He read it and two weeks later I signed the contract. The editors told me not to be disappointed if it doesn't do well and that they were publishing it because they loved it." The public loved the book too. *A Wrinkle in Time* won the Newbery Medal in 1963, the Lewis Carroll Shelf Award in 1965, and was a runner-up for the Hans Christian Andersen Award in 1964.

Speaking with Roy Newquist in his *Conversations,* L'Engle recalled winning the Newbery Medal: "The telephone rang. It was long distance, and an impossible connection. I couldn't hear anything. The operator told me to hang up and she'd try again. The long-distance phone ringing unexpectedly always makes me nervous:

is something wrong with one of the grandparents? The phone rang again, and still the connection was full of static and roaring, so the operator told me to hang up and she'd try once more. This time I could barely hear a voice: 'This is Ruth Gagliardo, of the Newbery Caldecott committee.' There was a pause, and she asked, 'Can you hear me?' 'Yes, I can hear you.' Then she told me that *Wrinkle* had won the medal. My response was an inarticulate squawk; Ruth told me later that it was a special pleasure to her to have me *that* excited."

In *A Wrinkle in Time,* young Meg Murry, with the help of her friend Calvin O'Keefe, must use time travel and extrasensory perception to rescue her father, a gifted scientist, from the evil forces that hold him prisoner on another planet. To release him, Meg must learn the power of love. In *A Critical History of Children's Literature,* Ruth Hill Viguers calls *A Wrinkle in Time* a "book that combines devices of fairy tales, overtones of fantasy, the philosophy of great lives, the visions of science, and the warmth of a good family story . . . . It is an exuberant book, original, vital, exciting. Funny ideas, fearful images, amazing characters, and beautiful concepts sweep through it. And it is full of truth."

The Newbery Award—winning Classic

Madeleine L'Engle

L'Engle's popular "Time Fantasy" series combines elements of science fiction with themes of love and responsibility.

According to L'Engle, writing *A Wrinkle in Time* was a mysterious process. "A writer of fantasy, fairy tale, or myth," she explained in *Horn Book,* "must inevitably discover that he is not writing out of his own knowledge or experience, but out of something both deeper and wider. I think that fantasy must possess the author and simply use him. I know that this is true of *A Wrinkle in Time.* I can't possibly tell you how I came to write it. It was simply a book I had to write. I had no choice. And it was only *after* it was written that I realized what some of it meant."

In his book *A Sense of Story: Essays on Contemporary Writers for Children,* John Rowe Townsend examines the themes in L'Engle's work: "L'Engle's main themes are the clash of good and evil, the difficulty and necessity of deciding which is which and of committing oneself, the search for fulfillment and self-knowledge. These themes are determined by what the author *is;* and she is a practising and active Christian. Many writers' religious beliefs appear immaterial to their work; Miss L'Engle's are crucial." Townsend sees a mystical dimension to *A Wrinkle in Time.* In that book, he writes, "the clash of good and evil is at a cosmic level. Much of the action is concerned with the rescue by the heroine Meg and her friend Calvin O'Keefe of Meg's father and brother, prisoners of a great brain called IT which controls the lives of a zombie population on a planet called Camazotz. Here evil is obviously the reduction of people to a mindless mass, while good is individuality, art and love. It is the sheer power of love which enables Meg to triumph over IT, for love is the force that she has and IT has not."

L'Engle went on to write *A Wind in the Door* and *A Swiftly Tilting Planet,* which feature the characters introduced in *A Wrinkle in Time* and further develop the theme of love as a weapon against darkness. By the third book in the series, Meg and Calvin have become husband and wife and are expecting their first child, Polly. Polly has adventures of her own in novels such as *A House Like A Lotus* and *An Acceptable Time.* Although the series has been criticized as too convoluted for young readers, and some reviewers find the Murry family a trifle unbelievable and elitist, most critics praise the series for its willingness to take risks. Michele Murray, writing of *A Wind in the Door* in the *New York Times Book Review,* claimed that "L'Engle mixes classical theology, contemporary family life, and futuristic science fiction to make a completely convincing tale." Speaking of this work, *School Library Journal* contributor Margaret A. Dorsey asserted: "Complex and rich in mystical religious insights, this is breathtaking entertainment."

"Austin Family" Books Explore Complex Issues

L'Engle has also created a second family, the Austins, in *Meet the Austins, The Moon by Night, A Ring of Endless Light,* and other works. These characters, like those in the "Time Fantasy" series, explore philosophical and spiritual issues as they negotiate their relationships and the challenges that growing up entails. But the Austins' journeys—unlike Meg and Calvin's voyages across galaxies and time—involve more familiar settings and events.

In *Meet the Austins,* L'Engle's 1960 novel, the four children—John, Vicky, Suzy, and Rob—face the prospect of adopting Maggy, a spoiled and unruly foster child who initially turns their household upside-down, but slowly adjusts to her new home and becomes a member of the family. A *Times Literary Supplement* contributor noted that although the family is "much too good to be real," Maggy's "gradual improvement and acceptance by the others are the best part of the book." *The Moon by Night,* published in 1963, takes place throughout the family's cross-country camping trip. Fourteen-year-old Vicky, who narrates the story, meets Zachary Gray at a camping ground. A complex, older boy whose ideas bear little resemblance to those of Vicky's small-town family and friends, Zachary both frightens and fascinates her. The Austins continue to encounter Zachary along the way, and later Vicky meets Andy, a sunny, down-to-earth boy who competes with Zachary for her affections. In the course of their travels, Vicky learns that the world is far more complicated than she had imagined.

A Ring of Endless Light, which was named a Newbery Honor Book in 1981, finds the Austins spending the summer caring for their dying grandfather at his home near the ocean. It is sixteen-year-old Vicky's first experience with death, and the concept raises new and difficult questions. Then Commander Rodney, a Coast Guard officer and cherished family friend, is killed rescuing a drowning young man. Vicky learns that the young man was Zachary Gray, who is once again trailing Vicky, and that his near-drowning was a suicide attempt. At the funeral, Vicky meets Adam Eddington, who works with Vicky's older brother John at the marine biology station. As the summer progresses, Vicky finds four men dependent on her in different ways. She reads to her grandfather, a wise minister who, in his coherent moments, helps her sort out her confusion. Troubled Zachary takes Vicky for exciting but dangerous adventures and leans on her emotionally. Vicky also befriends Commander Rodney's grieving son Leo, who seeks more than friendship, and assists Adam with his project at the marine biology station. Although Adam thinks of Vicky as John's younger sister, thwarting her hopes for a romantic relationship, it is their work with dolphins that reveals Vicky's gift for telepathic communication and helps her find a new understanding of life and death. Carol Van Strum, writing in the *Washington Post Book World,* commented, "The cosmic battle between light and darkness, good and evil, love and indifference, personified in the mythic fantasies of the *Wrinkle in Time* series, here is waged compellingly in its rightful place: within ourselves."

L'Engle's practice of reviving characters from earlier novels makes all her works for young people—whether realistic or fantasy—part of an intricately connected whole. The Murry, O'Keefe, and Austin characters become increasingly real as they age and progress

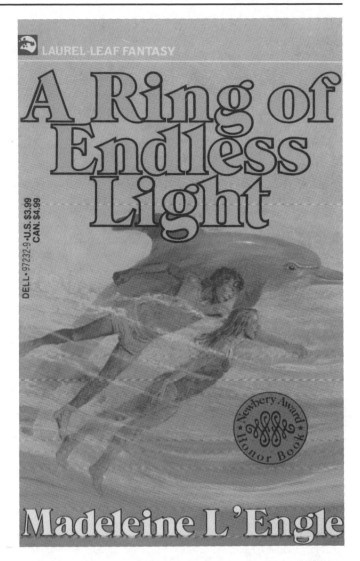

LAUREL-LEAF FANTASY

A Ring of Endless Light

DELL-97232-9-U.S. $3.99 CAN. $4.99

Newbery Award Honor Book

Madeleine L'Engle

In this Newbery Honor Book, a young woman grapples with her spiritual confusion when she must face issues of death and love in one summer on a picturesque island.

through their life-cycles. Similarly, new facets of Zachary Gray and Adam Eddington emerge when they are placed in diverse situations. Originally associated with Vicky Austin, Zachary meets Polly O'Keefe in Greece in *A House Like a Lotus.* In *An Acceptable Time,* Zachary visits Polly at her grandparents' house, and the two travel three thousand years into the past, to the same community that Polly's uncle, Charles Wallace, visits as a teenager in *A Swiftly Tilting Planet.* Before he meets the Austins, Adam Eddington is featured in a dangerous escapade involving Dr. Calvin O'Keefe's biological research and his twelve-year-old daughter Polly in *The Arm of the Starfish.*

Explaining her storytelling method in *Something about the Author Autobiography Series,* L'Engle stated, "I start with what I know with all five senses, what I have experienced, and then the imagination takes over and says, 'But what if—' and the story is on." The author's ability to entertain is evident in her popularity with readers. A *Publishers Weekly* survey of the nation's booksellers ranked her in the top six best-selling children's authors, while in an overview of children's book publishing, *American Bookseller* ranked L'Engle among the ten most popular children's authors in the country. But the writing process also fulfills an essential need for the author. As she stated in *Something about the Author Autobiography Series,* "Often I am asked, 'Are you writing anything now?' Of course I'm writing something now. I'm not nice when I'm not writing."

■ Works Cited

Dorsey, Margaret A., review of *A Wind in the Door, School Library Journal,* May, 1973, p. 81.

Farrell, Michael J., "Madeleine L'Engle: In Search of Where Lion and Lamb Abide," *National Catholic Reporter,* June 20, 1986.

Hopkins, Lee Bennett, *More Books by More People,* Citation, 1974.

L'Engle, Madeleine, "The Expanding Universe," *Horn Book,* August, 1963.

L'Engle, Madeleine, *A Circle of Quiet,* Farrar, Straus, 1972.

L'Engle, Madeleine, *Something about the Author Autobiography Series,* Gale, Volume 15, 1993, pp. 187-199.

L'Engle, Madeleine, *The Summer of the Great-Grandmother,* Farrar, Straus, 1974.

Review of *Meet the Austins, Times Literary Supplement,* May 19, 1966, p. 433.

Murray, Michele, review of *A Wind in the Door, New York Times Book Review,* July 8, 1973, p. 8.

Newquist, Roy, *Conversations,* Rand McNally, 1967.

Parker, Marygail G., "Madeleine L'Engle," *Dictionary of Literary Biography,* Volume 52: *American Writers for Children since 1960: Fiction,* Gale, 1986.

Rausen, Ruth, "An Interview with Madeleine L'Engle," *Children's Literature in Education,* Number 19, winter, 1975.

Townsend, John Rowe, "Madeleine L'Engle," *A Sense of Story: Essays on Contemporary Writers for Children,* Lippincott, 1971, pp. 120-129.

Van Strum, Carol, "Glimpses of the Grand Design," *Washington Post Book World,* May 11, 1980, pp. 15-16.

Viguers, Ruth Hill, "Golden Years and Time of Tumult, 1920-1967: Worlds without Boundaries and Experiences to Share," *A Critical History of Children's Literature,* edited by Cornelia Meigs, Macmillan, revised edition, 1969, p. 481.

■ For More Information See

BOOKS

Authors and Artists for Young Adults, Volume 1, Gale, 1989.

Authors in the News, Volume 2, Gale, 1976.

Children's Literature Review, Gale, Volume 1, 1976, Volume 14, 1988.

Contemporary Literary Criticism, Volume 12, Gale, 1980.

Huck, Charlotte S., *Children's Literature in the Elementary School,* 3rd edition, Holt, 1976, pp. 246-303.

Nodelman, Perry, editor, *Touchstones: Reflections on the Best in Children's Literature,* Volume 1, Children's Library Association, 1985, pp. 123-131.

Norton, Donna E., *Through the Eyes of a Child: An Introduction to Children's Literature,* 2nd edition, Merrill Publishing, 1987, pp. 294-295.

Viguers, Ruth Hill, *Margin for Surprise: About Books, Children, and Librarians,* Little, Brown, 1964, pp. 3-34.

PERIODICALS

Children's Literature in Education, summer, 1976, pp. 96-102; winter, 1983, pp. 195-203; spring, 1987, pp. 34-44.

Christian Century, April 6, 1977, p. 321; November 20, 1985, p. 1067.

Christianity Today, June 8, 1979.

Horn Book, December, 1983.

Language Arts, October, 1977, pp. 812-816.

Lion and the Unicorn, fall, 1977, pp. 25-39.

Ms., July-August, 1987.

LAUREL-LEAF CONTEMPORARY FICTION

The Moon by Night

Madeleine L'Engle

Author of *A Wrinkle in Time,* the Newbery Medal Winner

The second in the Austin Family series

L'Engle's characters continually grow and explore complex emotional and philosophical questions in her "Austin Family" series.

New York Times Book Review, January 11, 1981, p. 29.
PEN Newsletter, September, 1988, p. 18.
Publishers Weekly, June 20, 1980, p. 67.
Washington Post Book World, April 12, 1981, p. 12;
   September 13, 1981, p. 12.

* * *

LEONARD, Laura 1923-

■ Personal

Born September 7, 1923, in Oakland, CA; daughter of James S. (an electrical engineer) and Olga (a homemaker; maiden name, Stenberg) Bunnell; married James W. L. Leonard (a chemist); children: three. *Education:* Attended University of Hawaii, 1941; University of California, Berkeley, B.A., 1944.

■ Addresses

Home—Concord, CA.

■ Career

Writer.

■ Writings

Saving Damaris (novel), Antheneum, 1989.
Finding Papa, Antheneum, 1991.

■ Work in Progress

Aloha Abby.

■ Sidelights

Laura Leonard told *SATA:* "It makes me happy to write children's books, and I hope it makes young people happy to read them."

* * *

LeSIEG, Theo.
See GEISEL, Theodor Seuss

* * *

LLOYD, (Mary) Norris 1908-1993

OBITUARY NOTICE —See index for *SATA* sketch: Born September 1, 1908, in Greenwood, SC; died February 10, 1993, in Winnetka, IL. Author and social activist. Lloyd was a participant in protests during the 1960s and 1970s, fighting for racial equality in the Civil Rights Movement and against the Vietnam War. She also wrote several works that were either written for or about children, including *Desperate Dragons, Billy Hunts the Unicorn, Katie and the Catastrophe, The Village That Allah Forgot,* and *A Dream of Mansions.*

OBITUARIES AND OTHER SOURCES:

PERIODICALS

Chicago Tribune, February 15, 1993, sec. 1, p. 11.

* * *

LOVERSEED, Amanda (Jane) 1965-

■ Personal

Born October 22, 1965, in London, England; daughter of Bruce (an antique dealer) and Ann (an actress; maiden name, Basset) Loverseed. *Education:* Attended Harrogate College of Arts and Technology, 1985-86; received degree from Cambridge College of Arts and Technology, 1988. *Hobbies and other interests:* Collecting old tea pots and books; "food—both eating and cooking!"

■ Addresses

Home—West Sussex, England.

■ Career

Writer and illustrator. *Member:* Society of Authors, Royal Academy.

■ Writings

SELF-ILLUSTRATED

Tickkatoo's Journey: An Eskimo Folk Tale, Peter Bedrick, 1990.
The Thunder King: A Peruvian Tale, Peter Bedrick, 1991.
The Count around Counting Book, HarperCollins, 1991.
Fandangoe's Fabulous Circus, Sadie Fields Productions, 1992.

■ Work in Progress

The Rhyme around Nursery Rhyme Book; *The Mermaid's Tale,* completion expected in June, 1993; an anthology of poems and stories about the sea.

■ Sidelights

Amanda Loverseed told *SATA:* "When I left school I was lucky enough to spend three months traveling through America where I fell in love with American Indian art. When I returned to college, I started to base a lot of my research and paintings on this new-found inspiration. During my final year at college, I started to write my first book, *Tickkatoo's Journey.* This allowed me the opportunity to study Inuit (Eskimo) art and mythology. I wrote an original story but tried to use traditional themes and images as inspiration.

"Because I am interested in folk tales and fairy tales, my writing very often falls into that genre. I then use images evoked by bone carvings, shamanism, and gods to create my drawings. I love experimenting with color and

AMANDA LOVERSEED

pattern and very often put borders around my work. After the pale colors of *Tickkatoo's Journey,* I chose Peru for the inspiration of *The Thunder King.* Using ancient textiles and the country's dramatic landscape, I tried to create a magical carpet of color. I also design books that pop up or have wheels and flaps. These books are a real challenge as the art work is like piecing together a jigsaw puzzle.

"I love visiting schools to talk to children about books and have become increasingly involved with workshops that make books and pop-ups. I believe that it is very important that all children have the opportunity to develop a love of books.

"I consider myself very lucky to be able to write and illustrate books, as I have wanted to do this since I was seven. I enjoy being able to use my work to study themes that I am especially interested in. How many jobs make visiting a circus or collecting seashells a legitimate part of one's work?"

M

MacKENZIE, Jill (Kelly) 1947-

■ Personal

Born August 12, 1947, in Boston, MA; daughter of Sumner Gage (a politician) and Jessie (a homemaker; maiden name, Johnston) Whittier; married James C. MacKenzie, April 17, 1971 (divorced May 23, 1991); married William Lewis Kelly (a lawyer), May 14, 1992; children: (first marriage) Jennifer, Heather, Elizabeth. *Education:* Mt. Holyoke College, B.A., 1969; Wayne State University, M.A. and Ph.D., 1972-78. *Politics:* Republican. *Religion:* Presbyterian.

■ Addresses

Office—The Birmingham Clinic, 802 South Worth, Birmingham, MI 48009.

■ Career

Clinical psychologist, Birmingham, MI, private practice, 1972—. *Member:* American Psychological Association, Michigan Psychological Association, Psychologists for Social Responsibility, Amnesty International.

■ Writings

The Golden Fairy, Winston-Derek, 1991.

Also author of "Jennifer," a novel chapter in *The Bridge,* 1992.

■ Work in Progress

Jennifer, an adult novel; *The Celtic Prince,* a chapter book for children; researching Celtic life and lore.

■ Sidelights

Jill MacKenzie told *SATA:* "When I was a very young child, my father would read to us in his wonderfully modulated voice. There was so much richness, both in the stories he chose and his involvement, that I was mesmerized. So much adventure! So much intensity! Just what a child needs in order to help her imagination thrive! When I learned to read, it felt like a miracle. I could suddenly bring all these new worlds to life all by myself! Each day I walked to the library and took out a book and read it through. Very often the reading, or re-reading, was under the covers with a flashlight after I was supposed to be asleep. I was fascinated by other peoples, other times, other places. And then began the years when we moved repeatedly and I was often alone

JILL MacKENZIE

123

or struggling again to make new friends. Reading was my refuge and companion into adolescence.

"And then friends took over my imagination, instead! The demands of a college preparatory course also consumed my time. And then preparation for graduate school, and graduate school itself, and marriage, and children. I grew more and more immersed in career and family. Time to read or dabble in writing was lost. It was not until my third and youngest daughter was well into childhood that I found, during her nap times, I had a few hours to myself to play. I read voraciously! It was magic all over again. I chose very different books than when I was young and they reflected who I had become and where I was going. It was a completion and a renewal all at once.

"It was at this time that I stumbled upon, or perhaps I was guided to, the Celtic culture. Their central belief in the oneness of all things and their deep reverence for all forms of life reached into me and drew out something in my soul which the struggles of the real world of today had not come close to at all. This closeness to the earth and reverence, so much missing in the modern world,

A lonely Scottish woman creates a very special Christmas gift in this story by MacKenzie. (Cover illustration by Patricia Taber.)

became central to me and became very much a part of my way of life, as well as my writings.

"At some point, I began to write, and it was a transformation. I wrote the rough draft of a novel in three weeks! I wrote during every spare moment, as soon as the children were in bed, before everyone got up, waiting at the doctor's office. I had no idea, until I began, what a terrible hunger I had to give voice to my own stories. And, while family life and work continued, there were telltale changes. Too many times I arrived at the wrong time at school to pick up the children, sometimes early, sometimes a bit late, because I'd lost all track of time writing, and then rushed off in a panic. Most of the time I was an hour or two early, for I'd written so much, I was certain it was much later and didn't even check the clock.

"*The Golden Fairy* was originally an adult short story. But it was too sad. So I put it away for a year and got it out one fall. I revised it to tell my children and then rewrote it this way. I wanted to communicate that death is not so final as everyone thinks. There are living threads and pathways left behind that weave themselves into the future. This was partly due to my own feelings that my mother, gone for ten years and so dear, is not all that far away, not nearly so far as I'd been led to believe. And, of course, some is due to that ubiquitous Celtic influence!

"'Jennifer' is the first chapter of that novel I wrote so quickly, the story of my oldest daughter's premature birth and amazing struggle to survive. I revise, unfortunately, to the point of compulsion. But this book is very nearly complete, to my level of satisfaction. There are so many more, two novels, plus poems and stories too numerous to count. I will polish and publish as many as I have time and energy for. But that is not the draw of writing. I love the freedom and flow of putting something of my essence, an essence that goes beyond myself, into words. I love the playfulness and challenge of changing colors and characters and settings. It is like blowing bubbles, only better! And always with a Celtic twist."

* * *

MARA, Barney
    See ROTH, Arthur J(oseph)

* * *

MARSHALL, Edward
    See MARSHALL, James (Edward)

MARSHALL, James (Edward) 1942-1992
(Edward Marshall)

■ Personal

Born October 10, 1942, in San Antonio, TX; died of a brain tumor, October 13, 1992, in Manhattan, NY; son of George E. (an insurance salesman) and Cecille (Harrison) Marshall. *Education:* Attended New England Conservatory of Music (Boston), 1960-61; Southern Connecticut State College, B.A., 1967; also attended Trinity College, 1967-68. "No art school (self-taught)."

■ Addresses

Home—Mansfield Center, CT. *Agent*—Sheldon Fogelman, 10 East 40th St., New York, NY 10016.

■ Career

Cathedral High School, Boston, MA, French and Spanish teacher, 1968-70; free-lance writer and illustrator, 1970-92.

■ Awards, Honors

Children's Book Showcase titles, Children's Book Council, 1973, for *George and Martha,* 1974, for *All the Way Home,* 1975, for *The Stupids Step Out,* and 1977, for *Bonzini! The Tattooed Man;* the American Institute of Graphic Arts Children's Book Show included *All the Way Home* and *The Piggy in the Puddle,* 1973-74, and *I Will Not Go to Market Today,* 1980; Academy Award nomination for best animated film, Academy of Motion Picture Arts and Sciences, 1978, for movie adaptation of *It's So Nice to Have a Wolf around the House;* Edgar Allan Poe Award nomination, Mystery Writers of America, 1978, for *Miss Nelson Is Missing!;* Children's Choice awards, International Reading Association, 1979, for *The Stupids Have a Ball* and *George and Martha One Fine Day,* and 1982, for *The Stupids Die* and *There's a Party at Mona's Tonight; School Library Journal* "Best of the Best 1966-1978" citation, 1979, for *The Stupids Step Out;* Parents' Choice awards, Parents' Choice Foundation, 1982, for *Miss Nelson is Back* and *Roger's Umbrella,* and 1983, for *Rapscallion Jones;* Caldecott honor book citation, American Library Association, 1989, for *Goldilocks and the Three Bears.*

Marshall has received several Outstanding Books of the Year and Ten Best Illustrated Books of the Year citations from the American Library Association, *Horn Book, New York Times,* and *School Library Journal,* as well as numerous librarians', parents', and children's choice awards from state organizations in Arizona, California, Colorado, Georgia, Kentucky, Nebraska, Ohio, and Washington; many of his books were Junior Literary Guild selections.

■ Writings

SELF-ILLUSTRATED

What's the Matter with Carruthers?, Houghton, 1972.

JAMES MARSHALL

Yummers!, Houghton, 1973.
Miss Dog's Christmas Treat, Houghton, 1973.
Willis, Houghton, 1974.
The Guest, Houghton, 1975.
Four Little Troubles (also see below), Volume I: *Eugene,* Volume II: *Someone Is Talking about Hortense,* Volume III: *Sing Out Irene,* Houghton, 1975.
Speedboat, Houghton, 1976.
A Summer in the South, Houghton, 1977.
(Selector) *James Marshall's Mother Goose,* Farrar, Straus, 1979.
Portly McSwine, Houghton, 1979.
(Under name Edward Marshall) *Troll Country,* Dial, 1980.
(Under name Edward Marshall) *Space Case,* Dial, 1980.
Taking Care of Carruthers, Houghton, 1981.
Rapscallion Jones, Viking, 1983.
Wings: A Tale of Two Chickens, Viking, 1986.
Yummers Too: The Second Course, Houghton, 1986.
Three up a Tree, Dial, 1986.
Merry Christmas, Space Case, Dial, 1986.
(Reteller) *Red Riding Hood,* Dial, 1987, published as *Little Red Riding Hood,* Collins, 1987.
(Reteller) *Goldilocks and the Three Bears,* Dial, 1988, published as *Goldilocks,* Collins, 1988.
(Reteller) *Hey, Diddle, Diddle,* Heath, 1989.
My Friends the Frogs, Heath, 1989.
(Reteller) *The Three Little Pigs,* Dial, 1989.
(Reteller) *Hansel and Gretel,* Dial, 1990.
Rats on the Roof: And Other Stories, Dial, 1991.
Mother Hubbard & Her Wonderful Dog, Farrar, Straus, 1991.
Pocketful of Nonsense, Western Publishing, 1992.
Rats on the Range and Other Stories, Dial, 1993.

"THE CUT-UPS" SERIES; SELF-ILLUSTRATED

The Cut-Ups, Viking, 1984.
The Cut-Ups Cut Loose, Viking, 1987.

Fox's day of babysitting results in some very silly moments in this book written and illustrated by Marshall. (Illustration from *Fox and His Friends*.)

The Cut-Ups at Camp Custer, Viking Kestrel, 1989.
The Cut-Ups Carry On, Viking, 1990.
The Cut-Ups Crack Up, Viking, 1992.

"GEORGE AND MARTHA" SERIES; SELF-ILLUSTRATED

George and Martha, Houghton, 1972.
George and Martha Encore, Houghton, 1973.
George and Martha Rise and Shine, Houghton, 1976.
George and Martha One Fine Day, Houghton, 1978.
George and Martha, Tons of Fun, Houghton, 1980.
George and Martha Back in Town, Houghton, 1984.
George and Martha 'Round and 'Round, Houghton, 1988.

"THE STUPIDS" SERIES; WRITTEN WITH HARRY ALLARD; SELF-ILLUSTRATED

The Stupids Step Out, Houghton, 1974.
The Stupids Have a Ball, Houghton, 1978.
The Stupids Die, Houghton, 1981.
The Stupids Take Off, Houghton, 1989.

"FOX" SERIES; SELF-ILLUSTRATED

(Under name Edward Marshall) *Three by the Sea,* Dial, 1981.
(Under name Edward Marshall) *Fox and His Friends,* Dial, 1982.

(Under name Edward Marshall) *Fox in Love,* Dial, 1982.
(Under name Edward Marshall) *Fox on Wheels,* Dial, 1983.
(Under name Edward Marshall) *Fox at School,* Dial, 1983.
(Under name Edward Marshall) *Fox All Week,* Dial, 1984.
(Under name Edward Marshall) *Four on the Shore,* Dial, 1985.
Fox on the Job, Dial, 1988.
Fox Be Nimble, Dial, 1990.
Fox Outfoxed, Dial, 1992.
Fox on Stage, Dial, 1993.

ILLUSTRATOR

Byrd Baylor, *Plink, Plink, Plink,* Houghton, 1971.
Lore Segal, *All the Way Home,* Farrar, Straus, 1973.
Norma Klein, *Dinosaur's Housewarming Party,* Crown, 1974.
Charlotte Pomerantz, *The Piggy in the Puddle,* Macmillan, 1974.
Jakob Grimm and Wilhelm Grimm, *The Frog Prince,* retold by Edith H. Tarcov, Four Winds Press, 1974.
Allard, *The Tutti-Frutti Case: Starring the Four Doctors of Goodge,* Prentice-Hall, 1975.
Russell Hoban, *Dinner at Alberta's,* Crowell, 1975.
Cynthia Jameson, *A Day with Whisker Wickles,* Coward, 1975.
Jeffrey Allen, *Mary Alice, Operator Number 9,* Little, Brown, 1975.
Laurette Murdock, *Four Little Troubles,* Volume IV: *Snake—His Story,* Houghton, 1975.
Allen, *Bonzini! The Tattooed Man,* Little, Brown, 1976.
Diane Wolkstein, reteller, *Lazy Stories,* Seabury, 1976.
Allard, *It's So Nice to Have a Wolf around the House,* Doubleday, 1977.
Allard, *Miss Nelson Is Missing!,* Houghton, 1977.
Frank Asch, *MacGoose's Grocery,* Dial, 1978.
Jan Wahl, *Carrot Nose,* Farrar, Straus, 1978.
Allard, *I Will Not Go to Market Today,* Dial, 1979.
Allard, *Bumps in the Night,* Doubleday, 1979.
Jane Yolen, *How Beastly! A Menagerie of Nonsense Poems,* Philomel, 1980.
John McFarland, reteller, *The Exploding Frog: And Other Fables from Aesop,* Little, Brown, 1981.
Allard, *There's a Party at Mona's Tonight,* Doubleday, 1981.
Allard, *Miss Nelson Is Back,* Houghton, 1982.
Daniel Pinkwater, *Roger's Umbrella,* Dutton, 1982.
Allard, *Miss Nelson Has a Field Day,* Houghton, 1985.
Clement C. Moore, *The Night before Christmas,* Scholastic, 1985.
Allen, *Nosey Mrs. Rat,* Viking, 1985.
Allen, *Mary Alice Returns,* Little, Brown, 1986.
Louis Phillips, *Haunted House Jokes,* Viking Kestrel, 1987.
Barbara Karlin, reteller, *Cinderella,* Little, Brown, 1989.

OTHER

(Contributor) *Once upon a Time ... : Celebrating the Magic of Children's Books in Honor of the Twentieth*

Anniversary of Reading Is Fundamental, Putnam, 1986.

(With Richard Beach) *Teaching Literature in the Secondary School,* Harcourt, 1990.

Marshall's manuscripts are included in the Kerlan Collection of the University of Minnesota, the de Grummond Collection of the University of Southern Mississippi, the University of Oregon Library, and the University of Connecticut at Storrs.

■ Adaptations

It's So Nice to Have a Wolf around the House was made into a full-length television cartoon feature by Learning Corporation of America, 1978, as was *Miss Nelson Is Missing* in 1979; *Miss Nelson Is Back* and *Three by Sea* were featured on *Reading Rainbow,* PBS-TV, 1983; *The Three Little Pigs* was adapted for video by Weston Woods, 1991. The following books have been made into filmstrip/cassette or book/cassette sets: *Miss Nelson Is Missing,* Weston Woods, 1984; *I Will Not Go to Market Today,* Random House, 1984; *Three by the Sea,* Listening Library, 1985; *The Night before Christmas,* Listening Library, 1986; *Fox and His Friends, Fox at School, Fox in Love,* and *Fox on Wheels,* Random House, 1986; *Miss Nelson Is Missing* and *George and Martha,* Hougton, 1987; and *George and Martha, George and Martha Encore, George and Martha Rise and Shine, George and Martha One Fine Day, The Stupids Step Out, The Stupids Have a Ball,* and *The Stupids Die,* all from Random House. Random House has also released *James Marshall's Mother Goose* as a cassette.

■ Sidelights

James Marshall wrote and illustrated several popular series of children's books, including the "George and Martha," "Fox," and "Cut-up" series, and, with Harry Allard, the "Stupids" and "Miss Nelson" books. Marshall's work is characterized by a matter-of-fact wit ranging from gentle to outrageous; his books also show his skill at depicting friendships. His trademark line drawings are simple yet capable of much expression, containing many humorous details. In his version of classic *Mother Goose* tales, for instance, "in his inimitable style he has filled the pages with a hilarious and memorable cast of characters," Karen M. Klockner noted in *Horn Book. Bulletin of the Center for Children's Books* critic Robert Strang, however, noted that while Marshall's drawings have always been praised for their wit, the author's "ear for the quirks and cliches of the American language" provided an important part of "his peculiar sense for what is funny."

Marshall relied on books for entertainment while growing up on an isolated farm near San Antonio, Texas. His family later moved to Beaumont, Texas. "Beaumont is deep south and swampy and I hated it," the author declared in an interview with Rachel Koenig for *Something about the Author.* "I knew I would die if I stayed there, so I diligently studied the viola, and eventually won a scholarship to the New England Conservatory in

Boston." Marshall earned praise there, but his music study was cut short by injury. "I flew out of my seat on a plane and injured my hand, but ignored the injury and continued to play," he explained. "As a result I developed a condition which forbad me to play more than twenty minutes a day.... Looking back, I think this turn of events was all for the good. It helped me realize something that had before been only subconscious. That is, I did not want to be a professional musician, and having the injury made it easier for me to stop."

Marshall then attended several colleges in Texas and Connecticut, eventually receiving a degree in French and history. He returned to Boston, where he taught French and Spanish at a private school. Not having studied Spanish previously, Marshall learned the language from Puerto Rican students in his Spanish class. While teaching, Marshall resumed his hobby of drawing, which he had abandoned in the second grade when a teacher laughed at his artwork. A friend who saw his sketches brought them to the attention of a neighbor who worked in publishing; the neighbor contacted the director of children's books at Houghton-Mifflin, and advised him of Marshall's skills. Marshall met with the director, and the next day was offered a contract to illustrate *Plink, Plink, Plink.*

Books for Children Provide Easy-to-Read Fun

A year later, Marshall wrote and illustrated *George and Martha,* the first book in a widely acclaimed series featuring a pair of hippopotamus friends. The author took the names of the protagonists from Edward Albee's play *Who's Afraid of Virginia Woolf?,* which was broadcast on television at the time that sketches for *George and Martha* were being made. However, "Albee's gladi-

Hippopotamus friends George and Martha are the subjects of one of Marshall's most popular self-illustrated series. (Illustration from *George and Martha One Fine Day.*)

Marshall provided the illustrations for Harry Allard's series of stories about the many ridiculous antics of the Stupid family.

atorial marriage partners are a far cry from the gently prankish hippo pals that Marshall describes as 'innocent, crafty and courtly' with 'exquisite manners and a sense of fun,'" asserted Leonard Marcus, who interviewed Marshall for *Publishers Weekly.* Marshall told Marcus about a dream in which his character Martha complained about the stories: "She had become very cross with me. She wanted better stories, better *lines.* And I distinctly remember her telling me that if she didn't get them she was going to a certain other illustrator's house. I woke up in a cold sweat!"

Marshall has also coauthored and illustrated a series of books about "the Stupids," described by Marcus as "a family of noodle-heads whose talent for getting backwards what every four-year-old can plainly understand is matched only by their boundless *joie de vivre* [joy of living]." The books "satirize the antics of the nuclear American family in the mass media of the 1950's," wrote *Twentieth-Century Children's Writers* contributor Hugh T. Keenan, who also asserted that the stories of

the Stupids "are calculated to amuse adults and children, though on different levels." A few critics have complained that "The Stupids" series derides stupid people. However, evaluating *The Stupids Step Out,* Nora L. Magid asserted in the *New York Times Book Review* that "these particular Stupids are so safe, snug and amiable in their context as to make the condition enviable."

Under the pseudonym Edward Marshall, the author began to produce his "Fox" books, which *Bulletin of the Center for Children's Books* reviewer Betsy Hearne called "a justifiably popular easy-to-read series." As described by Keenan in *Dictionary of Literary Biography,* "Fox tries for the upper hand, but more often than not ... is outfoxed by his younger sister Louise or by fate." Marshall related to Koenig his reason for using a pseudonym: "I wanted to do an easy-to-read book, but I was under an exclusive contract at a publishing house so I made up Edward, supposedly a cousin of mine from San Antonio. One day an editor called me and said,

Miss Nelson's students make their own substitute when their beloved teacher is home sick one day. (Text by Harry Allard.)

'We're having so much trouble reaching your cousin to get publicity material, could *you* tell me something about him?' 'Well,' I said, 'It's very difficult for him living way out there near the crematorium with his eighteen children . . . .' I just spun a whole yarn about this so-called cousin, and before I knew it, it was printed in a publication."

Created with Harry Allard, the "Miss Nelson" series, about a nice teacher who disguises herself as a mean substitute in order to bring her class under control, has received attention from teachers as well as young readers. Referring to Miss Nelson's harsh alter ego, Marshall told Marcus that "all over America, teachers are dressing up as Viola Swamp." Marshall has also been involved with retellings of classic stories, such as *Little Red Riding Hood, Cinderella,* and *Goldilocks and the Three Bears,* which was named a Caldecott honor book in 1989. Critics praised Marshall for bringing a fresh perspective to these classic tales; as Caroline Ward observed in *School Library Journal:* "Through simple words and a restrained use of line in the art, Marshall masterfully imbues his characters with humorous personality traits."

Marshall commented in his *SATA* interview: "A book must have a good beginning and a strong middle, but without a knockout ending, you're shot. I've done books which featured wonderful characters, and some of the funniest lines I've ever written, but I blew the endings and they just don't work. You have to make a full circle because ending is emotionally satisfying. If not, everything valuable which precedes your bad ending will go out the window, no matter how hard you worked on it. I also teach that pacing is essential. You don't kill a story from page to page, you kill it by stalling. You have to

make a book *move,* there always has to be a reason to turn the next page."

In 1992, Marshall's career was cut short when he died of a brain tumor at age fifty. His passing inspired many tributes; as recounted in *Publishers Weekly,* Houghton editor Walter Lorraine called Marshall "a creator without peer. He could convey more in a line and a word than most authors can in a volume . . . . His work always left room for the experience of the reader and yet he never left doubt about his message." "His stories were as wonderful as his art," Phyllis Fogelman and Toby Sherry of Dial Books similarly wrote, "and even if he had never drawn a picture, he would have been celebrated for his writing." Noting that Marshall left many fine works behind, Michael di Capua of HarperCollins concluded, "Surely they will give pleasure to many generations of children and will also inspire creators of children's books well into the twenty-first century."

■ Works Cited

Hearne, Betsy, review of *Fox on the Job, Bulletin of the Center for Children's Books,* April, 1988, p. 161.

"James Marshall Remembered," *Publishers Weekly,* December 7, 1992, pp. 30-31.

Keenan, Hugh T., *Dictionary of Literary Biography,* Volume 61: *American Writers for Children since 1960: Poets, Illustrators, and Nonfiction Authors,* Gale, 1987, pp. 189-199.

Keenan, Hugh T., "James Marshall," *Twentieth-Century Children's Writers,* 3rd edition, St. James Press, 1989, pp. 637-639.

Klockner, Karen M., review of *James Marshall's Mother Goose, Horn Book,* February, 1980, p. 48.

Magid, Nora L., review of *The Stupids Step Out, New York Times Book Review,* May 5, 1974, p. 19.

Marcus, Leonard, "James Marshall," *Publishers Weekly,* July 28, 1989, pp. 202-203.

Marshall, James, interview with Rachel Koenig in *Something about the Author,* Volume 51, Gale, 1988, pp. 109-121.

Strang, Robert, review of *The Cut-ups Cut Loose, Bulletin of the Center for Children's Books,* December, 1987, p. 71.

Ward, Caroline, review of *Red Riding Hood, School Library Journal,* September, 1987, p. 176.

■ For More Information See

BOOKS

Children's Literature Review, Volume 21, Gale, 1990.

PERIODICALS

Newsweek, December 16, 1982, p. 132.

New York Times Book Review, November 18, 1973, p. 8; October 26, 1980, p. 26; January 18, 1981, p. 35; May 3, 1981, p. 40; May 21, 1989, p. 33; November 12, 1989, p. 27.

School Library Journal, October, 1988, p. 134.

Times Literary Supplement, July 24, 1981, p. 841.

Washington Post Book World, July 8, 1990, p. 10.

OBITUARIES:

PERIODICALS

New York Times, October 15, 1992.
School Library Journal, December, 1992, p. 17.*

*   *   *

McCANN, Helen 1948-
(Elinor Dean)

Personal

Born August 20, 1948, in Scotland; daughter of Hugh and Margaret (Foley) McCann; married William Magee (a lawyer), August 19, 1972; children: Stephen, Matthew. *Education:* Glasgow University, LL.B., 1969; London University, B.Sc., 1979. *Religion:* Roman Catholic. *Hobbies and other interests:* Painting, music, yoga, printmaking.

Addresses

Agent—Lesley Hadcroft, Laurence Pollinger, 18 Maddox St., Mayfair, London W1R 0EU, England.

Career

Lauder College, Dunfermline, Fife, Scotland, lecturer in law, 1982—. *Member:* Society of Authors, Scottish Artists and Artist Craftsmen, Dunfermline Print Workshop.

Awards, Honors

Scottish Arts Council Award, 1990, for research on ninth-century Viking Scotland.

Writings

JUVENILE

A Ghost Called Clarence, Educational Publishers, 1990.
What Do We Do Now, George?, Simon & Schuster, 1991.
What's French for Help, George?, Simon & Schuster, 1993.

Also contributor of stories to periodicals.

UNDER PSEUDONYM ELINOR DEAN

False Enchantment, Hale, 1984.
Master of Dryford, Hale, 1985.

Work in Progress

A humorous contemporary story; ongoing research into Viking history.

Sidelights

Helen McCann told *SATA:* "I suppose my interest in storytelling goes right back to when I was a child. My sister and I were blessed with a father who could spin

HELEN McCANN

tales like nobody else I have ever known. He had the true storyteller's gift of gaining complete acceptance from his audience no matter how fantastical his stories were. He created three little characters especially for us. I can still picture them though my sister and I can only remember odd snippets of stories. He never told the same one twice. They just seemed to come to him, effortlessly.

"It was only in later years that we wondered why he had never written them down, and I suppose that thought changed my direction from writing for adults to writing for children. It was storytelling that interested me—that and fun. George [the protagonist in two of McCann's books] and his gang are definitely not serious people. I have always loved verbal slapstick and that particular anarchy that kids can create when they get the chance. That's what I see in the George stories—total anarchy.

"Recently I've become really interested in Viking Scotland and Ireland. I've done a lot of research into the sagas and legends and I love the romance of it—longships and raven banners and sea battles. I thought I had got it out of my system when I completed a series of three shortish stories called 'A Legend, A Tale and A Magical Dragon,' then I found myself with another idea and I was off again, this time with a full length story called 'A Footprint in Time.' It never fails to amaze me how caught up I get in what I'm writing. Sometimes it's like living a double life with the real world going on around you and all this stuff going on in your head. No wonder writers get a reputation for being absent-minded.

"I love writing for children. I love the thought of them reading what I've written—getting absorbed in it, living with the characters. And I suppose at the end of the day what I'm trying to do is pass on the kind of pleasure I got from a much loved storyteller when I was a child."

*   *   *

McCAUGHREN, Tom 1936-

■ Personal

Born August 11, 1936, in Ballymena, County Antrim, Northern Ireland; son of John (a gardener) and Ethel (Smyth) McCaughren; married Frances Byrne, April 4, 1970; children: Michelle, Amanda, Samantha, Simone. *Education:* Attended primary and secondary schools in Ireland. *Religion:* Presbyterian.

■ Addresses

Home—137 Whitehall Rd., Terenure, Dublin 6, Ireland. *Office*—Radio Telefis Eirann, Donnybrook, Dublin 4, Ireland.

■ Career

Writer, journalist and broadcaster. Radio Telefis Eirann, Dublin, Ireland, security correspondent, 1978—. *Member:* Irish Writers' Union

■ Awards, Honors

Book award, Reading Association of Ireland, 1985, for *Run with the Wind;* "White Raven" selection, International Youth Library, Munich, 1988, for *Run Swift, Run Free;* Book of the Decade (1980-1990) Award, Irish Children's Book Trust, for *Run with the Wind, Run to Earth,* and *Run Swift, Run Free;* Oscar Wilde Literary Recognition Award, 1992.

■ Writings

The Peacemakers of Niemba (nonfiction), Richview Press, 1966.
Run with the Wind, Wolfhound Press, 1983.
The Legend of the Golden Key, Children's Press, 1983.
The Legend of the Phantom Highwayman, Children's Press, 1983.
Run to Earth, Wolfhound Press, 1984.
The Legend of the Corrib King, Children's Press, 1984.
The Children of the Forge, Children's Press, 1985.
Run Swift, Run Free, Wolfhound Press, 1986.

TOM McCAUGHREN

The Silent Sea, Children's Press, 1987.
Rainbows of the Moon, Anvil Press, 1989.
Run to the Ark, Wolfhound Press, 1991.
Run Wild, Wolfhound Press, 1993.

■ Work in Progress

Researching the Irish Rebellion of 1798; *Wildlife Diary.*

■ Sidelights

Tom McCaughren writes: "When I was in my twenties, I had one book published, *The Peacemakers of Niemba.* This was a documentary account of the first casualties suffered by Irish troops serving with the United Nations overseas and was set in the Congo in Africa. At the same time I had a lot of ideas for young people's books. (I don't like calling them children's books, as I find children no longer regard themselves as children when they reach the age of about 12).

"Few if any books for young people were being published in Ireland at that time, and I soon found out why. Publishers thought they weren't a viable proposition. How wrong they were! Most books came from Britain and the U.S. and there seemed to be a general belief that books written and set in Ireland couldn't be as good as books from elsewhere. I said to myself, *why not?* So I went ahead and put my ideas into practice.

"Soon I ended up with three books I couldn't get published. Irish publishers weren't interested, and British publishers didn't want to know an unknown Irish author. However, I persisted. Among other things I lobbied the Arts Council, and in 1981 the council introduced a scheme by which it gave to publishers the same financial support for young people's fiction as adult fiction. Since then publishing of young people's fiction has been a growth industry in Ireland with many titles being exported and published abroad. Thus it was that I had three titles published in 1983.

"My books fall into three categories. First are the adventure books for 9-to 14-year-olds published by Children's Press. They are, as I say, set in Ireland, in a real place and with a flavour of folklore or history as a backdrop. *The Legend of the Golden Key* is set in my native County Antrim and takes place against the backdrop of the 1798 rebellion. It includes a lot of my own childhood and some of the colourful characters from that childhood. *The Legend of the Phantom Highwayman* centres around a highwayman who was supposed to have hijacked a stagecoach and taken it to the famous Glens of Antrim. In the course of the story young readers learn much about the stagecoaches and of the real highwaymen, usually fugitives from one rebellion or another, who inhabited the highways and byways of Ireland in times past.

Irish Setting Colors Mystery Novels

"*The Legend of the Corrib King* is set on Lough Corrib in the west of Ireland, at the village of Cong, where the film *The Quiet Man* was made. Not only do young people read about John Wayne and Maureen O'Hara, they learn about the folklore of the west of Ireland in a time when people suffered greatly and believed in 'the little people.' *The Children of the Forge* is a mystery set in County Wicklow against the backdrop of a gold rush that took place there in 1795. *The Silent Sea* is set in County Cork. It harks back to a famous feud between the O'Driscolls and the Waterfordmen, and features pirates from Algeria, a mysterious yacht from the Far East, and suggestions of stolen jewels and drugs.

"*Rainbows of the Moon* is a novel for teenagers, a group I felt was being neglected in Ireland as far as home-grown reading material was concerned. It is a thriller set on the Irish border, involving two games of "chess"—one between a British Special Air Services patrol and an Irish Republican Army (IRA) active service unit, the other between two boys, one from either side of the religious divide in Northern Ireland. The battle between the boys concerns the many misunderstandings and misconceptions that exist between the two communities. The underlying theme is for the need for mutual understanding, and this book is now used in the EMU course for mutual understanding in schools in Northern Ireland.

A BEST SELLING CLASSIC

Run WITH THE *Wind*

Tom McCAUGHREN

ILLUSTRATED BY JEANETTE DUNNE

McCaughren's concern that the fox might be exterminated from his native Ireland led him to write this novel from the foxes' point of view. (Cover illustration by Debbie Rawlinson.)

"My other four books are about foxes. These came out over a ten-year period when foxes were being widely trapped in Ireland for their fur. The trapping occurred at a time when the fox was being exterminated in Europe because of rabies, and it gave rise to fears that the species might be wiped out in Ireland. The experts say there never was any real possibility that the fox would be wiped out, but I wrote the stories from the point of view of the foxes, who believed otherwise. Needless to say, they are very strong on the need to protect the environment and to look after species which might be endangered. These books are for the 9 to 90 age group and have been very popular with both young people and adults." These books have been translated into many languages, including French, German, Swedish, and Japanese, as well as in English outside of the United States.

"I get many letters from young readers, not only in Ireland but also abroad. While the books are not yet published in America, I've had correspondence from schools as far apart as Toronto and New Jersey where pupils told me they had enjoyed them immensely."

McGURK, Slater
  See ROTH, Arthur J(oseph)

*   *   *

McKAUGHAN, Larry (Scott) 1941-

■ **Personal**

Surname is pronounced "ma-coin"; born December 14, 1941, in Ross, CA; son of James Wesley (a Presbyterian minister and missionary to Mexico) and Dorothy Marie (a choir director and organist; maiden name, Ward) McKaughan; married Nancy Jane Gordon (a secretary and elementary teacher), July 3, 1965; children: Lara Sue, Daniel Jon. *Education:* Whitworth College, B.A., 1963; University of Illinois, M.A., 1965, Ph.D., 1968. *Religion:* "Mennonite, Presbyterian and Baptist."

■ **Addresses**

Home and office—2985 Ellen Avenue, Eugene, OR 97405.

■ **Career**

Adolph Meyer Zone Center, Decatur, IL, psychologist, 1967-68; University of Oregon, Eugene, teaching assistant, 1970-71; St. Meinrad College, St. Meinrad, IN, assistant professor of psychology, 1971-72; Alderson-Broaddus College, Philippi, WV, associate professor of psychology, 1972-79; University of California at Berkeley, Berkeley, research associate, 1979-80; Lane Community College, Eugene, part-time instructor, 1981-84; Institute for the Study of Human Action and Responsibility, Eugene, research associate and director, 1981-86; free-lance writer, 1985—. Cook Inlet, AK, commercial salmon fisherman, 1982—; newspaper carrier, 1990—.

■ **Awards, Honors**

Excellence in teaching award.

■ **Writings**

Why Are Your Fingers Cold?, illustrated by Joy Dunn Kennan, Herald Press, 1992.

Contributor to periodicals, including *Journal of Experimental Child Psychology* and *Imagination, Cognition and Personality.*

■ **Work in Progress**

On Following a Rule, a psychology book which tests the clash between freedom and determinism; several children's stories.

■ **Sidelights**

Larry McKaughan told *SATA:* "I have taught a wide variety of psychology courses. Most enjoyable was a

LARRY McKAUGHAN

history and theory of psychology course in which I impersonated several important psychologists who 'came to campus to give a lecture.' Also pleasant were courses in human development, thinking, and problem solving. I have done research on the thought processes of children of various ages during a problem solving task. I am interested in exploring the nature of human freedom and responsibility. In the summers I am a set net salmon fisherman in Cook Inlet, Alaska. I fish in a sixteen foot dory working either as skipper or crew. We mend lots of nets and pick seaweed from the nets. It is best of all when a school of fish hits the nets. In Eugene I get up early every morning to look at stars and deliver a newspaper. When it rains I pull my Scotch golf cap over my eyebrows and collect droplets in my beard. I now have numerous stories about children dancing around in my head and hope to share them with children."

*   *   *

MIKOLAYCAK, Charles 1937-1993

OBITUARY NOTICE —See index for *SATA* sketch: Surname is pronounced "*mike*-o-lay-chak"; born January 26, 1937, in Scranton, PA; died of cancer, June 23, 1993, in Manhattan, NY. Illustrator and author. An award-winning illustrator and book designer, Mikolaycak primarily worked on children's books because, he explained, he loved to draw and also loved to design—and children's literature offered him the opportunity to combine both his talents. A graduate of Pratt Institute, Mikolaycak joined the staff of Time-Life Books as a designer in 1963. He left thirteen years later to concentrate on illustrating children's books. The illustrator of over sixty books and the designer of hundreds of book covers, Mikolaycak was the recipient of numerous awards for his work, including the Charles W. Follett Award for *Banner Over Me,* the New York Graphics Award for *The Surprising Things Maui Did,* and the Golden Kite Honor Book Award for *Juma and the Magic Jinn.* Mikolaycak also wrote as well as illustrated several works, such as *Babushka: An Old Russian Folktale,* which won the *New York Times* best illustrated book award in 1984. That same year, Mikolaycak illustrated Eve Bunting's *Man Who Could Call Down Owls,* which became one of his most popular books. His more recent illustrations include *Orpheus,* written and illustrated by the author in 1992, and *The Hero of Bremen,* written by Margaret Hodges and published in 1993.

OBITUARIES AND OTHER SOURCES:

BOOKS

Who's Who in the World, 10th edition, Marquis, 1990.

PERIODICALS

Chicago Tribune, June 27, 1993, section 2, p. 6.
New York Times, June 25, 1993, p. B7.

* * *

MOOSER, Stephen 1941-

■ Personal

Born July 4, 1941, in Fresno, CA; son of Joseph Nathan (in business) and Lillian (a librarian; maiden name, Davidson) Mooser; married Etta Kralovec (a teacher), November 20, 1971; children: Chelsea, Bryn. *Education:* University of California, Los Angeles, B.A., 1963, M.A., 1968. *Hobbies and other interests:* Treasure hunting, collecting tin toys, playing basketball.

■ Addresses

Home—8 Arata Dr., Bar Harbor, ME 04609. *Agent*—Marilyn Marlow, Curtis Brown, Ltd., 10 Astor Place, New York, NY 10003.

■ Career

Photographer and producer of documentary films, Los Angeles, CA, 1964-65; McGraw-Hill Book Co., Los Angeles, reporter, 1966-67; Southwest Regional Laboratory for Educational Research and Development, Los Angeles, story writer, 1969-74; free-lance writer, 1974—. Speaker at conferences. *Military service:* National Guard, 1965-68. *Member:* Society of Children's Book Writers and Illustrators (co-founder and president, 1971—).

■ Writings

JUVENILES

101 Black Cats, Scholastic Inc., 1975.
The Ghost with the Halloween Hiccups, illustrated by Tomie de Paola, F. Watts, 1977.
(Coeditor) *The New York Kid's Book,* Doubleday, 1978.
Monster Fun, Messner, 1979.
Into the Unknown: Nine Astounding Stories, Lippincott, 1980.
Funnyman's First Case, illustrated by de Paola, F. Watts, 1981.
Lights! Camera! Scream!: Making Your Own Monster Movies, Messner, 1983.
Funnyman and the Penny Dodo, illustrated by de Paola, F. Watts, 1984.
Orphan Jeb at the Massacree, illustrated by Joyce Audy dos Santos, Knopf, 1984.
Shadows on the Graveyard Trail, Dell, 1986.
Lost in the Woods, Weekly Reader Books, 1986.
Funnyman Meets the Monster from Outer Space, Scholastic, 1987.
(Coauthor) *The Fat Cat,* Warner Juvenile Books, 1988.
(With Lin Oliver) *Tad and Dad,* Warner Juvenile Books, 1988.
The Hitchhiking Vampire, Dell, 1989.
It's a Weird, Weird School, Dell, 1989.
Elvis Is Back! And He's in the 6th Grade, Dell, in press.
Disaster in Room 101, Troll, in press.

STEPHEN MOOSER

"WHICH WAY" INTERACTIVE SERIES

Space Raiders and the Planet of Doom, Archway, 1983.
Starship Warrior, Archway, 1984.
Nightmare Planet, Archway, 1985.
Invasion of the Mutants, Archway, 1985.
Mind Bandits, Archway, 1985.
Monster Express, Archway, 1986.

"TREASURE HOUND" SERIES

The Case of the Slippery Sharks, illustrated by Leslie Morrill, Troll, 1988.
The Mummy's Secret, illustrated by Morrill, Troll, 1988.
The Secret Gold Mine, illustrated by Morrill, Troll, 1988.
Secret in the Old Mansion, illustrated by Morrill, Troll, 1988.

"GIGGLEMAJIG" SERIES

Numbers Up!, Modern Publishing, 1989.
A Square Deal, Modern Publishing, 1989.
Flying Colors!, Modern Publishing, 1989.
Tons of Fun from A-Z, Modern Publishing, 1989.

"CREEPY CREATURE CLUB" SERIES

Monsters in the Outfield, illustrated by George Ulrich, Dell, 1989.
My Halloween Boyfriend, illustrated by Ulrich, Dell, 1989.
Monster Holiday, illustrated by Ulrich, Dell, 1989.
The Fright Face Contest, illustrated by Ulrich, Dell, 1990.
Monster of the Year, illustrated by Ulrich, Dell, 1990.
That's So Funny, I Forgot to Laugh, illustrated by Ulrich, Dell, 1990.
Crazy Mixed-Up Valentines, illustrated by Ulrich, Dell, 1990.
Secrets of Scary Fun, illustrated by Ulrich, Dell, 1991.
The Night of the Vampire Kitty, illustrated by Ulrich, Dell, 1991.
The Man Who Ate a Car, illustrated by Ulrich, Dell, 1991.

"ALL-STAR MEATBALLS" SERIES

Babe Ruth and the Home Run Derby, illustrated by George Ulrich, Dell, 1992.
The Terrible Tickler, illustrated by Ulrich, Dell, 1992.
Scary Scraped Up Skaters, illustrated by Ulrich, Dell, 1992.
The Headless Snowman, illustrated by Ulrich, Dell, 1992.
The Snow Bowl, illustrated by Ulrich, Dell, 1992.
Muscle Mania, illustrated by Ulrich, Dell, 1993.
Amazing Stories, illustrated by Ulrich, Dell, 1993.
April Fools, illustrated by Ulrich, Dell, 1993.

OTHER

Also author of a number of small books for major instructional reading series. Author of educational film-strips for independent film companies, and chief author of a number of video game programs for both the Mattel and Disney Corporations. Stories and novels have been anthologized in many national programs. Contributor of stories to magazines.

■ Sidelights

An adventure seeker himself, Stephen Mooser fills his many humorous children's books with creepy monsters, buried treasure, and hair-raising escapades. The "Creepy Creature Club" series, the "Treasure Hound" series, and the "All-Star Meatballs" series, which are directed at beginning readers, each feature a regular cast of characters who often encounter strange things and experience the unexpected. In an interview for *SATA,* Mooser says that he believes children enjoy these types of books "because for kids the world is still a wide open, incredible place—a place where flying saucers and things just might exist somewhere, where you actually might be able to go out on a weekend and find a treasure. There are a lot of times when kids are not very mobile, they're stuck in some place, and a book can help transport them into something that's magical."

Mooser spent his own childhood in Fresno, California, which he describes as "a relatively small town. It was very quiet. It was very hot there, so I did a lot of swimming, rode my bike around, and walked to school. It was very much like the fifties, which is what it was." Both of Mooser's parents were college-educated, so there were a lot of books around the house. His father, who ran an auto parts business, was very supportive of anything that Mooser wanted to do, and his mother, a part-time librarian, was always trying to get him to read. He didn't always read what his mother wanted him to, but Mooser did make his way through two newspapers a day, a number of magazines, and numerous adventure stories and tales of the weird and unexpected.

Looking back at his childhood now, Mooser remembers, "I was always very aware that I was a child, and that this was a time that was not going to come again. I think probably that was something that I gained from my parents as well. So I tried to have as much fun, and to get away with as many things as I could, because I knew I would be forgiven for being a child. I think of that now with my own kids. I know that they have that consciousness, that they can get away with a lot of stuff, and I certainly did that. So I tried to have as many kinds of adventures as I could. I still do for that matter."

Love of Writing Appears Early

Being aware of the freedom of childhood was not enough to compensate for the fact that Mooser was very short for his age, however. So, he became the class clown. He was also the writer for the class, penning all the plays and skits that were put on. "The first thing that I know I wrote was in the second grade," Mooser tells *SATA.* "I wrote a play that my class put on, and I still have a copy of that, so it must have really impressed me. I suspect before that I was probably writing little dumb stories and things. In looking back, I sort of assumed that everybody wrote all the time. It was only in retrospect that I realized that I was probably the only one in class that was doing a lot of writing. I've just been very fortunate in that I had people all along the way that encouraged me in what I was doing."

Mooser's overall school experience was average; "I just sort of got through it because I figured what choice did I have," he explains in his interview. By the time high school rolled around, Mooser was involved in various outside activities, including some local television work. At one point he even considered moving to Los Angeles and starting a television career. In addition to his acting, Mooser was also on the diving team at school and spent a great deal of time practicing. And even though he continued writing throughout high school, Mooser never really thought of this as a career option. "I never knew that writing was a possible career, because I'd never met a writer, and certainly no writer had never come to my school to say that this was something that you could make a living out of. So writing was something that I always enjoyed doing. I liked making up stories and writing letters and doing things like that, but it really wasn't until I'd gotten out of college and got my first job that involved writing that I thought that this was something that I could make a living doing."

After majoring in film at the University of California, Los Angeles, Mooser decided that he was never going to have a career in this field and ended up working at a variety of jobs that eventually led to his first writing

A DELL YEARLING BOOK

40542-4 •U.S. $3.25
CAN. $3.99

What *is* a family anyway?

All-Star Meatballs
THE HEADLESS SNOWMAN

Stephen Mooser
Illustrated by George Ulrich

Mooser fills his books, including this installment of the "All-Star Meatballs" series, with the kind of adventures he enjoyed plotting when he was a child. (Cover illustration by George Ulrich.)

position. Finally realizing that writing was something that he wanted to pursue, Mooser went on to earn his master's degree in journalism and worked for a magazine for a short period of time. He next found a job writing a reading series for children, and it was then that he really started getting into children's books. Mooser stayed at Southwest Regional Lab for five years, writing approximately 250 books for grades kindergarten through four.

Founds Society of Children's Book Writers

A year after Mooser started at Southwest Regional Lab, Lin Oliver also came on staff as a writer, "and we both realized we needed more help on what to do as far as writers and so we looked around for an organization to join, one for children's writers," comments Mooser. "When we didn't find anything we started the Society of Children's Book Writers in 1971. Because of the Society of Children's Book Writers I ended up meeting all kinds of people, and I ended up going to all kinds of conferences because I was putting them on. When I left Southwest Regional Lab in 1975 I had just published my first book, *101 Black Cats,* so I thought I'd try to make it as a free-lance writer, and I've been free-lancing since."

The origins of this first book go all the way back to Mooser's childhood. "In growing up I had been a treasure hunter, and I'd spent about two years off in Panama and off in the desert looking for treasures," Mooser relates. "As a child I had collected lots of true treasure stories because I thought when I grew up that I was going to be a treasure hunter. So I was making scrapbooks and collecting stories of treasures." Among the many stories Mooser accumulated was one which became the basis for *101 Black Cats.* Having recently met Sid Fleischman, Mooser was impressed with his books, which are adventure stories written mostly for boys, and read them over and over again. With this "education," Mooser then took a story of a black cat with a treasure hidden in it and wrote what became *101 Black Cats.* "I gave it to Sid to look at and he taught me probably the most important lesson I ever learned in writing," reveals Mooser. "He said, 'This is a very good story, but you haven't really sweated over it, you haven't really rewritten it enough.' And I went back and worked for a couple weeks on it and discovered the power of rewriting." When the book was finally finished, Mooser sent it off to Scholastic, and eventually a number of other publishers. After losing the manuscript and then finding it again, Scholastic finally published *101 Black Cats* about a year and a half later.

Mooser's first few books after *101 Black Cats* were a little bit of everything; he had a hard time finding a publisher who would buy more than just one or two books. So he did what he could sell, which included a few nonfiction books revolving around weird things and monsters, and a few picture books, including *The Ghost with the Halloween Hiccups, Funnyman's First Case,* and *Funnyman and the Penny Dodo. The Ghost with the Halloween Hiccups* is built around sound effects. It is Halloween and Mr. Penny, dressed as a ghost, has a horrible case of the hiccups. He spends most of the day trying the remedies offered by various members of the community, only to have the hiccups scared out of him on the way home when a couple of children dressed like monsters block his path. Sally H. Lodge, writing in *Publishers Weekly,* asserts that *The Ghost with the Halloween Hiccups* "is a nifty tale that beginners will easily read and chuckle over." The two *Funnyman* books feature young detective Archie, whose screwball and corny sense of humor gets him fired from his job in one book, and enables him to catch a thief in another. Reviewing *Funnyman's First Case,* a *School Library Journal* contributor points out that "the jokes *are* awful, but they crack right along and make sense within the story's framework."

At the same time he was writing his first children's books, Mooser was also writing filmscripts, reading programs, and a show at Sea World. "I guess I was in some ways searching for what I could do best, and at the same time selling stuff," remembers Mooser. His association with Dell finally took off after he met one of their editors through a writing group in New York. The publisher bought one of Mooser's westerns, *Shadows on the Graveyard Trail,* and went on to publish two hardcovers, *The Hitchhiking Vampire* and *It's a Weird, Weird School,* and two of his series, the "Creepy Creature Club" series and the "All-Star Meatballs" series.

Young Adult Novels Feature Teen Predicaments

The two hardcovers—*The Hitchhiking Vampire* and *It's a Weird, Weird School*—are written for a somewhat older audience than Mooser's series books. In the first, thirteen-year-old Jamie Plufphanger and her older brother Luke must travel from San Diego to Utah after their father throws a birthday party for Jamie and ends up in jail. Luke and Jamie convince their mother, who is visiting her sick father in Utah, that they can drive themselves, and set out across the desert with only thirty dollars. Along the way, they pick up an old prospector, Hank, who looks like a vampire—his teeth are cracked and jagged and his lips are red from all the pistachios he eats. Hank is on his way to Las Vegas to bet a bag full of money; Jamie persuades him to put it all on her favorite baseball team. They lose the bet, throw away the ticket, discover they didn't really lose the bet, search for the ticket, collect their money, and then lose most of what they've won. "This is an easy-to-read fantasy/farce/satire that's saturated with silly humor and moves with lightning speed from one implausible episode to another," maintains Jack Forman in *School Library Journal.*

Jamie Plufphanger also finds her way into Mooser's *It's a Weird, Weird School.* In this adventure, Jamie's best friend Carrie takes over the Madison Junior High School Board after the school librarian is fired and certain books are banned and removed from the shelves. One of Carrie's first moves is to make Jamie principal, and chaos almost immediately follows. The student school board eventually gives control back to the adults,

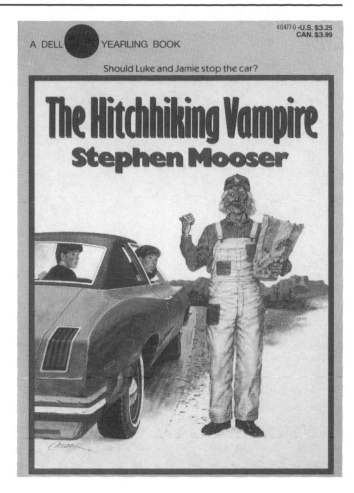

A DELL YEARLING BOOK   40477-0 ·U.S. $3.25
                                                    CAN. $3.99

Should Luke and Jamie stop the car?

The Hitchhiking Vampire
Stephen Mooser

Jamie and Luke pick up a suspicious-looking passenger and are led on an outlandish wild-goose-chase in Mooser's fast-paced novel. (Cover illustration by Carl Cassler.)

but only after the librarian is reinstated and the books are returned to the library. A *Voice of Youth Advocates* reviewer believes that the "off-the-wall characters" and "zany plot" will attract readers, and Joanne K. Hammond writes in the *School Library Journal* that *It's a Weird, Weird School* "is a realistic look at school life."

While his relationship with Dell was still developing (before *The Hitchhiking Vampire* and *It's a Weird, Weird School* were published), Mooser did his first series for Archway—the "Which Way" interactive science fiction series. Consisting of six books published between 1983 and 1986, this series allows readers to choose their own adventures and includes such titles as *Space Raiders and the Planet of Doom* and *Mind Bandits.* The first is a space fantasy in which two missions are presented and readers must make choices to get through them. And *Mind Bandits* casts the reader as the only person left on the ship the Star Voyager, facing the challenges of the universe alone. "I loved doing those because I love science fiction," remarks Mooser. "I read a lot when I was growing up and I went to every horror movie and science fiction movie I could see. I still go to all the science fiction films, so writing those was a highlight for me."

When Jamie's best friend Carrie engineers a takeover of the school board, Jamie is appointed principal of her junior high. (Cover illustration by Cassler.)

Other highlights for Mooser include the "Treasure Hound" series and the "Creepy Creature Club" series. Such books as *The Case of the Slippery Sharks* and *Secret in the Old Mansion* present Mooser's three young treasure hunters who spend their time searching for riches and solving mysteries at the same time. Their adventures include everything from diving for sunken treasure to searching for lost treasure in an old mansion. "Each case features amusing and eccentric characters," asserts Ruth Sadasivan in the *School Library Journal,* concluding that the series is "good, clean fun that should be popular with mystery fans." The "Creepy Creature Club" series presents a similar group of grade school children, but their main interests are monsters and other scary things, which are the basis for the club they've formed. In each new adventure, the gang manages to get into some sort of trouble, but always learns something along the way. Janice C. Hayes, writing in *School Library Journal,* describes one of the books in the series, *Monsters in the Outfield,* as "light, entertaining reading" that is "packed with action and dialogue."

Mooser's most recent series, the "All-Star Meatballs" series, features a group of Bayview school students who are into sports, but can't really be classified as jocks. The group earns their name in the first book of the series, *Babe Ruth and the Home Run Derby,* when they are involved in a lunchtime food fight which includes flying meatballs. Another book in the series, *The Terrible Tickler,* presents a more serious topic through the character of Kate, a blind student who turns into a heroine during a blackout at school. *Publishers Weekly* contributor Sybil Steinberg writes that "kid-pleasing silliness abounds" in the series.

Encounters with the Unexpected Make Series a Favorite

Out of all the different types of books he writes, it is the books like those in the "Creepy Creature Club" series that Mooser prefers most. "I enjoy writing middle-grade fiction with real-life characters who encounter something a little strange, something a little off-center," he explains. "I like to go to movies where you're surprised, and I like the same thing to happen in a book, where something unexpected happens. It may start off as a very regular story, then suddenly something you totally do not expect happens. So, my books are a little bit off-center, but they're based on reality. I think like that." Along with the unexpected, humor is another recurring element in Mooser's works; the "Creepy Creature Club" books even include a collection of monster jokes on the last few pages. Mooser believes that children are drawn to this aspect of his writing: "I think that most kids are looking for a little bit of escape, and I think that humor is such a universal thing that kids can enjoy sharing strange and weird tales. They can't resist being the first to tell their friends about something weird that happened, and they like to tell them jokes or something funny that happened, too."

Not only does Mooser want kids to enjoy and share stories, but he wants them to continue reading. That's why he writes humorous adventure stories. "I guess that if most people have some kind of crusade, I think that mine is getting kids to be able to read. I don't think there's a skill that's as important to acquire in this life as reading. If you can read, you can go to the library, you can fill out an application form. I know for my own kids, when I found out they could read I breathed a sigh of relief because I knew that they would always be okay in this world. I want to write books that give kids an enjoyable reading experience so that they'll pick up another book after that—not necessarily my book, but another book—and they'll keep reading and that reading will be fun for them. I would say that the most important thing for me is to write books that are fun to read."

■ Works Cited

Forman, Jack, review of *The Hitchhiking Vampire,* *School Library Journal,* April, 1989, pp. 103-04.
Review of *Funnyman's First Case,* *School Library Journal,* December, 1981, p. 74.
Hammond, Joanne K., review of *It's a Weird, Weird School,* *School Library Journal,* May, 1990, p. 108.
Hayes, Janice C., review of *Monsters in the Outfield,* *School Library Journal,* February, 1990, p. 92.

A DELL YOUNG YEARLING

40338-3 • U.S. $2.99
CAN. $3.50

SECRETS OF SCARY FUN
Stephen Mooser

Illustrated by George Ulrich

WEIRD PLAYS, MONSTER JOKES, FLIP MOVIES INSIDE

The members of Mooser's "Creepy Creature Club" reveal their spookiest skills in this volume. (Cover illustration by Ulrich.)

Review of *It's a Weird, Weird School, Voice of Youth Advocates,* April, 1990, p. 32.

Lodge, Sally H., review of *The Ghost with the Halloween Hiccups, Publishers Weekly,* September 25, 1981, p. 92.

Mooser, Stephen, in an interview with Susan M. Reicha for *Something about the Author,* April 21, 1993.

Sadasivan, Ruth, review of the "Treasure Hound" series, *School Library Journal,* May, 1988, pp. 99-100.

Steinberg, Sybil, review of *Babe Ruth and the Home Run Derby* and *The Terrible Tickler, Publishers Weekly,* September 7, 1992, p. 96.

■ **For More Information See**

PERIODICALS

Horn Book, August, 1984, pp. 408-09.

New York Times Book Review, November 13, 1977, p. 45.

Publishers Weekly, June 9, 1989, p. 68.

School Library Journal, December, 1977, p. 59; March, 1980, p. 135; March, 1984, p. 163; December, 1984, p. 97.

Voice of Youth Advocates, December, 1983, p. 283; February, 1986, pp. 399-400.

—*Sketch by Susan M. Reicha*

*   *   *

MOTT, Evelyn Clarke 1962-

■ **Personal**

Born August 22, 1962, in Portchester, NY; daughter of William (a mechanical engineer) and Kimiko (a social worker; maiden name, Kajikawa) Clarke; married Douglas Kenneth Mott, June 9, 1984; children: Christopher Douglas. *Education:* Bucks County Community College, A.A., 1983; Thomas Edison College, B.S. (summa cum laude), 1986. *Hobbies and other interests:* Art, travel, music, hiking, stargazing.

■ **Addresses**

Home and office—325 Hillside Ave., Morrisville, PA 19067.

■ **Career**

Photographer, 1987—; free-lance writer and photo-illustrator of children's books, 1989—. Founder and president of Lakeside Writers for Young People, 1990—; volunteer author for a homeless shelter; resident author for an elementary school. *Member:* Authors Guild, Society of Children's Book Writers and Illustrators, Lakeside Writers for Young People, Canon Professional Photographers, Philadelphia Children's Reading Round Table.

■ **Writings**

(And photographer) *Steam Train Ride,* Walker and Co., 1991.

(And photographer) *Balloon Ride,* Walker and Co., 1991.

(And photographer) *A Day at the Races with Austin and Kyle Petty,* Random House, 1993.

(And photographer) *Baby Face—A Mirror Book* (board book), Random House, 1994.

Contributor to *For All the Write Reasons: Forty Successful Authors, Publishers, Agents, and Writers Tell You How to Get Your Book Published,* Gallagher Jordan, 1992.

■ **Work in Progress**

Hot Dog!, a photographic book "about man's best friend"; research on Native American dance.

■ **Sidelights**

Evelyn Clarke Mott told *SATA:* "When I was ten years old, I decided to become a writer. The three dollars I won in a writing contest sponsored by the *Philadelphia Inquirer* were enough to convince me that writing was a great way to make a living! Two years later, I entered a local newspaper's contest. I won again, but this time I won my wish—to spend a day at the newspaper writing my own column. It was exciting to see my words in the newspaper the next day! In high school, I was published in *Seventeen* magazine and worked as an assistant editor and columnist for my high school newspaper.

"*Steam Train Ride* is my celebration of America's romance with the steam train. Through the photographs and text I hope children will feel the thrills and excitement their grandparents and great-grandparents felt as they watched the steam train come to town.

"I have always felt passionate about trains. As a little girl, I enjoyed watching the trains from my backyard. Everyday, I listened for the sounds of train whistles and the clickety-clacks of wheels along the railroad tracks. When trains whizzed past, I waved to the engineers and passengers.

"As a toddler, my son, Christopher, had an incredible passion for steam trains. Christopher's appetite for train books was insatiable, and the book he really wanted—a picture book with photographs of steam trains—didn't exist. I decided that with my love of photography and writing, I should create the book Christopher wanted so desperately to read.

EVELYN CLARKE MOTT

Books Combine Love of Writing and Photography

"During my research, I read about Strasburg Railroad in Lancaster County, Pennsylvania. Christopher and I visited Strasburg and immediately fell in love with the well-preserved, lovingly maintained steam trains, the rural countryside, and the friendly people. I hope that children and adults have as much fun reading *Steam Train Ride* as I had photographing it.

"For me, children's book writing allows me to combine the things I love the most—research, writing, photography, and teaching. I truly do what I love and love what I do.

"*Balloon Ride* was an important book for me because it helped me conquer one of my greatest fears—the fear of heights! I had several ideas for a transportation photo-essay when my editor suggested hot air balloons. I was immediately mortified but said that I would be happy to try it. I flew several times with shaking knees and chattering teeth; on one occasion, I completely forgot how to operate my camera! Considering the difficulty I experienced in trying to keep my hands steady, no one was more surprised than I was at how well the pictures turned out.

"Writing children's books has been a growth process. My first book helped me conquer my fear of failure (I didn't think I could complete *Steam Train Ride*—every step was a challenge), my second book helped allay my fear of heights, my third book ended my fears of revision, and my fourth book let me speak out against something that has deeply disturbed me since my childhood: prejudice.

"*A Day at the Races with Austin and Kyle Petty* was my most difficult book to complete. I spent months researching and writing the story and an intense week at Charlotte Motor Speedway in Charlotte, North Carolina, photographing the book. When I sent the photographs to my editor, I was certain that most of the work was complete. But after looking at the many interesting garage photographs, she suggested I include them, change the book's angle, and rewrite it. It was difficult for me because I had grown so attached to the original story. After several months of research and many difficult rewrites, however, I realized that my editor was right. *A Day at the Races* had become more visual, interesting, and exciting. My appreciation for the art of revision increased considerably.

"Photographing Kyle Petty, a celebrity race car driver, provided many interesting challenges. It was extremely difficult to take a photograph of Kyle without people asking for autographs, shaking his hand, and talking to him. Just when I thought I had time to photograph Kyle, someone else would come along with another request.

"Photographing Kyle's car, Mello Yello, was easier. It was gorgeous! Visually, there was so much to look at and so many wonderful colors and angles. The greatest

Christopher learns how a real steam train runs as he takes a tour in Mott's book.

challenge was to photograph it when it travelled at speeds of over 180 miles per hour—I had never photographed anything that fast before. It was fun to travel in areas of the race track that most people only see on television. Charlotte Motor Speedway was a noisy and busy place, and, for a photographer who loves auto racing, a visual feast!

"*Baby Face—A Mirror Book* grew out of what I felt was a need for a book for very young children that spoke out against prejudice. I am extremely passionate about *Baby Face* because of my own childhood experiences with racism—growing up half-Japanese was not easy for me.

Some of my early childhood memories are still very painful. Many of my classmates would not play with me simply because of the way I looked. A few threw rocks at me and called me 'slanty eyes.'

"Having grown up wishing I looked like most everyone else, I understand how important it is to give children an awareness and appreciation of our external differences and a realization that, underneath it all, we are very much the same. I feel that through teaching children to respect others we give them something even more important: self-respect."

N

NILAND, Kilmeny

■ Personal

Born in Sydney, Australia; daughter of D'Arcy (a writer) and Ruth (a writer; maiden name, Park) Niland; married Rafe Champion (a writer) in 1975; children: Leo, Hugh, Patrick, Thomas. *Education:* Julian Ashton Art School, diploma in drawing, 1968.

■ Addresses

Home—77 Holt Ave., Cremorne, New South Wales 2090, Australia. *Agent*—Curtis Brown, 27 Union St., Paddington, New South Wales 2021, Australia.

KILMENY NILAND

■ Career

Children's book author, illustrator, and painter. Worked as a free-lance book illustrator and card designer, England, 1968-70; also worked in animation, 1970-73; poster, mural, and card design for Portal Publications. *Exhibitions:* Barry Stern galleries, Sydney, Australia (three showings); Medici Gallery, London, England; and several other mixed shows. *Member:* Australian Society of Illustrators, Australian Society of Miniature Art, Australian Guild of Realist Artists, Australian Wildlife Fund.

■ Awards, Honors

Visual Arts Board best illustrated children's book of the year citation, and Australian Book Publishers Association Book Design Award, both 1974, and outstanding picture book of the year citation, 1975, all for *Mulga Bill's Bicycle;* Children's Book Council of Australia picture book of the year commendation, 1977, for *Tell Me Another Tale;* Australian Book Publishers Association Book Design Award, and Royal Zoological Society of New South Wales best children's book certificate, both 1980, both for *Feathers, Fur and Frills;* Leipzig Award for Book Design, 1986, for *Bright Eyes and Bushy Tails;* Mosman Residents' Prize at the Mosman Art Prize, and several prizes for miniature art painting, all 1992.

■ Writings

SELF-ILLUSTRATED

(With others) *Animal Tales,* Angus & Robertson, 1974.
Feathers, Fur and Frills, Hodder & Stoughton, 1980.
My World, Hodder & Stoughton, 1981.
Bright Eyes and Bushy Tails, Hodder & Stoughton, 1984.
A Bellbird in a Flame Tree, Angus & Robertson, 1989, Tambourine, 1991.

ILLUSTRATOR

(With sister) *The Little Goat,* Transworld, 1971; published as *The Lost Goat,* Reader's Digest Services, 1977.

The Farm Alphabet, Transworld, 1973.

(With sister) A. B. Paterson, *Mulga Bill's Bicycle,* Collins, 1973, Parents Magazine Press, 1975.

What Am I, Transworld, 1974.

Tell Me A Tale, Hodder & Stoughton, 1974.

Ruth Park, *Callie's Castle,* Angus & Robertson, 1974.

(With sister) Park, *The Gigantic Balloon,* Collins, 1975, Parents Magazine Press, 1976.

Barbara Ireson, *One Eyed Jack and Other Rhymes,* Transworld, 1975.

Birds on a Bough, Hodder & Stoughton, 1975.

Tell Me Another Tale, Hodder & Stoughton, 1976.

The Corrugated Violin Show, Australian Broadcasting Commission, 1976.

(With sister) Park, *Roger Bandy,* Rigby, 1977, new edition, Nelson, 1987.

Ruth Manning Sanders, *The Haunted Castle,* Angus & Robertson, 1978.

Sanders, *Old Witch Bonyleg,* Angus & Robertson, 1978.

Jane Wilton Smith, *The Fairytale Picture Dictionary,* Hodder & Stoughton, 1979.

The Zoo Alphabet, Transworld, 1980.

Jean Chapman, *Pancakes and Painted Eggs,* Hodder & Stoughton, 1981.

Pieta Letchford, *Matthew and the New Baby,* Hodder & Stoughton, 1986.

Mem Fox, *Just Like That,* Hodder & Stoughton, 1986.

Hazel Edwards, *Fey Mouse,* Nelson Publishers, 1988.

Kristine Church, *Grandad Barnett's Beard,* Angus & Robertson, 1988.

Park, *Callie's Family,* Angus & Robertson, 1989.

Church, *My Brother John,* Angus & Robertson, 1990, Tambourine, 1990.

Sally Odgers, *The Window Book,* Walter McVitty Books, 1992.

Lydia Pender, *The Land and the Spirit,* Margaret Hamilton Books, 1992.

Marcia Vaughan, *Sheep Shape,* Margaret Hamilton Books, 1993.

A Finnish edition of *Birds on a Bough* was published by Kirjateos in 1979.

■ Work in Progress

Concentrating on painting for exhibition; learning printmaking.

■ Sidelights

Kilmeny Niland's affection for depicting animals of her native Australia is evident in two of her self-illustrated children's books, *Bright Eyes and Bushy Tails* and *A Bellbird in a Flame Tree.* The first, published in 1984, contains full page illustrations and textual descriptions of various exotic animals. "It is essentially a pin-up album of ... Niland's attractive pictures of exotic

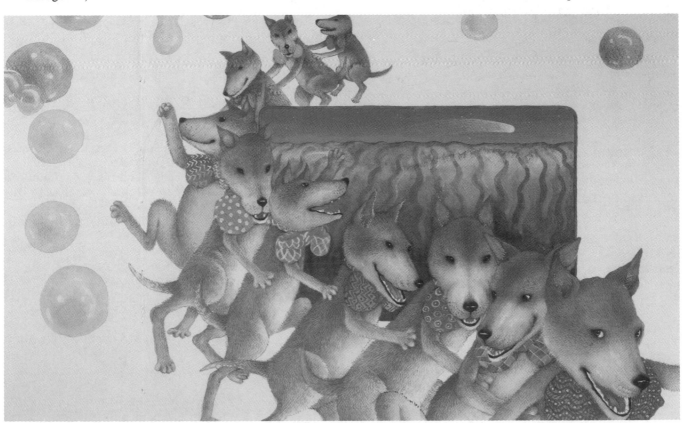

Niland brings an Australian perspective to her self-illustrated version of the traditional holiday carol *The Twelve Days of Christmas.*

creatures, in poses which combine heraldic solemnity with a precise, breathing, caught-in-the-act fidelity," describes Eric Korn in the *Times Literary Supplement.* And a *Junior Bookshelf* contributor maintains that Niland "has a way of portraying animals with a quivering sensitivity which goes straight to the heart." This insight into animals is also present in *A Bellbird in a Flame Tree,* an Australian version of the traditional song, "The Twelve Days of Christmas." Instead of the usual characters, Niland fills her book with creatures native to her own country, including crocodiles, dingoes, lorikeets, and koalas. The background illustrations included with these many celebrants also offer visual information about Australian fauna and flora. "The animals, brightly painted in tropical colors, are just right for an Australian celebration," observes a *School Library Journal* contributor. And a *Publishers Weekly* contributor finds *A Bellbird in a Flame Tree* to be a "fresh, winsome take on the favorite holiday song."

■ Works Cited

Review of *A Bellbird in a Flame Tree, Publishers Weekly,* September 27, 1991, p. 57.
Review of *A Bellbird in a Flame Tree, School Library Journal,* October, 1991, p. 32.
Review of *Bright Eyes and Bushy Tails, Junior Bookshelf,* June, 1985, p. 145.
Korn, Eric, "Natural Acts," *Times Literary Supplement,* August 2, 1985, p. 862.

■ For More Information See

PERIODICALS

Times Literary Supplement, July 23, 1982.

*   *   *

NUNES, Lygia Bojunga 1932-

■ Personal

Born August 26, 1932, in Pelotas, Brazil; married.

■ Addresses

Home—26 Cressy Rd., London NW3 2LY, England; and Rua Eliseu Visconti 425, 20251 Rio de Janeiro, RJ, Brazil.

■ Career

Writer, translator, and actor. Member of theatre troupe Theatre Duse and of the Repertoire Theatre of Henriette Morineau; cofounder of rural school TOCA. Presenter of dramatic monologues at libraries, universities, and cultural centers.

■ Awards, Honors

Hans Christian Andersen Award, 1982, for body of children's books; Moliere Prize, Theatre Critics of Paris,

LYGIA BOJUNGA NUNES

and Mambembe Trophy, Ministry of Education and Culture, Brazil, both 1986, both for play *O pintor.*

■ Writings

Os colegas (title means "The Companions"), Sabia (Rio de Janeiro), 1972.
Angelica, illustrated by Vilma Pasqualini, Artes Graficas Industrias Reunidas (AGIR; Rio de Janeiro), 1975.
A bolsa amarela (title means "The Yellow Bag"), illustrated by Marie Louise Nery, AGIR, 1976.
A casa de madrinha (title means "Godmother's House"), illustrated by Regina Yolanda, AGIR, 1978.
Corda bamba (title means "Tightrope"), Civilizacao (Rio de Janeiro), 1979.
O sofa estampado (title means "The Chintz Sofa"), illustrated by Elvira Vigna, Olympio, 1980.
Tomie Ohtake, [Rio de Janeiro], 1983.
Tchau, AGIR, 1984.
Livro (autobiography; title means "Book"), AGIR, 1988.
O meu amigo pintor (for children), Olympio, translation by Giovanni Pontiero published as *My Friend the Painter,* Harcourt, 1991.

Also author of *O pintor* (play; based on *O meu amigo pintor*), *Nos tres* (children's book and play; title means "The Three of Us"), *Fazendo Ana Paz* (title means "Creating Ana Paz"), and *Paisagem* (title means "Landscape"), all published by AGIR.

Nunes's works have been translated into several languages, including French, German, Spanish, Swedish, Norwegian, Danish, Finnish, Basque, Hebrew, Italian, Dutch, Czech, Bulgarian, Galician, Catalan, and Icelandic.

■ Sidelights

Winner of the 1982 Hans Christian Andersen Award, Brazilian author Lygia Bojunga Nunes has written several children's books that have been translated into a variety of languages. Her first work to be translated into English is 1991's *My Friend the Painter,* which is aimed at older elementary and middle school readers. In the book young Claudio must cope with the suicide of his adult friend, a painter who encouraged his interest in art. According to some critics, Nunes's treatment of her subject is emotionally intense, while other reviewers found the book too abstract and subtle for young readers. A *Kirkus Reviews* critic praised *My Friend the Painter* as "a rich, poetic glimpse of universal feelings filtered through an unfamiliar culture." And a reviewer in the *Bulletin of the Center for Children's Books* called the story's conclusion "a lyrical celebration of a remembered friendship."

Nunes told *SATA:* "Since I was seven I began reading stories, and right from the beginning I fell in love with books. But it was a love of reading, not doing. My affair took me by surprise because it was so overwhelming, so much a part of me, that before I realized what was happening, I'd been taken over entirely by literature."

■ Works Cited

Review of *My Friend the Painter, Bulletin of the Center for Children's Books,* May, 1991, p. 224.
Review of *My Friend the Painter, Kirkus Reviews,* May 1, 1991, p. 607.

■ For More Information See

PERIODICALS
School Library Journal, October, 1991, p. 125.

O–P

O'CONNOR, Genevieve A. 1914-

■ Personal

Born September 5, 1914, in Raton, New Mexico; daughter of Myrton Grover Young (a teacher) and Mary Hellen (a teacher; maiden name, Hill) Connors; married James A. O'Connor, Jr. (an aircraft assembler), August 22, 1934 (died, 1984); children: James, Mary Pusey, Kathleen Jaworski, Elizabeth Anderson, William. *Education:* San Diego State University, B.A., 1988. *Politics:* Democratic. *Religion:* Roman Catholic.

■ Addresses

Home—San Diego, California.

■ Career

San Diego Community Colleges, San Diego, CA, secretary, 1965-76; writer.

■ Writings

The Admiral and the Deck Boy: One Boy's Journey with Christopher Columbus, Shoe Tree Press, 1991.

Also author of short stories; contributor to periodicals, including *Family Circle, Our Sunday Visitor, St. Joseph* and *Catholic Digest.*

■ Work in Progress

The Tree Troll Mystery; The Long Road Home (tentative title), a historical novel about a boy's journey with his family from New England to Ohio in 1790; research for a novel about Mayan young people.

■ Sidelights

Genevieve A. O'Connor told *SATA:* "I don't remember a time when I was not either telling stories or trying to write stories. My very strict great-grandmother told me when I was a child that I was going to hell someday if I kept telling lies. Her daughter, my great-aunt, however, said that I wasn't telling lies, I was using my imagination. She said that someday I would become an actress or a writer. I believed her and kept on imagining stories. I also read all the books I could in my childhood. When I had children later, I saw that they had books to read, or for me to read to them.

"I was fourteen when my first published story appeared in my high school annual. The following year I entered a national essay contest, winning second place, and the essay was published by *American Girl* magazine. By then I knew I had to become an author. I enrolled in San Diego Teacher's College (later San Diego State Univer-

GENEVIEVE A. O'CONNOR

sity), but dropped out after one semester when I realized that I didn't want to be a teacher. I went to a commercial college and became a secretary; after only one year in the work world, however, I met 'Mr. Right' and married.

"In the years following my marriage, while I was pretty much tied down at home with small children, I wrote and wrote without much success. I found a copy of Dorothea Brande's book *Becoming a Writer* in the public library. I read it carefully and wrote and wrote some more. Finally, I had two short stories published by a national Catholic newspaper, *Our Sunday Visitor.* Next followed a rash of short fillers in *Family Circle* and *Catholic Digest.* Then a short story about Abe Lincoln's boyhood, 'Wilderness Journey,' was published by F.A. Owen in their magazine for primary school teachers, *The Instructor.* As a result, the editor, Mary Owen, asked me if I would submit other stories for a projected primary grades reader. Three historical stories were accepted, although the reader was never published. In 1966 I wrote the story of my intensely emotional part in my son's wedding; although he was to marry a Mexican girl whom I loved at once, I had grave doubts that their marriage could succeed due to their differing cultural backgrounds. The story, 'Lazo de Amor' (bond of love), focused on how this Mexican *lazo* resolved my fears. It was published by *St. Joseph's* magazine in October, 1967.

"After my children were grown and gone from home, I had an opportunity to return to college. I spent the next eight years finishing my work at the history department at San Diego State University, finally getting my B.A. in history on December 17, 1988—fifty-seven years after I had first enrolled at the school. It was probably one of the most satisfying accomplishments in my life. If only my husband of fifty years had lived to share it, my happiness would have been complete. He had died in 1984.

College Research Inspires Sailing Tale

"One of the last requirements I had to fulfill at San Diego State was a class in the history of writing. The professor's assigned subject for the class was to explore some aspect of Christopher Columbus's voyages, a topic which entailed a lot of research and writing. I will always remember my last evening in that class. As I sat there the thought came to me as clearly as handwriting on the classroom chalkboard: 'I have enough material for a children's book about the young deck boy who was at the tiller the night the *Santa Maria* was wrecked.' That was it! For all these years I had fond memories of those afternoons in my sixth grade year when the teacher had read aloud to us from the sea adventure book *The Log of Tom Dark.* I don't remember the author's name, but the flavor of that book remained with me. I'm sure it influenced the writing of my first novel for children.

"All I needed to write the book was a computer. Writing and rewriting a whole book on the old typewriter would

be hard. When my children, their spouses, and my grandchildren gathered at my home that Christmas Eve, a week after my graduation, they presented me with a box that held a framed picture of the computer I had dreamed of and a card signed by all twenty-two of them. They all had faith in me. I knew I had to get to work and really write. The result was *The Admiral and the Deck Boy: One Boy's Journey with Christopher Columbus.*

"Presently I have a second children's book, *The Tree Troll Mystery,* making the rounds looking for a publisher, and another historical story is in the works. The writing seems to keep generating more and more ideas as I go. It makes my life seem truly fulfilled. My age was no handicap in college, and it is certainly a plus now to have free time in my 'retirement' to research and to write."

*   *   *

OWEN, Annie 1949-

■ Personal

Born August 23, 1949, in Dartford, Kent, England; daughter of John F. and Margaret O. (Baldwin) Jones; married C. J. Owen, August 14, 1971 (divorced December 7, 1981); children: Thirza Halcyon Margaret, Rufus Henry Rowan. *Education:* Attended Goldsmith's College of Art and Design, London, 1968-69; London College of Printing, B.A., 1972.

■ Addresses

Home and office—Eastwood Hall, South Lopham, Diss, Norfolk 1P22 2HL, England. *Agent*—Laura Cecil, 17 Alwyne Villas, London N1 2HG, England.

■ Career

Worked for a design group in London, England, 1972-73; *Photo News Weekly,* London, picture editor and art director, 1973-74; *British Journal of Photography,* London, picture editor and art director, 1974-76; free-lance graphic designer; writer and illustrator. Taught life drawing and illustration at Suffolk College, 1984; taught illustration at Norfolk Institute of Art and Design, 1987-92.

■ Writings

SELF-ILLUSTRATED

Annie's ABC, Orchard Books, 1986.
Annie's One to Ten, Orchard Books, 1987.
Cats, Kings, and Other Things (nursery rhymes), Hodder & Stoughton, 1988.
Models, Two-Can Books, 1989.
Traffic Jam, Orchard Books, 1989, published in the United States as *Bumper to Bumper,* Knopf, 1991.
Is It Hairy? Is It Scary?, Orchard Books, 1991.
(Compiler) *Pigeons* (poetry anthology), Pan/Macmillan, 1992.

ILLUSTRATOR

Elizabeth MacDonald, *My Aunt and the Animals,* Aurum Press, 1985.

Robert Louis Stevenson, *A Child's Garden of Verses,* Aurum Press, 1985.

■ Work in Progress

A set of board books for Kingfisher Books.

■ Sidelights

Annie Owen told *SATA:* "My reasons for doing the work I do with children's books stem from a passionate love of books and a belief that books have always had a very crucial role in a child's development and imagination, and this remains the case today despite television and video interests. Books are still very special."

* * *

PARSONS, Ellen
See DRAGONWAGON, Crescent

* * *

PILGRIM, Anne
See ALLAN, Mabel Esther

* * *

POMEROY, Pete
See ROTH, Arthur J(oseph)

* * *

POWER, Margaret (M.)

■ Personal

Born October 29, in Melbourne, Australia; daughter of Richard and Sylvia (an artist and potter; maiden name, McPherson) Power; divorced. *Education:* Royal Melbourne Institute of Technology Art School, diploma of illustration, 1964. *Politics:* "Green."

■ Addresses

Home and office—6/6 Sidwell Ave., East St. Kilda, Victoria 3183, Australia.

■ Career

Children's book illustrator, 1986—. Has worked as fashion illustrator for stores in London and Australia and as freelance illustrator for magazines and newspapers. *Member:* Society of Children's Book Writers and Illustrators, Australian Society of Book Illustrators.

MARGARET POWER

■ Awards, Honors

Children's Book of the Year picture book honor prize, 1988, for *The Long Red Scarf.*

■ Illustrator

Margaret Wild, *Creatures in the Beard,* Omnibus, 1986.
Nette Hilton, *The Long Red Scarf,* Omnibus, 1987.
Edel Wignell, *Spider in the Toilet,* Lothian, 1988.
Robert Klein, *The Ghost in Abigail Terrace,* 1989.
Christina Dwyer, *Jimmie Jean and the Turtles,* Walter McNutty Books, 1992.

Also illustrator of *Dad's Camel* and *Anna Pavlova.* Illustrated covers for *Anne of Green Gables* paperback series.

■ Work in Progress

Illustrating *Daisy Drew an Elephant,* a picture book, for CIS Publishers; working on reading series for Educational Books; magazine work.

■ Sidelights

Margaret Power told *SATA:* "All I ever wanted to do was draw—and this even before I began school. It must have been written on the slate when I was born!

"My first children's book was called *Dad's Camel* and was part of the Heineman 'Red Apple' series. *Dad's Camel* was done in pen and ink, and it was printed in two colors with a three-color overlay. I was clearly at the height of my pen and ink period! In those early days I worked with Janet Ahlberg in a studio in London; she illustrated *The Jolly Postman* and is one of my favorite illustrators.

"I love watercolors, but strangely enough I haven't used them in any of my picture books so far, though *Spider in the Toilet* and the covers I did for the *Anne of Green Gables* paperback series are a combination of pantoue markers, watercolor, and pencil. My other picture books are all in pastels, so clearly *this* is my pastel period! I am often asked if I draw in other styles, and I do use a more cartoonish style for some of the reading scheme books I'm involved in. I love the freedom this gives me. But I try to bring a sense of fun and fantasy even to my realistic works.

"With all my books, I do a tremendous amount of research to get the details right. Before I began *Jimmie Jean and the Turtles,* for example, I read and studied books about turtles and vegetation and landscape particular to those areas of Queensland where the turtle rookeries are located. I also asked my brother, who is one of the scientists in the story, to take photographs of beachscapes and vegetation around turtle rookeries near where he was vacationing—just to add to the mountain of references I already had. I really feast on this part of the creative process, drenching my brain with all the appropriate data. Then the really fun part begins— deciding what the characters in the story will look like. I do working drawings and take photographs of different people; the granddaughter of some friends was the model for Jimmie Jean.

"For *The Long Red Scarf,* I didn't use models at all. I had a strong idea already as to how I wanted the characters to look—particularly the Grandpa. When I had completed the artwork for the book and sent it off to the publishers, the very next day I was crossing the street near my home and the very 'character' of Grandpa, complete with woolly cap, peddled by on a battered old bike. I was so astonished! I stared after him and wanted to call out, 'You're in my book!' Though I have no recollection of it, I must have seen him somewhere before and filed him away in my mind as a wonderful character to draw."

*   *   *

PUSHKER, Gloria (Teles) 1927-

■ Personal

Born January 12, 1927, in New Orleans, LA; daughter of Abraham (a retail merchant) and Rose (Pesses) Teles; married Benjamin Pushker (a retail merchant), 1948 (deceased, June 7, 1992); children: Judy, Elizabeth, Gail. *Education:* Loyola University, B.A., 1982; University of New Orleans, M.Ed., 1987. *Religion:* Jewish.

■ Addresses

Home—302 West Gatehouse Dr., Metairie, LA 70001.

■ Career

Writer. Storyteller, New Orleans, 1983—. Also worked variously as a retail store manager, fashion coordinator, and Sunday school teacher. *Member:* National Association for the Preservation and Perpetuation of Storytelling.

■ Writings

Toby Belfer Never Had a Christmas Tree, Pelican, 1990.
Toby Belfer's Seder: A Passover Story Retold, Pelican, 1994.

■ Work in Progress

A book about eyes; other stories for young children.

■ Sidelights

Gloria Pushker told *SATA:* "In 1971, I had a conversation with my sister about people who were jealous. She added that I don't have a jealous bone in my body. My reply was 'Yes, I have. I sincerely wish I had a master's degree and a flat tummy.' Her reply was, 'If you wanted either one badly enough you could have them both!' I heard an ad on the radio the same day about continuing education for women at Loyola University in New Orleans. I thought that must be some kind of omen, so I registered the very next day for one course in English with the understanding that if I passed, I would continue. I was forty-four years old. I have, therefore, been taking one subject at a time for twenty-two years. I now have a B.A. from Loyola with a concentration in psychology and sociology, and a master's degree in education from the University of New Orleans with a concentration in children's literature. I am presently doing postgraduate work in children's literature which may lead to a Ph.D. I will be teaching children's literature at Loyola University beginning in the fall of 1993.

GLORIA PUSHKER

"My first book was published in 1990 about a young Jewish girl living in a totally Christian community. She has Christmas with her friends and they learn about Hanukkah from her and her family. I dedicated this book to my 'magnificent seven' grandchildren, my major professor, and one of my sisters. My second book, *Toby Belfer's Seder: A Passover Story Retold,* is about a little Christian girl invited to her first Seder who agonizes over what to wear. I have had great fun being a storyteller-author, my goal being to make storytellers out of my audiences. My repertoire includes stories from literature, Southern classics, Jewish tales, as well as original poems and stories."

R

REGAN, Dian Curtis 1950-

■ Personal

Born May 17, 1950, in Colorado Springs, CO; daughter of Donald (Denver & Rio Grande Railroad worker) and Katherine (a homemaker; maiden name, French) Curtis; married John Regan (an engineer), August 25, 1979. *Education:* University of Colorado, Boulder, B.S. (honors), 1980. *Politics:* Independent. *Religion:* Protestant. *Hobbies and other interests:* Travel, study of herbal healing, reading, camping.

■ Addresses

Home—Box 1875, Edmond, OK 73083. *Agent*—Curtis Brown Ltd., 10 Astor Place, New York, NY 10003.

■ Career

Hewlett Packard, Colorado Springs, CO, inspector, 1968-70; Colorado Interstate Gas Corporation, Colorado Springs, clerk, 1971-78; Adams County District 12, Denver, CO, elementary school teacher, 1980-82; full-time author and speaker, 1982—. Society of Children's Book Writers and Illustrators, regional advisor, 1984-92; National Association for Young Writers, board member, 1987-91. *Member:* Society of Children's Book Writers and Illustrators, Authors Guild, Science Fiction and Fantasy Writers of America.

■ Awards, Honors

I've Got Your Number was named an International Reading Association/Children's Book Council Children's Choice Award book, 1987; *Game of Survival* was honored as an American Library Association Recommended Book for Reluctant Readers, 1990; Oklahoma Cherubim Award, 1990, for *Game of Survival,* 1991, for *Jilly's Ghost,* and 1992, for *Liver Cookies.*

DIAN CURTIS REGAN

■ Writings

YOUNG ADULT NOVELS

I've Got Your Number, Avon, 1986.
The Perfect Age, Avon, 1987.
Game of Survival, Avon, 1989.
Jilly's Ghost, Avon, 1990.
The Initiation, Avon, 1993.

I've Got Your Number and *The Perfect Age* have appeared in German translation.

MIDDLE-GRADE NOVELS

The Kissing Contest, Scholastic, 1990.
Liver Cookies, Scholastic, 1991.
My Zombie Valentine, Scholastic, 1993.
The Vampire Who Came for Christmas, Scholastic, 1993.
Princess (working title), Scholastic, in press.

CHAPTER BOOKS

The Class with the Summer Birthdays, illustrated by Susan Guevara, Holt, 1991.
The Curse of the Trouble Dolls, illustrated by Michael Chesworth, Holt, 1992.
The Peppermint Race, Holt, in press.

PICTURE BOOKS

Thirteen Hours of Halloween, illustrated by Lieve Baeten, Albert Whitman, 1993.
Dad and Me, Scholastic, in press.
Mom and Me, Scholastic, in press.

OTHER

Juvenile market columnist, *Byline* magazine, 1983-89; on assignment for *Writer's Digest,* 1987—.

■ Work in Progress

Writing *Callan's Song,* a historical fiction middle-grade novel set in 1480, and *Monster of the Month Club,* a contemporary humor/fantasy novel; researching the Oklahoma Land Run for a middle-grade novel entitled *Morning Star,* set in 1889.

■ Sidelights

Dian Curtis Regan told *SATA:* "Even though I have more than fifteen books to my credit, I still feel as if I'm on the brink of my career with much to write about and much to learn.

"Letting my imagination run wild in the course of everyday living probably accounts for my being a writer of children's books. Being caught daydreaming is embarrassing when one is an adult, but it makes for good story ideas.

"When I was in elementary school, I loved hearing the teacher say, 'We're going to write a story.' Everyone would groan except me. I'd already be writing. The reason, I suppose, was that I always surprised myself with the end result—something I *still* try to do. And when the teacher chose my story to read to the class, it reinforced my instinct that what I'd written was good, or, at least, different from what everyone else had written.

"One of the surprises of my writing career has been the many invitations to speak at schools and conferences. Yet, once a teacher, always a teacher; I find it easy to talk about books and to share my enthusiasm.

Regan combines humor and fantasy in many of her works, including this book about some sinister toys. (Cover illustration by Michael Chesworth.)

"I'm pleased that the Whole Language Movement has resulted in author visits to the schools. If I'd had the opportunity to meet an author when I was growing up, it would have had a tremendous impact on me. I'm certain I would have chosen writing as a career at an earlier age, instead of more or less stumbling upon the realization that my hobby could become a full-time occupation.

"I've experimented in all genres: picture books, chapter books, middle-grade, young adult, mystery, suspense, romance, humor, historical fiction, and fantasy. I was 'warned' not to do this, and advised to stick to one area and become good at it. But the idea of writing the same kind of book over and over didn't appeal to me. Right now, the niche I've carved for myself seems to be humor/fantasy, or 'scary funny' as one editor called it.

"The process of creativity constantly amazes me. Many of my books are sparked by a single premise, phrase, or title, such as *My Zombie Valentine.* It's also curious to me how circumstances in my past, present, and the way I foresee the future find their way into my books.

"I'm often asked if I will ever 'grow up' and write for adults. I think I've already found the best audience. If writing for children means I'll never grow up, then so be it."

■ For More Information See

PERIODICALS

Writer's Digest, winter, 1987; fall, 1992.

* * *

REID BANKS, Lynne 1929-

■ Personal

Listed in some sources under Banks; born July 31, 1929, in London, England; daughter of James Reid (a doctor) and Muriel Alexander (an actress; maiden name, Marsh); married Chaim Stephenson (a sculptor), 1965; children: Adiel, Gillon, Omri (sons). *Education:* Attended high school in Canada; attended Italia Conti Stage School, London, 1946, and Royal Academy of Dramatic Art, London, 1947-49. *Religion:* None. *Hobbies and other interests:* Theater, gardening, teaching English as a second language abroad.

■ Addresses

Home—Dorset, England. *Agent*—Sheila Watson, Watson, Little Ltd., 12 Egbert St., London NW1 8LJ, England.

■ Career

Actress in English repertory companies, 1949-54; freelance journalist, London, England, 1954-55; Independent Television News, London, television news reporter, 1955-57, television news scriptwriter, 1958-62; taught English as a foreign language in Israel, 1963-71; writer, 1971—. *Member:* Society of Authors (London).

LYNNE REID BANKS

■ Awards, Honors

Yorkshire Arts Literary Award, 1976, and Best Books for Young Adults Award, American Library Association, 1977, both for *Dark Quartet;* West Australian Young Readers' Book Award, Library Association of Australia, 1980, for *My Darling Villain;* Outstanding Books of the Year Award, *New York Times,* 1981, Young Reader's Choice Award, Pacific Northwest Library Association, 1984, California Young Readers Medal, California Reading Association, 1985, Children's Books of the Year Award, Child Study Association, 1986, Young Readers of Virginia Award, 1988, Arizona Young Readers' Award, 1988, and Rebecca Caudill Young Reader's Books Award, Illinois Association for Media in Education, 1988, all for *The Indian in the Cupboard;* Parents' Choice Award for Literature, Parents' Choice Foundation, 1986, Notable Books Award, *New York Times,* 1986, Children's Books of the Year Award, 1987, and Indian Paintbrush Award, Wyoming Library Association, 1989, all for *The Return of the Indian.*

■ Writings

JUVENILE

One More River, Simon & Schuster, 1973, revised edition, Morrow, 1992.

The Adventures of King Midas, illustrated by George Him, Dent, 1976, illustrated by Jos. A. Smith, Morrow, 1992.

The Farthest-Away Mountain, illustrated by Victor Ambrus, Abelard Schuman, 1976.

I, Houdini: The Autobiography of a Self-Educated Hamster, illustrated by Terry Riley, Dent, 1978, Doubleday, 1988.

My Darling Villain, Harper, 1977.

Letters to My Israeli Sons: The Story of Jewish Survival, H. W. Allen, 1979, F. Watts, 1980.

The Indian in the Cupboard, illustrated by Robin Jacques, Dent, 1980, Doubleday, 1981.

The Writing on the Wall, Chatto & Windus, 1981, Harper, 1982.

Maura's Angel, illustrated by Robin Jacques, Dent, 1984.

The Fairy Rebel, illustrated by William Geldart, Dent, 1985, Doubleday, 1988.

The Return of the Indian, illustrated by Geldart, Doubleday, 1986.

Melusine: A Mystery, Hamish Hamilton, 1988, Harper, 1989.

The Secret of the Indian, Collins, 1988, Doubleday, 1989.

The Mystery of the Cupboard, illustrated by Tom Newsom, Morrow, 1993.

The Magic Hare, illustrated by Barry Moser, Morrow, 1993.

PLAYS

It Never Rains (produced by British Broadcasting Corp. [BBC], 1954), Deane, 1954.

All in a Row, Deane, 1956.

The Killer Dies Twice (three-act), Deane, 1956.

Already It's Tomorrow (produced by BBC, 1962), Samuel French, 1962.

The Unborn, produced in London, England, 1962.

The Wednesday Caller, produced by BBC, 1963.

Last Word on Julie, produced by ATV, 1964.

The Gift (three-act), produced in London, 1965.

The Stowaway (radio play), produced by BBC, 1967.

The Eye of the Beholder, produced by ITV, 1977.

Lame Duck (radio play), produced by BBC, 1978.

Purely from Principal (radio play), produced by BBC, 1985.

Travels of Yoshi and the Tea Kettle (for children), produced in London, 1991.

OTHER

The L-Shaped Room, Chatto & Windus, 1960, revised edition, Longman, 1977.

House of Hope, Simon & Schuster, 1962, published in England as *An End to Running,* Chatto & Windus, 1962.

Children at the Gate, Simon & Schuster, 1968.

The Backward Shadow, Simon & Schuster, 1970.

The Kibbutz: Some Personal Reflections, Anglo-Israel Association, 1972.

Two Is Lonely, Simon & Schuster, 1974.

Sarah and After: The Matriarchs, Bodley Head, 1975, published as *Sarah and After: Five Women Who Founded a Nation,* Doubleday, 1977.

Dark Quartet: The Story of the Brontes, Weidenfeld & Nicholson, 1976, Delacorte, 1977.

Path to the Silent Country: Charlotte Bronte's Years of Fame, Weidenfeld & Nicholson, 1977.

Defy the Wilderness, Chatto & Windus, 1981.

Torn Country: An Oral History of the Israeli War of Independence, F. Watts, 1982.

The Warning Bell, Hamish Hamilton, 1984.

Casualties, Hamish Hamilton, 1986.

Contributor to numerous periodicals, including *Ladies' Home Journal, Observer, Guardian, Sunday Telegraph, Independent,* and *Sunday Times.*

■ Adaptations

The L-Shaped Room, starring Leslie Caron, was released by Davis-Royal Films, 1962.

■ Work in Progress

An adult novel; *The Broken Bridge,* a sequel to *One More River,* set twenty-five years later.

■ Sidelights

Lynne Reid Banks has written about a number of complex subjects—single parenthood, alcoholism, the Middle East, Zionism—but she is best known to young audiences for imaginative stories such as *The Indian in the Cupboard, The Adventures of King Midas,* and *Melusine.* Many of Reid Banks's titles for younger readers, such as the "Indian" books, feature magic as a central theme. Teen readers are attracted to works such as *The Writing on the Wall,* in which Reid Banks deals

with typical teenage problems, including dating and family relationships. In writing, Reid Banks often draws on personal experience. "I have learned a fundamental lesson," she wrote in an essay for the *Sixth Book of Junior Authors.* "Nothing is ever wasted. And for a writer, there's something more: nothing one ever experiences or feels is wasted. Even the bad things, the negative emotions.... While one is suffering them, I mean at the time, a little voice is saying 'Hold on to it. Remember.' Because one day you may need it."

Like many English children her age, Reid Banks had her childhood interrupted by World War II, when she and her mother moved to Canada for five years. "Since my mother was evacuated with me, I was very happy, and though we were poor, I hardly noticed it, except that I couldn't have fashionable clothes," the author noted in an interview. "I didn't really realise what the war meant, or the terrible things that had been happening, until I got back to England, at the very formative age of fifteen. I found my city in ruins, and learned what had been happening to my family, left behind, and, in Europe, to the Jews. I felt like a deserter." The experience marked Reid Banks for life.

Reid Banks originally planned on being an actress like her mother. In order to prepare for this career, she attended drama school. "I adored every minute of

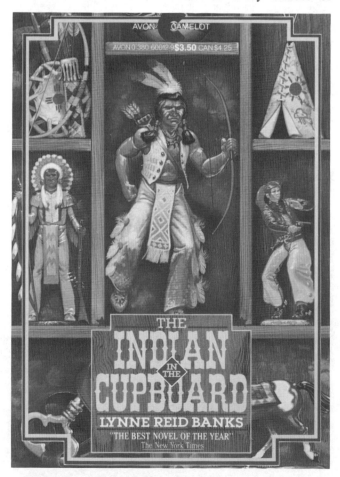

A locked wardrobe is the key to bringing Omri's toys to life in Reid Banks's popular novel.

it .... I was going to take the theater world by storm! Little did any of us know the heartbreak and hardships ahead. Very few of us made it. The vast majority left the profession—we simply couldn't make a living," she noted in her *Junior Authors* essay. After five years as an actress, Reid Banks found a steadier job as a television writer and reporter. At the same time, she wrote plays for stage, radio, and television, many of which were produced, and worked on her first novel.

Novels Tackle Difficult Issues

That novel, *The L-Shaped Room,* became Reid Banks's first literary success. The book chronicles the life of unmarried, twenty-seven-year-old Jane Graham, who goes to live in run-down lodgings when she becomes pregnant. Janice Elliott of the *New Statesman* called the novel "ambitious and mature," while Otis Kidwell Burger commented in the *New York Times Book Review* that "love is the book's theme, developed in bright, warm prose, through diverse and interesting characters." Reid Banks eventually wrote two more novels featuring Jane Graham, *The Backward Shadow* and *Two Is Lonely,* as well as five other adult books, which are still in print in Britain.

The success of her novel also gave the author the means to accomplish another dream, as she recounted in her interview: "Throughout my late teens and twenties, when Israel was going through its early traumas, I had a great desire to go there." So in 1960, Reid Banks traveled to Israel, where she met her future husband "and my life was to turn off at a tangent. Perhaps emigrating to Israel, living in a kibbutz, working the land, teaching and having my babies in that 'alien' country that I came to love so much, was a sublimation for my lingering feelings of guilt for having missed the War." Reid Banks began teaching English as a second language in 1963, and found her theatrical training a great help to her. "Every lesson was a performance— how else could I make them understand me?," she remarked in her *Junior Authors* entry. "And it worked. I was more successful at teaching than I ever was on the stage."

Reid Banks and her family returned to England in 1972, and she published her first children's book in 1973—*One More River,* the story of a pampered Canadian girl's adjustment to living in an Israeli kibbutz. Since that time, she has delighted scores of young fans with tales of magical kings, brave fairies, toys that come to life, and intrepid hamsters. Two of her most popular works are *The Indian in the Cupboard* and its sequel, *The Return of the Indian.* In both volumes, a boy's plastic Indian comes to life every time it is locked in a cupboard. Young Omri soon discovers that his toy, Little Bear, has a taste for adventure—sometimes with near-disastrous results. A reviewer for the *Times Literary Supplement* found *The Indian in the Cupboard* to be "original, lively, compulsive writing" that "will well stand through repeated readings." The author has since published further books about Omri and his magical adventures, *The Secret of the Indian* and *The Mystery of*

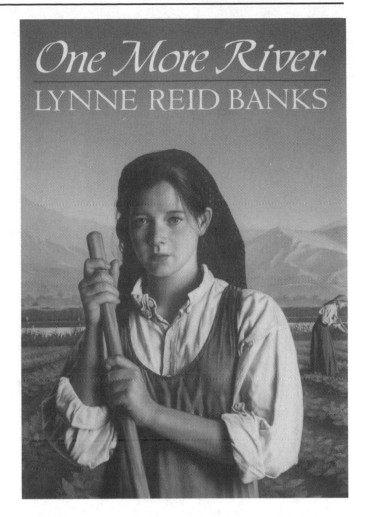

The author's experience as a teacher in Israel informs this novel about a teenage girl's adjustment to life on a kibbutz. (Cover illustration by Michael Deas.)

the Cupboard, in which Omri discovers the family history behind the magic cupboard.

While Reid Banks enjoys writing for audiences of all ages, she is especially fond of writing tales for the younger set. "Writing for young people is a much pleasanter, and easier, thing than writing for adults," she once commented. "I especially enjoy writing wish-fulfillment tales for younger children in which real, everyday life co-exists with magic .... In the end, one has to write what one wants to write, or what one is commissioned to write, and hope for the best. You can't win 'em all."

■ Works Cited

Burger, Otis Kidwell, "Someone to Love," *New York Times Book Review,* April 6, 1961, p. 38.

Elliott, Janice, "Old Hat," *New Statesman,* July 26, 1968, p. 116.

Review of *The Indian in the Cupboard, Times Literary Supplement,* November 21, 1980.

Reid Banks, Lynne, essay in *Sixth Book of Junior Authors,* edited by Sally Holmes Holtze, Wilson, 1989, pp. 22-24.

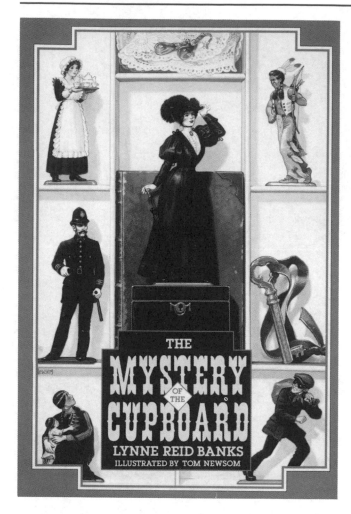

Omri attempts to solve the secret of the cupboard's magical powers in this fourth installment of the "Indian" series. (Cover illustration by Tom Newsom.)

Reid Banks, Lynne, interview with Marc Caplan published in *Authors and Artists for Young Adults*, Volume 6, Gale, 1991, pp. 189-194.

■ For More Information See

BOOKS

Contemporary Literary Criticism, Volume 23, Gale, 1983, pp. 40-43.
Twentieth Century Children's Writers, edited by Tracy Chevalier, St. James, 1989, pp. 56-58.

PERIODICALS

Los Angeles Times Book Review, April 23, 1989, p. 10.
New York Times Book Review, April 16, 1989, p. 26.
Times Literary Supplement, December 1, 1988.

* * *

RESCINITI, Angelo G. 1952-

■ Personal

Surname pronounced "ress-in-neat-tee"; born January 21, 1952, in New York, NY; son of Vito Angelo (an insurance and real estate agent) and Dolores (a homemaker; maiden name, Papa) Resciniti; married Karen Pepper (a children's librarian), April 3, 1982; children: Emily Rose. *Education:* Attended University of Miami, 1970, and Broward Community College, 1974; University of South Florida, B.A., 1977. *Politics:* Independent.

■ Addresses

Home—7805 Chaperon Court, Tampa, FL 33637. *Office*—Armwood High School, 12000 U.S. Highway 92, Seffner, FL 33584.

■ Career

High school English teacher in Hillsborough County, FL, 1977-80 and 1981—; freelance writer in Tampa, FL, 1980-81; author. Park ranger and teacher in Tampa, summers, 1985-89. *Member:* Hillsborough Council of Teachers of English.

■ Awards, Honors

Teacher of the Year, Armwood High School, 1988 and 1991; finalist, Hillsborough County Teacher of the Year, 1991.

■ Writings

NONFICTION; SPORTS

Basketball's Biggest Stars, School Book Fairs, Inc., 1979, revised edition, 1980, revised edition published as *Basketball Super Shooters*, 1983.
Countdown to 13 Super Bowls, School Book Fairs, Inc., 1979, revised editions published as *Victory at the Super Bowl*, 1982, *Super Bowl Victories*, 1985, *Hot Super Bowl Battles*, 1988, and (with Ann Steinberg) *Incredible Super Bowl Action*, 1991.
New Superstars in Sports, School Book Fairs, Inc., 1980.
Soccer Stars, School Book Fairs, Inc., 1980.
Hockey's Hottest Stars, School Book Fairs, Inc., 1981.
Star Running Backs, School Book Fairs, Inc., 1981.
Stars of the Diamond, School Book Fairs, Inc., 1981.
Kick Off!, School Book Fairs, Inc., 1983.
Baseball Heavy Hitters, School Book Fairs, Inc., 1983.
A Day at the Stock Car Races, School Book Fairs, Inc., 1984.
Dynamite Defenses, School Book Fairs, Inc., 1984.
Racing Dragsters, School Book Fairs, Inc., 1986.
Radio Controlled Racing, School Book Fairs, Inc., 1988.

"LIZ AND WILL" SERIES

Liz and Will Solve Mini-Mysteries, School Book Fairs, Inc., 1979.
More Mini-Mysteries for Liz and Will, School Book Fairs, Inc., 1980.

"C. J. WATSON" SERIES

The Mystery Cases of C. J. Watson, School Book Fairs, Inc., 1980.
C. J. Watson Solves the Dragon's Blood Mystery, School Book Fairs, Inc., 1980.

C. J. Watson Solves the Spaceport Mystery, School Book Fairs, Inc., 1980.

NOVELS

The Treehouse Gang, School Book Fairs, Inc., 1980.
The Baseball from Outer Space (science fiction), School Book Fairs, Inc., 1980.
The Treehouse Gang's Racing Revenge, School Book Fairs, Inc., 1981.
To Be a Dancer, School Book Fairs, Inc., 1981, revised edition published as *Vanessa's First Love,* 1987.
The Ketchup Kid, School Book Fairs, Inc., 1984.

NONFICTION

Pirates, School Book Fairs, Inc., 1981.
Shark Attack!, School Book Fairs, Inc., 1982.

OTHER

(With Duane Damon) *Bigfoot and Nessie,* School Book Fairs, Inc., 1979.

Sportswriter and music columnist for various publications, including *Miami Herald* and *Hollywood Sun-Tattler,* 1968-75.

■ Work in Progress

"I am currently outlining a young adult novel with the working title of *The Bird Boy.* It is a coming-of-age novel with an environmental sub-text."

ANGELO G. RESCINITI

■ Sidelights

Angelo G. Resciniti told *SATA:* "It was in second grade at Madie Ives Elementary that I received my first rave reviews for my writing, winning the school's writing contest with a story entitled 'The Perfect Pancake.'

"My family moved to nearby Hollywood, Florida, in my mid-teens and I attended Chaminade High School there. I became involved with the school newspaper, *The Lion's Den,* and served as editor-in-chief during my senior year. But it was during the summer of 1968, between my sophomore and junior years, that I entered the realm of professional journalism. I took a position as a stringer with the 'Teen-Tattler,' a weekly teen-oriented supplement to the *Hollywood Sun-Tattler.* For my first article I interviewed the 'Disco-Tea' girls, one from India and one from England, who were touring the country promoting tea-drinking. I probably spent fifteen hours 'perfecting' that first thousand-word article, for which I was paid the astounding sum of three dollars. Despite the modest income, I was hooked on writing and on getting published. So I continued with the 'Teen-Tattler,' carving out a niche as a rock-and-roll music columnist, until returning to college in 1974.

"1974 marked a turning point in my career. I left the *Sun-Tattler* for good, traveled around the country one last time, and returned to college, paying my way by writing music and entertainment articles for the newly-established *Miami Phoenix,* an off-shoot of the well-known *Boston Phoenix.* I earned my associate of arts degree in 1975 and moved to Tampa to attend the University of South Florida. I worked briefly in a mall bookstore, and then became the entertainment editor of the *Oracle,* the daily student newspaper. Thus cheerfully writing and being published, I worked my way through school, earning my B.A. in English (creative writing) and in English education in 1977. I began a rewarding teaching career in the Hillsborough County school system and writing faded into the occasional freelance piece for the *Tampa Tribune* weekly entertainment section.

"About a year later, my writing career took on a whole new life. Dr. Margaret Holland, an inspirational professor of English education at the University of South Florida, contacted me to talk about my writing for a children's book-publishing firm established by her father, J. Hilbert Sapp. I wrote a 22,000-word manuscript entitled *Basketball's Biggest Stars,* and with Dr. Holland's help tailored it for a pre-teen reading audience. Sapp's company, School Book Fairs, Inc., bought the book for publication. Thus began a children's book-writing career that has spanned thirty-three books, so far.

"My literary heroes are Ernest Hemingway, Kurt Vonnegut, Harlan Ellison, and Theodore Sturgeon. All of these writers speak of a chaotic universe wherein men and women can and must strive to find meaning, be it in themselves, in each other, or in something larger than themselves. I try to imbue some of these same qualities of self-discovery in the characters in my fiction."

* * *

RICHMOND, Robin 1951-

Personal

Born November 7, 1951, in Philadelphia, PA; daughter of Edwin (in business) and Patricia (a writer) Richmond; married James Hampton (a university professor of psychology) July 15, 1972; children: Adam, Saskia. *Education:* Attended St. Georges English School, Rome; Chelsea School of Art, received B.A. and M.F.A.

Addresses

Home—20 Calabria Rd., London N5 15A, England.

Career

Professional artist. Taught adult education courses, 1977-85; volunteer teacher of fine art and art history in primary schools. Regular broadcaster for British Broadcasting Corporation (BBC). Visiting professor, Camberwell School of Art, 1982-85, and University of California—Santa Cruz, 1984-85. Lecturer, University of London, 1983-85. *Exhibitions:* Galleria Ariete, Rome, 1971; Ben Uri Gallery, London, 1976; Off Centre Gallery, London, 1980; Boundary Gallery, London, 1987; Mercury Gallery, London, 1989-90; Barbican Gallery, London, and Mercury Gallery, London, 1992. *Member:* Society of Authors.

Awards, Honors

Joseph Mendelson Memorial Award, 1982.

Writings

(Illustrator) John Goldsmith, *Oliver and the Magic Hat,* MacDonald, 1982.
Add a Pinch of Pepper, G. B. Press, 1983.
The Magic Flute, Faber & Faber, 1989.
Introducing Michelangelo, Little, Brown, 1992.
Michelangelo and the Creation of the Sistine Chapel, Barrie & Jenkins, 1992.
The Story in a Picture, Ideals, Volume 1: *Children in Art,* 1992, Volume 2: *Animals in Art,* 1993.

Also contributor to *Modern Painters.*

Work in Progress

Frita Kahlo, Volume 1: *Painters and Places,* publication expected spring 1994; *Masaccio in Florence; Tales from the Earth.*

Sidelights

Robin Richmond writes, "I am an American who is by now a seasoned expatriate. I've lived in London for 23

ROBIN RICHMOND

years. I am primarily a painter, with a very strong interest in writing about art for adults and children in a clear, accessible voice. As a working artist, I hope that I am able to illuminate the study of what is considered an 'elitist' subject. I can explain the 'cooking' skills needed to make a painting from a practical angle, rather than a solely theoretical one. I have a strong interest in Renaissance art, having spent my childhood in Rome, but my new series *The Story in a Picture* looks at art from pre-history up until 1992. The books, (Volume 1, *Children in Art,* and Volume 2, *Animals in Art*) are fun, eclectic and immediate. I hope that they will de-mystify art history for a new generation of children, including my own—Adam and Saskia."

* * *

ROSENBERG, Liz 1958-

■ Personal

Born February 3, 1958, in Glen Cove, NY; daughter of Ross and Lucille Rosenberg; married John Gardner (a novelist), February 14, 1980 (died, 1982); married David Bosnick (a writer, teacher, and bookstore owner), 1983; children: (second marriage) Eli. *Education:* Received B.A. from Bennington College and M.A. from

Johns Hopkins University. *Politics:* "Bleeding heart liberal." *Religion:* Jewish Unitarian.

■ Addresses

Home—32 Highland Ave., Binghamton, NY 13905. *Office*—English Department, State University of New York at Binghamton, Binghamton, NY 13902-6000.

■ Career

Children's book author and poet. State University of New York at Binghamton, Binghamton, associate professor of English, 1979—. Cofounder of the Indoor Playground of the City of Binghamton; member of the preschool school board and the kindergarten task force. *Member:* Associated Writing Program, Poets and Writers.

■ Awards, Honors

National Kellogg fellow, 1982-85; Agnes Starrett Poetry Prize, 1986.

■ Writings

The Fire Music (poems), University of Pittsburgh Press, 1986.
Adelaide and the Night Train, illustrated by Lisa Desimini, Harper, 1989.
Window, Mirror, Moon, illustrated by Ruth Richardson, Harper, 1990.
The Scrap Doll, illustrated by Robin Ballard, Harper-Collins, 1992.

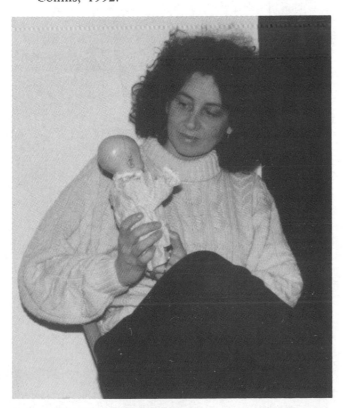

LIZ ROSENBERG

Monster Mama, illustrated by Stephen Gammell, Philomel, 1993.
Children of Paradise (poems), University of Pittsburgh Press, 1993.

Regular contributor to periodicals, including *New York Times Book Review* and *Chicago Tribune.* Editor, *Manuscript* magazine, 1980-87; children's book review editor for *Parents* magazine.

■ Work in Progress

The Loneliest Girl, a young adult novel, for Philomel; five children's books, for Philomel.

■ Sidelights

Liz Rosenberg told *SATA:* "Reading children's books was a large part of how I survived childhood. I read constantly, and never stopped reading books written for children. That mountain of books became a kind of leviathan—and I rode on its back through waves and storms. My childhood was happy, but seldom calm. In writing for children, I remember that past and repay that debt.

"The truly great books for children—*Charlotte's Web, A Wrinkle in Time,* among others—I still read them. Children love passionately; I think these first books stay with us, grow with us, for life. I believe there is nothing holier or higher than to write something fine for children. As A. A. Milne once said, 'It is impossible to take too much care when one is writing for children.'

"To me, writing children's books and writing poetry is two sides of the same activity. They are both visionary, illuminated art forms. They try to go directly to the heart of the matter, whatever is at stake—friendship, homesickness, immortality, love. In a way, both forms short-cut to the things that matter most, what C. G. Jung called 'the big dreams.' Poetry and children's books are big dreams written out in short-hand.

"I still have the original 'ugly old thing'—the doll I write about in *The Scrap Doll,* and sometimes my son likes to play with her. My belief in that book—as in life—is that the more you care for something, the more closely you look at it, the more you love it. Love and understanding go along hand in hand. I hope children will always find things in their lives to care for and to love, because from those activities come joy and peace of mind."

■ For More Information See

PERIODICALS

Los Angeles Times Book Review, January 28, 1990, p. 15.
New York Times Book Review, July 6, 1986, p. 23; April 1, 1990, p. 15.

ROTH, Arthur J(oseph) 1925-1993
(Nina Hoy, Barney Mara, Slater McGurk, Pete Pomeroy)

OBITUARY NOTICE—See index for *SATA* sketch: Born August 3, 1925, in the Bronx, New York, NY; died of liver cancer, March 5, 1993, in Amagansett, Long Island, NY. Columnist, novelist, and author. Roth was perhaps best known for his *East Hampton Star* column, "From the Scuttlehole," which he wrote for twenty-seven years beginning in 1966. He held various jobs as a budding author, including bartender, coalminer, logger, college English instructor, and truck driver. His first novel, *A Terrible Beauty,* was based on his personal experience in the Irish Republican Army during the 1940s. Roth's other adult works include *The Shame of Our Wounds* and the nonfiction volume, *Eiger: Wall of Death.* He also wrote mystery novels under the pseudonym Slater McGurk, such as *The Grand Central Murders* and *The Big Dig.* But it is for young adults that Roth wrote the majority of his books, including *Wipeout!, The Iceberg Hermit, Two for Survival, Demolition Man,* and *The Caretaker.*

OBITUARIES AND OTHER SOURCES:

BOOKS

Authors of Books for Young People, 3rd edition, Scarecrow, 1990.
Something about the Author Autobiography Series, Volume 11, Gale, 1991.

PERIODICALS

New York Times, March 22, 1993, p. D8.

* * *

RUNNERSTROEM, Bengt Arne 1944-

■ Personal

Born December 19, 1944, in Helsingborg, Sweden; son of Bengt G. (a post office employee) and Karin I. A. (a nurse; maiden name, Lindskog) Runnerstroem; married Margaret R. Marie (a caterer), 1973; children: Jessica, Jacob. *Education:* Attended Konstfackskolan, 1962-71, passed art teacher examination.

■ Addresses

Home and office—Iskallebol, S-590 34 Tjaellmo, Sweden. *Agent*—Opal, Box 20113, S-161 02 Bromma, Sweden.

■ Career

Commercial artist for a newspaper in Stockholm, Sweden, 1962-66; art teacher in Sweden, 1973-79; illustrator of children's books and television programs in Sweden, 1980—. Universidad Metropolitana, Mexico, instructor in illustration, 1988. Contributor to three films about South American Indians in the Amazon and the Andes for Swedish television; lecturer and creator of exhibi-

BENGT ARNE RUNNERSTROEM

tions about Native South Americans. *Exhibitions:* Work has been shown in numerous exhibitions in Sweden, including shows at Galleri Nyttokonst, Goeteborgs Etnografiska Museum, Konstfoereningen i Finspang, Galleri Kulturkapellet, Galleri 1, Karlskoga Konsthall, Galleri Smedbyn, Kulturhuset, Kulturcentrum, Norrkoepings Konstmuseum, Bohuslaens Museum, and Vaenersgorgs Konsthall; participant in the show *The Meeting: Europe and America, 1492-1992. Military service:* Swedish Navy, 1966-67.

■ Awards, Honors

Litteratur Framiandet ("Promoter of Literature"), 1984, for *Cubeo Amazonas;* Elsa Beskow Medal, 1985, for *Arhuaco Sierra Nevada;* grant from Garanterad Forfattar Penning ("Guaranteed Salary for Authors and Illustrators"), 1991.

■ Writings

SELF-ILLUSTRATED

Cubeo Amazonas (title means "The Cubeo Indians of the Colombian Amazon"), AWE/Gebers, 1983.
Arhuaco Sierra Nevada (title means "The Arhuaco Indians of Colombia"), AWE/Gebers, 1984.
Shipibo, cockes droem (title means "The Shipibo Indians of the Peruvian Amazon"), Opal, 1993.

Runnerstroem's works in Swedish have been translated into Danish, Dutch, English, Finnish, German, Japanese, Kurd, Lapp, Norwegian, and Spanish.

ILLUSTRATOR

Rose Lagercrantz, *Jaettevainner,* R & S, 1981.
Ingamaj Beck, *Mamma groen,* Korpen, 1982.
Roald Dahl, *Kalle och chokladfabriken,* Tiden, 1983.
Lasse Carlsson, *Sveket,* Prisma, 1984.
Dahl, *Kalle och den stora glashissen,* Tiden, 1984.
Per Helge, *Mjoelnarkungen,* Awe/Gebers, 1985.
Langa lansen, Nok, 1985.
Ebbe Schoen, *Trollguld,* R & S, 1985.
Beck, *Pappa blast,* Nordan, 1986.
Monica Zak, *Radda min djungel,* Opal, 1987, translated
     by Nancy Schimmel as *Save My Rainforest,* Volca-
     no Press, 1992.
Cecil Boedker, *Maria fran Nasaret,* R & S, 1987,
     translated by Eric Bibb as *Mary of Nazareth,* Farrar,
     Straus, 1989.
Beck, *Banantraedet,* Nordan, 1987.
Zak, *Paloma och pyramidstadens hemlighet* (title means
     "Paloma and the Secret of the Pyramid City"),
     Opal, 1989.
Goeran Bergengren, *Kaerrhoekens Vildmark,* Var Skola,
     1989.
Zak, *Pojken med vralaporna* (title means "The Boy and
     His Howlermonkeys"), Opal, 1990.
Zak, *Uggleflickan* (title means "The Owlgirl"), Opal,
     1991.
Sex Folksagor, Almqvist & Wiksell, 1991.
Britt Engdal, *Gengangare,* Opal, 1992.
Engdal, *Spoekskeppet i dimman,* Opal, 1993.
Hans Dahlgren, *Alexandra, sista resan,* Bild och Pedago-
     gik, 1993.

■ Sidelights

Bengt Arne Runnerstroem told *SATA:* "I was born in
1944 in Helsingborg, a town in the southern part of
Sweden. I was brought up on the Swedish west coast, in
a town called Uddevalla. I learned to sail and was taught
love and respect for nature by my father, an ornitholo-
gist, who also got me interested in traveling.

"I have traveled a lot all over the world (over fifty
countries). This has given me a great interest in the way
of life of other people and an understanding of different
cultures—not only in Europe and the United States, but
also people from the so-called Third World and especially the Fourth World, the ethnic minority groups.

**Runnerstroem's interest in the environment has led him
to write and illustrate books such as *Cubeo Amazonas,*
about the Cubeo Indians of the Amazon.**

"I have also gained an interest in our environment. We
are looking for paradise on earth, spending a great deal
of money to go to certain places on holidays, but once
we have been there, it is destroyed. In my books I want
to teach children to take care of our planet, to make it
that paradise that it is if we work together to preserve it.
We have a lot to learn from people that treat the earth
like it is sacred. This is one of the reasons why I am
mostly interested in nonfiction children's books. The
real world is so interesting that I feel that I can fill ten
lifetimes trying to describe just a small part of it.
Paradise is here and now—so few grown-ups understand that. But the children do."

S

SAIDMAN, Anne 1952-

■ Personal

Born July 25, 1952, in New York, NY; daughter of Edward (a landlord) and Jeanette (a secretary; maiden name, Greenberg) Gottlieb; married Philip Saidman (a musician and storyteller), September 3, 1972; children: Matthew. *Education:* Brooklyn College of the City University of New York, B.A., 1976; Pratt Institute, M.L.S., 1980; School of Visual Arts, 1988—. *Politics:* Liberal Democrat. *Religion:* Jewish. *Hobbies and other interests:* Juggling, photography, youth ice hockey.

■ Addresses

Home—Brooklyn, NY.

■ Career

New York Public Library, children's librarian, 1980-82; Brooklyn Public Library, Brooklyn, NY, children's librarian, 1982-85; New York City Board of Education, school librarian in Brooklyn, 1986—. Team mother for ice hockey and Little League baseball.

■ Writings

Oprah Winfrey: Media Superstar, Lerner Publications, 1991.
Stephen King, Lerner Publications, 1992.

■ Work in Progress

A biography of musician Leonard Bernstein, for Lerner Publications.

■ Sidelights

Anne Saidman told *SATA:* "I've always loved books and reading. As a child, my favorite thing to do was to curl up with a good book. The longer the book was, the more I liked it. There was a used bookstore in my neighbor-

ANNE SAIDMAN

hood, and my father would take me there and let me choose whatever I wanted.

"In college I studied literature and studio art, but I never thought about a career. One day I walked into the public library and saw the librarian reading the *New York Times Book Review.* It occurred to me that she was being paid to do what I did for fun, and I enrolled in library school and ended up with a master's degree in library science.

"Once I had my degree, I got a job working as a children's librarian for the New York Public Library. I had always enjoyed writing, and before long I realized that I could write books that would be at least as good as those I saw on the library's shelves.

"The creative process has always interested me, and I decided to write a biography of a creative, talented person. I tried to think of someone who was contemporary, whose name children would recognize, whom I would enjoy learning and writing about, and whom—at that point, anyway—no one else had written about in a book designed for children. The person I came up with was actress and talk-show host Oprah Winfrey, and my first book was born.

"The first book is the hardest one of all. Writing it takes time away from your family and it's hard to justify. When it was finished I discovered that it also takes time finding a publisher. Luckily, in the end the time and effort paid off. I suppose what I would advise other aspiring writers is that the most important things are to believe in yourself and not give up. It's hard to describe the thrill of actually holding your own book in your hands."

*   *   *

SARA
See De La ROCHE SAINT ANDRE, Anne

*   *   *

SCARRY, Richard (McClure) 1919-

■ Personal

Surname rhymes with "carry"; born June 5, 1919, in Boston, MA; son of John James (a department store proprietor) and Barbara (McClure) Scarry; married Patricia Murphy (a children's book writer), September 7, 1949; children: Richard McClure (Huck). *Education:* Attended Boston Museum School of Fine Arts, 1938-41. *Hobbies and other interests:* Skiing, sailing, traveling.

■ Addresses

Home—Schwyzerhus, 3780 Gstaad, Switzerland.

■ Career

Magazine and children's book illustrator, 1946—; writer. *Military service:* U.S. Army, 1941-46; served as art director, editor, writer, and illustrator, Morale Services Section, Allied Forces Headquarters, North African and Mediterranean theaters; became captain.

■ Awards, Honors

Edgar Allan Poe nomination for children's mystery, 1976, for *Richard Scarry's Great Steamboat Mystery.*

RICHARD SCARRY

■ Writings

SELF-ILLUSTRATED

The Great Big Car and Truck Book, Simon & Schuster, 1951.
Rabbit and His Friends, Simon & Schuster, 1953.
Nursery Tales, Simon & Schuster, 1958.
Tinker and Tanker (also see below), Garden City Books, 1960.
The Hickory Dickory Clock Book, Doubleday, 1961.
Tinker and Tanker Out West (also see below), Doubleday, 1961.
Tinker and Tanker and Their Space Ship (also see below), Doubleday, 1961.
Tinker and Tanker and the Pirates (also see below), Doubleday, 1961.
Tinker and Tanker, Knights of the Round Table (also see below), Doubleday, 1963.
Tinker and Tanker in Africa (also see below), Doubleday, 1963.
Best Word Book Ever, Golden Press, 1963.
The Rooster Struts, Golden Press, 1963, published as *The Golden Happy Book of Animals,* 1964 (published in England as *Animals,* Hamlyn, 1963).
Polite Elephant, Golden Press, 1964.
Feed the Hippo His ABC's, Golden Press, 1964.
Richard Scarry's Animal Mother Goose, Golden Press, 1964.
Busy, Busy World, Golden Press, 1965.
Richard Scarry's Teeny Tiny Tales, Golden Press, 1965.
The Santa Claus Book, Golden Press, 1965.
The Bunny Book, Golden Press, 1965.
Is This the House of Mistress Mouse?, Golden Press, 1966.
Storybook Dictionary, Golden Press, 1966.
Planes, Golden Press, 1967, published as *Richard Scarry's Planes,* Western Publishing, 1992.

Trains, Golden Press, 1967, published as *Richard Scarry's Trains*, Western Publishing, 1992.

Boats, Golden Press, 1967, published as *Richard Scarry's Boats*, Western Publishing, 1992.

Cars, Golden Press, 1967, published as *Richard Scarry's Cars*, Western Publishing, 1992.

Richard Scarry's Egg in the Hole Book, Golden Press, 1967.

What Animals Do, Golden Press, 1968.

Best Storybook Ever, Golden Press, 1968.

The Early Bird, Random House, 1968.

What Do People Do All Day?, Random House, 1968.

The Adventures of Tinker and Tanker (contains *Tinker and Tanker*, *Tinker and Tanker Out West*, and *Tinker and Tanker and Their Space Ship*), Doubleday, 1968.

The Great Pie Robbery (also see below), Random House, 1969.

The Supermarket Mystery (also see below), Random House, 1969.

Richard Scarry's Great Big Schoolhouse, Random House, 1969.

Richard Scarry's Best Mother Goose Ever, Golden Press, 1970.

More Adventures of Tinker and Tanker (contains *Tinker and Tanker and the Pirates*, *Tinker and Tanker, Knights of the Round Table*, and *Tinker and Tanker in Africa*), Doubleday, 1971.

ABC Word Book, Random House, 1971.

Richard Scarry's Best Stories Ever, Golden Press, 1971.

Richard Scarry's Fun with Words, Golden Press, 1971.

Richard Scarry's Going Places, Golden Press, 1971.

Richard Scarry's Great Big Air Book, Random House, 1971.

Richard Scarry's Things to Know, Golden Press, 1971.

Richard Scarry's Mother Goose, Golden Press, 1972.

Funniest Storybook Ever, Random House, 1972.

Nicky Goes to the Doctor, Golden Press, 1972.

Richard Scarry's Great Big Mystery Book (contains *The Great Pie Robbery* and *The Supermarket Mystery*), Random House, 1972.

Hop Aboard, Here We Go, Golden Press, 1972.

Babykins and His Family, Golden Press, 1973.

Silly Stories, Golden Press, 1973.

Richard Scarry's Find Your ABC's, Random House, 1973.

Richard Scarry's Please and Thank You Book, Random House, 1973.

Richard Scarry's Best Rainy Day Book Ever, Random House, 1974.

Cars and Trucks and Things That Go, Golden Press, 1974.

Richard Scarry's Great Steamboat Mystery, Random House, 1975.

Richard Scarry's Best Counting Book Ever, Random House, 1975.

Richard Scarry's Animal Nursery Tales, Golden Press, 1975.

Richard Scarry's Early Words, Random House, 1976.

Richard Scarry's Color Book, Random House, 1976.

Richard Scarry's Busiest People Ever, Random House, 1976.

Richard Scarry's Collins Cubs, Collins, 1976.

Richard Scarry's Picture Dictionary, Collins, 1976.

Richard Scarry's Random Laugh and Learn Library, four books, Random House, 1976.

Learn to Count, Golden Press, 1976.

All Year Long, Golden Press, 1976.

At Work, Golden Press, 1976.

Short and Tall, Golden Press, 1976.

My House, Golden Press, 1976.

On Vacation, Golden Press, 1976.

About Animals, Golden Press, 1976.

On the Farm, Golden Press, 1976.

Six Golden Look-Look Books, six volumes, Golden Press, 1977.

Richard Scarry's Lowly Worm Storybook, Random House, 1977.

Richard Scarry's Best Make-It Book Ever, Random House, 1977.

Tinker and Tanker Journey to Tootletown and Build a Space Ship, Golden Press, 1978.

Richard Scarry's Bedtime Stories, Random House, 1978.

Richard Scarry's Punch-Out Toy Book, Random House, 1978.

Richard Scarry's Postman Pig and His Busy Neighbors, Random House, 1978.

Richard Scarry's Lowly Worm Sniffy Book, Random House, 1978.

Richard Scarry's Stories to Color: With Lowly Worm and Mr. Paint Pig, Random House, 1978.

Storytime, Random House, 1978.

Little Bedtime Story, Random House, 1978.

Things to Learn, Golden Press, 1978.

Mr. Fixit and Other Stories, Random House, 1978.

Busy Town, Busy People, Random House, 1978.

Little ABC, Random House, 1978.

Richard Scarry's Mix or Match Storybook, Random House, 1979.

Richard Scarry's Best First Book Ever, Random House, 1979.

Richard Scarry's Busytown Pop-Up Book, Random House, 1979.

Richard Scarry Huckle's Book, Random House, 1979.

Richard Scarry's Tinker and Tanker Tales of Pirates and Knights, Golden Press, 1979.

Richard Scarry's to Market, to Market, Golden Press, 1979.

Richard Scarry's Peasant Pig and the Terrible Dragon, Random House, 1980.

Richard Scarry's Lowly Worm Word Book, Random House, 1981.

Richard Scarry's Best Christmas Book Ever, Random House, 1981.

Richard Scarry's Busy Houses, Random House, 1981.

Richard Scarry's Funniest Storybook Ever, Random House, 1982.

Richard Scarry's Four Busy Word Books, four volumes, Random House, 1982.

Christmas Mice, Golden Press, 1982.

Lowly Worm Coloring Book, Random House, 1983.

Lowly Worm Cars and Trucks Book, Random House, 1983.

The Best Mistake Ever!, Random House, 1984.

Richard Scarry's Lowly Worm Bath Book, Random House, 1984.

drugstore delivery car

taxi

ABC GLASS COMPANY

bookstore delivery van

TAXI STAND

shopping cart

glass-window truck

old-time buggy

motorbikes

Did you see that? Dingo Dog has knocked down almost all the parking meters. What a terrible driver! I think Officer Flossy is going to give him a ticket. At least, she is going to try. We'll see if she succeeds.

baby buggy

STOP

a frightened parking meter

Officer Flossy and her bicycle

a terrible driver

7

Scarry's popular self-illustrated books, such as *Richard Scarry's Cars and Trucks and Things That Go,* introduce young children to various objects using humorous drawings.

Richard Scarry's Busy Fun and Learn Book, Western Publishing, 1984.

Richard Scarry's Pig Will and Pig Won't: A Book of Manners, Random House, 1984.

Richard Scarry's Biggest Word Book Ever!, Random House, 1985.

My First Word Book, Random House, 1986.

Fun with Letters, Random House, 1986.

Fun with Numbers, three volumes, Random House, 1986.

Norwegian Dictionary: Min Forste Ordbok (subtitle means "My First 'Word Book'"), Arthur Vanous Co., 1986.

Fun with Words, Random House, 1986.

Fun with Reading, Random House, 1986.

Richard Scarry's Splish-Splash Sounds, Western Publishing, 1986.

Big and Little, Western Publishing, 1986.

Things to Love, Western Publishing, 1987.

Richard Scarry's Things That Go, Western Publishing, 1987.

Richard Scarry's Lowly Worm's Schoolbag, Random House, 1987.

Getting Ready for Numbers, Random House, 1987.

Getting Ready for School, Random House, 1987.

Getting Ready for Writing, Random House, 1987.

Busy Workers, Western Publishing, 1987.

Smokey the Fireman, Western Publishing, 1988.

Sniff the Detective, Western Publishing, 1988.

Play Day, Western Publishing, 1988.

Dr. Doctor, Western Publishing, 1988.

Farmer Patrick Pig, Western Publishing, 1988.

Frances Fix-It, Western Publishing, 1988.

Harry and Larry the Fishermen, Western Publishing, 1988.

Richard Scarry's Best Times Ever: A Book about Seasons and Holidays, Western Publishing, 1988.

Richard Scarry's Simple Simon and Other Rhymes, Western Publishing, 1988.

Richard Scarry's Little Miss Muffet and Other Rhymes, Western Publishing, 1988.

Scarry's Best Ever, Random House, 1989.

Richard Scarry's Best Ride Ever, Western Publishing, 1989.

Richard Scarry's Best Friend Ever, Western Publishing, 1989.

Richard Scarry's Mother Goose Scratch and Sniff Book, Western Publishing, 1989.

Richard Scarry's Naughty Bunny, Western Publishing, 1989.

Richard Scarry's All about Cars, Western Publishing, 1989.

Richard Scarry's Best Two-Minute Stories Ever!, Western Publishing, 1989.

Richard Scarry's Counting Book, Western Publishing, 1990.

Richard Scarry's Just Right Word Book, David McKay Co., 1990.

Be Careful, Mr. Frumble, Random House, 1990.

Richard Scarry's Cars and Trucks from A to Z, Random House, 1990.

Best Read It Yourself Book Ever, Western Publishing, 1990.

Watch Your Step, Mr. Rabbit!, Random House, 1991.

Richard Scarry's ABC's, Western Publishing, 1991.

Richard Scarry's Best Year Ever, Western Publishing, 1991.

Richard Scarry's the Cat Family Takes a Trip, Western Publishing, 1992.

Richard Scarry's the Cat Family's Busy Day, Western Publishing, 1992.

Mr. Frumble's Worst Day Ever!, Random House, 1992.

Richard Scarry: Sergeant Murphy's Busiest Day Ever, Western Publishing, 1992.

Richard Scarry's Best Little Word Book Ever!, Western Publishing, 1992.

Richard Scarry's Biggest Pop-up Book Ever!, Western Publishing, 1992.

Bananas Gorilla: Richard Scarry's Smallest Pop-up Book Ever!, Western Publishing, 1992.

Mr. Fix-It: Richard Scarry's Smallest Pop-up Book Ever!, Western Publishing, 1992.

Mr. Frumble: Richard Scarry's Smallest Pop-up Book Ever!, Western Publishing, 1992.

Richard Scarry's Little Red Riding Hood, Western Publishing, 1993.

Richard Scarry's The Little Red Hen, Western Publishing, 1993.

Richard Scarry's The Three Bears, Western Publishing, 1993.

Richard Scarry's The Three Little Pigs, Western Publishing, 1993.

Huckle Cat's Busiest Day Ever, Random House, 1993.

Also author of *Richard Scarry's Busy Busy World,* Western Publishing.

ILLUSTRATOR

Kathryn Jackson, *Let's Go Fishing,* Simon & Schuster, 1949.

Jackson, *Mouse's House,* Simon & Schuster, 1949.

Jackson, *Duck and His Friends,* Simon & Schuster, 1949.

Jackson, *Brave Cowboy Bill,* Simon & Schuster, 1950.

Jackson, *The Animals' Merry Christmas,* Simon & Schuster, 1950.

Oliver O'Connor Barrett, *Little Benny Wanted a Pony,* Simon & Schuster, 1950.

Patricia Scarry, *Danny Beaver's Secret,* Simon & Schuster, 1953.

Leah Gale, *The Animals of Farmer Jones,* Simon & Schuster, 1953.

Margaret Wise Brown, *Little Indian,* Simon & Schuster, 1954.

P. Scarry, *Pierre Bear,* Golden Press, 1954.

Jane Werner, *Smokey the Bear,* Simon & Schuster, 1955.

Jackson, *Golden Bedtime Book,* Simon & Schuster, 1955.

Mary Maud Reed, *Mon petit dictionnaire geant,* Editions des deux coqs d'or, 1958.

P. Scarry, *Just for Fun,* Golden Press, 1960.

My Nursery Tale Book, Golden Press, 1961.

Selligmann and Levine Milton, *Tommy Visits the Doctor,* Western Publishing, 1962.

Edward Lear, *Nonsense Alphabet,* Doubleday, 1962.

Peggy Parish, *My Golden Book of Manners,* Golden Press, 1962.

M. Reed and E. Oswald, *My First Golden Dictionary Book,* Western Publishing, 1963.

(And editor and translator) Jean de la Fontaine, *Fables,* Doubleday, 1963.

Barbara Shook Hazen, *Rudolph the Red-nosed Reindeer,* Golden Press, 1964.

Jackson and others, *My Nursery Tale Book,* Western Publishing, 1964.

Jackson, *The Golden Book of 365 Stories,* Golden Press, 1966.

Ole Risom, *I Am a Bunny,* Golden Press, 1966.

Roberta Miller, *Chipmunk's ABC,* Golden Press, 1976.

The Gingerbread Man, Golden Press, 1981.

My First Golden Dictionary, Western Publishing, 1983.

The Golden Treasury of Fairy Tales, Western Publishing, 1985.

Jackson, *Richard Scarry's Best House Ever,* Western Publishing, 1989.

Also illustrator of coloring activity books and children's foreign language dictionaries. Scarry's works are included in the Kerlan Collection at the University of Minnesota.

■ Adaptations

Cacdmon produced recordings, read by Carol Channing, of *What Do People Do All Day and Other Stories,* 1978, and *What Do People Do All Day and Great Big Schoolhouse,* 1979; *Richard Scarry's Best Electronic Word Book Ever!,* computer software for Commodore 64/128 or Apple computers, was produced by CBS Interactive Learning, 1985.

■ Sidelights

Richard Scarry is "one of the world's best-selling superstars of children's literature," according to Barbara Karlan in the *West Coast Review of Books.* The skillful blend of education and entertainment found in Scarry's books makes them appealing both to children and their parents. Each book, be it a dictionary, an alphabet, or a fairy tale, features the author's bright, lively illustrations of such anthropomorphic animal characters as Huckle Cat, Lowly Worm, and Mr. Paint Pig. Publishing statistics testify to the popularity of Scarry's works. His books have been translated into twenty-eight languages and sold over one hundred million copies. Elaine Moss summarizes the books' appeal in *Signal:* "Totally unpretentious, bubbling with humour, alive with activity, peppered with words of wisdom and corny jokes ... Scarry books are a marvellous combination of entertainment, always on a child's level, and incidental instruction. They occupy a unique place in the learning-to-read process."

Scarry was born and raised in Boston, Massachusetts, where his father was the owner of a small chain of department stores. He was not an enthusiastic student; he spent five years struggling through high school. "I couldn't even get into college because I didn't have enough credits," he recalls in an article by Rob Wilder

The citizens of Busytown prepare for the holidays in *Richard Scarry's Best Christmas Book Ever.*

14 fourteen

Suddenly Willy discovers fourteen travelers who have stopped beside the lane.

Five are sleeping.

Five are eating.

And four are playing a game.

Here! Here! Stop fighting over the cards, you rascals!

Scarry acquaints children with numbers from 1 to 100 in *Richard Scarry's Best Counting Book Ever.*

in *Parents* magazine. Scarry did try a short stint at a Boston business school, but soon dropped out. Since he had always liked drawing and had spent every Saturday morning as a child studying art at the Boston Museum of Fine Arts, he was finally accepted at the Boston School for Fine Arts.

World War II interrupted Scarry's art studies, however. He spent five years in the United States Army. "I had a bit of a problem getting in," he explains in the *Third Book of Junior Authors.* "Because I wore glasses they wouldn't accept me as a volunteer but preferred to draft me instead." Although Scarry was originally scheduled to become a radio repairman, he soon secured a place at an Officer Candidate school. After graduation, he went on to serve as art director for the troops in North Africa and Italy, where he drew maps and designed graphics.

After the war Scarry moved to New York City, originally intending to pursue a career as a commercial artist. However, in 1946 he completed illustrations for a children's book called *The Boss of the Barnyard,* published by Golden Press, and he was ensured a steady flow of work. He illustrated other authors' books for several years before beginning to write and illustrate original stories of his own. "During his free-lance period," writes Bobbie Burch Lemontt in the *Dictionary of Literary Biography,* "he met Patsy Murphy, from Vancouver, British Columbia, who, he says, writes kids' books, 'but can't draw.' After being married in 1949, the couple lived on a farm in Ridgefield, Connecticut, and collaborated on several books."

Illustrated Children's Books Gain Popularity

Scarry's first big commercial success came in 1963 with the publication of *Richard Scarry's Best Word Book Ever.* The book was filled with colorful illustrations and pages of information—it "contains more than 1,400 defined and illustrated objects which can engage a preschooler's interest by the infectious vitality and purposefulness of the selections," states Lemontt—and established Scarry's popularity with children. *New York Times* contributor Richard Flaste writes that the book "seems to identify everything children meet in their world, and some things in more exotic worlds."

Scarry's work, however, is not without its critics. Some librarians feel that Scarry's use of slapstick humor in his books, with its overtones of violence, could be dangerous for young children. But "it's not true violence, it's fun," Scarry told Rudi Chelminski in *People.* "I have cars pile up and people get into trouble. It's the old banana peel or custard pie in the face. The only thing that really suffers is dignity. Kids love that—and they're right." "A typical 'violent' encounter," explains Edwin McDowell in the *New York Times,* "... is likely to show, for example, canine cop Sergeant Murphy on collision course with a birthday cake. Even then the moment of impact is left to the imagination."

Other critics object to what they see as sexual stereotyping in Scarry's work. But the author told Arthur Bell in

Publisher's Weekly that one reason he uses animals as subjects is to eliminate the problem of sexual and racial stereotypes: "Children can identify more closely with pictures of animals than they can with pictures of another child. They see an illustration of a blond girl or a dark-haired boy who they know is somebody other than themselves, and competition creeps in. With imagination—and children all have marvelous imagination—they can easily identify with an anteater who is a painter or a goat who is an Indian or a honey-bear schoolteacher."

In 1969 Scarry, his wife, and their son, Huck (now an author-illustrator) moved to a mountain chalet in Gstaad, Switzerland. The decision was made after a skiing trip. "It was the usual 21-day excursion," he told Bell. "But coming home, we had to pass through Lausanne in order to catch our plane from Geneva. From the train window I caught a glimpse of a child throwing a snowball—just that, nothing more—and I thought, 'Now is the time to move to Switzerland.'" "The move was not a political one—we had always hoped at sometime to live in Europe," Scarry continues, "but couldn't make plans because of Huck's being in school. But Huck was 15, and Switzerland was magnificent, and suddenly the time seemed right.... We settled our affairs and leased our house, and ... with little more than the clothes on our backs, we moved to Lausanne."

From his European residence Scarry continues to produce highly popular children's books which enchant young people. "One of the greatest compliments any author can receive from a preschool audience," declares Lemontt, "is to have his or her books held together with more tape than there is paper in the book itself. Tearing is an accidental toddler pastime that often suggests a book is good enough to be reread. Richard Scarry's books usually display an abundance of such mending."

■ Works Cited

Chelminski, Rudi, "This Is the House the Menagerie of Richard Scarry Built," *People,* October 15, 1979, pp. 105-10.

Bell, Arthur, "Richard Scarry's Best Switzerland Ever," *Publishers Weekly,* October 20, 1969, pp. 41-42.

De Montreville, Doris, and Donna Hill, editors, *Third Book of Junior Authors,* H. W. Wilson, 1972.

Flaste, Richard, "Richard Scarry and His People," *New York Times,* March 16, 1976.

Karlan, Barbara, *West Coast Review of Books,* December, 1975.

Lemontt, Bobbie Burch, "Richard Scarry," *Dictionary of Literary Biography,* Volume 61: *American Writers for Children since 1960: Poets, Illustrators, and Nonfiction Authors,* Gale, 1987, pp. 248-57.

McDowell, Edwin, "Behind the Best Sellers: Richard Scarry," *New York Times,* April 27, 1980.

Moss, Elaine, "Richard Scarry," *Signal,* January, 1974, pp. 42-46.

Wilder, Rob, "Richard Scarry: The Wizard of Busytown," *Parents,* August, 1980, pp. 62-65.

For More Information See

BOOKS

Children's Literature Review, Volume 3, Gale, 1978.

Kingman, Lee, and others, editors, *Illustrators of Children's Books: 1957-1966,* Horn Book, 1968.

Lanes, Selma G., *Down the Rabbit Hole: Adventures and Misadventures in the Realm of Children's Literature,* Atheneum, 1972.

Ward, Martha E., and Dorothy A. Marquardt, *Authors of Books for Young People,* Scarecrow, 1971.

Wintle, Justin, and Emma Fisher, *The Pied Pipers: Interviews with the Influential Creators of Children's Literature,* Paddington Press, 1974.

PERIODICALS

New Yorker, December 14, 1968.

New York Times Book Review, November 6, 1966; December 14, 1968; April 5, 1968; October 1, 1972; May 6, 1973; November 14, 1976; May 27, 1980.

Times Literary Supplement, December 3, 1971.

Young Readers Review, September, 1968.

* * *

SCHIELDS, Gretchen 1948-

Personal

Born March 31, 1948, in Tokyo, Japan; married Robert Foothorap (a photographer), 1985. *Education:* Art Center College of Design, B.A., 1969.

Addresses

Home—San Francisco, CA. *Agent*—Sandra Dijkstra Literary Agency, P.O. Box 4500, 1155 Camino Del Mar, Del Mar, CA 92014.

Career

Illustrator in fashion and advertising as well as for children's books, textbooks, filmstrips, and cookbooks. Creator of pattern covers for Folkwear Patterns, and of "Secrets" line of notecards for Portal Publications.

Awards, Honors

Three awards of merit, Los Angeles Society of Illustrators, all 1982, all for "Secrets" line of notecards.

Illustrator

Sara Lea Chase, *Cold Weather Cooking,* Workman, 1990.

Amy Tan, *The Moon Lady* (children's book), Macmillan, 1992.

Tan, *The Chinese Siamese Cat,* Macmillan, in press.

Also provided cover art for Tan's novels *The Joy Luck Club* and *The Kitchen God's Wife.* Schields's illustrations have appeared in magazines, including *Seventeen* and *Cosmopolitan,* and on a 1990 Easter Seal stamp.

Work in Progress

The Water Shell, publication by Harcourt expected in 1995; two books set in Australia and the Yucatan.

Sidelights

A respected illustrator for more than twenty years, Gretchen Schields illustrated her first children's book, Amy Tan's *The Moon Lady,* in 1992. The book, intended for readers ages five to nine, follows seven-year-old Ying-ying as she attends China's autumn moon festival. Ying-ying is eager to meet Lady Chang-o, who lives on the moon and who grants wishes once a year. Writing in the *New York Times Book Review,* Ellen Schecter praised the "handsome" book's "glowing illustrations." The reviewer further observed that "Schields's vigorous illustrations capture the mood and tone of the story. Each picture is wonderfully evocative, lavish in design, color and drama."

Schields told *SATA:* "Intricate pictures, in which I could get lost finding stories within stories, have always been my favorite kind. I was a very nearsighted child and saw the world as strong compositions of color and shape, a graphic sense that is very evident in my pictures today. Perhaps that's why I so loved the close-up, delicate detail of the Asian decorative art that followed my family's household in our travels throughout the world!

GRETCHEN SCHIELDS

A childhood spent living in exotic places prepared Schields for illustrating Amy Tan's Chinese tale *The Moon Lady*.

"A childhood of travel made me rely on my imagination for friends and entertainment, and I was always drawing worlds and creating adventures and characters to populate them. Living in so many exotic places—Japan, China, Africa, Australia—brought with it a taste for the fables and myths of the people I encountered. My second book with Amy Tan, *The Chinese Siamese Cat,* is a playful fable of how the Chinese Siamese cat came to have the dark markings on her feet and face and tail, and in my own story, *The Water Shell,* I tell a tale of how a little girl's world was born from volcanic fire and the magic water of life, based on the many myths and folktales of the South Pacific. Two future books will take the young reader and viewer into the outback of Australia, where the world was sung into creation, and down into the steamy jungles of the Yucatan, for a look into the dark disappearance of the Mayan civilization."

■ Works Cited

Schecter, Ellen, "Girl Overboard," *New York Times Book Review,* November 8, 1992, p. 31.

SCHINDLER, S(teven) D. 1952-

■ Personal

Born September 27, 1952, in Kenosha, WI; son of Edwin C. and Bettie L. (maiden name, Pfefferkorn) Schindler; married. *Education:* Graduated with a degree in biology from the University of Pennsylvania. *Politics:* "Green." *Religion:* Christian. *Hobbies and other interests:* Playing the piano, recorder, and harpsichord, tennis, squash, and gardening. Also an amateur naturalist who enjoys wildflower propagation and creating ponds to attract amphibians like frogs and toads.

■ Addresses

Home—Philadelphia, Pennsylvania. *Office*—c/o Amy Parsons, Children's Publicity, Orchard Books, 95 Madison Ave., New York, NY 10016. *Agent*—Publishers' Graphics Inc., 251 Greenwood Ave., Bethel, CT 06801.

■ Career

Illustrator.

■ Awards, Honors

Parent's Choice Award for Illustration, Parents' Choice Foundation, 1982, for *The First Tulips in Holland;* best book selection, *School Library Journal,* 1985, for *Every Living Thing.*

■ Illustrator

G. C. Skipper, *The Ghost in the Church,* Childrens Press, 1976.
Susan Saunders, *Fish Fry,* Viking, 1982.
Phyllis Krasilovsky, *The First Tulips in Holland,* Doubleday, 1982.
Morrell Gipson, reteller, *Favorite Nursery Tales,* Doubleday, 1983.
Leon Garfield, *Fair's Fair,* Doubleday, 1983.
Deborah Perlberg, *Wembley Fraggle Gets the Story,* Holt, 1984.
Cynthia Rylant, *Every Living Thing,* Bradbury, 1985.
Elizabeth Bolton, *The Tree House Detective Club,* Troll, 1985.
Laurence Santrey, *Moon,* Troll, 1985.
Virginia Haviland, reteller, *Favorite Fairy Tales Told around the World,* Little, Brown, 1985.
Eric Suben, editor, *The Golden Goose and Other Tales of Good Fortune,* Golden Books, 1986.
Rylant, *Children of Christmas; Stories for the Season,* Orchard, 1987.
Ursula K. Le Guin, *Catwings,* Orchard, 1988.
Margery Williams, *The Velveteen Rabbit,* adapted by David Eastman, Troll, 1988.
Le Guin, *Catwings Return,* Orchard, 1988.
Steven Kroll, *Oh, What a Thanksgiving!,* Scholastic Inc., 1988.
(And text) *My First Bird Book,* Random House, 1989.
Bobbi Katz, *The Creepy, Crawler Book,* Random House, 1989.

Deborah Hautzig, *The Pied Piper of Hamelin,* Random House, 1989.

Melvin Berger, *As Old As the Hills,* F. Watts, 1989.

Morgan Matthews, *The Big Race,* Troll, 1989.

William H. Hooks, *The Three Little Pigs and the Fox,* Macmillan, 1989.

Christian, *Penrod's Party,* Macmillan, 1990.

Mark Twain, *The Prince and the Pauper,* retold by Raymond James, Troll, 1990.

Carollyn James, *Digging Up the Past: The Story of an Archaeological Adventure,* F. Watts, 1990.

Joanne Oppenheim, *Could It Be?,* Bantam, 1990.

Jonathan Swift, *Gulliver's Travels,* retold by Raymond James, Troll, 1990.

Megan McDonald, *Is This a House for Hermit Crab?,* Orchard, 1990.

Janet Craig, *Wonders of the Rain Forest,* Troll, 1990.

Betsy Rossen Elliot and J. Stephen Lang, *The Illustrated Book of Bible Trivia,* Tyndale, 1991.

Evan Levine, *Not the Piano, Mrs. Medley!,* Orchard, 1991.

Oppenheim, *Eency Weency Spider,* Bantam, 1991.

Mary Blount Christian, *Penrod's Picture,* Macmillan, 1991.

McDonald, *Whoo-oo Is It?,* Orchard Books, 1992.

The Twelve Days of Christmas, music copying and calligraphy by Christina Davidson, HarperCollins, 1991.

Erica Silverman, *Big Pumpkin,* Macmillan, 1992.

(With others) Walter Retan, *Piggies, Piggies, Piggies,* SilverPress, 1992.

Susanne Santoro Whayne, *Night Creatures,* Simon & Schuster, 1992.

Dawn Langley Simmons, *The Great White Owl of Sissinghurst,* Macmillan, 1992.

Each of Schindler's illustrated books complements the unique subject matter of the text, in this case, a traditional Christmas song.

Elizabeth Jaykus, editor, *For Dad,* Peter Pauper Press, 1992.

Christina Anello, editor, *For Grandma,* Peter Pauper Press, 1992.

Jennifer Habel, editor, *For Mom,* Peter Pauper Press, 1992.

Rita Freedman, editor, *For My Daughter,* Peter Pauper Press, 1992.

Noah Lukas, *The Stinky Book,* Random, 1993.

Constance C. Greene, *Odds on Oliver,* Viking, 1993.

Leah Komaido, *Great Aunt Ida and Her Great Dane, Doc,* Doubleday, in press.

Oppenheim, *Floratorium,* Bantam, in press.

William Kennedy, *Charlie Marlarkie and the Singing Moose,* Viking, in press.

■ Work in Progress

Catwings III and *I Love My Buzzard,* both for Orchard Books; *Don't Fidget a Feather,* Macmillan; *Spooky Tricks,* Dell.

■ Sidelights

Accomplished in many mediums and diverse styles, Steven D. Schindler has illustrated over forty books since 1976. Schindler says in an interview for *Something about the Author* (*SATA*): "I began drawing and coloring at an early age. My first award was when I was four; I won a red wagon at a coloring contest at a summer playground program. My favorite kinds of pictures were of animals. I had a total fascination with animals and their habitats. I loved going out looking for animals to bring home as pets as much as I loved drawing. I would bring home rabbits, snakes, pollywogs, rats, mice, and even a bat once. I have an older brother and we would do coloring or drawing together. He was more advanced and was certainly a stimulus. We continued to draw together until he was in junior high school, then he stopped drawing."

Schindler relates that he is self-taught. Even though he never took art courses, he was known as the class artist throughout school and he took care of the class bulletin boards and posters in grade school. Like other young children, Schindler liked to copy cartoons and characters, especially from *Mad* magazine and Disney films. His parents acknowledged his talent, but also encouraged him to work towards a technical degree because of the difficulty of making a living in the art field. During junior high school, Schindler began giving his drawings as presents, then in high school he decided to set up at a local outdoor art exhibit to sell his botanical drawings. Schindler was so successful that he continued to set up at art exhibits to earn money for college. When he began college, he entered as a premed major. "The first two years I goofed off and did a lot of drawing. I didn't really care too much for the biology courses which was a surprise," Schindler recalls. "I guess they were too microscopic/molecular and I disliked organic chemistry. I realized in my junior year in college that I wanted to be an artist." After graduation Schindler decided to go to New York to obtain a job in the art field. When a job did not develop, he returned to selling his artwork at outdoor exhibits. An agent visiting an exhibit noticed some pieces of Schindler's work that related to children and got him involved in textbook illustration for two years. Another agent approached him about illustrating a children's story and his career as a children's book illustrator was launched.

Since then, Schindler has built a reputation as an illustrator accomplished in a variety of styles and mediums and known for his balanced vision. Schindler typically works on five to six projects at a time and must be able to jump from one style to the next without carrying over the previous style of work. The illustrator states that the style called for in any book "depends on the feel of the story," and he determines this by reading "the text over and over until I'm sure of its tone, then the pictures appear." Schindler often finds that after he draws the characters, he finds them in real life. He relates, for example, that while working on *Not the Piano, Mrs. Medley* he went to the New Jersey shore to take photographs for his research on the book and, while there, found a woman that matched the image of the character, Mrs. Medley. The artist's work is also known for the humor it lends. Schindler asserts: "Visual humor is so easy; I never have to think of ways to achieve it." He has a reputation for detail as well. The detail is inspired by "the appeal of diversity. I've always enjoyed observing the details and what they mean. And in drawing or painting them I enjoy combining them to achieve a whole," comments Schindler. When asked how long it takes to complete a particular book, Schindler explains that it depends on how detailed the characters and background are and the type of medium he uses. On the average, he finds it takes four weeks of work, working eight to ten hours per day, to finish a book.

Illustrations Garner Praise from Reviewers

In 1982, Schindler's illustration for *The First Tulips in Holland* received the Parents' Choice Illustration award. Written by Phyllis Krasilovsky, *The First Tulips in Holland* tells Krasilovsky's version of how tulips, originally a Middle Eastern flower, first came to Holland in the seventeenth century. Krasilovsky imagines a Dutch merchant who, after visiting Persia, returns with some flower bulbs for his daughter, Katrina. Katrina plants the flower bulbs in a pot in her window. When the tulips bloom, they receive much public attention and the merchant is offered huge sums of money for the tulips. He refuses the offers and, instead, gives the flower bulbs to Katrina as a dowry when she marries a young florist. The florist eventually builds them into a Holland trademark for everyone to enjoy. Schindler's artwork in *The First Tulips in Holland* is praised by critics. "Brilliantly colored illustrations that echo Dutch paintings," hails the *New York Times Book Review*'s Joyce Maynard, "spill out to the edges of nearly every page." Schindler's work is "reminiscent of the Dutch masters" according to the *School Library Journal*'s Eva Elisabeth Von Ancken, who praises Schindler's sense of detail. A contributor to *Booklist* describes Schindler's

work as a "visual feast," and a *Publishers Weekly* contributor calls them "marvelous paintings." Commenting on the accurate detail of architecture, costume, and rendering of tulips, a *Bulletin of the Center for Children's Books* contributor finds "the book is lovely to look at."

Schindler also illustrated one of his favorite author's books, Cynthia Rylant's *Every Living Thing*. This collection of short stories relates the positive influence animals have on people. One story relates how getting a hermit crab as a pet helps a young orphaned child relate to his old aunt who has become his new caretaker. Another story demonstrates how a turtle assists a learning impaired child develop a friendship. Schindler's artwork is represented as "decorations" because small pen and ink renderings of the featured animal of each story are the book's only illustrations. His skill is nonetheless evident. A *Publishers Weekly* contributor notes the drawings "adorn as well as illustrate" the tales in the book. "Finely detailed" comments the *School Library Journal*'s Ruth Vose, who also stated that the drawings beginning each short story "express its tone" as well.

Schindler's pen-and-ink drawings capture the delicate grace of flying felines in Ursula K. LeGuin's *Catwings*.

Schindler also illustrated the popular Ursula K. Le Guin book, *Catwings* and the sequel *Catwings Return.* The story of four kittens born with wings who are encouraged by their mother to flee the dangerous city for the safety of the countryside is richly detailed by Schindler's work. Crescent Dragonwagon, in the *New York Times Book Review,* points out that Le Guin's story and Schindler's "marvelous ink and watercolor illustrations, especially the kitten closeups: personable, enchanting, believable" captivate the reader. "Fine illustrations show the delightfully furry and winged cats to perfection. Every cat lover will wish for one of his or her own," asserts Ann A. Flowers in her *Horn Book* review.

For all his successes, Schindler acknowledges that illustrating is not an easy career to establish. He points out that even though his style has not changed since his graduation from college, when he first went to New York no one was initially interested in his work. Interest in Schindler's work began when an agent started representing him. "Art directors do not have to look for illustrators for children's books," he notes, adding, "It is easier to get work once you have been published." Schindler advises young readers interested in a career as an illustrator to "be sure of yourself" and "draw, draw, draw."

■ Works Cited

Dragonwagon, Crescent, review of *Catwings, New York Times Book Review,* November 13, 1988.

Review of *Every Living Thing, Publishers Weekly,* September 20, 1985, p. 108.

Review of *The First Tulips in Holland, Booklist,* May 15, 1982, p. 1258.

Review of *The First Tulips in Holland, Bulletin of the Center for Children's Books,* June, 1982, pp. 190-91.

Review of *The First Tulips in Holland, Publishers Weekly,* April 23, 1982.

Flowers, Ann A., review of *Catwings, Horn Book,* November/December, 1988, p. 781.

Maynard, Joyce, review of *The First Tulips in Holland, New York Times Book Review,* April 25, 1982, p. 38.

Schindler, Steven D., interview for *Something about the Author,* conducted by Pamela S. Dear on May 26, 1993.

Von Ancken, Eva Elisabeth, review of *The First Tulips in Holland, School Library Journal,* March, 1982, p. 136.

Vose, Ruth S., review of *Every Living Thing, School Library Journal,* December, 1985, p. 106.

■ For More Information See

PERIODICALS

Horn Book, March/April 1989, pp. 205-06.

New York Times Book Review, November 12, 1989, p. 27.

Publishers Weekly, July 5, 1985, p. 67.

School Library Journal, October, 1991, p. 22.

SCHUETT, Stacey 1960-

■ Personal

Born October 9, 1960, in Elmhurst, IL; daughter of Marvin D. Schuett (a woodworker) and Rita (Hassenhauer) Kimball (a personnel director). *Education:* Sierra College, A.A., 1980; University of California, Davis, B.A., 1983.

■ Addresses

Home—P.O. Box 15, Duncans Mills, CA 95430.

■ Career

Illustrator. *Member:* Society of Children's Book Writers and Illustrators, Graphic Artists Guild, Phi Kappa Phi Honor Society.

■ Awards, Honors

The Moon Comes Home was a Junior Library Guild selection and was included on the John Burroughs List of Nature Books for Young Readers, both 1990.

■ Illustrator

Mavis Jukes, *Lights around the Palm,* Knopf, 1987.
Mary Jo Salter, *The Moon Comes Home,* Knopf, 1989.
Anne Mazer, *Watch Me,* Knopf, 1990.
Mary D. Lankford, *Is It Dark? Is It Light?,* Knopf, 1991.
Natalie Kinsey-Warnock, *When Springs Comes,* Dutton, 1993.
Jukes, *I'll See You in My Dreams,* Knopf, 1993.

■ Work in Progress

Illustrations for Eileen Spinelli's *If You Want to Find Golden,* to be published by Albert Whitman, and Anna Smucker's *Outside the Window,* to be published by Knopf; a self-written book titled *Midnight, Lost and Found,* to be published by Knopf; research for a book by Barbara Younger, tentatively titled *Traveling to Purple Mountains,* the story of Katherine Lee Bates, the poet whose work was adapted into the song "America the Beautiful."

■ Sidelights

Stacey Schuett told *SATA:* "As a kid, I spent almost all my time reading, drawing, and making things; putting words to pictures, and vice versa, was a natural thing to do. I was fortunate in that I had a supportive family who not only tolerated, for the most part, my state of preoccupation, but encouraged it. I was given a constant supply of materials: paper, paint, etc., and my grandparents hung my paintings beside prints by artists like Dutch painter Jan Vermeer. I also received one memorable gift from my grandmother, a box of brilliant glass mosaic pieces—I was mesmerized by the color, depth, and clarity of the glass, and the way it was illuminated by light.

STACEY SCHUETT

"In school, I was lucky to have understanding teachers who gave me plenty to read and look at, but let me wander and find out things for myself. Being a dreamy sort of kid, I usually paid little attention to what was going on in class, but instead filled notebooks with pages of labored poetry, snatches of what was meant to be meaningful dialogue, and drawings. Horses, especially, figured big; though there was almost always some other kid in class who drew more perfectly rendered, realistic horses than I did, I persisted.

"When I was twelve, I was allowed to spend my entire savings account on a horse of my own—an elderly roan mare named Snorky. After that, the world opened up for me. Even though I grew up in a suburban tract-home neighborhood, we lived at the very edge of a valley bordered by undeveloped foothills. On horseback, I had much freedom, and I wandered farther than my parents ever knew. Being outside so much, often by myself, gave me the opportunity to pay close attention to the way things look—particularly how objects are affected by different qualities of light and the sensations certain kinds of lighting can produce. The way a shadow fell or how a branch divided evenly into light and dark seemed enormously significant and mysterious. It was important, I thought, to notice everything. Now, when I make paintings to illustrate a story, I put a lot of what I've noticed, remembered, and imagined, to use.

"I have strong memories of books I loved as a child, particularly stories and pictures that made me see a little differently and gave me another angle on the world. I like to think and hope that the pictures I make might sometimes affect other imaginations in a similar way."

* * *

SCHWARTZ, Perry 1942-

■ Personal

Born January 22, 1942, in Minneapolis, MN; son of Herbert Jesse (a cab owner and driver) and Ann Loraine (in sales; maiden name, Borken) Schwartz; married Vicky Engel, January 24, 1964 (divorced 1976); married Mary Jane Miller (a graphic designer), June 2, 1978; children: Catherine, Elizabeth, Carolyn, Michael. *Education:* University of Minnesota at Minneapolis, B.A., 1964.

■ Addresses

Home—Illinois.

■ Career

Executive producer, writer, and director of motion pictures, television programs, business theater, and special events. Staff producer/director at several public television stations, moving to film, special events and multi-image production, beginning 1969; Pan American World Airways, producer and director of travel destination films and business theater events; The Filmakers, Inc., founding president, 1971-c. 1989; Business Incentives, Inc., Minneapolis, MN, executive producer; currently executive producer, Motivational Media, Chicago, IL.

■ Awards, Honors

Received over 60 national and international film festival awards.

■ Writings

Making Movies, Lerner, 1989, 2nd edition, 1991.
How to Make Your Own Video, Lerner, 1991.

TELEVISION SPECIALS

Wrote the script for *The 11th Annual World Popular Song Festival.*

■ Work in Progress

A Family in Georgia, referring to the former Soviet republic.

■ Sidelights

Executive producer, writer, and director Perry Schwartz has made over 200 motion pictures, television presentations, and business theater and special events in the last 24 years. This wealth of media experience provided a useful background for Schwartz's instructional book, *How to Make Your Own Video.* While working for Pan

American World Airways, he produced and directed travel destination films and business theater events, including *The Introduction of the 747,* a multi-media production involving a multi-lingual stage, 35mm film, and 24-slide projectors.

In 1971, Schwartz founded his own business communication production company, The Filmakers, Inc. The company's productions have won more than 60 national and international film festival awards. Schwartz was president of the company for 18 years, during which time he travelled all over the world, including South American jungles, the deserts and villages of West Africa, the Orient, and Europe. Schwartz has written, directed, and produced on a variety of topics, including writing and directing the television music special, *The 11th Annual World Popular Song Festival.* Featuring such artists as Mary MacGregor, the hour-long program was shot on location in Tokyo. Furthermore, Schwartz co-directed a film, *Perspectives on Peace,* for the Third Annual Nobel Peace Prize Forum, held in Decorah, Iowa.

* * *

SEUSS, Dr.
See GEISEL, Theodor Seuss

* * *

SHEPARD, Aaron 1950-

■ Personal

Born October 7, 1950.

■ Addresses

Home and office—P.O. Box 73613, Davis, CA 95617. *Agent*—Barbara Kouts, P.O. Box 558, Bellport, NY 11713.

■ Career

Professional storyteller and performer in reader's theater, 1985-1991; children's author, 1987—. Has also worked as a publisher, journalist, computer programmer, musician, instrument maker and repairer, printer, and salesman. *Member:* International Reading Association, Society of Children's Book Writers and Illustrators, Association of Booksellers for Children, Association of Children's Librarians of Northern California, California Reading Association, California Library Association, Northern California Children's Booksellers Association, Northern California Booksellers Association, Southern California Booksellers Association, Sacramento Area Reading Association.

■ Awards, Honors

Celebrate Literacy Award, International Reading Association, 1991.

■ Writings

FICTION

Savitri: A Tale of Ancient India, illustrated by Vera Rosenberry, Albert Whitman, 1992.
The Legend of Lightning Larry, illustrated by Toni Goffe, Scribner, 1993.
The Legend of Slappy Hooper: An American Tall Tale, illustrated by Goffe, Scribner, 1993.

OTHER

Stories on Stage: Scripts for Reader's Theater, Wilson, 1993.

Also contributor of stories to *Cricket.*

■ Work in Progress

The Gifts of Wali Dad: A Tale of India and Pakistan, illustrated by Daniel San Souci, for Scribner; *The Baker's Dozen: A Saint Nicholas Tale,* for Scribner; *The Enchanted Storks: A Tale of the Middle East,* for Clarion; *The Maiden of Northland,* a picture book adaptation of Finland's *Kalevala,* for Scribner; researching world religions and mythology.

AARON SHEPARD

■ Sidelights

Aaron Shepard told *SATA:* "I've loved books and wanted to be a writer for longer than I can remember. As a kid, I wanted to be a fireman and a writer, or a policeman and a writer, or a lawyer and a writer—but always a writer! I think that's partly because my mother read wonderfully to me when I was very young. Reading books to kids is the best way to get them to love reading and writing.

"Around 1985, I got involved in storytelling and reader's theater. For the next few years, I performed and taught workshops part-time. My audiences were all ages, but I soon learned I enjoyed young people the most.

"So in 1987, I started also writing for kids. I sold my first children's magazine story in 1989—to *Cricket Magazine*—and my first picture book in 1990. Four more picture books were accepted in 1991, so at the age of 40 I became a full-time children's author. And I can't imagine a more wonderful career.

"Each of my stories is an artistic creation by itself, but it is also a building block in a larger artistic creation: the career of a children's author. I'm excited about this career of mine, and I'm learning a lot as I work on it. For instance, I've discovered there's much more to being a successful author than just writing. There's also answering the mail, talking on the phone, visiting schools and bookstores, attending conferences, teaching workshops, and writing profiles like this one.

"For me, the most fun part of being an author—even more fun than writing stories—is going out and reading them to kids. In fact, I get high on kid energy. I've never married or had kids of my own, though I still might someday.

"I feel very lucky, because I'm doing exactly the kind of work I want. Some people can't do that, because they have too many responsibilities. Others *could* do it, but they don't—because it seems too hard, or they don't want to live on less money, or they're just afraid. So they stay unhappy. If there's one thing I want to tell young people, it's this: Follow your dreams!"

*   *   *

SHERMAN, Josepha

■ Personal

Born in New York, NY; daughter of Nat (a theatre manager) and Alice (a writer and teacher; maiden name, Altschuler) Sherman. *Education:* Hunter College of the City University of New York, B.A., M.A.

■ Addresses

Home—Riverdale, NY. *Office*—c/o Publicity Director, Walker & Co., 720 5th Ave., New York, NY 10019.

JOSEPHA SHERMAN

■ Career

Writer and editor. *Member:* Science Fiction and Fantasy Writers of America, Society of Children's Book Writers and Illustrators, Authors Guild, American Folklore Society, Sierra Club.

■ Awards, Honors

Compton Crook Award, 1990; Nebula Award nominee, 1991. Best Book citation, American Library Association, 1993, for *Child of Faerie, Child of Earth*.

■ Writings

JUVENILE NOVELS

The Invisibility Factor, Ballantine, 1986.
The Crystal of Doom, Ballantine, 1986.
Vassilisa the Wise: A Tale of Medieval Russia, illustrated by Daniel San Souci, Harcourt, 1988.
Secret of the Unicorn Queen (fantasy), Ballantine/Fawcett, *Book 1: Swept Away!,* 1988, *Book 5: Sorcery of the Dark Gods,* 1989.

FANTASY NOVELS

Song of the Dark Druid (interactive novel), TSR, Inc., 1987.
The Shining Falcon, Avon, 1989.
The Horse of Flame, Avon, 1990.
Child of Faerie, Child of Earth, Walker & Co., 1992.
(With Mercedes Lackey) *Castle of Deception,* Baen, 1992.
A Strange and Ancient Name, Baen, January, 1993.
Windleaf, Walker & Co., 1993.
The Chaos Gate, Baen, in press.
Gleaming Bright, Walker & Co., in press.
(With Lackey) *A Cast of Corbies,* Baen, in press.

OTHER

Indian Tribes of North America, Portland House, 1990.
A Sampler of Jewish-American Folklore, August House, 1992.
Rachel the Clever and Other Jewish Folktales, August House, 1993.

Also author of "The Space Sorcerers," an episode for the television series *Adventures of the Galaxy Rangers.* Contributor of numerous short stories to anthologies, including *Sword and Sorceress IV,* DAW Books, 1987; *Vampires,* HarperCollins, 1991; *Horse Fantastic,* DAW, 1991; and *Sisters in Fantasy,* New American Library, 1993. Also contributor to various periodicals, including *Cricket, Children's Digest, Jack and Jill, Highlights for Children,* and *Dragon.* Consulting editor for Baen Books and field editor for Walker & Company.

■ Work in Progress

Oathbreaker, book one of *The Sidhe Prince* duology, Baen, 1995; *The Sundered Realm,* book two of *The Sidhe Prince* duology, Baen, 1995; *The Demons of Khervina,* a juvenile science fiction novel; several fantasy novels.

■ Sidelights

Josepha Sherman told *SATA:* "I've led the usual checkered life of a writer, having been everything from archaeologist to scientific book indexer, and am right now a writer/editor/folklorist. Like many a fantasy writer, I came under the influence of J. R. R. Tolkien at an early age. But it was his essay 'On Fairy-Stories' that turned me onto the fascinating world that is comparative folklore. Many of my books and stories reflect my love of folklore."

One of Sherman's books inspired by folklore is *Vassilisa the Wise: A Tale of Medieval Russia,* her retelling of a 12th-century Russian legend. The main character, Vassilisa, is very intelligent and the most beautiful woman in the kingdom. Her husband foolishly boasts about this in front of royalty, claiming that his wife is lovelier than the Princess and smarter than the Prince; unsurprisingly the husband is imprisoned in the dungeon. Vassilisa is warned by a servant that the Prince is also intending to abduct her, so she cuts off her beautiful blonde hair, dresses as a man, and creates a plan to rescue her husband. Disguised as a Tartar nobleman, Vassilisa cleverly outwits the Prince by meeting three seemingly impossible tasks and rescues her husband. According to *Washington Post Book World'*s Michael Dirda, *Vassilisa the Wise* is "a fine book."

■ Works Cited

Dirda, Michael, review of *Vassilisa the Wise, Washington Post Book World,* October 9, 1988, p. 10.

■ For More Information See

PERIODICALS

New York Times Book Review, May 8, 1988, pp. 23, 34.

* * *

SHRIVER, Jean Adair 1932-

■ Personal

Born December 9, 1932, in Philadelphia, PA; daughter of Frederic Adair (an interior decorator) and Margaret (Pierce) Milholland; married Charles Shriver (a consultant), June 23, 1956; children: Stephen, Sarah, Frederic. *Education:* Vassar College, B.S., 1954; University of Southern California, M.S., 1968. *Politics:* Independent. *Religion:* Presbyterian. *Hobbies and other interests:* Gardening, reading, visiting with friends and family.

■ Addresses

Home—21 Pomegranate Rd., Portuguese Bend, CA 90274. *Agent*—William Reiss, John Hawkins and Associates Inc., 71 West Twenty-third St., Suite 1600, New York, NY 10010.

■ Career

Writer. Worked as a librarian. Palos Verdes Friends of the Library, president, 1965 and 1980; San Francisco Theological Seminary, board member. Elder in Presbyterian church. *Member:* PEN, Society of Children's Book Writers, Surfwriters, Amnesty International, Nature Conservancy, Vassar Club.

JEAN ADAIR SHRIVER

Writings

Mayflower Man, Delacorte, 1991.

Work in Progress

Writing *The Turning Worm* and *Gromwell Carpenter, The Shake King,* books for young readers; researching World War II for a young adult novel.

Sidelights

Jean Adair Shriver told *SATA:* "I was an old-fashioned romantic child who read all the time to escape what I considered 'dull reality.' The best times of my life were spent at a rambling ancient Massachusetts farmhouse with an unmarried great aunt who told me tales going back three generations of our family and showed me their treasures and their photographs. The past became as real to me as the present, and I learned to value continuity.

"I value character in books over action—Anne Tyler over a spy thriller. I'm interested in eccentrics and in tangled relationships. Children are gratifying to write for—their lives are not yet totally jelled. There is possibility for change. But then, adults, too, are learning to change these days. Since there will never be a short supply of interesting, oddball people who get into situations they didn't expect, I'll never run short of raw material to write about."

For More Information See

PERIODICALS

Booklist, June 1, 1991.
School Library Journal, July, 1991.

*   *   *

SIMS, Blanche (L.)

Personal

Born November 5, in Cleveland, OH; daughter of Hugh (a house-painter) and Theodosia (a homemaker; maiden name, Sekulic) Lombardy; married William J. Sims (divorced); children: Loretta Chaney, Greg Hepting (daughter), Deborah Macaskill, William J. *Hobbies and other interests:* Music (especially classical), *New York Times* crossword puzzles.

Addresses

Home and office—8 Wakenor Rd., Westport, CT 06880.

Career

Famous Artists School, Westport, CT, began as researcher, became instructor in young people's art; Xerox Corp., Middletown, CT, illustrator in art department; book illustrator. Also worked as a waitress.

Blanche Sims brings the characters of Patricia Reilly Giff's popular "Polk Street School" series to life with illustrations such as this classroom portrait from *Beast and the Halloween Horror.*

■ Illustrator

FICTION

Elizabeth Levy, *Running Out of Magic with Houdini,* Knopf, 1981.
Dean Hughes, *Nutty for President,* Atheneum, 1981.
Jane Flory, *Miss Plunkett to the Rescue,* Houghton, 1983.
Ann M. Martin, *Stage Fright,* Holiday House, 1984.
Kathy Feczko, *Halloween Party,* Troll, 1985.
Martin, *Me and Katie (the Pest),* Holiday House, 1985.
Elizabeth Spurr, *Mrs. Minetta's Carpool,* Atheneum, 1985.
Elizabeth Bolton, *Secret of the Magic Potion,* Troll, 1985.
Kathy Bieger Roche, *Weekly Reader Books Presents Andy and Sandy's Yummy Summer Snack Book,* Weekly Reader Books, 1985.
E. W. Hildick, *The Case of the Muttering Mummy: A McGurk Mystery,* Macmillan, 1986.
Abby Levine and Sarah Levine, *Sometimes I Wish I Were Mindy,* A. Whitman, 1986.
Jean Marzollo, *Cannonball Chris* (part of "Step into Reading" series), Random House, 1987.

Caron Lee Cohen, *Renata, Whizbrain, and the Ghost,* Atheneum, 1987.

Marzollo, *Soccer Sam* (part of "Step into Reading" series), Random House, 1987.

Madeleine Yates, *It's School Picture Day,* Abingdon, 1987.

Barbara Brooks Wallace, *The Interesting Thing That Happened at Perfect Acres, Inc.,* Atheneum, 1988.

Marzollo, *Red Ribbon Rosie,* Random House, 1988.

Marzollo, *The Pizza Pie Slugger,* Random House, 1989.

Eric A. Kimmel, *I Took My Frog to the Library,* Viking, 1990.

Gery Greer, *Jason and the Aliens down the Street,* HarperCollins, 1991.

Greer and Bob Ruddick, *Let Me off This Spaceship!,* HarperCollins, 1991.

Linda Walvoord Girard, *Alex, the Kid with AIDS,* A. Whitman, 1991.

Kate Banks, *The Bunnysitters,* Random House, 1991.

Gladys Yessayan Cretan, *Joey's Head,* Simon & Schuster, 1991.

Greer and Ruddick, *Jason and the Lizard Pirates,* HarperCollins, 1992.

Suzy Kline, *Mary Marony and the Snake,* Putnam, 1992.

Terrance Dicks, *Sally Ann and the School Show,* Simon & Schuster, 1992, originally published in England as *Sally Ann and the School Play,* Piccadilly Press.

Dicks, *Sally Ann on Her Own,* Simon & Schuster, 1992.

"POLK STREET SCHOOL" SERIES; BY PATRICIA REILLY GIFF

The Beast in Ms. Rooney's Room, Dell, 1984.
December Secrets, Dell, 1984.
Sunny-Side Up, Dell, 1986.
Pickle Puss, Dell, 1986.
All about Stacy, Dell, 1988.
Fancy Feet, Dell, 1988.
Watch Out! Man-Eating Snake, Dell, 1988.
Spectacular Stone Soup, Dell, 1989.
Matthew Jackson Meets the Wall, Delacorte, 1990.

"OLIVER AND COMPANY" SERIES

Page McBrier, *Oliver and the Lucky Duck,* Troll, 1986.
P. McBrier, *Oliver's Lucky Day,* Troll, 1986.
Michael McBrier, *Oliver and the Runaway Alligator,* Troll, 1987.
M. McBrier, *Oliver's Back-Yard Circus,* Troll, 1987.
M. McBrier, *Oliver's High-Flying Adventure,* Troll, 1987.
M. McBrier, *Getting Oliver's Goat,* Troll, 1988.
M. McBrier, *Oliver and the Amazing Spy,* Troll, 1988.
M. McBrier, *Oliver Smells Trouble,* Troll, 1988.
M. McBrier, *Oliver's Barnyard Blues,* Troll, 1988.

NONFICTION

William Ostrow, *All about Asthma,* A. Whitman, 1989.
Gretchen Super, *Drugs and Our World,* Twenty-first Century Books, 1990.
Super, *What Are Drugs?,* Twenty-first Century Books, 1990.
Super, *You Can Say "No" to Drugs,* Twenty-first Century Books, 1990.

OTHER

Caroline F. Bauer, editor, *Valentine's Day: Stories and Poems,* HarperCollins, 1993.

■ Work in Progress

Illustrating *How to Write a Play* and *Count Your Pennies,* both for Dell; *Mary Marony Mummy Girl,* for Putnam; and *Nurse Sally Ann,* for Simon & Schuster.

■ Sidelights

Blanche Sims is the illustrator of numerous works of fiction and nonfiction for young readers, including the popular "Kids of the Polk Street School" and "New Kids of the Polk Street School" series by Patricia Reilly Giff. Sims also lent her watercolor skills to Caron Lee Cohen's picture book, *Renata, Whizbrain, and the Ghost.* The story, a wild west tale, concerns Red River Renata, the mayor, sheriff, fire marshall, postmaster, and patent agent of Amarillo. Her enemy is Fearless Bones Kelly, the ghost of a drowned pirate who is now able to create instant floods, drenching anyone who tries to recover his gold from the Red River. However, when Whizbrain Wallerbee approaches Renata with his latest invention—an ice box railroad car—Renata comes up with a plan to freeze Fearless and win his treasure. Sims portrayed the pirate ghost using a light, nearly transparent film and a soft outline, prompting Donnarae Mac-

Sims's soft watercolors convey a ghost's frustration at being trapped by Sheriff Renata and her inventor cohort, Whizbrain Wallerbee. (Illustration by Sims from *Renata, Whizbrain, and the Ghost* by Caron Lee Cohen.)

Cann and Olga Richard to note in the *Wilson Library Bulletin* that the figure seems to disappear and reappear as the reader scans the cloudy horizon. The reviewers called Fearless Bones the artist's "crowning achievement." A *Bulletin of the Center for Children's Books* contributor called the paintings "breezy and expressive, a fine match for the text except that the ghost looks like he's scattering raindrops instead of 'a walking flood.'" A *Publishers Weekly* critic commented that the "well-designed" illustrations "convey the story's rollicking flavor."

Sims told *SATA:* "I am basically self-taught. My grandfather on my father's side was an Italian painter. He was a professor of art at Mount Holyoke College and died at ninety-six years of age. When I was a child in Cleveland, he would send me assignments—'draw a hand,' 'draw a foot,' etc.—and reward me with chocolate bars, lockets, and rings.

"I remember a teacher, Miss Cassatt, who taught history. She knew I couldn't bring lunches and would always have me drawing maps or historical figures at lunchtime to 'feed' me.

"I had a wonderful high school art teacher, Mr. Paul Ulen, who had studied in London. In my first year of high school we were learning at an art school level. He stressed drawing and that's what we did—from live models to plaster casts. A scholarship was certain, but I had to drop out of school and get out on my own due to an unpleasant home life.

"I left Cleveland and moved to New York City, married an illustrator, had four wonderful children, and now have eight grandchildren. I divorced long ago and needed to work to support my brood. I took a few odd jobs which I was horrible at. I even worked as a cocktail waitress part-time while I worked days as a researcher and instructor for a young people's art course at Famous Artist School. The school closed and I went on to Xerox in Middletown, Connecticut, as an illustrator. This pulled me together and I became a book illustrator. I had an agent for about ten years, and have been on my own since 1989."

■ Works Cited

MacCann, Donnarae, and Olga Richard, "Picture Books for Children," *Wilson Library Bulletin,* September, 1987, pp. 66-67.
Review of *Renata, Whizbrain, and the Ghost, Bulletin of the Center for Children's Books,* May, 1987, p. 164.
Review of *Renata, Whizbrain, and the Ghost, Publishers Weekly,* February 27, 1987, p. 164.

■ For More Information See

PERIODICALS

Kirkus Reviews, January 15, 1987, p. 134.

SMALL, Terry 1942-

■ Personal

Born May 10, 1942, in St. Louis, MO; son of Frederick Ruse (an electrical engineer) and Adele Naomi (a homemaker; maiden name, Edwards) Small; married Kathy McDowell (a teacher), August 25, 1979; children: Alysander McDowell, Catlin Edwards. *Education:* University of Missouri, B.A. (with honors), 1965; University of California, Berkeley, M.A., 1966; attended American School of Classical Studies (Athens, Greece), 1967-68. *Hobbies and other interests:* Ancient and medieval history, archaeology, linguistics, legends and myth.

■ Addresses

Home—Oakland, CA. *Agent*—The Jane Rotrosen Agency, 318 East 51st St., New York, NY 10022.

■ Career

Worked as an archaeologist in the Pacific Northwest of the United States, 1963-66, Gordion, Turkey, 1967, and Old Corinth, Greece, 1968; antique dealer in Berkeley, CA, 1971-78; special education teacher's aide in Richmond, CA, 1979—; history teacher in El Cerrito, CA, 1983-85; author and illustrator. Creator of poster for "Second Start Adult Literacy Program" sponsored by the Friends of the Oakland Library.

TERRY SMALL

■ Awards, Honors

Book design award, American Institute of Graphic Arts, 1988, for *The Pied Piper of Hamelin.*

■ Writings

SELF-ILLUSTRATED

(Reviser) Robert Browning, *The Pied Piper of Hamelin,* Harcourt, 1988.
Tails, Claws, Fangs, and Paws, Bantam, 1990.
The Legend of William Tell, Bantam, 1991.
The Legend of Pecos Bill, Bantam, 1992.
John Henry, Doubleday, 1993.

ILLUSTRATOR

Paul Panish and Anna Belle Panish, *Mother Goose Your Computer,* Sybex, 1984.

■ Sidelights

Terry Small told *SATA:* "I always understood from my earliest days that my inborn artistic talent was a rare and precious gift, yet not something I could expect to base a career on. The earliest buzz of excitement stirred by my art came, as near as I can remember, in kindergarten; and throughout grade school I rode that reputation as far as it would take me. Many a dinosaur mural, school play backdrop, and holiday window was painted by me, the school artist—coincidentally excusing me from the more tedious aspects of formal education, like memorizing the 'times' tables. The eventual development of the hand calculator has saved me from the embarrassment of such educational gaps.

"Later, when it came time to choose a direction in life, I had already absorbed the notion that art was no more than a wonderful hobby. Consequently, I studied in no art school, enrolled in no art classes, and generally shunned the too-too arty types I met. Fortunately I had always generally loved to read, and in reading I had discovered a love of history, especially ancient and medieval times. I studied archaeology in various departments of various universities; depending on the school, archaeological studies were found in anthropology, art history, or classics departments. In fact, I have two degrees in the subject, and neither document mentions the word 'archaeology.' You rarely meet a real archaeologist because, as I found out (rather late), archaeologists are in even less demand than artists. Fortunately, through the efforts of one of my professors, I had my very first writing published—an unbearably dull article in an obscure technical journal published mainly in Greek on the island of Cyprus. What a thrill!

"It wasn't until years later—after many odd jobs and adventures—that my art finally came together with some words to create a real book. At first the words weren't even mine. A friend, who happened to be an editor for a local publisher of computer books, asked me to illustrate a humorous take-off on Mother Goose rhymes that was written by one of her coworkers. I almost turned her down! But good sense prevailed, and half a year later my very first book was on the shelves. (Not all shelves, I found out, but some.) After that I revised and illustrated a classic poem by Robert Browning. Finally, I wrote and illustrated an alphabet book that grew completely out of my own whirling brain. Still it took one more book and a couple of weeks on the *San Francisco Chronicle* bestseller list before I could actually choke out the long-hidden truth: 'I am Terry Small, and I'm an author and illustrator of children's books.'

"It was true. Publishers were actually paying me money for the words I wrote and the picture I made. It was no longer a hobby. It was a career. I feel I am one of the fortunate few who are allowed to do exactly what they want in life. Not only do I get great personal satisfaction from my work, but I can pass on to others some of the joys and pleasures I found in my own childhood."

*   *   *

SMITH, Barry (Edward Jervis) 1943-

■ Personal

Born April 27, 1943, in Sydney, Australia; son of Allen Jervis Walter (a musician) and Myrtle Lillian (a toy manufacturer) Smith. *Education:* University of Melbourne, B.A., 1967. *Hobbies and other interests:* Reading, writing, listening, talking, painting, travelling.

■ Addresses

Home and office—P.O. Box 846, London E8 1ER, England. *Agent*—Susan Elliott, Elaine Greene Ltd., 4 Lord Napier Pl., Upper Mall, London W6 9UB, England.

BARRY SMITH

■ Career

Self-employed artist and writer, 1975—.

■ Awards, Honors

Parents' Choice Honor in Illustration, 1990.

■ Writings

Tom and Annie Go Shopping, Pavilion Books/
   Houghton, 1989.
Cumberland Road, Pavilion Books/Houghton, 1989.
Minnie and Ginger: A Twentieth-Century Romance,
   Pavilion Books/Clarkson N. Potter, 1990.
A Child's Guide to Bad Behavior, Pavilion
   Books/Houghton, 1991.
The First Voyage of Christopher Columbus, 1492, Vik-
   ing, 1993.
(With Annabel Shulton Thomas) *A First Book of Bible
   Stories,* Viking, 1993.

■ Work in Progress

"Preparation for my next exhibition; designing new
ceramics; working on the words and images for my new
book on European railway travel; assembling a collection of domestic photographs from the Victorian and
Edwardian eras to the present day; occasional research
into European and U.S. history."

■ Sidelights

Barry Smith writes, "My introduction to working for
children was a commission to illustrate a series of games
and puzzles with an educational bias for the British firm
of James Galt.

"At this time (about 1985) my career lay in painting
pictures for an adult audience. Exhibitions of my work
were held in the United Kingdom, France, Sweden, U.S.
and Australia. My pictures were reproduced in a variety
of formats—cards, prints, ceramics—and were sold
world-wide. This work was largely based on my close
observation of everyday life in England.

"The English publishing house of Pavilion Books saw
my work and perceived its potential for children's
illustration and commissioned my first two books, *Tom
and Annie Go Shopping* and *Cumberland Road* (published in the U.S. by Houghton Mifflin). The latter book
won a Parents' Choice Honor in illustration in January
1990.

"Pavilion Books expressed an interest in what could be
described as 'crossover books'—books having appeal to
adults as well as children. In 1990 *Minnie and Ginger: A
Twentieth-Century Romance* was published. This book
told of an Edwardian working class couple in the North
of England who fell in love, married, had children and
grew old together. With this book, I saw the creative
potential of books for children, to match mature,

The residents of *Cumberland Road* are all having
trouble with misplaced items in Smith's self-illustrated
search-and-find book.

complex, and interesting themes with accessible, informative, friendly drawings.

"Viking Children's Books also saw my potential for
creating informative, entertaining and enjoyable books
for children with a strong educational bias. A collaboration between me and Viking resulted in *The First
Voyage of Christopher Columbus, 1492.* This sideways
look at that infamous journey was published in 1992 in
five languages. My most recent book is *A First Book of
Bible Stories,* where my illustrations complement Annabel Shulton Thomas's retelling of stories from both the
Old and New Testaments.

"My influences range from classic books of the nineteenth and twentieth centuries to the early work of the
Disney studio and the comic books, movies, and TV I
grew up with in the 1950s and 1960s. I am always
looking, and the work of many artists in and out of the
galleries and museums of Europe are part of my
education.

"I like to create clear, coherent, richly-coloured and
friendly illustrations for children that, together with a
simple, thoughtful, and entertaining text, will nudge a
new reader or pre-reader into curiosity and thought.

"I share with children a fascination for the minutiae of everyday life and I hope through my illustrations and my words I can communicate that fascination and enjoyment."

*   *   *

SMITH, Doris Buchanan 1934-

■ Personal

Born June 1, 1934, in Washington, DC; daughter of Charles A. (a business executive) and Flora (an executive secretary; maiden name, Robinson) Buchanan; married R. Carroll Smith (a building contractor), December 18, 1954 (divorced, 1977); married Bill Curtis, November 1, 1989; children: (first marriage) Robb, Willie, Randy, Susan, Matthew. *Education:* Attended South Georgia College, 1952-53. *Religion:* None. *Hobbies and other interests:* Travel, biking, reading, walking, canoeing, pottery, ceramic sculpture, music, stargazing.

■ Addresses

Home—P.O. Box 266, Canton, MO 63435. *Office*—c/o Viking Penguin, Inc., 375 Hudson St., New York, NY

10014. *Agent*—John Hawkins & Associates, Inc., 71 West 23rd St., Suite 1600, New York, NY 10010.

■ Career

Writer, 1971—.

■ Awards, Honors

American Library Association notable book citation, and Child Study Association Book of the Year Award, both 1973, Georgia Children's Book Author of the Year, and Georgia General Author of the Year Award, both Dixie Council of Authors and Journalists, both 1974, Georgia Children's Book Award, 1975, Sue Hafner Award, and Kinderbook Award, both 1977, all for *A Taste of Blackberries;* Georgia Children's Book Author of the Year Award, and National Council for Social Studies notable children's book citation, both 1975, both for *Kelly's Creek;* Breadloaf fellowship, 1975; Georgia Children's Book Author of the Year Award, and *School Library Journal* best book of the year citation, both 1982, both for *Last Was Lloyd;* Parents' Choice Literature Award, 1986, for *Return to Bitter Creek.*

■ Writings

YOUNG ADULT NOVELS

A Taste of Blackberries, illustrated by Charles Robinson, Crowell, 1973.
Kick a Stone Home, Crowell, 1974.
Tough Chauncey, illustrated by Michael Eagle, Morrow, 1974.
Kelly's Creek, illustrated by Alan Tiegreen, Crowell, 1975.
Up and Over, Morrow, 1976.
Dreams and Drummers, Crowell, 1978.
Salted Lemons, Four Winds, 1980.
Last Was Lloyd, Viking Kestrel, 1981.
Moonshadow of Cherry Mountain, Four Winds, 1982.
The First Hard Times, Viking Kestrel, 1983.
Laura Upside-Down, Viking Kestrel, 1984.
Return to Bitter Creek, Viking Kestrel, 1986.
Karate Dancer, Putnam, 1987.
Voyages, Viking Kestrel, 1989.
The Pennywhistle Tree, Putnam, 1991.
Best Girl, Viking, 1993.
Remember the Red-Shouldered Hawk, Putnam, 1994.

■ Work in Progress

An untitled fictional autobiography, for Viking.

■ Sidelights

Doris Buchanan Smith's numerous award-winning young adult novels are praised for their realism and relevance, and deal with such topics as death, divorce, obesity, juvenile delinquency, unwed mothers, dyslexia, and child abuse. Despite the weighty topics she covers, however, Smith stays away from making these issues the focus of her books and concentrates instead on realistic,

DORIS BUCHANAN SMITH

likable characters who grow, change, and cope as a result of their difficulties. "As a writer," asserts Hugh T. Keenan in the *Dictionary of Literary Biography,* "Smith's greatest asset is her effectiveness at portraying the inner life of her protagonists; whether they are nine or seventeen, boy or girl, she writes assuredly and honestly from that character's point of view, and, consequently, critics and ordinary readers have responded well to the integrity of her novels for children."

In looking back on her reasons for becoming a writer, Smith muses in *Something about the Author Autobiography Series* (*SAAS*): "I truly don't know when I became a storyteller, or why. I did not grow up in a storytelling tradition with people sitting around on porches, or in front of fireplaces, telling stories. But my mother read to me and read to me, and those nursery rhymes and stories must have infused me and compelled me to spin my own." By the time she was two, Smith knew all her nursery rhymes by heart, and as she grew older she began to create stories of her own to entertain others. "From the time I was small," she recalls in *SAAS,* "I sat with two even smaller cousins in their sandbox and regaled them with stories, sculpting the geography of the story in the sand." When asked by adults what kind of stories she was telling, she was embarrassed to admit that she made them up.

In 1943, the family moved to Atlanta, Georgia, and Smith found herself feeling surprised when other children called her a yankee. She later intensified these feelings in fiction in her book *Salted Lemons.* After several more moves within the city, the outgoing Smith became shy and reclusive. However, a kind sixth grade teacher made an impact on Smith's world by noticing that she had talent in writing and asking her if she wanted to be a writer one day. Smith was hit hard with this question. "Be a writer? I didn't even know it was something you could be," she relates in *SAAS.* "I'm not sure I ever gave her an audible answer but inside me were flashing lights and eureka bells and a huge 'Yeah-hhh!' that has never left me." Still shy, Smith became a closet writer, working privately in her room. She showed an eighth grade teacher a story and was mortified when the teacher read it aloud to each of her classes. Joining the school newspaper, Smith submitted anonymous articles to the editor, but never came forward to reveal her identity. She kept her desired vocation so secret that many years later, when she told her father about her ambitions, he was surprised because he had never heard it mentioned before.

Smith married in 1954 and settled down to raise four children of her own, one adopted child, and scores of foster children. While she adored motherhood, there was something nagging inside her to continue writing. Never very disciplined at her art, Smith began to carve out times in the day when she could be alone to write. Attending workshops also helped her to focus. At first, however, she was disappointed in the seemingly endless rejections she received. One summer, threatened by the loss of serenity from her children being home, Smith decided to write an adventure novel with them as the

Based on the author's own childhood experiences during World War II, *Salted Lemons* tells of a young girl's struggle to be accepted in a new neighborhood. (Cover illustration by Lloyd Bloom.)

characters. While this book was never published, she decided to write another children's book while she was waiting to hear from publishers.

Death of Child Discussed in First Book

This other book was to be her first published novel, *A Taste of Blackberries,* which was released in 1973. It focuses on the guilt and sorrow felt by the narrator when his best friend dies from an allergic reaction to a bee sting. Up until this work, no other modern children's book had tackled this tough topic—the death of a child's playmate. Setting was an important element of this book, also, since it really did not seem complete in Smith's mind until she put it in a familiar Maryland suburb. "The sensitive, introspective character of the narrator emerges as he recalls the daring, mugging, fun-loving nature of his friend," describes Keenan, adding: "The telling of the story is natural, unforced, and sympathetic to the young boy's point of view. He learns to accept death as a fact, without relying on the cliches society offers."

Dealing with her own parents' divorce when she was a child provided Smith with material for writing her second novel, *Kick a Stone Home.* This story tells of a young girl, Sara, who feels alienated after her parents' divorce. Saul J. Amdursky, writing in *School Library Journal,* points out that Smith adeptly portrays Sara's maturation and creates "an engaging, believable, and likeable character." In another novel published in 1974, *Tough Chauncey,* Smith probes juvenile delinquency, showing in the end that the protagonist had a better chance dealing with life in a foster home rather than with his own abusive and neglectful family. *New York Times Book Review* contributor Alix Nelson observes that in *Tough Chauncey* "the writing is as crisp, honest, wry, tough and tender as is Chauncey himself—a charming gutsy book with a moral: you don't have to be 'pushed around like a leaf in front of a rake,' you can determine your own shape and direction." Both *Kick a Stone Home* and *Tough Chauncey* show characters learning to cope with their lives instead of presenting an unlikely, storybook ending.

More novels soon followed. In *Kelly's Creek,* published in 1975, young Kelly O'Brien confronts his dyslexia and learns how to best use his talents. "Both the biological description of the fertile marsh life and the sterile therapeutic exercises that Kelly must repeat to over-

HARPER
TROPHY

$3.95 US
$5.25 CDN

Doris Buchanan Smith

A Taste of Blackberries

One of the first children's books to address the death of a friend, Smith's 1973 debut *A Taste of Blackberries* recounts the guilt and sorrow Jamie feels after his best friend dies. (Cover illustration by Mike Wimmer.)

come dyslexia are authentically detailed," asserts Keenan. *Up and Over,* published in 1976, looks at the crazy days of the early 1970s, when streaking, racial tension, and teenage pregnancy were the issues of the day. A *Horn Book* contributor points out that "a ring of truth characterizes this contemporary novel about high schoolers during three weeks of crises." *Dreams and Drummers,* published two years after *Up and Over,* departs from Smith's usual themes, looking at a ninth grade girl who has no problems aside from her high maturity level, which brings her feelings of isolation. Although *Dreams and Drummers* "lacks a strong story line," contends a *Bulletin of the Center for Children's Books* contributor, "Smith has good style and solidly-constructed characters."

Teens Overcome Difficulties in YA Novels

In other books, Smith has written about bigotry and sexual awakenings. *Salted Lemons,* set during World War II, is a semi-autobiographical story which deals with Smith's experiences when she moved to Atlanta. Darby Bannister is the young girl in the story who finds her hopes of making new friends dashed when she is discriminated against because she is a yankee. Smith "displays penetrating insight with the depiction of relationships among Darby and her classmates, as the girl slowly wins their friendship and respect," relates a *Horn Book* contributor. Troy Matthews, the protagonist of *Karate Dancer,* must also face ridicule when he takes up ballet to please his new girlfriend. Both a cartoonist and karate student, Troy is eventually able to integrate elements of dance into his fighting. Cathryn A. Camper, writing in *School Library Journal,* maintains that *Karate Dancer* "breaks down stereotypes by presenting karate as a real-life mastery of body and mind."

In *Voyages,* published in 1989, Smith introduces elements of fantasy into her usual realistic style. Twelve-year-old Janessa Kessel is shoved from a speeding car after being abducted outside a local grocery store. Seriously injured, Janessa is resentful of the random violence while recuperating in the hospital, finding solace in only the daily hospital routine. A tutor introduces her to Norse mythology, and Janessa takes a series of fantasy journeys amongst the gods. There Janessa learns about fate, the power of the individual, and the strength to face adversity. "Smith ... enters new ground here by stepping into fantasy," observes Ruth S. Vose in *School Library Journal,* "yet retains her sure touch in creating believable human characters who learn and grow." Wendy Martin, writing in the *New York Times Book Review,* finds *Voyages* to be "both tautly and elegantly written," adding that Smith's "readers, young and old, will respond to the complex and deeply moving journey she describes in *Voyages.*"

A critically acclaimed author, Smith often ventures onto untraveled ground. Although her works discuss serious issues that are pervasive today, she keeps from being solely an "issues author" by focusing on the characters' growth and development. Smith feels strongly about her vocation and stresses discipline as one of the reasons for

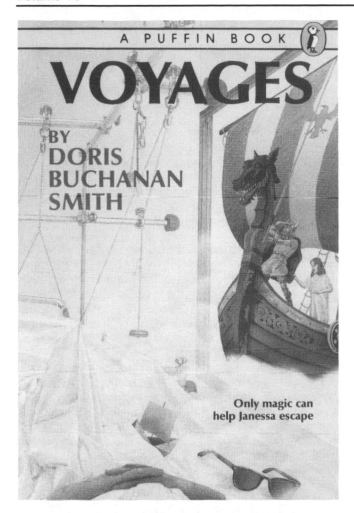

A PUFFIN BOOK

VOYAGES

BY DORIS BUCHANAN SMITH

Only magic can help Janessa escape

Smith turns to fantasy in this story of how Janessa's attempts to deal with a violent injury introduce her to the gods of Norse legends. (Cover illustration by Lonnie Knabel.)

her success. However, she enjoys this line of work greatly, commenting that the "most wonderful thing in the world to me is doing what I love to do and earning my living at it."

■ Works Cited

Amdursky, Saul J., review of *Kick a Stone Home, School Library Journal,* March, 1975, pp. 101-02.

Camper, Cathryn A., review of *Karate Dancer, School Library Journal,* December, 1987, p. 88.

Review of *Dreams and Drummers, Bulletin of the Center for Children's Books,* October, 1978.

Keenan, Hugh T., in an essay for *Dictionary of Literary Biography,* Volume 52: *American Writers for Children since 1960: Fiction,* Gale, 1986.

Martin, Wendy, review of *Voyages, New York Times Book Review,* March 4, 1990.

Nelson, Alix, review of *Tough Chauncey, New York Times Book Review,* June 23, 1974, p. 8.

Review of *Salted Lemons, Horn Book,* February, 1981.

Smith, Doris Buchanan, in an essay for *Something about the Author Autobiography Series,* Volume 10, Gale, pp. 305-18.

Review of *Up and Over, Horn Book,* August, 1976, p. 408.

Vose, Ruth S., review of *Voyages, School Library Journal,* November, 1989, pp. 114-15.

■ For More Information See

BOOKS

Twentieth-Century Children's Writers, 3rd edition, St. James Press, 1989.

PERIODICALS

Bulletin of the Center for Children's Books, June, 1976; April, 1983; January, 1985; April, 1986; March, 1988.

Horn Book, June, 1981, p. 305; May/June, 1986, pp. 328-29; March/April, 1990, pp. 203-04.

Library Journal, September 15, 1973, p. 2657; September 15, 1974, p. 2278.

School Library Journal, September, 1975, p. 112; September, 1976, p. 139; October, 1978, p. 150; May, 1981, pp. 86-87; September, 1986, p. 140.

Voice of Youth Advocates, February, 1988, p. 283; February, 1992, pp. 376-77.

Wilson Library Bulletin, January, 1987, pp. 60-61; February, 1988, pp. 78-79; May, 1988, pp. 75-77.

*   *   *

SMITH, Sandra Lee 1945-

■ Personal

Born June 28, 1945, in San Francisco, CA; daughter of John H. (a hospital administrator) and Bettelee (in personnel; maiden name, Zahn) Wardman; married Edward L. Smith, Jr. (a teacher), March 4, 1967. *Education:* California State University at Long Beach, B.A., 1967; University of California at Humboldt, teaching certificate, 1970; Arizona State University, M.A., 1980. *Politics:* Conservative. *Religion:* Christian. *Hobbies and other interests:* Reading, hiking, bicycling, museums, travel.

■ Addresses

Home—5433 South Mill Ave., Tempe, AZ 85283.

■ Career

McKinleyville School District, Arcata, CA, teacher, 1967-70; Ft. Bragg Elementary School District, Leggett, CA, teacher, 1970-73; Phoenix Elementary School District, Phoenix, AZ, teacher, 1975—. Consultant to Arizona State University, 1984—, and California State Universities, 1987—. Presenter of workshops at conferences and on the radio. Member of writers and educational associations.

■ Awards, Honors

Silver Pen Award, and Special Achievement Award, both 1989, both for *Love's Miracles.*

■ Writings

FICTION

Love's Miracles, Popular Library, 1989.
Dream Song, Popular Library, 1990.

NONFICTION

Coping with Decision Making, Rosen Publishing, 1989.
Coping with Cross-Cultural and Interracial Relationships, Rosen Publishing, 1990.
Value of Self Control, Rosen Publishing, 1990.
Coping through Self-Control, Rosen Publishing, 1991.
Drug Abuse Prevention Library—Marijuana, Rosen Publishing, 1991.
Drug Abuse Prevention Library—Heroin, Rosen Publishing, 1991.
Discovering Your Personal Resources, Rosen Publishing, 1991.
Setting Goals, Rosen Publishing, 1991.
Discovering Your Own Space, Rosen Publishing, 1991.
Great Grooming for Girls, Rosen Publishing, 1992.
Coping with Changing Schools, Rosen Publishing, 1993.

OTHER

Contributor of poetry and articles to periodicals.

■ Sidelights

Sandra Lee Smith currently lives in Arizona with her husband of twenty-five years and their dog Bo. "Ed and I grew up in California," Smith tells *SATA*. "We taught in redwood country for several years and then took off for a year of traveling in Central and South America. After that we ended up in Arizona and have grown to love the desert."

Smith's trip to Latin America instilled in her a love for other cultures. Because of this, she went on to earn her master's in bilingual multicultural education and even-

SANDRA LEE SMITH

tually started teaching English as a second language in the Phoenix School District. It was a research project that Smith was involved in at Arizona State University that first prompted her interest in writing. While developing methods for teaching bilingual students, Smith, and other Phoenix teachers, evolved a holistic, whole language approach to teaching. One of the major components of this program involved writing. "It became more and more evident that the writing process was an important factor in the success of literacy," asserts Smith. Trying to set an example for her own students, Smith began to write. "I fell in love with writing right then," she explains. "And I began to direct my goals toward becoming published."

Always an avid reader, Smith proceeded to write two mainstream fiction novels first. The books she takes the most pride in, however, are the numerous self-help books she writes for teens. "I love working with young adults," she relates. "And have deep respect for the decisions they have to make and live with in this present age." In addition to her novels and nonfiction works, Smith has also published poems and articles. Her favorite poem is one she wrote for her mother that was published on Mother's Day. "My mother is special to me as is my whole family," comments Smith. Other special things in Smith's life include family get togethers and desert camp-outs with the stars and the silence of nature. A spiritual person, Smith also enjoys time alone with her thoughts and prayers for God.

*   *   *

SNODGRASS, Mary Ellen 1944-

■ Personal

Born February 29, 1944, in Wilmington, NC; daughter of William Russell (a building contractor) and Lucy Ella (a hosiery worker; maiden name, Hester) Robinson; married Hugh Edwin Snodgrass (a chemist), November 16, 1984; children: Deborah Ann Eckard (foster daughter). *Education:* University of North Carolina at Greensboro, A.B., 1966; Appalachian State University, M.A., 1968; Lenoir-Rhyne College, certification in gifted education, 1980, graduate study, 1986-88. *Politics:* Independent. *Religion:* Presbyterian. *Hobbies and other interests:* Travel, classical ballet, piano, choral music, gardening, volunteer work, movies.

■ Addresses

Home and office—5591 Ashley Ct., Gold Creek, Hickory, NC 28601.

■ Career

Hickory High School, Hickory, NC, teacher of English and Latin, 1966-85, English department chair, 1968-75; free-lance writer, 1985—. Consultant to Perma-Bound; reviewer for Salem Books. Local president of Friends of the Library; local scholarship chair of Mensa. Meals on Wheels volunteer. *Member:* National Council of Teachers of English, International Reading Association, North Carolina Writer's Network, Phi Beta Kappa, American Civil Liberties Union, People for Choice.

■ Awards, Honors

Hickory Chamber of Commerce Star Teacher Award, 1971 and 1972; winner, Hickory *Daily Record* writing contest, 1983, for an essay, and Anchorage Education Association writing contest, 1988.

■ Writings

55 Lessons in Latin I and II, J. Weston Walch, 1986.
The Great American English Handbook, Perma-Bound, 1987.
Library Skills, J. Weston Walch, 1988.
Poetry Skills, E.S.P., 1988.
Greek Classics Notes, Cliffs Notes, 1988.
Roman Classics Notes, Cliffs Notes, 1988.
Wise Words, The Gifted Child Today, 1989.
(With Peter Gammond) *Bluffer's Guide to Bluffing,* Cliffs Notes, 1989.
Bluff Your Way in the Deep South, Centennial Press, 1990.
The English Book, Perma-Bound, 1990.
Cliffs Notes in the Classroom, Cliffs Notes, 1990.
Reading the Newspaper, Media Materials, 1990.
Writing Letters, Media Materials, 1990.
(Editor) *Contests for Students: All You Need to Know to Enter and Win 600 Contests,* Gale, 1990.
Characters from Young Adult Literature, Libraries Unlimited, 1991.
Environmental Awareness, Volume 1: *Acid Rain,* Volume 2: *Air Pollution,* Volume 3: *Land Pollution,* Volume 4: *Solid Waste,* Volume 5: *Toxic Waste,* Volume 6: *Water Pollution,* Bancroft-Sage, 1991.
Silver: A Study Guide, LRN Links, 1991.
Late Achievers: Famous People Who Succeeded Late in Life, Libraries Unlimited, 1992.
Crossing Barriers: People Who Overcame, Libraries Unlimited, 1993.
Auctori Latini, AMSCO School Publications, 1993.
Japan vs. U.S.A., Millbrook Press, 1993.

Also series editor for Cliffs Notes, 1985-93, and author of several Cliffs Notes pamphlets, 1988-92. Contributing editor of several books, including *The Short Story and You,* National Textbook Co., 1986; *Reading for Success,* Continental Press, 1990; *The Writer's Craft,* Macmillan, 1991; *Inventors and Inventions,* Gale, 1992; and *African-American Encyclopedia,* Salem Press, 1992. Columnist, Charlotte *Observer,* 1990-93. Contributor to periodicals, including *Ms., On the Issues, Islands, School Library Media Activities Monthly,* and *Canadian Medical Association Journal.*

■ Work in Progress

Black History Month: A Resource Book, for Gale; *News Leaders; Indian Terms* and *Literary Maps,* for Libraries Unlimited; *Voyages: The Eternal Quest,* for ABC-Clio; and *Improving Your Writing Skills.*

MARY ELLEN SNODGRASS

■ Sidelights

Mary Ellen Snodgrass told *SATA:* "Serendipity has blessed my life. Although it was difficult to cope with my father's frail health and my family's limited finances, from the time I was eight years old until my dad's death in 1976, I treasured our relationship. With barely a fifth-grade education, he taught me geography and algebra, politics and the Bible. From early times, I took to the rudiments of debate and became, in his words, 'a hard-headed young 'un,' which was a necessary preface to becoming a writer.

"In addition to the good fortune of having a loving, humanistic father, in late youth I encountered other riches. Three times in my undergraduate years, unforeseen scholarships kept me in college. When I taught my first Latin and English classes (in the high school that I graduated from), I felt that I had inherited an empire. For twenty years, I taught other people how to write. Then, when the regimentation, dehumanization, and test mania of the mid-1980s made teaching miserable, I escaped into textbook writing. I've tackled all sorts of jobs—a book on Japanese economics, genealogical research, a book about how to be southern, a regular column for the Charlotte *Observer,* even translating British humor into palatable American English.

"Now, writing seems as much a part of life as breathing. I sink nose-deep into research projects, such as my books on contests, pollution, Latin readings, Indian terms, and black history month celebrations. For a break, I speak to book clubs and conventions, civic and school groups. I've always been a 'sampler'—I've sung in a couple of operas, served as a church organist, composed music, played the piano in a French restaurant, and danced in a few ballets, once as the queen in *Sleeping Beauty.* I keep a garden and work out twice a week with an adult ballet group. Serendipity remains a constant companion: I just happen to be at the right place when satisfying, fulfilling challenges crop up."

* * *

SNYDER, Zilpha Keatley 1927-

■ Personal

Born May 11, 1927, in Lemoore, CA; daughter of William Solon (a rancher and driller) and Dessa J. (Jepson) Keatley; married Larry Allan Snyder, June 18, 1950; children: Susan Melissa, Douglas; foster children: Ben. *Education:* Whittier College, B.A., 1948; additional study at University of California, Berkeley, 1958-60. *Politics:* Democrat. *Religion:* Episcopalian. *Hobbies and other interests:* "My hobbies seem to change from time to time, but reading and travel remain among the top favorites. And of course writing which, besides being my occupation, is still and always will be my all-time favorite hobby."

■ Addresses

Home—52 Miller Ave., Mill Valley, CA 94941.

■ Career

Writer. Public school teacher at Washington School, Berkeley, CA, and in New York, Washington, and Alaska, 1948-62; University of California, Berkeley, master teacher and demonstrator for education classes, 1959-61; lecturer.

■ Awards, Honors

George G. Stone Recognition of Merit from Claremont Graduate School, Lewis Carroll Shelf award, Spring Book Festival first prize, all 1967, and Newbery honor book, 1968, all for *The Egypt Game;* Christopher Medal, 1970, for *The Changeling;* William Allen White Award, Newbery honor book, Christopher Medal, all 1972, and Hans Christian Andersen International honor list of the International Board on Books for Young People, 1974, all for *The Headless Cupid; New York Times* Outstanding Book, 1972, National Book Award finalist and Newbery honor book, both 1973, all for *The Witches of Worm; New York Times* Outstanding Book, 1981, for *A Fabulous Creature;* PEN Literary Award, 1983, and Parent's Choice Award, both for *The Birds of Summer;* Bay Area Book Reviewers Award, 1988, William Allen White Master Reading List, 1989-90, and Georgia

Children's Book Award Master List, 1990-91, all for *And Condors Danced;* New Mexico State Award, 1989-90, and Notable Trade Books in the Language Arts citation, National Council of Teachers of English, both for *The Changing Maze; Season of Ponies, The Egypt Game, The Headless Cupid, The Witches of Worm,* and *A Fabulous Creature* were all named American Library Association Notable Books; *The Velvet Room* and *The Egypt Game* were named to the *Horn Book* honor list; *The Velvet Room, The Changeling, The Headless Cupid, Below the Root, Until the Celebration,* and *Blair's Nightmare* were all Junior Literary Guild selections; *Blair's Nightmare* was included on state awards master lists in Missouri, Texas, Nebraska, Pacific Northwest, and New Mexico; *Libby on Wednesday* was on the Virginia state award master list.

■ Writings

FOR CHILDREN

Season of Ponies, illustrated by Alton Raible, Atheneum, 1964.

The Velvet Room, illustrated by Raible, Atheneum, 1965.

Black and Blue Magic, illustrated by Gene Holtan, Atheneum, 1966.

The Egypt Game, illustrated by Raible, Atheneum, 1967.

Eyes in the Fishbowl, illustrated by Raible, Atheneum, 1968.

Today Is Saturday (poetry), photographs by John Arms, Atheneum, 1969.

The Changeling, illustrated by Raible, Atheneum, 1970.

ZILPHA KEATLEY SNYDER

The Headless Cupid, illustrated by Raible, Atheneum, 1971.

The Witches of Worm, illustrated by Raible, Atheneum, 1972.

The Princess and the Giants (picture book), illustrated by Beatrice Darwin, Atheneum, 1973.

The Truth about Stone Hollow, illustrated by Raible, Atheneum, 1974, published in England as *The Ghosts of Stone Hollow,* Lutterworth, 1978.

Below the Root (first volume in the "Green-sky" trilogy), illustrated by Raible, Atheneum, 1975.

And All Between (second volume in the "Green-sky" trilogy), illustrated by Raible, Atheneum, 1976.

Until the Celebration (third volume in the "Green-sky" trilogy), illustrated by Raible, Atheneum, 1977.

The Famous Stanley Kidnapping Case, illustrated by Raible, Atheneum, 1979.

Come On, Patsy (picture book), illustrated by Margot Zemach, Atheneum, 1982.

Blair's Nightmare, Atheneum, 1984.

The Changing Maze (picture book), illustrated by Charles Mikolaycak, Macmillan, 1985.

The Three Men, Harper, 1986.

And Condors Danced, Delacorte, 1987.

Squeak Saves the Day and Other Tooley Tales, illustrated by Leslie Morrill, Delacorte, 1988.

Janie's Private Eyes, Delacorte, 1989.

Libby on Wednesday, Delacorte, 1990.

Song of the Gargoyle, Delacorte, 1991.

Fool's Gold, Delacorte, 1993.

YOUNG ADULT NOVELS

A Fabulous Creature, Atheneum, 1981.
The Birds of Summer, Atheneum, 1983.

OTHER

Heirs of Darkness (adult novel), Atheneum, 1978.

Snyder's manuscript collection is kept in the Kerlan Collection, University of Minnesota, Minneapolis.

■ Adaptations

Black and Blue Magic was made into a filmstrip with tape, Pied Piper, 1975; *The Egypt Game* was recorded by Miller-Brody, 1975, and produced as a filmstrip and tape by Piped Piper; *The Headless Cupid* was recorded for *Newbery Award Cassette* stories by Miller-Brody, 1976, and made into a filmstrip with tape by Pied Piper, 1980; *The Witches of Worm* was recorded by Miller-Brody, 1978; *Below the Root* was made into a computer game by Spinnaker Software's Windham Classics, 1985.

■ Sidelights

"I was eight years old when I decided I was a writer," Zilpha Keatley Snyder recalls in Lee Bennett Hopkins's *More Books by More People,* "and in spite of many detours, I never entirely gave up the idea." It was not until after she had become a mother of two and spent nine years working as an elementary school teacher that the author finally found time to write. Inspired by childhood memories and her experiences with children,

Snyder's penchant for combining everyday problems with the magical is evident in this story of a lonely city boy who is suddenly given a pair of wings. (Cover illustration by Dave Henderson.)

Snyder decided to write stories that combined typical themes about the problems that children face with an element of fantasy. Snyder's stories, writes Jean Fritz in the *New York Times Book Review,* "suggest that magic lies within the power of imagination itself."

As a child growing up in California, Snyder's imagination was very active. According to her, this was a matter of necessity. "We lived in the country during the Depression and World War II," she says in Hopkins's book. "Due to shortages of such things as gasoline and money, I didn't get around much or do many exciting things. In fact, my world might have been quite narrow and uninteresting if it had not been for two magical ingredients—animals and books." As for animals, the author's family lived in a country house and raised everything from cats, dogs, and rabbits to cows, goats, and horses, so there were plenty of four-legged friends to keep her happy. A nearby library supplied the young Snyder with her other magical ingredient. Having learned to read at the very early age of four years, she borrowed many books from the library, reading about one per day during her first years in school.

When she entered the seventh grade, as she recounts in the *Something about the Author Autobiography Series*

(*SAAS*), she felt she "was suddenly a terrible misfit" because she had been allowed to skip one grade and was younger than the other children. "So I retreated further into books and daydreams," she later remarked. Snyder began to feel less shy by the time she entered high school. "I became a little less afraid of my peers. I had some good teachers and made some exciting new friends, such as Shakespeare and Emily Dickinson." The author continued to grow as a student at Whittier College, where she also met her husband Larry, who was a music major at the time.

Snyder had romantic dreams of becoming a struggling writer in New York City, but after graduating from Whittier she found that she did not have the money for a ticket to get there, let alone try to live in the city with no dependable income. She took a teaching job instead; and not only did she enjoy teaching elementary school children, but she was so talented at it that she eventually became a master teacher at the University of California at Berkeley. Snyder held several teaching jobs around the United States because her husband transferred to different graduate schools and also was assigned to several bases while he served in the Air Force during the Korean War. They finally ended up in Berkeley, California, where Larry finished his degree. After moving fifteen times and having two children, the Snyders were finally ready to settle down. "I was still teaching but there seemed to be a bit more time and I caught my breath and thought about writing."

Books Drawn from Childhood Memories

For Snyder the appeal of writing lies in the author's power to create an entire world and populate it with people who have never existed before, so she was naturally drawn toward writing stories that dealt with imagination and fantasy. A large source of her inspiration, especially in her earlier books, has been her childhood memories. "Remembering a dream I'd had when I was twelve years old about some strange and wonderful horses," Snyder says, she sat down to write her first book, *Season of Ponies,* and submitted it to Atheneum for publication. Although the editor there, Jean Karl, did not immediately accept the author's manuscript, she encouraged Snyder to revise the book and, after the author rewrote the story twice, it was published.

Other early works like *The Velvet Room* and *The Egypt Game* also originated from Snyder's childhood. *The Velvet Room* echoes experiences Snyder had as a child growing up during the Depression. The story itself is based on one that Snyder wrote when she was only nineteen years old about a migratory worker and his family. Despite the realistic subject, magic enters the tale as it is told through a child's imaginative eyes. The inspiration for *The Egypt Game* came from what Snyder calls the "Egyptian period" of her childhood, a year during which she became completely absorbed in anything having to do with ancient Egypt. "However, the actual setting and all six of the main characters came

The author recalls her childhood love of animals in her first book, where a young girl's unhappy summer is enlivened by a ghostly herd. (Cover illustration by Henderson.)

from my years as a teacher in Berkeley," the author related.

"*The Egypt Game* is probably one of this author's most popular novels, and one of her best," claims *Twentieth Century Children's Writers* contributor Kay E. Vandergrift. "The Egypt game is an elaborate game played in a secret 'temple' and filled with ritualistic gestures. Through his observations of the game, an old professor takes a new interest in life and ultimately saves the children from unexpected danger. Although there is no special note taken of the fact, the players are a mixed group racially and ethnically which was at the time of publication (1967) still somewhat rare in American books for children."

The Egypt Game was published one year after the Snyders adopted their son Ben, a native of Kowloon, China. A few years later, in 1970, the Snyders left their home near Berkeley to tour Europe. When they returned they settled into a century-old farmhouse near Santa Rosa, California. It was here that Snyder wrote many of her books, including the science fiction "Green-sky" trilogy. Mystery and magic continue to be important elements in books like *The Changling, The Witches of Worm,* and *The Truth about Stone Hollow.* The reappearance of paranormal subjects in these books led a *Dell Carousel* interviewer to ask Snyder whether she was interested in the occult. Snyder responds that she was, "but only because I'm interested in everything that suggests a wider reach to knowledge and experience than what is readily available to the five senses." In Hopkins's book she notes: "A long time ago I accepted the fact that I'm probably incurably superstitious.... I've also known for some time that it's not too wise to admit that I still believe in fairy godmothers and some kinds of ghosts and all kinds of magical omens."

Switch to Science Fiction Yields Success

Snyder's imagination switched from stories about ghosts and witches to science fiction in the "Green-sky Trilogy," which includes *Below the Root, And All Between,* and *Until the Celebration.* "Like so many of my books," Snyder comments in *SAAS*, "the trilogy's deepest root goes back to my early childhood when I played a game that involved crossing a grove of oak trees by climbing from tree to tree, because something incredibly dangerous lived 'below the root.'" The game is first mentioned in *The Changling,* in which two of the characters play in the trees much as Snyder did, but it is given life in the trilogy. The people of Green-sky, known as the Kindar,

What secrets will Robin find?

Based on a story Snyder wrote at nineteen, *The Velvet Room* tells of a Depression-era girl faced with a decision between a magical place and her migrant family. (Cover illustration by Henderson.)

are settlers from another planet who live peacefully in the treetops. The only thing they fear are the Erdlings, an evil race who live beneath the trees and capture and enslave Kindar children. The Green-sky books focus on the adventures of three children and is told from the viewpoints of both the Kindar and the Erdlings in an attempt to deliver a message about peace and brotherhood.

Snyder did not at first plan to write a trilogy, but she enjoyed writing *Below the Root* so much that she returned to the world of Green-sky twice more. The same thing happened with Snyder's books about the Stanley family, which include *The Headless Cupid, The Famous Stanley Kidnapping Case, Blair's Nightmare,* and *Janie's Private Eyes.* The five Stanley children—David, Blair, Esther, Janie, and Amanda—are "favorites of mine," Snyder says in a *Junior Literary Guild* article. "Every so often I get an irresistible urge to find out what they're up to now, and the result is another book."

As to what Snyder is up to, in 1985 she finally fulfilled a childhood dream and traveled to Egypt. She also lived for a time in Italy before returning to the United States and settling in Mill Valley near San Francisco, where she continues to write and occasionally gives talks to adults and school children about her work. Her writing has become increasingly diverse, as her more recent books testify. Since returning to California she has written a historical novel, *And Condors Danced,* a fanciful collection of stories about tiny people called "Tiddlers" in *Squeak Saves the Day and Other Tooley Tales,* a mainstream children's book, *Libby on Wednesday,* a fantasy novel, *Song of the Gargoyle,* and contemporary novel set in California gold country, *Fool's Gold.*

During one of her lectures a member of the audience asked Snyder why she became an author. Recalling the incident in her *SAAS* entry, Snyder responds that "the maximum reward is simply—joy; the storyteller's joy in creating a story and sharing it with an audience. So I write for joy, my own and my imagined audience's—but why for children? Unlike many writers who say that they are not aware of a particular audience as they write, I know that I am very conscious of mine." She later concludes, "I enjoy writing for an audience that shares my optimism, curiosity and freewheeling imagination."

■ Works Cited

Dell Carousel, fall/winter, 1985-86.

Fritz, Jean, "For Young Readers: 'The Witches of Worm,'" *New York Times Book Review,* December 10, 1972, pp. 8, 10.

Hopkins, Lee Bennett, *More Books by More People,* Citation, 1974, pp. 318-322.

Junior Literary Guild, March, 1984.

Snyder, Zilpha Keatley, *Something about the Author Autobiography Series,* Volume 2, Gale, 1986, pp. 215-226.

Janie's search for a neighborhood dognapper takes center stage in this novel featuring the spirited Stanley family. (Cover illustration by Henderson.)

Vandergrift, Kay E., "Zilpha Keatley Snyder," *Twentieth Century Children's Writers,* 3rd edition, edited by Tracy Chevalier, St. Martin's, 1989, pp. 903-905.

■ For More Information See

BOOKS

Contemporary Literary Criticism, Volume 17, Gale, 1981, pp. 469-475.

PERIODICALS

Book World, December 3, 1967.
Bulletin of the Center for Children's Books, June, 1974; December, 1979, p. 82; March, 1982; January, 1983; April, 1984; November, 1985; November, 1987; May, 1988.
Christian Science Monitor, February 29, 1968.
Growing Point, September, 1976, p. 2939.
Horn Book, June, 1964, p. 284; April, 1965, p. 173; April, 1967, pp. 209-210; April, 1968, pp. 182-183; October, 1970, p. 479; October, 1971; December, 1972; October, 1973, p. 459; August, 1974, p. 380.
Junior Bookshelf, December, 1978, p. 324.

Kirkus Reviews, March 1, 1974, p. 245; March 1, 1975, p. 239; February 1, 1977, p. 95; September 1, 1978, p. 973.
New York Times Book Review, May 9, 1965; July 24, 1966, p. 22; July 23, 1967; May 26, 1968; November 7, 1971, pp. 42-44; May 4, 1975, pp. 32, 34; May 23, 1976, p. 16; May 8, 1977, p. 41; July 8, 1984; December 27, 1987.
Saturday Review, May 13, 1967, pp. 55-56.
School Library Journal, April, 1990, p. 124.

* * *

STERN, Judith M. 1951-

■ Personal

Born July 8, 1951, in Cleveland, OH; daughter of Bernard (a social worker) and Raula (an employment counselor) Stern; married Uzi Ben-Ami (a psychologist), May 23, 1976; children: Talia, Naomi. *Education:* State University of New York at Buffalo, B.A., 1972; Columbia University, M.A., 1973.

■ Addresses

Home—205 Watts Branch Parkway, Rockville, MD 20850.

■ Career

Charles E. Smith Jewish Day School, Rockville, MD, coordinator of special education services, 1983—; educational consultant in private practice, Rockville, 1985—.

■ Writings

WITH PATRICIA QUINN

Putting on the Brakes: Young People's Guide to Understanding Attention Deficit Hyperactivity Disorder (ADHD), Magination Press, 1991.
Putting on the Brakes: An Activity Book for Children with Attention Deficit Hyperactivity Disorder (ADHD), Magination Press, 1993.

■ Work in Progress

A children's book explaining learning disabilities.

■ Sidelights

Judith M. Stern told *SATA:* "Having worked in the field of education for twenty years, I became increasingly involved in the areas of learning disabilities and attention disorders. I have worked extensively with children in classroom settings, conducted teacher workshops, and have led parent information/support groups. I found that people were eager for information on attention deficit hyperactivity disorder (ADHD). Although there was a wealth of literature available directed to parents and professionals on ADHD, our book was one of the first nonfiction works published for the children them-

JUDITH M. STERN

selves. The response was exceptional. In less than a year, the book underwent three printings, and comments from parents, professionals, and children have been very positive. Readers have found the book useful and have noted that it is written in a style that is respectful and personal to the child reading it."

*   *   *

STOCK, Carolmarie 1951

■ Personal

Born December 25, 1951, in Cincinnati, OH; daughter of William H. and Mary (Bachmann) Stock; divorced; children: Sarah M. Fischesser. *Education:* College of Mount Joseph, A.A.; attended College of Lake County. *Religion:* Catholic.

■ Addresses

Home—3354 Gerold Dr., Cincinnati, OH 45238. *Office*—Summit Country Day School, 2161 Grandin Rd., Cincinnati, OH 45208.

■ Career

Writer. Free-lance professional storyteller, Cincinnati, OH, 1984—; WLWT-TV, Cincinnati, associate producer of "Live at 5," 1990-91; Summit Country Day School, Cincinnati, librarian, 1990—. Active in community theatre groups; director of middle school plays at Summit Country Day School. *Member:* National Association for the Preservation and Perpetuation of Storytelling, Cincinnati Storytellers Guild.

■ Writings

Sassafras Holmes and the Library Mysteries, Alleyside Press, 1991.

Also author of verse.

■ Work in Progress

Grandpa's Shoes and *The Three Little Pigs—A Modern Fairytale,* both picture books; *Shadow Memories* (a mystery) and *My Mom Married Sherlock Holmes?,* both chapter books; research for a biography of St. Julie Billiard.

■ Sidelights

Carolmarie Stock told *SATA:* "My mother says that I was born telling a story! Well, I'm not exactly sure I was actually born telling a story, but for as long as I can remember, I have been 'making up,' writing, and telling stories. My first 'captive' audience for my stories was my baby brother. I would make up a story and make him listen as I told it. After I started school, I would write little story books and read them to other 'captive' audiences—my teddy bear and dolls. I kept on writing stories and when I grew up and had a little girl of my own, I told my stories to her.

"All this time, I never really thought anyone else (besides my daughter and my teddy bear) would like my stories. Then, while I was taking a library technology course in college, I had to write a paper to complete the course. The paper had to explain a problem that people had when they came into the library and what I would do to correct that problem. Since I was working in the children's room of my local public library while I was taking this course, I knew immediately what problem I would write about. Every day, I would see children come into the library and not know how to find what they were looking for. I knew these children needed something to help them discover how to use the library, but this something had to be fun as well as educational.

"I decided that a story that would be fun to read while explaining how to use the card catalog was the answer. I chose a mystery and used characters from two of my favorite authors, Sir Arthur Conan Doyle and Edgar Allan Poe. Sassafras Holmes, girl detective was born! My instructor enjoyed the story so much that she had me read it to the class and then suggested I send it to a publisher. I decided to take her advice and give my story a chance.

"Alleyside Press, a publisher that specializes in library-related materials, decided that Sassafras Holmes' story was a great idea, too! They asked me if I could write stories about other problems that children encounter in the library. Then all the stories could be chapters in one larger book. I agreed to try and before I knew it, *Sassafras Holmes and the Library Mysteries* was finished.

CAROLMARIE STOCK

"Now, when I am working as a storyteller, I frequently use stories that I have 'made-up.' These stories have become so popular that children who know me as a storyteller ask me to tell my stories again and again. I am currently working on writing these stories down, so they can be published as books. I always try to put things in my stories that I know something about. That way the person reading or listening to the story will believe what I have written because it is believable! When teachers tell their students to write about 'what you know,' it is the best advice that a young writer can follow.

"I hope that children will always have fun reading and listening to the stories I write. And that they will always remember that reading is the key that unlocks their tomorrow!"

*   *   *

STONE, Rosetta
   See GEISEL, Theodor Seuss

*   *   *

STORMCROW
   See TALIFERO, Gerald

STRAUSS, Susan (Elizabeth) 1954-

■ Personal

Born December 21, 1954, in New York, NY; daughter of Robert (an electrical engineer) and Doris (a homemaker; maiden name, Dose) Strauss; married Ted Wise (an ecologist), June 22, 1991. *Education:* University of Virginia, B.A. (cum laude), 1977, M.Ed., 1979. *Politics:* Progressive Democrat. *Religion:* "Interested in all." *Hobbies and other interests:* Visual and theatrical arts, animals, environmental issues (especially old growth forests, water, and predator control), skiing, swimming, and running.

■ Addresses

Home—66280 White Rock Loop, Bend, OR 97709. *Office*—P.O. Box 1141, Bend, OR 97701.

■ Career

Professional storyteller, 1979—; has performed at schools, universities, museums, and festivals, including Columbia University, Smithsonian Museum of Natural History, Bay Area Storytelling Festival, with the Oregon symphony, and on television and radio; has produced videos and audio tapes of her performances. English teacher at Oregon Episcopal School, 1979-83, and High Country School, 1981-82; visiting professor at San Diego State University, 1989; affiliate faculty member at Colorado State University, 1990—. Speaker at educational conferences; participant in interpretive workshops. Consultant to National Forest and Park Services; member of board of directors, Star Mountain Waldorf School. *Member:* National Association of Interpretation (NAI), Society of Children's Book Writers and Illustrators.

■ Awards, Honors

Second place in interpretive media, NAI, 1991, for audio tape "Coyote Gets a Cadillac."

■ Writings

Coyote Stories for Children, Beyond Words, 1991.

Also contributor to *National Journal of Interpretation.*

■ Sidelights

Susan Strauss told *SATA:* "In my wildest childhood daydreams, I never imagined that I would be an author. I dreamt of becoming the first woman orchestra conductor or a political leader, among other things ... but not an author. I was a very poor reader and writer and I hated to work at a desk.

"Reading and writing was very important to my father. Every Sunday he would read very intellectual pieces from the *Washington Post Book Review* section and marvel at the craftsmanship of written thought. I

SUSAN STRAUSS

remember that I didn't understand much of what he read, but only that it was so important to him. He would speak about a particular writer's skill as if it was something mystical—one of life's nearly impossible, but awesomely worthwhile skills to attain.

"What was interesting to me? Not the world of printed paper at all, but the world of nature. I was always outside having adventures with bees, climbing trees, sharing telepathic moments with my dog, or building secret forts deep in the woods. I remember that one summer my father made me stay in my room for an hour every day to read. I would just fall asleep.

"In Miss Shoemaker's fifth grade and Mrs. Sundberg's high school English classes, the world of literature began to breathe with the same force and beauty as the world of nature. Both women played recordings of famous poets reading their own works. Through my ears, I entered the world of language and ideas. I was so love-struck by this world that I disciplined myself to read more and eventually graduated from college with an honors degree in English. I have carried that passion for the beauty of the spoken word into my work as a professional storyteller to this day. In my view, the full fervor of nature and life is freeze-dried in written text. Through spoken performance and orally-based writing, I feel that I release life experience and the world of nature into its true and exquisite self."

T

TAFURI, Nancy 1946-

■ Personal

Born November 14, 1946, in Brooklyn, NY; daughter of Otto George (a retired naval officer and an engineer) and Helen (Kruger) Haase; married Thomas Michael Tafuri (a graphic designer), June 14, 1969; children: Cristina. *Education:* Graduated from School of Visual Arts, New York City, 1967.

■ Addresses

Home and office—One Plus One Studio, 44 Tophet Rd., Roxbury, CT 06783.

■ Career

Simon & Schuster (publisher), New York City, assistant art director, 1967-69; One Plus One Studio (graphic design firm), Roxbury, CT, co-founder, graphic designer, and illustrator, 1971—. *Exhibitions:* Work exhibited by Society of Illustrators, 1977.

■ Awards, Honors

"Children's Choice" citation, International Reading Association, 1982, for *The Piney Woods Peddler;* "Best books of 1983" citation, *School Library Journal,* for *Early Morning in the Barn;* Jane Addams honor book, 1983, for *If I Had a Paka: Poems in Eleven Languages;* Caldecott Honor Book, American Library Association, 1985, for *Have You Seen My Duckling?*

■ Writings

FOR CHILDREN; SELF-ILLUSTRATED

All Year Long, Greenwillow, 1983.
Early Morning in the Barn, Greenwillow, 1983.
Have You Seen My Duckling?, Greenwillow, 1984.
Rabbit's Morning, Greenwillow, 1985.
Who's Counting?, Greenwillow, 1986.
In a Red House, Greenwillow, 1987.
Where We Sleep, Greenwillow, 1987.

My Friends, Greenwillow, 1987.
Do Not Disturb, Greenwillow, 1987.
Spots, Feathers, and Curly Tails, Greenwillow, 1988.
Two New Sneakers, Greenwillow, 1988.
One Wet Jacket, Greenwillow, 1988.
Junglewalk, Greenwillow, 1988.
The Ball Bounced, Greenwillow, 1989.
Follow Me!, Greenwillow, 1990.
This Is the Farmer, Greenwillow, 1993.

ILLUSTRATOR

Jean Holzenthaler, *My Hands Can,* Dutton, 1977.
George Shannon, *The Piney Woods Peddler,* Greenwillow, 1981.
Charlotte Zolotow, *The Song,* Greenwillow, 1982.
Mirra Ginsburg, *Across the Stream,* Greenwillow, 1982.
Charlotte Pomerantz, *If I Had a Paka: Poems in Eleven Languages,* Greenwillow, 1982.
Pomerantz, *All Asleep,* Greenwillow, 1984.

NANCY TAFURI

Crescent Dragonwagon, *Coconut,* Harper, 1984.

Helen V. Griffith, *Nata,* Greenwillow, 1985.

Ginsburg, *Four Brave Sailors,* Greenwillow, 1987.

Pomerantz, *Flap Your Wings and Try,* Greenwillow, 1989.

Ginsburg, *Asleep, Asleep,* Greenwillow, 1992.

Patricia Lillie, *Everything Has a Place,* Greenwillow, 1993.

Tafuri's work has also appeared in *Children's Book Illustration and Design,* edited by Julie Cummins; *Literature and the Child,* 2nd edition, by Bernice E. Cullinan; and *1990 Children's Writers and Illustrators Market.*

■ Sidelights

Nancy Tafuri has been illustrating books for very young children since the late 1970s. Whether providing pictures for other authors, such as Charlotte Pomerantz and Mirra Ginsburg, or creating her own works, she is praised by critics for her simple and uncluttered yet imaginative art. *If I Had a Paka: Poems in Eleven Languages,* which Tafuri illustrated for Pomerantz, was selected as a Jane Addams honor book; Tafuri's own *Have You Seen My Duckling?* was runner up for the prestigious Caldecott Medal.

Tafuri was born Nancy Haase on November 14, 1946, in Brooklyn, New York. For the first ten years of her life she was an only child and, as she once related, "I learned to enjoy my own company—coloring in my books, trying earnestly never to go out of the lines or break a crayon. Painting was fun, too, and mother would always set me up with whatever I needed for long hours of enjoyment." Tafuri noted in her *Something about the Author Autobiography Series* (*SAAS*) entry that when she discovered the possibility of studying children's book illustration, "just the thought of having a major that would deal in creating books for young children was overwhelmingly exciting."

Tafuri entered the School of Visual Arts in New York City in 1964. Although the commute was long, "just to enter the school with its smell of oil, paint, and turpentine lingering through the halls made it worth all the travel. I thrived in the environment." She followed a course of studies in journalistic design, which included classes in graphic design, type, book design, magazine illustration, and children's book illustration. Though the last class caught her interest, she concentrated more on her other studies in order to make a living. Her first job was as an assistant art director for the publishing firm Simon & Schuster, which she began upon graduating from the School of Visual Arts in 1967. Two years later, however, she left this post to marry Thomas Tafuri, a fellow student whom she had met during her years of study.

Together the Tafuris opened their own graphic design studio, One Plus One, in 1971. Their primary product was dustjackets for hardcover books. Though the Tafuris began this enterprise in New York City, they eventually gained enough of a reputation to move their studio to their home in Roxbury, Connecticut. "The time had come when I could devote my energies to just illustration," the artist recounted in *SAAS.* "But the illustration I found myself doing wasn't really what I had seen being published. I adored shapes—big, round, inviting shapes ... which I felt would be perfect for the very young. But in the late seventies the youngest reader was not a priority." Nevertheless, Tafuri worked on a portfolio of children's illustrations, taking them around to various publishing houses. "But at first," she revealed in *Horn Book,* "publishers felt my images were too graphic, and I got a lot of rejections. Now, when I read my early work, I realize that it wasn't half as good as I thought it was then. I was still learning a craft, the process of putting a book together, but I was determined to make things work."

Illustration Assignment Leads to Publishing Success

Tafuri's first assignment for Greenwillow Books, *The Piney Woods Peddler* by George Shannon, was to be the turning point in her career. "I knew this was going to be a tough one," she related in her *SAAS* entry, adding that "my experience with the human figure wasn't the strongest ... but I had to take it, I had to try." When the artist saw her husband coming out of one of the rooms in an old mill the couple had just rented, she was inspired. "It was exhilarating for me to be working on a book that I could be putting my real design feelings into.

Tafuri's farm in Roxbury, Connecticut, provided the inspiration for this picture book about break-of-day barnyard activities. (Illustration by the author from *Early Morning in the Barn.*)

Have you
seen my
duckling?

This near-wordless picturebook, which follows a mother duck's search for her stray baby, earned Tafuri a Caldecott Honor citation. (Illustration by the author from *Have You Seen My Duckling?*)

Even if it didn't get accepted, I would still know the feeling of trying to make it work." Tafuri's illustrations for the Shannon book were approved, leading to a contract with Greenwillow where she illustrated Charlotte Zolotow's *The Song* and Charlotte Pomerantz's *If I Had a Paka;* then she published her own *All Year Long* with that firm in 1983.

Tafuri's next two self-illustrated creations came about from ideas she got living on her farm in Roxbury. *Early Morning in the Barn* was inspired by the change of scenery from her former home in New York; her Caldecott Honor Book *Have You Seen My Duckling?* stems from a more specific incident. "We have a pond on our property," Tafuri explained in *Horn Book.* "Tom and I went down to look at it one day, and there was a mallard mother and her ducklings. Tom said, 'A story about them would make a great book.' *Have You Seen My Duckling?* came the most easily to me of all my books and was the most pleasurable to work on." Wordless except for the repeated question of the title,

Have You Seen My Duckling? shows a mother duck searching for her stray baby. A *Parents' Choice* reviewer calls the illustrations "beautifully precise yet emotionally affecting," while a *Horn Book* contributor terms the book "as fresh as spring—a delightful variation on a familiar theme." The book was awarded a Caldecott Honor citation in 1985.

Tafuri has also received critical acclaim for her work for other authors. Of her illustrations for Mirra Ginsburg's *Four Brave Sailors,* Donnarae MacCann and Olga Richard asserted in the *Wilson Library Bulletin:* "Tafuri's spacious designs mark *her* as an audacious explorer. Empty space is a challenge in the visual arts. There is a compulsion to fill it, to clutter it, to get rid of what is considered a void . . . . This style leans toward minimalist art. But that does not make it less dynamic, especially since . . . Tafuri has a gift for characterization."

Tafuri revealed in *SAAS* that "part of me still reacts the same every time I sit down at the drawing board to start a new book. It's that exuberance which comes over me, making every book just like the first one." She continued: "Working on children's books, whether totally my own or another author's, has always been one of life's joys for me ... being able to take short lines of text or, in most cases, none at all and turn them into a package that can be held by small hands." Tafuri's pleasure in creating books for the very young was enhanced when she and her husband had their first child in 1991. "I feel that what I'm doing is more important," she explained; "what I'm trying to say means more.... I feel honored to be creating literature for young children. Seeing how very important these early years are in a person's life, I can only hope that my books can contribute in some small way to that growth, with the feelings that I so hope I project within those pages, through line, color, shape, and story."

■ Works Cited

Review of *Have You Seen My Duckling?, Horn Book,* April, 1984.
Review of *Have You Seen My Duckling?, Parents' Choice,* spring, 1988.
MacCann, Donnarae, and Olga Richard, "Picture Books for Children," *Wilson Library Bulletin,* February, 1988, p. 77.
Tafuri, Nancy, "The Artist at Work: Books for the Very Young," *Horn Book,* November/December, 1989, pp. 732-735.
Tafuri, Nancy, entry for *Something about the Author Autobiography Series,* Volume 14, Gale, 1992, pp. 279-293.

■ For More Information See

PERIODICALS

Bulletin of the Center for Children's Books, June, 1987; February, 1988.
Chicago Tribune, May 5, 1985.
Horn Book, April, 1984.
Junior Literary Guild, March, 1984.
Parents' Choice, Spring, 1988.

*   *   *

TALIFERO, Gerald 1950-
(Stormcrow)

■ Personal

Born January 7, 1950, in Detroit, MI; son of Robert and Betty (maiden name, Lewis) Talifero. *Education:* Attended Santa Barbara City College, 1986-92. *Hobbies and other interests:* Sailing, scuba diving, chess, tennis, biking, mountain climbing.

■ Addresses

Home—133 East De La Guerra, Suite 237, Santa Barbara, CA 93101. *Office*—c/o Publicity Director, Carolrhoda Books, Inc., 241 1st Ave. North, Minneapolis, MN 55401.

GERALD TALIFERO

■ Career

Artist. Deja Vu Studios of Graphic Arts, Santa Barbara, CA, founder, director, and designer; Santa Barbara City College, Santa Barbara, graphic artist; Ravenwood Studios, Santa Barbara, founder and owner, developer of the Challenge Program. Works variously as teacher, designer, and consultant in the field of art and as a musician. Founder, organizer and counselor of the Sudden School and the Rainy Mountain Foundation. Santa Barbara Arts Council, director, 1989.

■ Illustrator

Carol Saller, *The Bridge Dancers,* Carolrhoda Books, 1991.
Student Voices, Santa Barbara City College, 1992.
The Ravenwood Collection (five volumes), Ravenwood, 1992.

Also illustrator of *Dark Summer Tears* (poetry with pen and ink drawings); designer and illustrator of greeting cards and clothing.

■ Work in Progress

A five volume edition of lithographic books encompassing a twenty-two year span of pencil drawing, for Ravenwood Press.

■ Sidelights

Gerald Talifero is a multi-media artist whose work demonstrates his skill with watercolors, pencil, and ink, as well as his ability to render both real and surreal characters and scenes. In addition to his art work, he is actively involved in creating positive outlets for troubled and disadvantaged children by establishing, organizing, and participating in programs that teach children about themselves. Participating children have been exposed to sailing, scuba diving, mountain climbing, wilderness exploration, archery, and kung fu. In an interview with *Ventura County and Coast Reporter* writer Elizabeth A. Thompson, Talifero explains that these programs help children "explore and develop their inner resources by outwardly coming in contact with nature."

■ Works Cited

Talifero, Gerald, in an interview with Elizabeth A. Thompson, "His Name is Stormcrow," *Ventura County and Coast Reporter,* April 17, 1986, pp. 4, 24.

*   *   *

TALLIS, ROBYN
See ZAMBRENO, Mary Frances

*   *   *

TAN, Amy 1952-

■ Personal

Born February 19, 1952, in Oakland, CA; daughter of John (a minister and electrical engineer) and Daisy (a vocational nurse; maiden name, Tu Ching) Tan; married Lou DeMattei (a tax attorney), 1974. *Education:* San Jose State University, B.A., 1973, M.A., 1974; postgraduate study at the University of California, Berkeley, 1974-76. *Hobbies and other interests:* Billiards, skiing, drawing, piano playing.

■ Addresses

Home—San Francisco, CA. *Office*—Sandra Dijkstra, 1155 Camino del Mar, Del Mar, CA 92014.

■ Career

Writer. Worked as a language consultant to programs for disabled children, 1976-81; worked as a reporter, a managing editor, and an associate publisher for *Emergency Room Reports* (now *Emergency Medicine Reports*), 1981-83; free-lance technical writer, 1983-87.

■ Awards, Honors

Commonwealth Club gold award for fiction, Bay Area Book Reviewers award for best fiction, American Library Association's best book for young adults citation, National Book Critics Circle award nomination for best novel, and *Los Angeles Times* book award nomination, all 1989, all for *The Joy Luck Club;* editor's choice citation, *Booklist,* 1991, and Bay Area Book Reviewers award nomination, both for *The Kitchen God's Wife.*

■ Writings

FOR CHILDREN

The Moon Lady (picture book), illustrated by Gretchen Schields, Macmillan, 1992.
The Chinese Siamese Cat, illustrated by Schields, Macmillan, in press.

OTHER

The Joy Luck Club (novel), Putnam, 1989.
The Kitchen God's Wife (novel), Putnam, 1991.
(With Ronald Bass) *The Joy Luck Club* (screenplay), Buena Vista, 1993.
The Year of No Flood (novel), Putnam, in press.

Also author of short stories, including "The Rules of the Game." Work represented in *State of the Language,* edited by Christopher Ricks and Leonard Michaels, second edition, University of California Press, 1989, and *Best American Essays, 1991,* edited by Joyce Carol Oates, Ticknor & Fields, 1991. Contributor to periodicals, including *Atlantic Monthly, McCalls, Threepenny Review,* and *Seventeen. The Joy Luck Club* was released on audiocassette by Dove, as was *The Kitchen God's Wife,* 1991.

AMY TAN

Ying-ying hopes to win a secret wish from Lady Chang-o during the Moon Festival in Tan's first children's book. (Cover illustration by Gretchen Schields.)

■ Sidelights

Amy Tan is the critically respected author of two best-selling novels for adults, *The Joy Luck Club* and *The Kitchen God's Wife*. Her third book, *The Moon Lady,* is based on a story Tan originally recounted in her first novel but which she has rewritten for children. In *The Moon Lady,* three fidgety young girls listen to their grandmother as she tells the story of her earliest memory, the Moon Festival that took place when she was seven years old. Celebrating the festival with her family, Ying-ying hopes that the Moon Lady, a character in the shadow theater, will grant her a secret wish. In the evening, Ying-ying is separated from her family and, as she wanders, she watches women cooking eels and accidentally falls into a lake. Back on shore after a fisherman saves her, Ying-ying's wish is granted: she is reunited with her family. Tan relates the beginning and ending of *The Moon Lady* in the grandmother's voice but shifts to Ying-ying's viewpoint to describe the young girl's memory of the Moon Festival. A *Publishers Weekly* contributor wrote of *The Moon Lady:* "Tan has done a superb job of distilling this incident for young readers, who will be ... mesmerized by the expressive narrative." "The Chinese setting comes vibrantly to life in Tan's warm narration, rich in detail and in saga-cious—but unobtrusive—observations," noted a *Kirkus Reviews* critic. And John Philbrook, writing in the

School Library Journal, called *The Moon Lady* "a successful collaboration of compelling text and absorbing illustrations that will make young readers crave more."

■ Works Cited

Review of *The Moon Lady, Kirkus Reviews,* September 1, 1992, p. 1135.
Review of *The Moon Lady, Publishers Weekly,* July 20, 1992, pp. 249-50.
Philbrook, John, review of *The Moon Lady, School Library Journal,* September, 1992, p. 255.

■ For More Information See

BOOKS

Bestsellers 89, Issue 3, Gale, 1989, pp. 69-71.
Contemporary Literary Criticism, Volume 59, Gale, 1990, pp. 89-99.

PERIODICALS

Chicago Tribune, August 6, 1989; March 17, 1991.
Detroit News, March 26, 1989, p. 2D.
Globe and Mail (Toronto), April 29, 1989; June 29, 1991, p. C8.
Los Angeles Times, March 12, 1989.
Los Angeles Times Book Review, March 12, 1989, p. 1.
New Statesman and Society, July 12, 1991, pp. 37-38.
Newsweek, April 17, 1989, pp. 68-69; June 24, 1991.
New York, March 20, 1989, p. 82; June 17, 1991, p. 83.
New York Times, July 5, 1989.
New York Times Book Review, March 19, 1989, pp. 3, 28; June 16, 1991, p. 9.
People, April 10, 1989, pp. 149-50.
Publishers Weekly, July 7, 1989, pp. 24-26; April 5, 1991, pp. 4-7.
Time, March 27, 1989, p. 98; June 3, 1991, p. 67.
Times (London), July 11, 1991, p. 16.
Tribune Books (Chicago), March 12, 1989, p. 1.
Washington Post, October 8, 1989.
Washington Post Book World, March 5, 1989, p. 7; June 16, 1991, pp. 1-2.*

*   *   *

TARLOW, Nora
See COHEN, Nora

*   *   *

TESSENDORF, K(enneth) C(harles) 1925-

■ Personal

Born August 18, 1925, in Neenah, WI; son of George A. (a factory worker) and Emma A. (a homemaker; maiden name, Christiansen) Tessendorf; married Marie Luise Schwender (a travel agent), January 6, 1968. *Education:* University of Wisconsin, B.S., 1950. *Politics:* Independent. *Religion:* Christian. *Hobbies and other interests:* World travel, reading.

■ Addresses

Home—500 Roosevelt Blvd. #612, Falls Church, VA 22044.

■ Career

United States Air Force, various locations, personnel clerk, 1943-46 and 1950-51; American Airlines, St. Louis, MO, reservationist, 1951-52; U.S. State Department, various locations, diplomatic courier, 1952-54; Enzor Travel Service, Arlington, VA, travel counselor and agent, 1955-85; writer.

■ Writings

Look Out! Here Comes the Stanley Steamer (Junior Literary Guild selection), illustrated by Gloria Kamen, Atheneum, 1984.
Kill the Tzar! Youth and Terrorism in Old Russia, Atheneum, 1986.
Uncle Sam in Nicaragua: A History, Atheneum, 1987.
Barnstormers and Daredevils (Junior Literary Guild selection), Atheneum, 1988.
Along the Road to Soweto, Atheneum, 1989.
Wings around the World: The American Flight of 1924, Atheneum, 1991.

Contributor to periodicals, including *Smithsonian, Airline Pilot,* and *MD.*

■ Work in Progress

An aviation history.

■ Sidelights

K. C. Tessendorf told *SATA:* "I come out of Neenah, a well kept paper-mill town in the pleasant Fox River

K. C. TESSENDORF

Valley of Wisconsin. Callow youth and public policy coincided to offer me an unexpected university education via World War II's G.I. Bill. My English instructors thought I showed modest promise, but I paid them no mind. My eye was on the wide world, and in the public weal I got my ticket punched as a professional globetrotter. Thereafter, as a career, I continued my affiliation and participation in world travel by marketing it to consumers.

"Most of the latter career occurred adjacent to Washington, DC, a repository of federal libraries including the greatest—the Library of Congress. My several years of salaried global wanderings afforded me a new matriculation in world pageantry. A great historical curiosity awakened. How had it all come to be? As an avocation I began delving into, then became captivated by, the mind-expanding resources available in the Library of Congress. You could find out about *anything* in infinite detail there. Then I evolved toward: 'Gee, this is *good stuff!* I want to tell others about it.' Enthusiasm!

"I'm empirically eclectic and productive in lee of the editorial maxim: 'A good nonfiction writer should be able to follow the latest scholarship in any field of human knowledge, and fill in the abstractions of scholarship for the benefit of the general reader by means of good, concrete, sensory reporting.' That's how I've been able to skip along, enjoying subjects from antique automobiles to Russian terrorism, to U.S. Central American intrigues, to the innocent 1920s era of 'I am a flyer and I am free!,' to racial bondage in South Africa, to the first around-the-world flight, to polar chapters from exploration's last stand."

*　　*　　*

TURNER, Bonnie 1932-

■ Personal

Born Bonnie Thomas, October 31, 1932, in Independence, MO; daughter of Sharon Earl Thomas (a cabinet maker) and Mildred Louise (Harter) Latimer (a homemaker); legally adopted by Orland "Bud" Stodgell and Dorothy Stodgell, 1943; married William R. Bowman, November 22, 1950 (divorced, June 1956); married Thomas W. Turner (a truck rental manager), November 7, 1957; children: (first marriage) James W.; (second marriage) Michael Stephen, Dana LeAnn, Jon Eric, Joseph Patrick. *Hobbies and other interests:* Yoga, metaphysics, parapsychology, self-hypnosis, telepathy, astronomy.

■ Career

Bank bookkeeper, Los Angeles, CA, and Kansas City and Independence, MO, 1950-60; Information Management Corp., Green Bay, WI, microfilm camera operator, 1985-90; writer, 1990—. *Member:* Society of Children's Book Writers and Illustrators, National Writers Club, Green Bay Writers Club, Children's Reading Round Table.

■ Awards, Honors

Several World of Poetry honorable mentions and Golden Poet awards.

■ Writings

The Haunted Igloo, Houghton Mifflin, 1991.

■ Work in Progress

Spirit Lights, a sequel to *The Haunted Igloo;* a sequel to *Spirit Lights;* an adult novel set during the Great Depression; researching the Arctic and Inuit people.

■ Sidelights

Bonnie Turner told *SATA:* "I am concerned about the declining moral values in our society, and the roles the media play in shaping young minds. I want to be a positive influence on children by providing them with wholesome reading material.

"Today, many children are growing up with the attitude that our government owes them a living. Welfare programs help promote the myth of 'I'm disadvantaged and will never amount to anything, so why try?' I believe children should be taught from the earliest grades that they can change their lives by changing the way they think, that negative thoughts draw to them the situations they wish to avoid. I'm convinced that by putting good ideas and images into children's minds through the books they read before middle school, they'll have solid foundations upon which to build.

"Since researching the Arctic, I've become sympathetic to the plight of the Inuits (Eskimos), whose culture—surviving many thousands of years—is fast going the way of 'civilization.' I have often thought that if modern families were suddenly forced to live in the close confines of igloos, they would, by necessity, learn to live

BONNIE TURNER

peacefully with each other. Over the centuries, the Inuits discovered that humans must live in harmony with nature in order to survive; modern man seems to fight life all the way. My philosophy of life is: 'What the mind of man can see and believe, can be achieved' (Napoleon Hill). And, 'Like always attracts like in the realm of mind' (Harold Sherman)."

U–V

UNGER, Harlow G. 1931-

◼ Personal

Born August 3, 1931, in New York, NY; son of Lester J. (a physician) and Beatrice (Raphael) Unger; children: Richard C. *Education:* Yale University, B.A., 1953; California State University, M.A., 1991. *Hobbies and other interests:* Skiing, horseback riding, reading.

◼ Addresses

Home—Teton Village, WY. *Office*—c/o Facts on File Publications, 460 Park Ave. S., New York, NY 10016.

◼ Career

New York Herald Tribune Overseas News Service, Paris, France, editor, 1956-60; free-lance journalist, 1960—; Canadian Broadcasting Corporation, radio commentator, New York City, 1964-80; *Times* and *Sunday Times* (based in London), New York City, U.S. correspondent, 1966-72. Briarcliff College, Briarcliff, NY, associate professor of journalism and chair of department, 1975-77; Sarah Lawrence College, Bronxville, NY, director of journalism certificate program, 1976-77. Sponsors for Educational Opportunity, vice president, 1965-75; Yale Class of 1953 Bequest and Endowment Program, chair, 1985—. *Member:* Yale Club of New York City.

◼ Writings

A Student's Guide to College Admissions: Everything Your Guidance Counselor Has No Time to Tell You, Facts on File, 1986, revised edition, 1990.
"What Did You Learn in School Today?" A Parent's Guide for Evaluating Your Child's School, Facts on File, 1991.
But What if I Don't Want to Go to College? A Guide to Successful Careers through Alternative Education, Facts on File, 1992.
How to Pick a Perfect Private School, Facts on File, 1993.

Contributor of numerous articles to periodicals.

◼ Work in Progress

History of American Education; The Encyclopedia of American Education.

◼ Sidelights

Harlow G. Unger told *SATA:* "I spent thirty exciting years as a journalist covering stories for magazines and newspapers around the world. I've seen the world (or at least most of it), written about the beautiful and the horrible, the interesting and the dull. Most of what I've written—and indeed what every journalist writes—seems important at the time, but is actually unimportant and gets tossed away or used to light fires or wrap fish. But a few of the stories I and other journalists have covered and written about are significant chunks of history that eventually get condensed into a chapter or a page or paragraph or perhaps just a line in the history books. And that's what has made journalism so exciting a career for me: the witnessing, describing, and interpreting of current and ultimately historic events, seeing and trying to understand how our world functions and why.

"One important aspect of that world that I have yet to understand, however, is the human animal's treatment of its young. No other animal sends its children to die by the millions in war the way we do. No other animal reproduces in so uncontrollable a fashion as to threaten the supply of natural resources on which the young (and indeed the entire population) must feed to survive. And no other animal routinely, almost purposefully ill-prepares its young for adulthood—as we here in the United States do by failing, even refusing, to give our children the kind of education and preparation for adult life that we can easily afford.

"According to the U.S. Department of Education, ninety percent of thirteen-year-olds in U.S. public schools are 'not adept at reading and are unable to understand complex information,' and more than twen-

HARLOW G. UNGER

ty-five percent of all students who graduate from high school are too illiterate to hold a job. Our public high schools have actually dumped forty-two percent of the kids they're supposed to educate—fifty-two million kids in all—into a kind of educational program called 'general studies,' which every educator in the country admits is an educational garbage can. One college president called general studies an 'academic and vocational desert [that] relates to nothing, leads to nothing and prepares for nothing.' It doesn't teach kids academic skills or a trade in which to earn a living. No wonder two-thirds of the kids in general studies drop out, and more than one-third of those dropouts never get a job. Those who do find work earn an average of less than six thousand dollars a year the rest of their lives.

"That's more than just a raw deal. That's criminal on the part of the schools—which is why I veered away from journalism about ten years ago and decided to start writing books for kids and their parents. I had worked as a volunteer counselor with economically deprived kids in New York City and was getting pretty angry about the bad education and bad advice the schools and guidance counselors were giving a lot of kids. And when my son came home from school one day having been told by his guidance counselor that he was not qualified to apply to an Ivy League college, I blew my top!

"I told him to ignore his guidance counselor and that we would handle the college admissions process ourselves:

schedule all the campus visits and personal interviews, deal with admissions offices directly, and do all the paperwork. Well, guess what? He was admitted to Yale and Brown, both of them top Ivy League colleges for which the guidance counselor had emphatically said my son was not qualified. My son now has a bachelor of arts degree from Yale.

Son's Experience Inspires First Book

"After his letters of admission arrived, all his friends at school were amazed and realized that had they not listened to that same guidance counselor, they might have been admitted to the Ivy League. Unfortunately, they didn't even send in any applications. That's why my son urged me to write my first book, *A Student's Guide to College Admissions: Everything Your Guidance Counselor Has No Time to Tell You.* My son said a lot of great kids were getting bad advice. He said they would love the book—and they have. The first edition went through four printings, and now it's in its second edition.

"In addition to not getting into the best possible colleges, millions of American kids aren't learning to read, write, and calculate adequately. Just as many guidance counselors aren't giving kids proper advice, a lot of teachers aren't giving students the proper courses to study. The trouble is most parents are not professional educators and have no way of knowing whether a local public school is good or not. And that's why I wrote *'What Did You Learn in School Today?' A Parent's Guide for Evaluating Your Child's School.* It gives parents checklists to determine whether the school and each of its teachers are any good. It also gives a complete sample 'course catalogue' listing and describing exactly what every child should be learning in every course, from kindergarten through twelfth grade.

"My next book was the result of research into colleges that uncovered the shocking fact that fifty percent of the kids who go to college drop out without graduating. That's an astonishing total of more than 750,000 students a year! I wondered, why did they ever go to college in the first place? Well, it turns out those guidance counselors—and a lot of misinformed parents—had told most of those kids that they couldn't get a good job without a college degree. What nonsense! The fact is that only twenty-three percent of all jobs in the United States require college degrees and that only three of the twenty fastest growing occupations, according the U.S. Department of Labor, require college degrees. By the year 2000, there will be fourteen million new jobs—three million in the hospitality industry, one million in construction, 850,000 in health care, and 750,000 in computer service and repair. Jobs for college professors, on the other hand, will shrink by four percent.

"So college is only one way to a good job. 'Alternative education' offers a dozen other ways to succeed, which is why I wrote *But What if I Don't Want to Go to College? A Guide to Successful Careers through Alternative Education.* An awful lot of young people don't belong in college, don't want to be there, and don't even have to be there to succeed as adults. But the adults who should be giving them good advice and preparing them for successful adult lives aren't doing their job properly. As I said before, a lot of kids are getting a raw deal, and I hope my books keep a few of them from getting hurt too badly."

* * *

VanCLEAVE, Janice 1942-

■ Personal

Born January 27, 1942, in Houston, TX; daughter of Raymond Eugene (a truck driver) and Frankie (a beautician; maiden name, Clowers) Pratt; married Wade Russell VanCleave (a postal carrier), August 29, 1959; children: Rajene Dianne, Russell Eugene, David Wade. *Education:* University of Houston, B.S., 1962; Stephen F. Austin State University, M.S., 1978. *Religion:* Southern Baptist.

■ Addresses

Home—Otto, TX. *Office*—c/o John Wiley & Sons, Inc., 605 Third Ave., New York, NY 10158-0012.

■ Career

Public school science teacher, 1966-91; writer, 1984—. Leader of science workshops for teachers and students. Bible study instructor.

■ Awards, Honors

Phi Delta Kappa Outstanding Teacher Award, 1983; Friend of Education Award, Beta Nu chapter of Delta Kappa Gamma Society International.

■ Writings

Teaching the Fun of Physics, Prentice-Hall, 1987.

"JANICE VanCLEAVE'S SCIENCE FOR EVERY KID" SERIES

Astronomy, Wiley, 1989.
Biology, Wiley, 1990.
Chemistry, Wiley, 1991.
Earth Science, Wiley, 1991.
Math, Wiley, 1991.
Physics, Wiley, 1991.
Geography, Wiley, 1993.
Microscopes, Wiley, 1993.

"JANICE VanCLEAVE'S SPECTACULAR SCIENCE FAIR PROJECTS" SERIES

Animals, Wiley, 1992.
Gravity, Wiley, 1992.
Molecules, Wiley, 1992.
Magnets, Wiley, 1993.
Earthquakes, Wiley, 1993.
Machines, Wiley, 1993.

"THE BEST OF JANICE VanCLEAVE" SERIES

200 Gooey, Slippery, Slimy, Weird and Fun Experiments, Wiley, 1993.

"A+ PROJECT" SERIES

A+ Biology, Wiley, 1993.
A+ Chemistry, Wiley, 1993.

■ Work in Progress

Dinosaurs, Volcanoes, and *More Math* for "Janice VanCleave's Science for Every Kid" series; *Electricity* for "Janice VanCleave's Spectacular Science Fair Projects" series; *Awesome Experiments* and *Elementary Science Encyclopedia* for "The Best of Janice Van-Cleave" series; a new series of preschool science experiment books.

■ Sidelights

Janice VanCleave told *SATA:* "I was born in Houston, Texas, and spent most of my childhood in the Houston area. We lived ten miles from downtown Houston and there were many trees and few people. It was a real adventure to go to 'town.' One of my fondest memories as a child was getting dressed up and riding the bus to town and shopping with my grandmother. She always let

JANICE VanCLEAVE

me buy one toy for myself and the one I remember the most was a wind-up car. Like most of the things I got my hands on, the car was taken apart to see what made it work, much to the chagrin of my mother. My curiosity did not stop at mechanical things and my insatiable appetite for reading only whetted my desire to discover things for myself. One of many memorable events in my home resulted from my usual negligence of cleaning up after completing a project. My mother, who had little curiosity about the scientific world around her, was most surprised—but not pleasantly—when she discovered some forgotten frogs in the vegetable bin of the refrigerator. I had wanted to see for myself if frogs really would hibernate when chilled. They did—until my mom screamed and threw them out. Another memorable moment resulted from my performing chemistry experiments in my bedroom. Mom did not buy the story that my bed was sitting in the middle of the room because I was trying a new decorating idea. Actually I had spilled acid on the carpet and moved the bed to cover up the problem. I learned how not to perform chemistry experiments, which was a valuable lesson since my interest in science led me to a career of teaching science.

"My mother started me in a private church school when I was five years old and during high school I attended summer school which allowed me to graduate at the age of sixteen. I was too young to get a good job, so I entered college. I majored in science with the desire to become a medical laboratory technician. A year later I married and dropped out of college to become a homemaker. At twenty and the mother of three children, I returned to college and changed my major to science education. It was a good choice for me and I taught for twenty-six years.

"I was never content with the curriculum in the text books and constantly searched for ideas to make each topic presented more fun. Experiments that required around-the-house supplies were especially coveted. These experiments took the science concept out of the formal laboratory setting and put them on a plane of being part of one's everyday life. Over the years I collected hundreds of ideas which I modified and adapted for use in the different science courses I taught.

"My family has been very transient during my twenty-six years of teaching. Our frequent moves provided me with the opportunity to teach every science course offered in grades six through twelve at a multitude of schools in several states and one foreign country (Germany). I was rarely given the advanced science classes, so I have appreciation for the problems in motivating those 'just try to teach me anything' students. In retrospect, it is this group that I used as a measuring instrument to determine if an experiment was fun and interesting. In seeking ways to provide more laboratory experiences for my students in classroom settings that too often had little or no formal laboratory equipment and few supplies, I started writing my own activities. Learning takes place when students are involved in discovering the solution to a problem, and to provide

my students with these learning experiences I designed experiments that every child could successfully perform. I had to use available supplies and these came from my home or a local store. This turned out to be a very positive factor because it allowed the children to repeat the experiments at home with parental supervision. This provided great public relations with parents and my students had fun while learning.

Series Based on Popular Classroom Activities

"I do not necessarily recommend my nomadic lifestyle, but it resulted in my gaining a broad science background that I can now share with students and teachers. My students eagerly performed the simple, safe, fun science experiments that I designed, and with their help each hands-on activity has improved, resulting in 'sure fire' workable activities. Part of this collection of pretested experiments has been printed in three separate series called *Janice VanCleave's Science for Every Kid, Janice VanCleave's Spectacular Science Fair Projects,* and *The Best of Janice VanCleave.*

"Like most people, I thought my ideas were worthy of being published but never took the time to organize them and submit a manuscript. I was teaching science at Southside High School in Ft. Smith, Arkansas, when Westark, a local community college, asked me to design and teach an after-school enrichment class for fourth-through sixth-graders. It was this college's catalog description of the children's course called 'The Magic of Science' that caught the eye of a New York publishing company and started my writing career. The publishing company contacted me and asked if I would like to write a children's experiment book. The result was my first book, *Teaching the Fun of Physics.*

"That first book was fun and frustrating. I was asked to only use around-the-house supplies: no glass tubing, no test tubes, and only chemicals that could be purchased at the grocery store. This presented a challenge that changed my home into a laboratory where I ate and slept. Every flat surface had experiments in some stage of development. My family was skeptical about eating things in the refrigerator since one of my projects was a printing gel made from gelatin and antifreeze. Mold growth on bread and fruit was encouraged and the house had an ample supply of fruit flies. I cannot say that these strange living conditions have changed much; in fact, if anything my home has acquired a more bizarre appearance. What would be considered an eccentric lifestyle for some is accepted as normal for a 'science writer.' Friends seem disappointed if they visit me after one of my rare housecleaning sprees and do not find strange bubbling and, of course, cobwebs.

"I am now a full-time science writer and work on many experiments at a time. It is a career that I find most satisfying. It is fun for me to read and test various ways of performing an experiment. It doesn't sound like much has changed in my life since I started testing and experimenting as a child. One major difference is that my husband does not scream when he finds frogs or

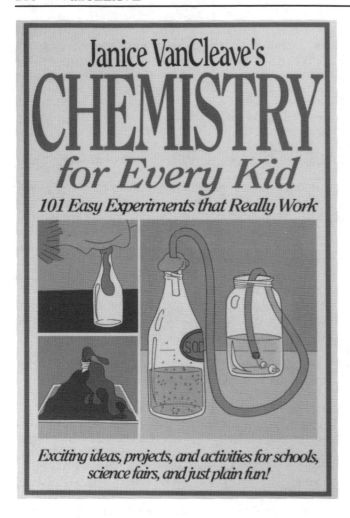

With this collection of exciting science experiments, VanCleave shows kids how to turn their house into a home laboratory. (Cover illustration by April Blair Stewart.)

earthworms in the refrigerator. He is careful not to wash coffee cups that have been left behind stacks of books. The colorful growths they contain just might be an important experiment that I am working on. My enthusiasm for writing has made me negligent in my housekeeping, but it also gives me excuses for having cobwebs in the corners. Like the forgotten coffee cups, cobwebs are viewed by those brave enough to visit me as possibly being part of an experiment for a book. I must confess that I encourage this idea, especially with my five grandchildren. Living in the country provides a variety of harmless spiders that gladly live inside the house. I am guilty of telling the kids that the spiders are my friends (which they are since they eat unwanted insects), and I call them by name: 'This black fuzzy fellow in the corner is Charlie.' The children's acceptance of Charlie (from a distance) allows me to teach them more about spiders and the wonders of web building. I never tire of studying a spider as it spins its trail of wispy, silky threads.

"My advice to children is to saturate your mind with as much knowledge as possible. You may or may not see the value now but store it all away for future use. In my youth I could not see the need for reading Shakespeare or learning about when and where to use semicolons. It was difficult at the time to relate any of this to studying science. Little did I know that later as a teacher I would seek literary examples to bring more excitement to my lectures. The frogs added to the witches' boiling cauldron in Shakespeare's play *Macbeth* provided a novel approach to introducing the frog's anatomy and the fact that the skin of some frogs contain hallucinogenic drugs. Read! Study everything! Do not limit yourself by zeroing in on one area of study to the exclusion of others. My interest has always been science, but in order to share this love with others I must be able to communicate, and this is where the language skills that I had little use for as a child now become coveted as an adult.

"My goal as a writer is to provide children young and old with experiments that will make them enthusiastic about learning science. Many of my experiment ideas come from just observing my surroundings. For example, while sitting in an airplane waiting for takeoff, I became fascinated by the designs the airplane propellers made in the air and that I could see through the spinning blades. I anxiously waited until we had landed to study the stationary blades and discover that a black stripe on each propeller created the design. My next thought was, 'How can I duplicate what I have seen in my home laboratory?' I designed paper blades with stripes that could spin around on a pencil point and used it to demonstrate how the planet Saturn can be seen through its moving rings. My point with this is that we too often are not observant enough of the world around us. You do not have to be a 'scientist' to be curious. I think it strange that people fly on airplanes without wondering how this massive weight can become airborne. I hope never to lose my curious nature. It is my desire that through the books that I write I will encourage others to share my love and curiosity of the scientific world around us."

*　　*　　*

VERNEY, John 1913-1993

OBITUARY NOTICE—See index for *SATA* sketch: Born September 30, 1913; died February 2, 1993. Artist and author. Verney was perhaps best known for his World War II text, *Going to the Wars,* a chronicle of his experiences in the British Army. A noted painter in oils and watercolor, Verney also worked with pottery, painted furniture, and created illustrations. Some of his drawings adorned his own books, including the children's story *Friday's Tunnel.* Verney also produced travel books such as *Verney Abroad,* children's literature, and other books on the topic of war. His works include the memoir *A Dinner of Herbs,* the juvenile mystery novels *February's World* and *Seven Sunflower Seeds,* the novels *Every Advantage* and *Fine Day for a Picnic,* and the volume *A John Verney Collection.*

OBITUARIES AND OTHER SOURCES:

BOOKS

The Writers Directory: 1992-1994, St. James Press, 1992.

PERIODICALS

Times (London), February 5, 1993, p. 17.

W

WARNER, J(ohn) F. 1929-

■ Personal

Born July 18, 1929, in Arlington, MA; son of John F. and Catherine (Hallisey) Warner; married Mary Moran, 1952 (divorced, 1972); married Margaret Brink, December 8, 1973; children: (first marriage) Kathleen, Norann, Margaret, Judd. *Education:* Clark University, M.A., 1957. *Hobbies and other interests:* Sailing; music; reading early histories of the U.S.; and following the Pawtucket Red Sox, a baseball farm team of the Boston Red Sox.

■ Addresses

Home and office—60 Bateman Ave., Newport, RI 02840. *Agent*—Andrea Brown, P.O. Box 429, El Granada, CA 94018.

■ Career

Worked as a high school teacher, 1955-62, and as an editor, 1962-75; B & W Associates, founder, 1976—; writer. *Military service:* U.S. Marine Corps, 1952-58, served in the Korean War; became captain. *Member:* International Reading Association, U.S. Marine Corps Reserve Officers Association.

■ Writings

The U.S. Marine Corps, Lerner Publications, 1991.
Rhode Island: A History, Lerner Publications, 1992.
Home Life in Colonial America, F. Watts, 1993.
Kerry Hill Casecrackers (mystery/adventure), Lerner Publications, 1993.

Contributor of stories, plays, and nonfiction to anthologies.

■ Work in Progress

Research on the history of the U.S., especially maritime affairs.

■ Sidelights

J. F. Warner told *SATA:* "I treat writing as I would any job. I try to work regular hours (nine a.m. to four p.m.) and stay at my desk producing whatever comes out of my typewriter, good or bad. Just as in *any* job, writers experience good days and bad days; the point is to give your *best* every day, and in the long run, the good days will outnumber the bad. Waiting around for inspiration never works for me. Sometimes I have to *drag* the ideas out of my mind. Sometimes they are too elusive to capture. We try."

*   *   *

WATERS, Tony 1958-

■ Personal

Born June 24, 1958, in Charleston, SC; son of Charles M. (a contractor) and Ruth (a homemaker; maiden name, Nowell) Waters. *Education:* Furman University, B.A., 1980. *Politics:* Independent. *Religion:* Christian. *Hobbies and other interests:* Portrait and landscape painting, photography, travel, and relaxing at the beach.

■ Addresses

Home—5584 Frisco Lane, Johns Island, SC 29455. *Office*—LS3P Architects, 24 North Market St., Charleston, SC 29401.

■ Career

Seabrook Island Resort Club, Charleston, SC, commercial reservations, 1982-88; LS3P Architects, Charleston, materials-resource librarian, 1988—. *Member:* Charleston Artists Guild, Beaufort Art Association.

■ Writings

(And illustrator) *The Sailor's Bride,* Doubleday, 1991.

■ Work in Progress

Two sequels to *The Sailor's Bride: The Sailor's Flight,* about a balloon trip to the mountains, and *The Sailor's Treasure; The Merlin Medallion,* a novel about magic, mermaids, sea gods, and sea witches; *The Almost Christmas Tree,* a picture book about a fir tree that isn't bought for Christmas, but leads a useful life nevertheless.

■ Sidelights

Tony Waters told *SATA:* "Ever since I could first hold a pencil, I have loved to draw, and through all the years since then, drawing has always given me the greatest pleasure and sense of achievement. Although I never outgrew children's books, it wasn't until college that I decided I wanted to illustrate them."

After graduation, Waters penned his first book, an adolescent novel, which attracted little interest from publishers. Waters didn't let that deter him, though. "After receiving a number of rejections," he recalled, "I decided that if I presented a package of both artwork and story to the publishers, they might show more interest. So I began *The Sailor's Bride* in early 1985, and after a number of unsolicited submittals, I found a publisher, Doubleday, in 1989. I never gave up because I've always felt I have something worthwhile to offer children."

TONY WATERS

The Sailor's Bride describes the efforts of a mouse named Susanna to locate her sailor-husband Whitewhiskers after he disappears at sea. "The subject for *The Sailor's Bride* came from a number of sources," Waters related. "Foremost, in my childhood, my brother and I raised mice. My brother created a whole fantasy world for them—and me—by building the most ornate, tiny homes for them with elaborate beds and settees, tables and chairs. He built boats for them, and we took them to the beach and to the creek by my great-grandmother's house. We gave dinners and picnics and Christmas parties for them; we planted a garden for them, complete with artistic 'ruins' (actually a cracked cinderblock); we painted their portraits in miniature. Truly, it was an imaginary world come to life."

The work of a famous children's author and a boyhood fascination with the sea also influenced Waters, who added: "When I 'discovered' Beatrix Potter—late in life, at age 12—I felt that she had written about my own pets. Also during my childhood, I was always enthralled by sea stories—whalers, pirates, yankee clippers, buried treasure. One day I came across a painting of a sailor marrying a demure girl in the justice of the peace's office; it provided me with the name of my book and the first illustration of my story as well.

"With all this background, I wrote about ... sailing mice! The sailor mice characters are taken from the Mother Goose rhyme 'I Saw a Ship A-Sailing,' about four-and-twenty white mice with a duck for their captain. Also, I wanted the book to show the value of friends and the strength of a determined mind. Susanna didn't know anything about sailing and was even a little afraid, but she knew that it was up to her to find Whitewhiskers.

"For the pictures, I poured in as much detail as possible. I love details! I even used some of the furniture my brother built as models for Susanna's bedroom furniture. Too, I wanted to make the pictures interesting enough so that children would look at the book again and again, and perhaps find something new each time."

*   *   *

WATT-EVANS, Lawrence 1954-

■ Personal

Born July 26, 1954, in Arlington, MA; son of Gordon Goodwin (a professor of chemistry) and Doletha (a secretary; maiden name, Watt) Evans; married Julie Frances McKenna (a chemist), August 30, 1977; children: Kyrith Amanda, Julian Samuel Goodwin. *Education:* Attended Princeton University, 1972-74 and 1975-77. *Hobbies and other interests:* Comic book collecting.

■ Addresses

Agent—Russell Galen, Scoville Chichak Galen, 381 Park Avenue South, 11th Floor, New York, NY 10016.

Career

Purity Save-Mor supermarket, Bedford, MA, sacker, 1971; Griffith Ladder, Bedford, worker, 1973; Arby's, Pittsburgh, PA, counterman and cook, 1974; Student Hoagie Agency, Princeton, NJ, occasional salesman, 1974-76; Mellon Institute of Science, Pittsburgh, bottle washer, 1976; free-lance writer, 1977—. *Member:* Science Fiction and Fantasy Writers of America, Horror Writers of America.

Awards, Honors

Hugo Award from World Science Fiction Society, Nebula Award nomination from Science Fiction Writers of America, and reader's poll award from *Isaac Asimov's Science Fiction Magazine,* all for best short story, all 1988, for "Why I Left Harry's All-Night Hamburgers"; reader's poll award for best short story from *Isaac Asimov's Science Fiction Magazine,* 1990, for "Windwagon Smith and the Martians."

Writings

"THE LORDS OF DUS" SERIES; FANTASY

The Lure of the Basilisk, Del Rey, 1980.
The Seven Altars of Dusarra, Del Rey, 1981.
The Sword of Bheleu, Del Rey, 1983.
The Book of Silence, Del Rey, 1984.

LAWRENCE WATT-EVANS

"WAR SURPLUS" SERIES; SCIENCE FICTION

The Cyborg and the Sorcerers, Del Rey, 1982.
The Wizard and the War Machine, Del Rey, 1987.

"LEGENDS OF ETHSHAR" SERIES; FANTASY

The Misenchanted Sword, Del Rey, 1985.
With a Single Spell, Del Rey, 1987.
The Unwilling Warlord, Del Rey, 1989.
The Blood of a Dragon, Del Rey, 1991.
Taking Flight, Del Rey, 1993.
The Spell of the Black Dagger, Del Rey, 1993.

OTHER

The Chromosomal Code, Avon, 1984.
Shining Steel, Avon, 1986.
Denner's Wreck (Science Fiction Book Club alternate selection), Avon, 1988.
Nightside City, Del Rey, 1989.
The Nightmare People (horror), New American Library, 1990.
(Editor and contributor) *Newer York* (anthology), New American Library, 1990.
The Rebirth of Wonder, Wildside Press, 1992, published with *The Final Folly of Captain Dancy,* Tor, 1992.
Crosstime Traffic (short stories), Del Rey, 1992.
(With Esther Friesner) *Split Heirs* (humorous fantasy), Tor, 1993.
Out of This World (Volume 1 of "Three Worlds" trilogy), Del Rey, 1993.

Author of column "Rayguns, Elves, and Skin-Tight Suits" for *Comics Buyer's Guide,* 1983-87, and of comic book scripts and stories for Marvel Comics and Eclipse Comics. Work represented in anthologies, including *One Hundred Great Fantasy Short Short Stories,* edited by Isaac Asimov, Terry Carr, and Martin H. Greenberg, Doubleday, 1984; and *"Why I Left Harry's All-Night Hamburgers" and Other Stories from Isaac Asimov's Science Fiction Magazine,* edited by Sheila Williams and Charles Ardai, Delacorte, 1990. Contributor of short stories, articles, poems, and reviews to periodicals, including *Amazing,* Louisville *Courier-Journal, Bedford Patriot, Dragon, Late Knocking, Movie Collector's World, Sagebrush Journal, Space Gamer,* and *Starlog.*

Work in Progress

In the Empire of Shadow and *The Brown Magician,* Volumes 2 and 3 of the "Three Worlds" trilogy, for Del Rey.

Sidelights

Lawrence Watt-Evans told *SATA:* "My parents both read science fiction—and lots of other things—so I grew up in a house filled with books and magazines, many of them with bright splashy covers showing spaceships and monsters and people firing rayguns. I loved it all.

"I was bored in school, so I would sneak in books and comic books and read them in class; fortunately, I had tolerant teachers, and as long as I kept up with the classwork they didn't object.

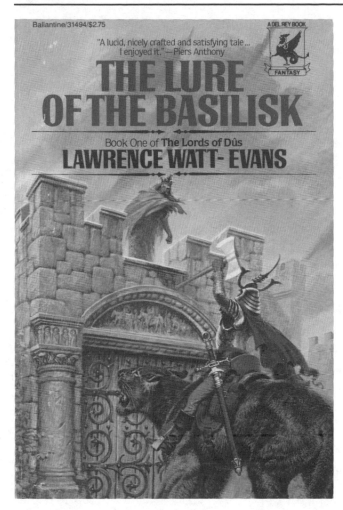

Ballantine/31494/$2.75   A DEL REY BOOK

"A lucid, nicely crafted and satisfying tale...
I enjoyed it." —Piers Anthony

FANTASY

THE LURE OF THE BASILISK

Book One of **The Lords of Dûs**

LAWRENCE WATT-EVANS

Watt-Evans's first novel begins the saga of an adventurer whose quest for fame leads him to become a pawn of the gods. (Cover illustration by Darrell K. Sweet.)

"I wasn't clear on the distinction between children's books and grown-up books (I'm still not always), so at age seven I started borrowing my mother's books as soon as she was done reading them—I figured if she liked them, I would too. So in second grade, while the other kids read 'Dick and Jane,' I read Ray Bradbury, and fell in love with words and stories. And I never got over it."

* * *

WEILERSTEIN, Sadie Rose 1894-1993

OBITUARY NOTICE—See index for *SATA* sketch: Born July 28, 1894, in Rochester, NY; died of a heart attack, June 23, 1993, in Rockville. Educator and author. Creator of the Jewish classic "K'tonton" series, Weilerstein won many honors for her contributions to children's literature, including the Jewish Book Council of America Award in 1956 and the National Women's League of the United Synagogue of America Yovel Award in 1968. A teacher for the deaf for three years after her graduation from the University of Rochester in 1917, Weilerstein began writing when her own children

were young. Responding to a need for books that would acquaint children with Jewish literature and legend, Weilerstein wrote down the stories she told her family, eventually creating the tiny character of K'tonton as a cross between the personalities of her husband and her son. Among Weilerstein's other popular works are *What Danny Did*, a Jewish book for very young readers; *What the Moon Brought*, published in 1942; *The Singing Way*, a book of verse; and *Ten and a Kid*, for which Weilerstein won a second Jewish Book Council of America Award.

OBITUARIES AND OTHER SOURCES:

BOOKS

Who's Who in World Jewry: A Biographical Dictionary of Outstanding Jews, Pitman, 1972, p. 941.

PERIODICALS

Washington Post, June 24, 1993, p. D4.

* * *

WELCH, Amanda (Jane) 1945-

■ Personal

Born May 3, 1945, in Radlett, Hertfordshire, England; daughter of Harvey Sidney (a nurseryman) and Vera Kathleen Jane (More) Frost; married John Hope Welch (a poet and teacher), April 14, 1973; children: Vanessa, Simon, Louise. *Education:* Chelsea School of Art, diploma in art and design, lower second, 1967. *Politics:* "Left of center." *Religion:* "None." *Hobbies and other interests:* Gardening, walking, reading, theatre.

■ Addresses

Home—15 Norcott Rd., Hackney, London N16 7BJ, England.

■ Career

Painter, 1967—; Camberwell School of Art, London, England, part-time art history teacher, 1968-73; Tollington Park School, London, part-time art teacher, 1973-75; free-lance illustrator, 1982—; Jubilee Primary School, part-time art teacher, 1989-92. *Member:* Association of Illustrators.

■ Awards, Honors

Shortlisted for Smarties Prize, 1985, for *The Enchanted Palace.*

■ Illustrator

Susheila Stone, *The Naughty Mouse,* Luzac, 1985.
Manchar Rakhe, *To Heaven and Back,* Luzac, 1985.
Ashim Bhattacharja and Champaka Basu, *The Enchanted Palace,* Luzac, 1985.
Niru Desai, *The Raja's Big Ears,* Luzac, 1986.
Roy Smith, *The Pond That Disappeared,* Nelson, 1988.
Susan Lacy, *Mussarat's Monster,* Methuen, 1988.

AMANDA WELCH

Odette Elliott, *Under Sammy's Bed,* Deutsch, 1989.
Naina Gandhi, *Sari Games,* Deutsch, 1990.
Elliott, *Sammy Goes Flying,* Deutsch, 1990.
Elliott, *Sammy and the Telly,* Deutsch, 1991.
Elliott, *Sammy's Christmas Workshop,* Deutsch, 1992.

Also illustrator of educational books. Contributor to periodicals, including *Cricket.*

■ Sidelights

Amanda Welch told *SATA:* "I am primarily a painter and became an illustrator almost accidently after doing a few unpaid black and white line drawings for some stories published by a local education authority. These were seen and I started getting a little modest work—this has gradually increased from educational work to trade picture books. I do what comes and in between I am a painter and, occasionally, I do workshops in schools.

"Illustrating is a relief from painting because at least you know what you're aiming at even if it doesn't always work out. It provides me with some money, a certain amount of self-esteem (being able to make something that someone else is prepared to pay for), and a considerable amount of pleasure. I enjoy expanding the story—often humorously in a way that is consistent with, but not explicit in, the text.

"I draw from life wherever possible. This has taken me up in a hot air balloon, inside a Sikh temple, into a premature baby unit, my Hindu grocer's living room, the London Zoo, Waterloo Station, etc. I have illustrated stories set in India, Puerto Rico, the United States, and Jamaica, but unfortunately the publishers have not been willing to pay travel expenses, so I've had to do my best with what's available, such as the Kew Gardens for a guava tree.

"People I always draw from life—family, friends, friends of friends, and the slightest acquaintances. I find drawing people immediately gives me something in common with them, so I don't feel shy. Hackney is a good place to live as its people come from all over the world. I also keep a sketch book for idle moments at bus stops, on the beach, etc. These people usually don't know they're being drawn and frequently move or go away so my sketch books are full of rapidly done fragments.

"I would like my finished work to keep more of this spontaneity and to get more atmospheric, but without losing its accurate detail. I hate generalizations. If I draw a table, it doesn't interest me that it has four legs and a top, but only that it's a particular table belonging to particular people."

*   *   *

WELFORD, Sue 1942-
(Fiona Kelly)

■ Personal

Born August 15, 1942, in Brighton, Sussex, England; daughter of Frederick (a police officer) and Stella (a homemaker) Ward; married Mick Welford, March 21, 1964; children: Melissa Jane, Adam Michael. *Education:* Crawley College, 1958-61. *Politics:* "Peace!" *Religion:* "Human beings!" *Hobbies and other interests:* Reading, watching science fiction and American teen movies, gardening, dogs, aerobics, shopping, lazing around in the sun, and getting together with family.

■ Career

Author. Has worked as a newspaper editorial writer.

■ Addresses

Home—Brisley Wood, Ruckinge, Ashford, Kent TN26 2PW, England. *Agent*—Lesley Hadcroft, Laurence Pollinger, 18 Maddox St., Mayfair, London W1R 0EU, England.

■ Writings

Catch the Moon, Macmillan, 1989.
Secrets, Macmillan, 1990.
Charlie in the Pink, Oxford University Press, 1992.
Ghost in the Mirror, Oxford University Press, 1993.

SUE WELFORD

"THE MYSTERY CLUB" SERIES, UNDER PSEUDONYM FIONA KELLY

Mischief at Midnight, Hodder and Stoughton, 1993.

Also author of *You've Got to Have the Heart,* Learning Difficulties Association. Contributor to periodicals, including *Country Living, Farmer's Weekly, Home and Country, Cross Country,* and *Countryman.* Contributor of short story to *Loving.*

Welford's work has been translated into Danish, German, and Dutch.

■ Work in Progress

A Song for Rosie, a novel about teenage pregnancy; *Siren Song,* a fantasy novel about the myth of the sirens, or mermaids; *Sally's Smelly Jumper,* a picture book about a girl's favorite article of clothing; *Charlie on the Spot,* a sequel to *Charlie in the Pink; Hen-rietta's Revenge,* a picture book; *First Patrol,* for Learning Difficulties Association; *Snowbird Winter.*

■ Sidelights

Sue Welford told *SATA:* "I'm probably what would be termed a 'late developer.' I disliked the discipline of school although I adored the social side of school life— being with other people, listening to different experiences and ideas. I'm sure my teachers would remember me more for the pictures of Elvis Presley stuck under my desk-lid than for my academic achievements."

After secondary school, Welford went to college for secretarial training, then unexpectedly landed a job writing editorials for a local newspaper. Spurred on by her success in that position, Welford later returned to college, studying English literature, sociology, and psychology. She also began writing fiction, but "it was another seven or eight years before I had my first novel accepted for publication; thanks to my husband I didn't starve."

Welford's great love is writing science fiction and fantasy, though she has a humorous novel, *Charlie in the Pink,* and a suspense novel, *Ghost in the Mirror,* among her works. Welford has also written books that explore contemporary social issues. In *Secrets,* Welford studies the effects of anorexia nervosa—an eating disorder—on the lives of Leigh, a teenage girl suffering from the disease, and her family. Discussing the novel, Welford stated, "My interest in anorexia stemmed from listening to conversations at my local gym and keep-fit center. I realized how fine the line was between just dieting and obsession. Then a friend's daughter was diagnosed anorexic. I spoke to her, did lots of research at my local hospital library and bingo—*Secrets* was born.

"I wanted particularly to show the effects the disease has upon the whole family, not just the anorectic. This is why I wrote the story from the point of view of Jason, Leigh's brother. The novel has been criticised for its 'neat' solution to Leigh's problem, but I wanted to write a positive novel, a novel of hope. From my research I learned that if the disease is diagnosed and the probable cause discovered within a year then the chances of recovery are great. I wanted readers to know that anorexia can be cured—with the help of the medical profession, the victim's family, and, of course, the victim herself." Welford's work in progress, *A Song for Rosie,* "explores the dilemma facing a pregnant sixteen-year-old—should she or should she not have an abortion. The main theme centers around young adults facing up to their problems and deciding their own destiny."

Welford maintains a busy schedule, balancing her writing, her family, and her many interests: "I'm in the throes of researching the history of my early nineteenth-century country cottage where I live with my husband, Mick, two rather crazy Jack Russell terriers, several hens, and a man-eating cockerel. My main ambition is to continue writing books that kids enjoy. Another ambition is to sell my novels in the United States. This has been a passion of mine ever since I began writing. Other ambitions? Well, like everyone else I suppose— just to be happy!"

WESTALL, Robert (Atkinson) 1929-1993

OBITUARY NOTICE—See index for *SATA* sketch: Born October 7, 1929, in Tynemouth, England; died of respiratory failure brought on by pneumonia, April 15, 1993, in Cheshire, England. Educator and writer. Westall was an award-winning author of children's books whose career spanned almost twenty years. His first work, 1975's *Machine-Gunners*, is a novel about a gang of British teenagers who, during World War II, find an undamaged German machine gun. Though some critics found the book controversial because of its realism in dealing with violence, emotions, sexuality, and family tensions, many others considered it a children's classic. The book won the renowned Carnegie Medal from the Library Association of Great Britain in 1976 and was later used as the basis for a television series. Westall, a teacher and member of the art department at Sir John Deane's College in Northwich for twenty-five years, left the teaching profession in 1985 to become an antiques dealer for a short time, then quit the antiques business to become a full-time writer. After his success with *The Machine-Gunners*, he went on to publish approximately forty books, including *Break of Dark; The Scarecrows,* for which he won the 1982 Carnegie Medal; *Blitzcat; Antique Dust,* a collection of ghost stories; and *The Kingdom by the Sea,* the winner of *Guardian*'s award for children's fiction in 1991. Among Westall's other works are *If Cats Could Fly,* published in 1990; *The Christmas Cat* and *Yaxley's Cat,* both released in 1991; and *Demons and Shadows,* the first of a two-part collection of ghost stories, to be published posthumously by Farrar, Straus and Giroux.

OBITUARIES AND OTHER SOURCES:

BOOKS

The Writers Directory: 1992-1994, St. James Press, 1991, p. 1038.

PERIODICALS

New York Times, April 20, 1993, p. B8.

* * *

WHITTINGTON, Mary K(athrine) 1941-

■ Personal

Born June 21, 1941, in Hollywood, CA; daughter of William (a metallurgist) and Jean Elizabeth (a homemaker; maiden name, Alliger) Whittington. *Education:* University of California, Santa Barbara, B.A., 1968. *Politics:* Democrat. *Hobbies and other interests:* Northwest history, animals, people, photography, recorder playing and early music, doll house miniatures, collecting antique children's books.

■ Addresses

Home and office—12920 North East 78th Place, Kirkland, WA 98033.

MARY K. WHITTINGTON

■ Career

Writer. Self-employed writing instructor, editor, public speaker, and workshop presenter. Piano and recorder instructor. *Member:* Society of Children's Book Writers and Illustrators (vice president and newsletter editor for local Seattle chapter, 1990-91), American Recorder Society, Eastside Writers Association.

■ Awards, Honors

Pacific Northwest Writers Conference finalist, 1981, 1985, and 1986; first prize in fiction category, Ferry Tales Contest, 1987; American Booksellers Association Pick of the Lists, 1991, for *The Patchwork Lady.*

■ Writings

PICTURE BOOKS

Carmina, Come Dance!, illustrated by Michael McDermott, Atheneum, 1989.
Troll Games, illustrated by Betsy Day, Atheneum, 1991.
The Patchwork Lady, illustrated by Jane Dyer, Harcourt, 1991.
Winter's Child, illustrated by Sue Ellen Brown, Atheneum, 1992.

OTHER

Contributor of short stories to anthologies, including *Werewolves,* Harper, 1988; *Northwest Ferry Tales,* Vashon Point Productions, 1989; *Things That Go Bump in the Night,* Harper, 1989; *Vampires,* HarperCollins, 1991; and *Haunted House,* HarperCollins, 1993.

■ Work in Progress

Braid, a fantasy novel; *And the Raven Shall Cry Him,* fantasy novel; various picture books; researching the pioneers of Willamette Valley, the supernatural, and folk and fairy tales.

■ Sidelights

Mary K. Whittington told *SATA:* "It's said there's a gene for writing stories in my mother's side of the family. Her father, whom I didn't meet until I was in my thirties and he was in his nineties, sold everything he submitted. He wrote a lot for the *Christian Science Monitor,* but also to other markets. When I was in my early teens, I remember reading one of his stories in *Jack and Jill.* My mother went to writing classes and wrote stories while my sisters and I were growing up. She came pretty close to selling a couple times. 'Rejection slip' entered my vocabulary early!

"All through my schooling I was expected to become a writer eventually. Recently, I was looking through my ninth grade school annual and discovered I'd 'willed' a copy of my first book to an eighth grader I've long since lost track of. In that same annual is a note from the school principal, asking for 'an autographed copy of your first book of poems—and I mean just that!' At that school, where the girls had to wear Scottish plaid (Campbell) uniforms, I wrote a lot of poetry, submitting with my English teacher's encouragement, a poem entitled, 'Dead Tree,' to a poetry contest sponsored by the Girl Scouts. To my delight, I won an honorable mention, a check for five dollars, and my poem was printed in their magazine, the *American Girl.* My parents were very proud; my father took the letter to work and made multiple copies of it, and showed it to people I didn't even know. How embarrassing! *American Girl* was not sold on magazine stands, so the only way I could obtain a copy was to send for one. The thought of my dad making a copy of my poem and showing that around stopped me cold, so I do not own a copy of my first published writing. Months later, I went to the library, sneaked the issue off the shelf, took it deep into the boring adult nonfiction section, sat on the floor, and privately savored seeing my own poem, my own name in print. I can still recite that poem.

"I spent a lot of time in the library; I was an insatiable reader. My younger sister, Val, used to try to get me to come out and play, but I just wanted to read. 'Bookworm!,' she'd mutter as she walked away in disgust. And mother says people could stand right next to me, talking very loudly, and I'd never hear a thing, I'd be so engrossed in my book. Several times I got in trouble at school for reading a book in my lap instead of doing my assigned work, usually arithmetic. I had no feel for math except fear, frustration and boredom. English and anything to do with reading were my favorite subjects

through high school, but while attending Hollywood High, I discovered biology and field trips. I became fascinated by marine biology in particular. During the summer before my senior year, I worked on a marine biology/geology project at the University of Southern California. Mostly I recorded thousands of numbers representing plankton counts on charts, and washed mud samples through fine screens to separate out the tiny foraminifera. The graduate students called me their mascot, and I learned a great deal about the non-romantic life of a scientist. I loved it. When I started college, I declared a biology major. Big mistake!

"I soon found out I didn't have the right kind of logical, scientific mind to be successful in biology. When it became apparent I would never be able to pass organic chemistry, I decided to change my major. I ended up in sociology. Two years before I graduated, I started working as a learning skills counselor in the Academic Skills Center of the University, tutoring English and writing skills to students. I did that full time for twelve years, learning to play and later teaching recorder playing in my spare time. Also during that time, I gravitated closer and closer to becoming a writer. When I left the university in 1979 to move to the Pacific Northwest, I decided to devote as much time as I could to writing fantasy for children.

"Between 1979 and 1985 I produced two novels which I think of as 'learning novels.' I didn't sell them, but I certainly learned a lot about the writing process while working on them. In the meantime I discovered the rich lode of children's writers who live in the Northwest, and in the summer of 1985, I went to the Port Townsend Writers Conference, attending a workshop taught by Jane Yolen, whose encouragement and support convinced me I was in the right field. Jane was the one who started me off writing picture books. I'd thought I was a

Whittington credits children's author Jane Yolen for giving her the inspiration to write books such as *The Patchwork Lady.* (Illustration by Jane Dyer.)

novelist. But one day I told her in a letter how I used to sit under the piano as a child and listen to my mother playing. 'It's a picture book,' said Jane, and gave me an informal deadline. No way could I pass up the challenge. I researched picture book writing, made a lot of false starts, and at last produced a draft of *Carmina, Come Dance!* It sold the first time out. I dedicated it to Jane.

"When I talk to children in elementary and middle schools, I always encourage them to read constantly if they want to be writers. And if they want to be doctors or engineers or teachers or secretaries, I tell them reading is one of the best ways to learn. But if they do want to be writers, I make sure to tell them how it feels to hold your very own book in your hands for the first time. That makes everything you went through in the years before worth it."

*   *   *

WILSON, Johnniece Marshall 1944-

■ Personal

Born September 25, 1944, in Montgomery, AL; daughter of John Morley Marshall, Jr. and Essie (Campbell) Marshall; children: Karin, Natalie, Tonya. *Education:* College coursework in institutional cooking and bacteriology. *Politics:* Democrat. *Religion:* Protestant. *Hobbies and other interests:* Taking long walks, reading, sketching, listening to music.

■ Addresses

Home—316 East End Ave., #4, Wilkinsburg, PA 15221. *Office*—St. Francis Medical Center, 4401 Penn Ave., Pittsburgh, PA 15201. *Agent*—Linda Allen Agency, 1949 Green, No. 5, San Francisco, CA 94123.

■ Career

Affiliated with St. Francis Medical Center, Pittsburgh, PA, 1988; writer. *Member:* National Writers Club, Society of Children's Book Writers and Illustrators, The Golden Penn.

■ Awards, Honors

Children's Choice Award, 1989, for *Oh, Brother.*

■ Writings

Oh, Brother, Scholastic, 1988.
Rubin on His Own, Scholastic, 1990.
Poor Girl, Rich Girl, Scholastic, 1992.

■ Work in Progress

Black Dog, Howl at the Moon and *The Angry Red Sky.*

JOHNNIECE MARSHALL WILSON

■ Sidelights

Johnniece Marshall Wilson told *SATA:* "I fell in love with books and words at an early age. I grew up in a household without a TV, but we always had lots of books. I've always wanted to be a writer. I wrote my first story at age eight, and read it to my family during storytime. That's how we entertained ourselves—by taking turns telling stories since we didn't have a TV. I was fourteen and a half when we got our first TV, but by then I was already hooked on books.

"Now, when I'm writing, I try to get a good first draft and go back over it, making sure my words say what I want them to say. I write at the same time every day.

"The writers who have influenced me most are Joan Aiken, Robert Newton Peck, and Virginia Hamilton. I also read Toni Morrison, Dean R. Koontz, Perry Mason novels, and Rex Stout.

"My only advice to aspiring young writers is to read everything you get your hands on, and write. Try to get into the habit of writing everyday, preferably at the same time each day so it will become automatic. It's hard, but hang in there!"

WINBORN, Marsha (Lynn) 1947-

■ Personal

Born December 24, 1947, in Dallas, TX, daughter of Claude D. (a physician) and Norma (a homemaker and real estate agent; maiden name, Wells) Winborn. *Education:* Attended Austin College, 1966, and Southern Methodist University, 1967; Art Center College of Design, B.F.A. (with distinction), 1971; University of Santa Monica, M.A., 1991. *Hobbies and other interests:* Hiking and walking, especially on nature trails; creating fun, dimensional cards and mobiles of cut paper; reading and studying subjects on changing and healing consciousness, self-awareness, and creative growth.

■ Addresses

Office—c/o Simon & Schuster, Inc., Simon & Schuster Bldg., 1230 Avenue of the Americas, New York, NY 10020.

■ Career

The Drawing Board, Inc., Dallas, TX, artist/designer, 1972-73; free-lance illustrator, Dallas, 1973-75, and Seattle, WA, 1975; Henri Fayette, Inc., Chicago, IL, artist/designer, 1975; Current, Inc., Colorado Springs, CO, artist/designer, 1976-79; Hallmark Cards Studio, Colorado Springs, 1979-80; free-lance illustrator, Dallas and Colorado Springs, 1980-82, New York City, 1983-87, and Los Angeles, CA, 1987—.

■ Illustrator

Deborah Apy, *Meals from Many Lands,* Current, Inc., 1978.
Apy, *The Birthday Dream,* Current, Inc., 1978.

MARSHA WINBORN

Apy, *Everything's Coming up Vegetables,* Current, Inc., 1979.
Valentine Space Mystery, Hallmark Cards, 1980.
Rose Greydanus, *Let's Pretend,* Troll, 1981.
Michaela Muntean, *I Have a Friend,* Golden Press, 1981.
Robyn Supraner, *Mystery of the Lost Ring,* Troll, 1982.
Joan Lexau, *Come! Sit! Stay!,* Watts, 1984.
Margery Cuyler, *Sir William and the Pumpkin Monster,* Henry Holt, 1984.
Lauren Swindler, *Big Brings Spring to Sesame Street,* Golden Press, 1985.
David Adler, *My Dog and the Knock-Knock Mystery,* Holiday House, 1985.
Rebecca Heller, *Little Red Riding Hood,* Golden Press, 1985.
Cuyler, *Freckles and Willie,* Henry Holt, 1986.
Inside Sesame Street, Golden Press, 1986.
Cuyler, *Fat Santa,* Henry Holt, 1987.
Jocelyn Stevenson, *Burt's New Collection,* Golden Press, 1988.
Barbara Baker, *Digby and Kate,* Dutton, 1988.
Baker, *Digby and Kate Again,* Dutton, 1989.
Benjamin Auster, *I Like It When . . . ,* Raintree Publishers, 1990.
Daniel C. Cutler, *One Hundred Monkeys,* Simon & Schuster, 1991.
Judy Nayer, *If I Could,* Modern Curriculum Press, 1992.

■ Sidelights

Marsha Winborn told *SATA:* "I moved into illustration out of a natural bent and flow toward art and picture making, and out of a natural bent to remain a child (or childlike) for as long as possible. I found myself most happy and rewarded when drawing kids, dogs, animals, bees, flowers—a young child's world! When I began *One Hundred Monkeys,* I said to the five-year-old inside of me, 'Okay, what would you like to do with this?' And as a result, boy, did we have fun. I feel that every monkey in that book is a portrait of *me.* It's a great way to make a living."

*   *   *

WYMAN, Andrea

■ Personal

Born in Indiana; daughter of Everett and Jane (Manship) Foust; married Richard Wyman (a professor); children: Susan Brazer, Drew Rush. *Education:* Westminster College, B.S., 1978; Western Oregon State College, M.S., 1979; University of Wisconsin—Milwaukee, M.L.I.S., 1985; Union Institute, Ph.D., 1992. *Religion:* Quaker. *Hobbies and other activities:* Gardening, weaving, collecting matroyshka dolls.

■ Addresses

Home—Mt. Morris Star Route, Mt. Morris, PA 15349.
Office—Waynesburg College, Miller Hall, Waynesburg, PA 15370.

■ Career

Waynesburg College, Waynesburg, PA, professor of early childhood education.

■ Awards, Honors

Ezra Jack Keats Award, 1991, for a children's novel in progress.

■ Writings

Red Sky at Morning, Holiday House, 1991.

■ Work in Progress

A sequel to *Red Sky at Morning;* writing and illustrating two works: *Bucket Full of Words,* a poetry book for children, and *Rural Women Teachers in America,* a sourcebook.

■ Sidelights

Andrea Wyman told *SATA:* "Born and raised in Indiana, I was fortunate to grow up in a beautiful part of the United States surrounded by farmland and wide-open spaces. During elementary school, I had two or three schoolteachers that I've wanted to find and thank because they really encouraged me to draw and write. I was also lucky enough to have parents and grandparents who spoke of our family history, telling stories about relatives and family members. *Red Sky at Morning* had its beginnings from those shared remembrances and memories.

"I particularly enjoy doing all the research that's needed for writing historical fiction, and, even better, I like the idea that history can come alive for readers in a pleasurable way by simply reading a book. Because of my work, I also write for a variety of magazines and journals—everything from academic articles to poetry. But none of my writing would be very worthwhile if it weren't for my family: my husband, Rick, daughter, Susan, and son, Drew—even our cat, Aslan, dog, Inua, and fish, Frank. If I succeed in making my characters

ANDREA WYMAN

come alive and seem real to readers, it's because of my family. They give me lots of ideas and offer helpful suggestions. I truly believe they enabled me to think of myself as a writer and creator of fiction."

■ For More Information See

PERIODICALS

Booklist, December 1, 1991, p. 698.
Kirkus Reviews, September, 1991, p. 1230.
Publishers Weekly, October 4, 1991, p. 88.
School Library Journal, September, 1991, p. 260.

Y–Z

YOLEN, Jane (Hyatt) 1939-

■ Personal

Born February 11, 1939, in New York, NY; daughter of Will Hyatt (an author and in public relations) and Isabelle (a social worker and homemaker; maiden name, Berlin) Yolen; married David W. Stemple (a professor of computer science), September 2, 1962; children: Heidi Elisabet, Adam Douglas, Jason Frederic. *Education:* Smith College, B.A., 1960; University of Massachusetts, M.Ed., 1976. *Politics:* Liberal Democrat. *Religion:* Jewish-Quaker. *Hobbies and other interests:* Folk music and dancing, reading, camping, politics, all things Scottish.

■ Addresses

Home—Phoenix Farm, 31 School Street, Box 27, Hatfield, MA 01038; and Wayside, 96 Hepburn Gardens, St. Andrews, Fife, Scotland KY16 9LN. *Agent*—Marilyn Marlow, Curtis Brown Ltd., 10 Astor Place, New York, NY 10003.

■ Career

Saturday Review, New York City, production assistant, 1960-61; Gold Medal Books (publishers), New York City, assistant editor, 1961-62; Rutledge Books (publishers), New York City, associate editor, 1962-63; Alfred A. Knopf, Inc. (publishers), New York City, assistant juvenile editor, 1963-65; full-time professional writer, 1965—. Editor of imprint, Jane Yolen Books, for Harcourt Brace Jovanovich, 1988—. Teacher of writing and lecturer, 1966—. Chairman of board of library trustees, Hatfield, MA, 1976-83; member of Arts Council, Hatfield. *Member:* International Kitefliers Association, Society of Children's Book Writers (member of board of directors, 1974—), Science Fiction Writers of America (president, 1986-88), Children's Literature Association (member of board of directors, 1977-79), Science Fiction Poetry Association, National Association for the Preservation and Perpetuation of Storytelling, Western New England Storyteller's Guild (founder), Bay State Writers Guild, Western Massachusetts Illustrators Guild (founder), Smith College Alumnae Association.

■ Awards, Honors

Boys' Club of America Junior Book Award, 1968, for *The Minstrel and the Mountain;* Lewis Carroll Shelf Award, 1968, for *The Emperor and the Kite,* and 1973, for *The Girl Who Loved the Wind; The Emperor and the Kite* was selected one of the *New York Times*'s Best Books of the Year and as a Caldecott Honor Book, both 1968; *World on a String: The Story of Kites* was named an American Library Association (ALA) Notable Book,

JANE YOLEN

223

1968; Chandler Book Talk Reward of Merit, 1970; Children's Book Showcase of the Children's Book Council citations, 1973, for *The Girl Who Loved the Wind,* and 1976, for *The Little Spotted Fish;* Golden Kite Award, Society of Children's Book Writers, 1974, ALA Notable Book, 1975, and National Book Award nomination, 1975, all for *The Girl Who Cried Flowers and Other Tales;* Golden Kite Honor Book, 1975, for *The Transfigured Hart,* and 1976, for *The Moon Ribbon and Other Tales;* Christopher Medal, 1978, for *The Seeing Stick.*

Children's Choice from the International Reading Association and the Children's Book Council, 1980, for *Mice on Ice,* and 1983, for *Dragon's Blood;* LL.D. from College of Our Lady of the Elms, 1981; Parents' Choice Awards, Parents' Choice Foundation, 1982, for *Dragon's Blood,* 1984, for *The Stone Silenus,* and 1989, for *Piggins* and *The Three Bears Rhyme Book; School Library Journal* Best Books for Young Adults citations, 1982, for *The Gift of Sarah Barker,* and 1985, for *Heart's Blood;* Garden State Children's Book Award, New Jersey Library Association, 1983, for *Commander Toad in Space;* CRABbery Award from Acton Public Library (MD), 1983, for *Dragon's Blood; Heart's Blood* was selected one of ALA's Best Books for Young Adults, 1984; Mythopoeic Society's Fantasy Award, 1984, for *Cards of Grief;* Daedelus Award, 1986, for "a body of work—fantasy and short fiction"; *The Lullaby Songbook* and *The Sleeping Beauty* were each selected one of Child Study Association of America's Children's Books of the Year, 1987; Caldecott Medal, 1988, for *Owl Moon;* World Fantasy Award, 1988, for *Favorite Folktales from around the World;* Kerlan Award for "singular achievements in the creation of children's literature," 1988; Parents' Choice Silver Seal Award, Jewish Book Council Award, and Association of Jewish Libraries Award, all 1988, Judy Lopez Honor Book and Nebula Award finalist, both 1989, all for *The Devil's Arithmetic;* Golden Sower Award from the Nebraska Library Association, 1989, and Charlotte Award from New York State Reading Association, both for *Piggins;* Smith College Medal for body of work, 1990; Skylark Award, New England Science Fiction Association, 1990; Regina Medal for body of writing in children's literature, 1992; thirteen of Yolen's books have been selected by the Junior Literary Guild.

■ Writings

YOUNG ADULT FICTION

(Editor) *Shape Shifters: Fantasy and Science Fiction Tales about Humans Who Can Change Their Shape,* Seabury, 1978.
The Gift of Sarah Barker, Viking, 1981.
Dragon's Blood: A Fantasy (first volume in trilogy), Delacorte, 1982.
Neptune Rising: Songs and Tales of the Undersea Folk (story collection), illustrated by David Wiesner, Philomel, 1982.
Heart's Blood (second volume in trilogy), Delacorte, 1984.
The Stone Silenus, Philomel, 1984.

Commander Toad and the Dis-Asteroid, illustrated by B. Degen, Coward, 1985.
(Editor with others) *Dragons and Dreams: A Collection of New Fantasy and Science Fiction Stories,* Harper, 1986.
Children of the Wolf, Viking, 1986.
Spaceships and Spells, Harper, 1987.
A Sending of Dragons (third volume in trilogy), illustrated by Tom McKeveny, Delacorte, 1987.
The Devil's Arithmetic, Viking, 1988.
(Editor with Martin H. Greenberg) *Werewolves: A Collection of Original Stories,* Harper, 1988.
The Faery Flag: Stories and Poems of Fantasy and the Supernatural, Orchard Books, 1989.
(Editor with Greenberg) *Things That Go Bump in the Night,* Harper, 1989.
(Editor) *2041 AD* (science fiction anthology), Delacorte, 1990.
(Editor with Greenberg) *Vampires,* Harper, 1991.
The Dragon's Boy, Harper, 1992.
Here There Be Dragons, Harcourt, 1993.

FOR ADULTS; FICTION

The Lady and the Merman, illustrated by Barry Moser, Pennyroyal, 1977.
Tales of Wonder (story collection), Schocken, 1983.
Cards of Grief (science fiction), Ace Books, 1984.
Merlin's Booke, Steel Dragon Press, 1984.
Dragonfield and Other Stories (story collection), Ace Books, 1985.
(Editor) *Favorite Folktales from around the World,* Pantheon, 1988.
Sister Light, Sister Dark, Tor Books, 1988.
White Jenna, Tor Books, 1989.
Briar Rose, Tor Books, 1992.
Xanadu, Tor Books, 1993.

FOR ADULTS; NONFICTION

Writing Books for Children, The Writer, 1973, revised edition, 1983.
Touch Magic: Fantasy, Faerie and Folklore in the Literature of Childhood, Philomel, 1981.
Guide to Writing for Children, Writer, 1989.

JUVENILE FICTION

The Witch Who Wasn't, illustrated by Arnold Roth, Macmillan, 1964.
Gwinellen, the Princess Who Could Not Sleep, illustrated by Ed Renfro, Macmillan, 1965.
(With Anne Huston) *Trust a City Kid,* illustrated by J. C. Kocsis, Lothrop, 1966.
The Emperor and the Kite, illustrated by Ed Young, World Publishing, 1967.
The Minstrel and the Mountain: A Tale of Peace, illustrated by Anne Rockwell, World Publishing, 1967.
Robin Hood (musical), first produced in Boston, MA, 1967.
Isabel's Noel, illustrated by Roth, Funk, 1967.
Greyling: A Picture Story from the Islands of Shetland, illustrated by William Stobbs, World Publishing, 1968.

The Longest Name on the Block, illustrated by Peter Madden, Funk, 1968.

The Wizard of Washington Square, illustrated by Ray Cruz, World Publishing, 1969.

The Inway Investigators; or, The Mystery at McCracken's Place, illustrated by Allan Eitzen, Seabury, 1969.

Hobo Toad and the Motorcycle Gang, illustrated by Emily McCully, World Publishing, 1970.

The Seventh Mandarin, illustrated by Young, Seabury, 1970.

The Bird of Time, illustrated by Mercer Mayer, Crowell, 1971.

The Girl Who Loved the Wind, illustrated by Young, Crowell, 1972.

(Editor) *Zoo 2000: Twelve Stories of Science Fiction and Fantasy Beasts*, Seabury, 1973.

The Girl Who Cried Flowers and Other Tales, illustrated by David Palladini, Crowell, 1974.

The Boy Who Had Wings, illustrated by Helga Aichinger, Crowell, 1974.

The Adventures of Eeka Mouse, illustrated by Myra McKee, Xerox Education Publications, 1974.

The Magic Three of Solatia, illustrated by Julia Noonan, Crowell, 1974.

The Rainbow Rider, illustrated by Michael Foreman, Crowell, 1974.

The Little Spotted Fish, illustrated by Friso Henstra, Seabury, 1975.

The Transfigured Hart, illustrated by Donna Diamond, Crowell, 1975.

Milkweed Days, photographs by Gabriel A. Cooney, Crowell, 1976.

The Moon Ribbon and Other Tales, illustrated by Palladini, Crowell, 1976.

The Seeing Stick, illustrated by Remy Charlip and Demetra Maraslis, Crowell, 1977.

The Sultan's Perfect Tree, illustrated by Barbara Garrison, Parents Magazine Press, 1977.

The Giants' Farm, illustrated by Tomie de Paola, Seabury, 1977.

The Hundredth Dove and Other Tales, illustrated by Palladini, Crowell, 1977.

Hannah Dreaming, photographs by Alan R. Epstein, Museum of Fine Art (Springfield, MA), 1977.

Spider Jane, illustrated by Stefan Bernath, Coward, 1978.

The Simple Prince, illustrated by Jack Kent, Parents Magazine Press, 1978.

No Bath Tonight, illustrated by Nancy W. Parker, Crowell, 1978.

The Mermaid's Three Wisdoms, illustrated by Laura Rader, Collins, 1978.

Dream Weaver and Other Tales, illustrated by Michael Hague, Collins, 1979.

The Giants Go Camping, illustrated by de Paola, Seabury, 1979.

Commander Toad in Space, illustrated by Degen, Coward, 1980.

Spider Jane on the Move, illustrated by Bernath, Coward, 1980.

Mice on Ice, illustrated by Lawrence DiFiori, Dutton, 1980.

Yolen's gentle tale of a father and daughter's night walk was perfectly complemented by John Schoenherr's Caldecott-winning illustrations.

The Robot and Rebecca: The Mystery of the Code-Carrying Kids, illustrated by Jurg Obrist, Knopf, 1980.

Shirlick Holmes and the Case of the Wandering Wardrobe, illustrated by Anthony Rao, Coward, 1981.

The Robot and Rebecca and the Missing Owser, illustrated by Lady McCrady, Knopf, 1981.

The Acorn Quest, illustrated by Susanna Natti, Harper, 1981.

Brothers of the Wind, illustrated by Barbara Berger, Philomel, 1981.

Sleeping Ugly, illustrated by Diane Stanley, Coward, 1981.

The Boy Who Spoke Chimp, illustrated by Wiesner, Knopf, 1981.

Uncle Lemon's Spring, illustrated by Glen Rounds, Dutton, 1981.

Commander Toad and the Planet of the Grapes, illustrated by Degen, Coward, 1982.

Commander Toad and the Big Black Hole, illustrated by Degen, Coward, 1983.

Commander Toad and the Intergalactic Spy, illustrated by Degen, Coward, 1986.

Owl Moon, illustrated by John Schoenherr, Philomel, 1987.

Commander Toad and the Space Pirates, illustrated by Degen, Putnam, 1987.

Piggins, illustrated by Jane Dyer, Harcourt, 1987.

(Reteller) *The Sleeping Beauty*, illustrated by Ruth Sanderson, Knopf, 1987.

Picnic with Piggins, illustrated by Dyer, Harcourt, 1988.

Piggins and the Royal Wedding, illustrated by Dyer, Harcourt, 1989.

Dove Isabeau, illustrated by Dennis Nolan, Harcourt, 1989.

Dream Weaver, Putnam, 1989.

Baby Bear's Bedtime Book, illustrated by Dyer, Harcourt, 1990.

Sky Dogs, illustrated by Barry Moser, Harcourt, 1990.

Tam Lin, illustrated by Mikolaycak, Harcourt, 1990.

Elfabet: An ABC of Elves, Little, 1990.

Letting Swift River Go, Little, 1990.

Wizard's Hall, Harcourt, 1991.

Welcome to the Green House, illustrated by Laura Reagan, Putnam, 1993.

Honkers, illustrated by Leslie Balker, Little, Brown, 1993.

JUVENILE NONFICTION

Pirates in Petticoats, illustrated by Leonard Vosburgh, McKay, 1963.

World on a String: The Story of Kites, World Publishing, 1968.

Friend: The Story of George Fox and the Quakers, Seabury, 1972.

(Editor with Barbara Green) *The Fireside Song Book of Birds and Beasts,* illustrated by Peter Parnall, Simon & Schuster, 1972.

The Wizard Islands, illustrated by Robert Quackenbush, Crowell, 1973.

Ring Out! A Book of Bells, illustrated by Richard Cuffari, Seabury, 1974.

Simple Gifts: The Story of the Shakers, illustrated by Betty Fraser, Viking, 1976.

(Compiler) *Rounds about Rounds,* illustrated by Gail Gibbons, F. Watts, 1977.

The Lap-Time Song and Play Book, musical arrangements by Stemple, illustrated by Margot Tomes, Harcourt, 1989.

Letter from Phoenix Farm, illustrated with photographs by Jason Stemple, Richard C. Owen, 1992.

JUVENILE POETRY

See This Little Line?, illustrated by Kathleen Elgin, McKay, 1963.

It All Depends, illustrated by Don Bolognese, Funk, 1970.

An Invitation to the Butterfly Ball: A Counting Rhyme, illustrated by Jane B. Zalben, Parents Magazine Press, 1976.

All in the Woodland Early: An ABC Book, illustrated by Zalben, Collins, 1979.

How Beastly!: A Menagerie of Nonsense Poems, illustrated by James Marshall, Philomel, 1980.

Dragon Night and Other Lullabies, illustrated by Demi, Methuen, 1980.

(Editor) *The Lullaby Songbook,* musical arrangements by Adam Stemple, illustrated by Charles Mikolaycak, Harcourt, 1986.

Ring of Earth: A Child's Book of Seasons, illustrated by John Wallner, Harcourt, 1986.

The Three Bears Rhyme Book, illustrated by Dyer, Harcourt, 1987.

Best Witches: Poems for Halloween, illustrated by Elise Primavera, Putnam, 1989.

Bird Watch, illustrated by Ted Lewin, Philomel, 1990.

Dinosaur Dances, Putnam, 1990.

(Compiler) *Street Rhymes around the World,* Boyds Mill Press, 1992.

Jane Yolen's Mother Goose Song Book, musical arrangements by Adam Stemple, illustrated by Rosecrans Hoffman, Boyds Mill Press, 1992.

(Compiler) *Weather Report,* illustrated by Annie Gusman, Boyds Mills Press, 1993.

Mouse's Birthday, illustrated by Bruce Degen, Putnam, 1993.

Raining Cats and Dogs, illustrated by Janet Street, Harcourt, 1993.

What Rhymes with Moon?, illustrated by Ruth Councell, Philomel, 1993.

OTHER

Also author of *The Whitethorn Wood,* a chapbook. Contributor to books, including *Dragons of Light,* edited by Orson Scott Card, Ace Books, 1981; *Elsewhere,* edited by Terri Windling and Mark Alan Arnold, Ace Books, Volume 1, 1981, Volume 2, 1982; *Hecate's Cauldron,* edited by Susan Schwartz, DAW Books, 1982; *Heroic Visions,* edited by Jessica Amanda Salmonson, Ace Books, 1983; *Faery!,* edited by Windling, Ace Books, 1985; *Liavek,* edited by Will Shetterly and Emma Bull, Ace Books, 1985; *Moonsinger's Friends,* edited by Schwartz, Bluejay, 1985; *Imaginary Lands,* edited by Robin McKinley, Greenwillow, 1985; *Don't Bet on the Prince: Contemporary Feminist Fairy Tales in North America and England,* by Jack Zipes, Methuen, 1986; *Liavek: Players of Luck,* edited by Shetterly and Bull, Ace Books, 1986; *Liavek: Wizard's Row,* edited by Shetterly and Bull, Ace Books, 1987; *Visions,* by Donald R. Gallo, Delacorte, 1987; *Liavek: Spells of Binding,* edited by Shetterly and Bull, Ace Books, 1988; *Invitation to Camelot,* by Parke Godwin, Ace Books, 1988; and *The Unicorn Treasury,* by Bruce Coville, Doubleday, 1988, and dozens more. Some of Yolen's manuscripts are held in the Kerlan Collection at the University of Minnesota.

Author of column "Children's Bookfare" for *Daily Hampshire Gazette* during the 1970s. Contributor of articles, reviews, poems, and short stories to periodicals, including *Writer, Parabola, New York Times, Washington Post Book World, Los Angeles Times, Parents' Choice, New Advocate, Horn Book, Wilson Library Bulletin, Magazine of Fantasy and Science Fiction, Isaac Asimov's Science Fiction Magazine,* and *Language Arts.* Member of editorial board, *Advocate* (now *New Advocate*), and *National Storytelling Journal,* until 1989. Some of Yolen's books have been published in England, France, Spain, Brazil, Germany, Austria, Sweden, South Africa, Australia, Japan, and Denmark.

■ Adaptations

The Seventh Mandarin (movie), Xerox Films, 1973.

The Emperor and the Kite (filmstrip with cassette), Listening Library, 1976.

The Bird of Time (play), first produced in Northampton, MA, 1982.

The Girl Who Cried Flowers and Other Tales (cassette), Weston Woods, 1983.

Dragon's Blood (animated television movie), *CBS Storybreak*, Columbia Broadcasting System, 1985.

Commander Toad in Space (cassette), Listening Library, 1986.

Touch Magic ... Pass It On (cassette), Weston Woods, 1987.

Owl Moon (filmstrip with cassette), Weston Woods, 1988.

Piggins and Picnic with Piggins (cassette), Caedmon, 1988.

■ Work in Progress

Two novels, *Many Mansions* and *The Wild Hunt;* picture books *Grandpa Bill's Song, The Traveler's Rose, Good Griselle, King Longshanks, Old Dame Counterpane, Miz Berlin Walks, Sacred Places, A Sip of Aesop, Beneath the Ghost Moon, The Girl in the Garden Bower;* poetry collections *Water Music, Animal Fare, Three Bears Holiday Book,* and *Sea Watch.*

■ Sidelights

Jane Yolen's many writings include fiction, poetry, and plays for young adults and children. Her creations range from ABC books to texts on kite flying to stories about vampires. She has spoken all over the United States to children and children's literature groups at schools, libraries, and conferences, and has won many awards. She is known as well as a folksinger, critic, essayist, and editor. However, she is probably best known for her literary folk and fairy tales, drawing on elements of old stories to illustrate modern themes. "In our need to update the educational standards," she writes in *Touch Magic: Fantasy, Faerie, and Folktale in the Literature of Childhood,* "we have done away with the old gods. And now we have names without faces, mnemonics without meaning." Yolen rebuilds, and in some cases creates from fragments, mythologies that apply to modern times while maintaining a timeless sense of wonder and beauty.

Jane Yolen was born in New York City, but, because of the Second World War, spent two years in Virginia, living with her grandparents while her father worked in England for the government. After the war the family moved back to New York until Jane was a teenager. Her parents gave her a strongly literary bent—her father, who wrote books and radio scripts, came from a line of Russian storytellers. Her mother wrote short stories and created crossword puzzles, and both parents read to Yolen as soon as she was old enough to listen. She herself learned to read before starting school at New York's PS 93. "I was a writer from the time I learned how to write," she tells Jean Ross in an interview for *Contemporary Authors.* "In first grade I wrote the class musical, and I was a performer in it too. It was all about vegetables. I played a carrot, and we all ended up doing the big finale in a salad together."

Kept in a walled house by her overprotective father, Danina hears the song of the wind and yearns to discover life on the outside. (Cover illustration by Ed Young.)

Yolen studied ballet for eight years, played fantasy games in Central Park, and loved music, especially folk songs. While in the sixth grade she scored highly on a test and was accepted at Hunter, a school for gifted girls. Having an alto voice, she played the male lead in *Hansel and Gretel* at the school even though she was a full head shorter than the girl who played Gretel. At Hunter she also wrote her eighth grade social studies paper in rhyme. She wrote her first two books at Hunter, a nonfiction one on pirates and a seventeen-page novel about the pioneer west, which in her *Something about the Author Autobiography Series* (*SAAS*) essay she sarcastically calls "a masterpiece of economy."

Religion and Music Influence Writings

In the summers of her twelfth and thirteenth years, Yolen attended a Quaker camp in Vermont, where she first became acquainted with pacifism and storytelling. Between high school and college, she spent a summer working in an American Friends Service Committee work camp in Yellow Springs, Ohio. These experiences led to an interest in Quaker beliefs; later, she wrote a biography called *Friend: The Story of George Fox and the Quakers.* Her religious horizons were also broadened in her teenage years when she was introduced to Catholicism by a friend. Many rituals in her fairy tales reflect this exposure; she writes in *SAAS,* "In *The Magic Three of Solatia,* the ceremony of Thrittem is a kind of bar mitzvah crossed with a silent Quaker meeting. In *Cards of Grief,* I worked in storytelling, seders, and the

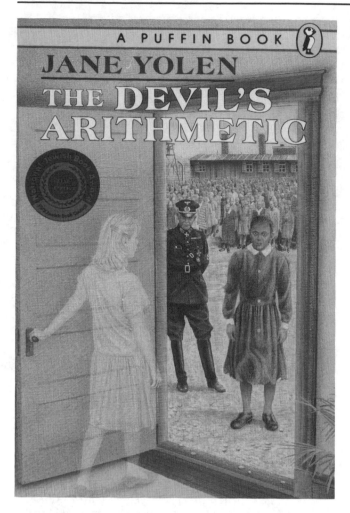

A PUFFIN BOOK

JANE YOLEN

THE DEVIL'S ARITHMETIC

A Jewish girl bored by her family's tales of the "Old World" is sudddenly transported into a Polish village during the Holocaust. (Cover illustration by Lonnie Knabel.)

Mass, along with Communion, Confession, and the Viaticum."

When Yolen was thirteen her family moved to Westport, Connecticut, where she attended Staples High School. Although she was captain of the girl's basketball team, served on the newspaper staff, was active in the jazz, Spanish, and Latin clubs, won the school's English prize, and toured and performed with the choir, her greatest inspiration during these years came from the woman who she always called a cousin, the sister of one of her aunts-by-marriage. Her name was Honey Knopp, and she really introduced Yolen to Quakerism and pacifism. She and her husband Burt also hosted music fests, called hootenannies, and helped Yolen realize another, more poetic side of her character. Yolen states in her *SAAS* entry that she drew on Honey Knopp's ideas and example for several of her works, including *The Minstrel and the Mountain* and *Friend: The Story of George Fox and the Quakers.*

The folk music she was exposed to has also influenced her work. Yolen tells Ross, "I can't listen to any music while I am writing because it forces a different rhythm.

Some of my prose can practically be sung—*Greyling,* for example, one of my picture books. All of my stuff is read out loud, because it's very important for me to please the ear as well as the eye. A lot of my themes, also, and magical figures come out of folk songs. And I have written music to go along with a number of my things. For example, *All in the Woodland Early* has a song at the end that I wrote. *Sister Light, Sister Dark* has seven or eight songs with piano accompaniment at the end of the book, poems that have appeared earlier in the book, but set to music at the end." She also reads her work out loud. "I write a sentence and then read it out loud before going on to the next," Yolen comments. "Then the paragraph is read aloud. Finally, the entire book is read and reread to the walls, to the bathtub, to the blank television, to my long-suffering husband."

Yolen attended Smith College, developing her writing skills there and having her stories published in magazines and newspapers. She had hoped to be a journalist, but found herself too emotional to do interviews. However, she won a journalism award at Smith as well as many poetry prizes. She even earned money at college by writing poetry and singing folk songs. After graduation Yolen, eager to see if she could be a successful writer, moved to Greenwich Village and began to work for various publishers in New York City. In 1962, she started a job with Alfred A. Knopf as an assistant editor of juvenile books. She had already started writing books for chiildren herself. Her first effort, *Pirates in Petticoats,* was published in 1963. In 1968 she researched, wrote, and published a book called *World on a String: The Story of Kites* for her father, a kite enthusiast.

In 1962, in the garden of her parents' home, Yolen married David Stemple, a photographer and computer programmer. Her fairy tale *The Girl Who Loved the Wind* is dedicated to him and celebrates their meeting. *The Girl Who Loved the Wind* is the story of a widowed merchant who tries to spare his daughter the heartbreak of everyday life, but only succeeds in isolating her from reality. Isolated, the girl receives a visit from the wind, who explains that while the world can be cruel and hurtful, it can also be joyful; but it is always changing. The girl, explains Marilyn R. Singer in *School Library Journal,* "is no longer content in her false dull world, and escapes with the wind," exchanging security for the everchanging world.

After five years of marriage, the couple ordered a Volkswagen Camper and went adventuring in Europe, where they toured for nine months. Yolen recalls in *SAAS* that during this time they climbed a mountain in Greece and worked in an orange grove in Israel, then back in the United States she "mushed" on a dog sled in Alaska and then went rafting down the Colorado River. Yolen and her husband have three children and currently live in a fifteen-room house in Hatfield, Massachusetts. For seven years a crafts center functioned in their large barn; now a T-shirt printer works there.

Work Ranges from Juvenile to Science Fiction

As her children grew older, Yolen's output broadened from children's books to include young adult and adult fiction; her first book for adults, *Cards of Grief,* was selected for the Science Fiction Book Club. Yet she does not see a sharp distinction between books for children and books for adults. "Mainly I simply tell a story or write a poem and think afterwards about the audience," she tells Ross. "Obviously with some things—if I'm writing a Commander Toad book, for example—it's clear that I'm not writing primarily for an adult audience, though there are a lot of adults who love those books. I don't normally say, 'All right, now I am going to write a children's book,' or, 'I am going to write a young adult book.' I tend first to figure out what the story is I want to tell, and the story itself tells me eventually who the audience is." She advises young people to read and write every day and conducts workshops across the country for aspiring authors.

The popularity of Yolen's work continues to grow; her humorous series books featuring the characters Piggins and Commander Toad are favorites with young readers. The "Commander Toad" series is science fiction, telling of the adventures of the title character and his crew—including Mr. Hop, Lieutenant Lily, and Jake Skyjumper—as they journey through the cosmos. Piggins, on the other hand, is a portly pig butler who solves mysteries in the "Edwardian world of 47 The Meadows," in which all the characters are animals, according to Marcia G. Fuchs in *Twentieth-Century Children's Writers.* Yolen's most popular work in recent years has been the Caldecott Medal-winning *Owl Moon.* Dedicated to her husband David, the book tells of a trip into a winter wood by a father and his young child in search of owls. Finally, after a long patient search, an owl answers the father's call, and bird and child confront each other for a long magical moment.

"The history of children's literature is very long and very wide, very varied," Yolen tells Ross. "Some of the best books that have been written in literature, especially in the English language, have been in the children's section. We tend to forget that. And ... the books that we read in childhood affect us more than anything else we read until the end of our days." "I consider myself a poet and a storyteller," she reflects in *SAAS.* "I just want to go on writing and discovering my stories for the rest of my life because I know that in my tales I make public what is private, transforming my own joy and sadness into tales for the people."

Yolen's books about "Commander Toad" and the crew of the *Star Warts* are favorites with children for their humor-filled adventures. (Cover illustration by Bruce Degen.)

■ Works Cited

Fuchs, Marcia G., "Jane Yolen," *Twentieth Century Children's Writers,* 3rd edition, St. James Press, 1989, pp. 1075-78.

Singer, Marilyn R., review of *The Girl Who Loved the Wind, School Library Journal,* March, 1973, p. 102.

Yolen, Jane, *Touch Magic: Fantasy, Faerie, and Folktale in the Literature of Childhood,* Philomel, 1981.

Yolen, Jane, essay in *Something about the Author Autobiography Series,* Volume 4, Gale, 1987, pp. 327-46.

Yolen, Jane, interview with Jean W. Ross, *Contemporary Authors New Revision Series,* Volume 29, Gale, 1990, pp. 463-69.

■ For More Information See

BOOKS

Authors and Artists for Young Adults, Volume 4, Gale, 1990, pp. 229-41.

Children's Literature Review, Volume 4, Gale, 1982, pp. 255-69.

de Montreville, Doris, and Elizabeth D. Crawford, editors, *The Fourth Book of Junior Authors and Illustrators,* H. W. Wilson, 1978.

Dictionary of Literary Biography, Volume 52: *American Writers for Children since 1960: Fiction,* Gale, 1986, pp. 398-405.

Roginski, Jim, *Behind the Covers: Interviews with Authors and Illustrators of Books for Children and Young Adults,* Libraries Unlimited, 1985.

Yolen, Jane, *Writing Books for Children,* The Writer, 1973, revised edition, 1983.

YUDITSKAYA, Tatyana 1964-

■ Personal

Born April 29, 1964, in Moscow, Russia; children: Sofya. *Education:* Technical School of Theater Arts, A.A.S., 1983; attended Moscow Technological Institute, School of Arts Technology, 1985-88, and Parsons School of Design, 1990 and 1992—.

■ Career

Worked in various theaters as a set and costume designer, Moscow, Russia, 1984-88; New York Shakespeare Festival, New York City, senior draper, 1989-90; Margaret Waterstone, Inc., New York City, fine art restorer and conservator, 1990-91; free-lance children's book illustrator, New York City, 1991—.

■ Illustrator

The Four Gallant Sisters, edited by Eric A. Kimmel, Holt, 1992.
Antony Pogorelsky, *The Black Hen: Or The Underground Inhabitants,* edited by Morse Hamilton, Dutton, 1994.

■ Work in Progress

Writing and illustrating *Siberia Is a Paradise.*

■ Sidelights

Tatyana Yuditskaya told *SATA:* "All my life in Russia I dreamt about becoming a children's book illustrator. But for me, the way to certain colleges was closed, so I chose the career of fashion and theater designer, which wasn't as elite as illustration. I was very successful, though I was always told that my sketches looked like illustrations. Then I came to America. I was already 25 years old, and I thought it was too late to pursue my childhood dream. But everybody around me encouraged me. So I started slowly—taking a class at Parsons School of Design in children's book illustration. That was just a twelve-session class! A month after completion, following a lot of presentations of my portfolio and some rejections, I had my first book at Henry Holt! I was so happy—it was like in the movies! My American Dream.

"Now I'm making illustrations for *The Black Hen: Or The Underground Inhabitants* (a tale from my Russian childhood which I'm happy to present to American kids), and I'm also almost finished with my manuscript of *Siberia Is a Paradise* using my own illustrations. The book is based on my grandmother's memories about her childhood in a small Siberian Orthodox village near the China border. I'm looking for a publisher for that project, although I have someone in mind already."

ZAMBRENO, Mary Frances 1954-
(Robyn Tallis)

■ Personal

Born January 16, 1954, in Oak Park, IL; daughter of Joseph Anthony (a lawyer and small business owner) and Elvira (a teacher; maiden name, Lombardi) Zambreno. *Education:* Northwestern University, B.A., 1976; University of Chicago, M.A. 1977, Ph.D., 1988.

■ Addresses

Office—c/o Publicity Director, Harcourt Brace Jovanovich, Inc., 6277 Sea Harbor Dr., Orlando, FL 32887. *Agent*—Valerie Smith, Rte. 44-55, R.D. Box 160, Modena, NY 12548.

■ Career

Writer. Rich South High School, Richton Park, IL, English teacher, 1977-80; Chicago State University, Chicago, IL, instructor, 1981; Loyola University, Chicago, lecturer, 1981-88; De Paul University, Chicago, instructor, 1986; University of Illinois at Chicago, Chicago, lecturer, 1987-91; Rosary College, River Forest, IL, visiting assistant professor, 1991-92. Kalamazoo Medieval Congress, session organizer, 1990-91. *Member:* Modern Language Association, Women's Caucus for Modern Languages, Science Fiction and Fantasy Writers of America, National Council of Teachers of English, Midwest Modern Language Association, Medieval Association of the Midwest, John Gower Society, Children's Reading Round Table, Illinois Medieval Association.

■ Writings

(Under pseudonym Robyn Tallis) *Children of the Storm,* Ballantine-Ivy, 1989.
A Plague of Sorcerers, edited by Jane Yolen, Harcourt, 1991.

Contributor of short stories to anthologies, including *Chilled to the Bone,* Mayfair; *Vampires,* Harper Jr. Books; *Things That Go Bump in the Night,* edited by Jane Yolen and Martin H. Greenberg, Harper Jr. Books; *Writers of the Future I,* Bridge Publications; *Sword and Sorceress III* and *V,* both DAW Books; and *Sword of Chaos,* DAW Books. Also contributor to periodicals, including *Medium Aevum Quotidianum, MZB's Fantasy Magazine,* and *Dragon Magazine.* Contributing editor to *American Fantasy Magazine.*

■ Work in Progress

Journeyman Wizard, a sequel to *A Plague of Sorcerers;* a young adult ghost story set in the upper peninsula of Michigan; researching medieval geography and medieval feasts.

MARY FRANCES ZAMBRENO

■ **Sidelights**

Mary Frances Zambreno told *SATA:* "I remember the day when I decided that I was a writer very clearly. I was about twelve years old, standing in my grammar school library, when I suddenly and for no logical reason looked at the books on the shelves and realized that every single one of those books had been written by *someone*—some real person with a supply of paper and an interest in telling stories. 'Hmm,' I said to myself reflectively. 'I could do that. Why don't I?' So I did.

"However, it didn't occur to me for a number of years that deciding to *be* a writer and *becoming* a writer were two very different things. The first was almost easy; the second took time and effort. Along the way, I also became first a high school English teacher and then a college professor. These days I have a doctorate in Medieval Languages and Literature; I teach Chaucer and Shakespeare and other courses in Medieval and Renaissance Literature, as well as Freshman Composition and Essay Writing; I read six languages (some more fluently than others)—and I'm still working on being and becoming a writer.

"From the first, I never had any doubt about what I wanted to write: I wanted to write science fiction and fantasy. I loved Robert Heinlein and Andre Norton and J. R. R. Tolkien and C. S. Lewis, as well as Lewis Carroll's *Alice* and a host of other books and stories that really would take forever to mention. My first published short stories were either science fiction or fantasy, published in anthologies for adults—I thought I had found my niche. Then something odd happened. I wrote a fantasy short story called 'Skinning a Wizard,' which was clearly a story for young adults. I hadn't been trying to write a story for young people; it just sort of happened. Jane Yolen bought the story for an anthology for young adults which she was editing, called *Things That Go Bump in the Night,* and the next thing I knew I was a 'young adult' writer. First I wrote a young adult series novel under the name of 'Robyn Tallis'—there were seven of us writing books in this science fiction series (mine was Number 7, *Children of the Storm*), and the whole thing was a lot of fun and good experience for me. Next I expanded 'Skinning a Wizard' into my first hard cover novel, *A Plague of Sorcerers,* which was published under my own name, with Jane Yolen editing the book for Harcourt. In other words, one thing led to another. I suppose the moral of this story is that you should never stop trying new things, because you never know what you are going to be good at.

"I still want to write mostly science fiction and fantasy, though—especially fantasy. I think the thing that attracts me to fantasy is similar to what caused me to want to study and teach Medieval Literature: both fields allow me to enter another world, like my own and yet not-like. It's the exploration and discovery that I enjoy, in teaching and in writing—and in reading, for that matter. The pleasure comes from the 'finding out.'"

Cumulative Indexes

Illustrations Index

(In the following index, the number of the volume in which an illustrator's work appears is given *before* the colon, and the page number on which it appears is given *after* the colon. For example, a drawing by Adams, Adrienne appears in Volume 2 on page 6, another drawing by her appears in Volume 3 on page 80, another drawing in Volume 8 on page 1, another drawing in Volume 15 on page 107, and so on and so on....)

YABC

Index citations including this abbreviation refer to listings appearing in *Yesterday's Authors of Books for Children,* also published by Gale Research Inc., which covers authors who died prior to 1960.

L

Author Index

The following index gives the number of the volume in which an author's biographical sketch, Brief Entry, or Obituary appears.

This index includes references to all entries in the following series, which are also published by Gale Research Inc.

YABC—*Yesterday's Authors of Books for Children: Facts and Pictures about Authors and Illustrators of Books for Young People from Early Times to 1960*
CLR—*Children's Literature Review: Excerpts from Reviews, Criticism, and Commentary on Books for Children*
SAAS—*Something about the Author Autobiography Series*

C

Frazetta, Frank 1928- *58*
Frazier, Neta Lohnes *7*
Frederic, Mike
  See Cox, William R(obert)
Freed, Alvyn M. 1913- *22*
Freedman, Benedict 1919- *27*
Freedman, Nancy 1920- *27*
Freedman, Russell 1929- *71*
  Earlier sketch in SATA *16*
  See also CLR *20*
Freeman, Barbara C(onstance) 1906- *28*
Freeman, Bill
  See Freeman, William Bradford
Freeman, Don 1908-1978 ....*17*
  See also CLR *30*
Freeman, Ira M(aximilian) 1905- *21*
Freeman, Lucy (Greenbaum) 1916- *24*
Freeman, Mae (Blacker) 1907- *25*
Freeman, Nancy 1932- *61*
Freeman, Peter J.
  See Calvert, Patricia
Freeman, Sarah (Caroline) 1940- *66*
Freeman, Tony
  Brief Entry *44*
Freeman, William Bradford 1938- *58*
  Brief Entry *48*
Fregosi, Claudia (Anne Marie) 1946- *24*
French, Allen 1870-1946
  See YABC *1*
French, Dorothy Kayser 1926- *5*
French, Fiona 1944- *75*
  Earlier sketch in SATA *6*
French, Kathryn
  See Mosesson, Gloria R(ubin)
French, Michael 1944- *49*
  Brief Entry *38*
French, Paul
  See Asimov, Isaac
Freund, Rudolf 1915-1969
  Brief Entry *28*
Frewer, Glyn 1931- *11*
Frick, C. H.
  See Irwin, Constance Frick
Frick, Constance
  See Irwin, Constance Frick
Friedlander, Joanne K(ohn) 1930- *9*
Friedman, Estelle 1920- *7*
Friedman, Frieda 1905- *43*
Friedman, Ina R(osen) 1926- *49*
  Brief Entry *41*
Friedman, Judi 1935- *59*
Friedman, Marvin 1930- *42*
  Brief Entry *33*
Friedrich, Otto (Alva) 1929- *33*
Friedrich, Priscilla 1927- *39*
Friendlich, Dick
  See Friendlich, Richard J.
Friendlich, Richard J. 1909- *11*
Friermood, Elisabeth Hamilton 1903- *5*
Friesner, Esther M. 1951- *71*
Friis, Babbis
  See Friis-Baastad, Babbis
Friis-Baastad, Babbis 1921-1970 ....*7*
Frimmer, Steven 1928- *31*
Friskey, Margaret Richards 1901- *5*
Fritz
  See Frazetta, Frank
Fritz, Jean (Guttery) 1915- *72*
  Earlier sketches in SATA *1, 29*
  See also CLR *2, 14*
  See also SAAS *2*
Froehlich, Margaret Walden 1930- *56*
Frois, Jeanne 1953- *73*
Froissart, Jean 1338(?)-1410(?) *28*
Froman, Elizabeth Hull 1920-1975 ......*10*
Froman, Robert (Winslow) 1917- *8*
Fromm, Lilo 1928- *29*
Frommer, Harvey 1937- *41*
Frost, A(rthur) B(urdett) 1851-1928 .....*19*
Frost, Erica
  See Supraner, Robyn
Frost, Lesley 1899(?)-1983 ....*14*
  Obituary *34*
Frost, Robert (Lee) 1874-1963 ....*14*
Fry, Christopher 1907- *66*
Fry, Edward Bernard 1925- *35*

Fry, Rosalie Kingsmill 1911- *3*
  See also SAAS *11*
Fuchs, Erich 1916- *6*
Fuchs, Lucy 1935-
  Brief Entry *52*
Fuchshuber, Annegert 1940- *43*
Fuge, Charles 1966- *74*
Fujikawa, Gyo 1908- *39*
  Brief Entry *30*
  See also CLR *25*
  See also SAAS *16*
Fujita, Tamao 1905- *7*
Fujiwara, Michiko 1946- *15*
Fuka, Vladimir 1926-1977
  Obituary *27*
Fuller, Catherine L(euthold) 1916- *9*
Fuller, Edmund (Maybank) 1914- *21*
Fuller, Iola
  See McCoy, Iola Fuller
Fuller, John G(rant, Jr.) 1913-1990 ......*65*
Fuller, Lois Hamilton 1915- *11*
Fuller, Margaret
  See Ossoli, Sarah Margaret (Fuller)
  marchesa d'
Fults, John Lee 1932- *33*
Funai, Mamoru (Rolland) 1932-
  Brief Entry *46*
Funk, Thompson
  See Funk, Tom
Funk, Tom 1911- *7*
Funke, Lewis 1912- *11*
Furchgott, Terry 1948- *29*
Furniss, Tim 1948- *49*
Furukawa, Toshi 1924- *24*
Fyleman, Rose 1877-1957 ....*21*
Fyson, J(enny) G(race) 1904- *42*

G

Gaan, Margaret 1914- *65*
Gabhart, Ann 1947- *75*
Gackenbach, Dick *48*
  Brief Entry *30*
Gaddis, Vincent H. 1913- *35*
Gadler, Steve J. 1905- *36*
Gaeddert, Lou Ann (Bigge) 1931- *20*
Gaffney, Timothy R. 1951- *69*
Gàg, Flavia 1907-1979
  Obituary *24*
Gàg, Wanda (Hazel) 1893-1946
  See YABC *1*
  See also CLR *4*
Gage, Wilson
  See Steele, Mary Q(uintard Govan)
Gagliardo, Ruth Garver 1895(?)-1980
  Obituary *22*
Gagnon, Cecile 1936- *58*
Gainer, Cindy 1962- *74*
Gál, László 1933- *52*
  Brief Entry *32*
Galdone, Paul 1907(?)-1986 ....*66*
  Obituary *49*
  Earlier sketch in SATA *17*
  See also CLR *16*
Galinsky, Ellen 1942- *23*
Gallant, Roy A(rthur) 1924- *68*
  Earlier sketch in SATA *4*
  See also CLR *30*
Gallico, Paul 1897-1976 ....*13*
Galloway, Priscilla 1930- *66*
Galt, Thomas Franklin, Jr. 1908- *5*
Galt, Tom
  See Galt, Thomas Franklin, Jr.
Gamerman, Martha 1941- *15*
Gammell, Stephen 1943- *53*
Ganly, Helen (Mary) 1940- *56*
Gannett, Ruth Chrisman (Arens)
  1896-1979 ....*33*
Gannett, Ruth Stiles 1923- *3*
Gannon, Robert (Haines) 1931- *8*
Gans, Roma 1894- *45*
Gantner, Susan (Verble) 1939- *63*
Gantos, Jack
  See Gantos, John (Bryan), Jr.
  See also CLR *18*
Gantos, John (Bryan), Jr. 1951- *20*

Ganz, Yaffa 1938- *61*
  Brief Entry *52*
Garbutt, Bernard 1900-
  Brief Entry *31*
Gard, Janice
  See Latham, Jean Lee
Gard, Joyce
  See Reeves, Joyce
Gard, Robert Edward 1910-1992 ....*18*
  Obituary *74*
Gard, (Sanford) Wayne 1899-1986
  Obituary *49*
Gardam, Jane 1928- *39*
  Brief Entry *28*
  See also CLR *12*
  See also SAAS *9*
Garden, Nancy 1938- *12*
  See also SAAS *8*
Gardiner, John Reynolds 1944- *64*
Gardner, Beau
  Brief Entry *50*
Gardner, Dic
  See Gardner, Richard
Gardner, Hugh 1910-1986
  Obituary *49*
Gardner, Jeanne LeMonnier *5*
Gardner, John (Champlin, Jr.)
  1933-1982 ....*40*
  Obituary *31*
Gardner, Martin 1914- *16*
Gardner, Richard 1931- *24*
Gardner, Richard A. 1931- *13*
Gardner, Robert 1929-
  Brief Entry *43*
Gardner, Sandra 1940- *70*
Gardner, Sheldon 1934- *33*
Garelick, May *19*
Garfield, James B. 1881-1984 ....*6*
  Obituary *38*
Garfield, Leon 1921- *32*
  Earlier sketch in SATA *1*
  See also CLR *21*
Garis, Howard R(oger) 1873-1962 ....*13*
Garland, Sarah 1944- *62*
Garland, Sherry 1948- *73*
Garner, Alan 1934- *69*
  Earlier sketch in SATA *18*
  See also CLR *20*
Garnet, A. H.
  See Slote, Alfred
Garnett, Eve C. R. 1900-1991 ....*3*
  Obituary *70*
Garou, Louis P.
  See Bowkett, Stephen
Garraty, John A. 1920- *23*
Garret, Maxwell R. 1917- *39*
Garretson, Victoria Diane 1945- *44*
Garrett, Helen 1895- *21*
Garrigue, Sheila 1931- *21*
Garrison, Barbara 1931- *19*
Garrison, Frederick
  See Sinclair, Upton (Beall)
Garrison, Webb B(lack) 1919- *25*
Garst, Doris Shannon 1894- *1*
Garst, Shannon
  See Garst, Doris Shannon
Garthwaite, Marion H. 1893- *7*
Garton, Malinda D(ean) (?)-1976
  Obituary *26*
Gascoigne, Bamber 1935- *62*
Gasperini, Jim 1952- *54*
  Brief Entry *49*
Gater, Dilys 1944- *41*
Gates, Doris 1901-1987 ....*34*
  Obituary *54*
  Earlier sketch in SATA *1*
  See also SAAS *1*
Gates, Frieda 1933- *26*
Gathorne-Hardy, Jonathan G. 1933- *26*
Gatty, Juliana Horatia
  See Ewing, Juliana (Horatia Gatty)
Gatty, Margaret Scott 1809-1873
  Brief Entry *27*
Gauch, Patricia Lee 1934- *26*
Gaul, Randy 1959- *63*
Gault, Clare S. 1925- *36*